ORIGINS *of the* SACRED

BOOKS BY DUDLEY YOUNG

Out of Ireland: The Poetry of W. B. Yeats

Origins of the Sacred: The Ecstasies of Love and War

ORIGINS *of*

the SACRED

The Ecstasies of Love and War

DUDLEY YOUNG

 HarperPerennial
A Division of HarperCollins*Publishers*

The art on the title pages and the part title pages is a representation of bull-vaulting from Knossos in Crete and is now displayed in the museum in Iraklion.

Permissions follow the index.

A hardcover edition of this book was published in 1991 by St. Martin's Press. It is here reprinted by arrangement with St. Martin's Press.

HarperCollins books may be purchased for educational, business, or sales promotional use. For information, please write: Special Markets Department, HarperCollins Publishers, Inc., 10 East 53rd Street, New York, NY 10022.

First HarperPerennial edition published 1992.

Designed by Janet Tingey

Library of Congress Cataloging-in-Publication Data

Young, Dudley.
    Origins of the sacred : the ecstasies of love and war / Dudley
Young. — 1st HarperPerennial ed.
      p. cm.
    Originally published: New York : St. Martin's Press, 1991.
    Includes bibliographical references and index.
    ISBN 0-06-097511-3 (pbk.)
    1. Religion. 2. Holy, The. 3. Sex—History. 4. Violence—
History. 5. Genetic psychology. 6. Human evolution. I. Title.
[BL48.Y59 1992]
200—dc20   92-52625

92 93 94 95 96 BI/MB 10 9 8 7 6 5 4 3 2 1

To my mother and the memory
of my father (1904–88)

I have kept my faith, though faith was tried,
To that rock-born, rock-wandering foot,
And the world's altered since you died,
And I am in no good repute
With the loud host before the sea,
That think sword-strokes were better meant
Than lover's music—let that be,
So that the wandering foot's content.

—W. B. Yeats

CONTENTS

PART THREE: OCCLUSIONS OF THE SACRED:
Moving from Myth into History

PREFACE AND ACKNOWLEDGMENTS

It is one of the nice inversions of prose composition that prefaces, which come first, are usually written last, as this one is; and hence my journey is about to end. Although my mental traveling was piously undertaken, it has not been without hazard, nor can it have been altogether free of the metaphorical rape and pillage; by which I mean the violation of context, tactless poking in dark places, things smothered in words, speediness. For these sins, though unwittingly committed, I have doubtless become in some measure bedevilled, and like Odysseus must now walk off my curse by further traveling down some road until my pen (like his oar) is no longer recognized by the locals. Such an expiatory rite, one of the finest things in the *Odyssey,* still has much to commend it.

On the positive side, my thanks for a safe passage are largely due, not to the watching of Penelope, but to the small farm which has anchored my body for the past eighteen years in seasonal sanities, real things, and natural beauty. And I would now ask the spirits presiding over the sheep and the pigs and the bees and the hens and the horse and the cats and the dogs from the Church Farm to come forward and be acknowledged. In a book that seeks to understand how the animal powers may be joined "in all innocence," as Goethe says, "with the divine life in man," it would indeed be strange were

I not to do so: these creatures have both underwritten the voyage and also informed it to no small degree.

In a work so involved with memory, with attempting to restore the connection between the living and the dead, the latter have naturally been much in evidence, and two of them should be mentioned: first of all my father's ghost, usually suggesting with eyes impatient to be gone that it was time to close the books and saddle the horses; and secondly Robert Lowell—a friend who used to spook me even when he was alive—usually suggesting with a quizzical look that what I had just written wasn't bad, but I could perhaps get down a little deeper.

Over the past ten years or so I have also been much aided by human help. I could not possibly list all the individuals who over such a long period have furthered the book's fortunes, but some of my thanks should be specified: to my students at the University of Essex, whose willingness for so long to answer my questions has been both instructive and encouraging; to Juliet Cashford, for years of good talk; to Carey Harrison, for good advice when it was needed; to Angela Livingstone, for her fine ear; to Andrew Marino, for teaching the teacher; to Julia Casterton, for help with beginnings; to Lionel Tiger, for significant suggestions; to James Spence, for enduring; to Charles Rycroft, also for enduring; to Donald Davie, for the grumps; to Sir Anthony, Lady Belinda, and all the Milbanks, for living locally; and to the Rev. Robert de Massey, for Evensong and the affectionate rigors of neighborliness. Absolutely important but not to be singled out are the traveling ladies who mused and moved on: craziness without them.

A large book such as this one naturally gathers its share of footnotes, and yet I am astonished at the length of the bibliography (which I have tried to restrict to the best books on the subjects concerned, and which omits those works that have been absolutely cited in the text). Even so, there are doubtless significant omissions; and it is also likely that certain authors will feel I have ineptly or unjustly transcribed their thoughts (particularly since the material is often of a contentious nature). And though I frequently mention this in the text, much of what I propose is both highly speculative and certainly shaped by my own background and convictions. If my mistakes and occluded vision can inspire others to improve the picture I shall be well satisfied.

On a mildly polemical note: In certain respects this book began at Cambridge University about twenty-five years ago, where I was lucky enough to teach some very bright students of English literature about Greek tragedy. The Tragedy paper was the mandatory intellectual focus for students of English in their final undergraduate year (a legacy from the Cambridge Anthropologists), and so it remains today. This seemed to me an admirable arrangement at the time, and the more so now that the study of things Greek is in serious decline not only in Britain but elsewhere in the West. Those of us in a position to know what folly is involved in so neglecting our passage from the primitive should speak out against it whenever we can. If the young are not given proper images to dream upon, they will dream the improper, and civilization will suffer. Some of our most important dreams are still in Greek keeping.

Two stylistic points, finally. Throughout the text the reader will find the word *Nature* spelled with a capital N, whereas *culture* is kept small. This is meant, quite simply, to manifest my own religious faith (*Deus sive Natura*, as Spinoza said); and those who might object to such tendentiousness should be at least somewhat mollified to discover that the practice is an old and not disreputable one: Darwin did it too.

The other point concerns the implicit sexism of words such as *mankind* and *human*, both of which shorten to *man* taking the pronoun *he*. It is absolutely clear to my mind that Adam's rib is embedded in this linguistic structure (even though the word *man* goes back to Sanskrit *manus*, which before it meant "mind," meant "born of woman"), and equally clear to my ear that there is no way of correcting this fault without falling into circumlocution and cacophony. But just as B.C. and A.D. began preemptively and have now arguably become innocuous, so the use of *man* for "all of us" can eventually be neutered (or at least house-trained) if authors who must employ it remember their Sanskrit and proffer appropriate apologies for the sins of the fathers in their prefaces.

A word of executive thanks, in conclusion, to Sylvia Sparrow, whose cheerfulness at the keyboard has kept the harvesting happy; to Robert Weil, David Burr, Richard Romano, and Leslie Sharpe at St. Martin's; to Helen Anderson and Helen Goodwin at Little, Brown; and to my agents John Brockman and Katinka Matson. For Alan Samson, my editor in London, sustained applause for gambling on a good thing when others wouldn't, and for then seeing it safely home. And for Robert Jones, finally, the power behind HarperCollins, *abrazzi*.

Accuse not Nature! She hath done her part;
Do thou but thine . . .

> —Milton

He who cannot give to himself
An account of the past three thousand years
Must remain unacquainted with the things of darkness,
Able to live only from day to day.

> —Goethe

When the last red man shall have perished from the earth and his
memory among the white man shall have become a myth, these
shores shall swarm with the invisible dead of my tribe . . .
 The white man will never be alone. Let him be just and deal
kindly with my people, for the dead are not altogether powerless.
Dead, did I say? There is no death, only a change of worlds.

> —Chief Seattle

Though pedantry denies,
It's plain the Bible means
That Solomon grew wise
While talking with his queens.

> —W. B. Yeats

The gods have not returned. "They have never left us."
They have not returned.
Cloud's processional and the air moves with their living.

> —Ezra Pound

Angel,
Be silent in your luminous cloud and hear
The luminous melody of proper sound.

> —Wallace Stevens

INTRODUCTION

> The world is too much with us; late and soon,
> Getting and spending, we lay waste our powers:
> Little we see in Nature that is ours;
> We have given our hearts away, a sordid boon!
> This Sea that bares her bosom to the moon;
> The Winds that will be howling at all hours,
> And are up-gathered now like sleeping flowers;
> For this, for every thing, we are out of tune;
> It moves us not—Great God! I'd rather be
> A Pagan suckled in a creed outworn;
> So might I, standing on this pleasant lea,
> Have glimpses that would make me less forlorn;
> Have sight of Proteus rising from the sea;
> Or hear old Triton blow his wreathèd horn.
> —William Wordsworth

This sonnet, though written some 200 years ago, nonetheless sketches with remarkable accuracy both the problems that this book addresses and the spirit in which it has been undertaken. Since Wordsworth's time we have gained a little ground here and lost a little there, but on the whole it seems to me that our major spiritual task, both its delights and its difficulties, remains substantially the same. Would we not still prefer to be pagans "suckled in a creed outworn" than to live, as most of us do, unmoved by beauty? And do we not still lay waste our imaginative powers, offering them up as if sacrificially in the service of those monster twins called "getting and spending"? In one sense, of course, our choice of whom to serve has been well rewarded, for we have all become rich in goods that replace what once we owned in Nature; and yet these goods frequently seem to own us rather than we them, and instead of helping us to realize the dream of "every man a king" they tend to leave us bemused and blinking in the cluttered playroom, not only "out of tune," as the poem says, but frequently intent on noisiness.

How are we to recall the damage done in our self-alienation and repossess what was originally given, the beauty of the bare-bosomed sea and the up-gathered winds? The poem suggests that one way back to such simple divinities may be *via* the elaborate fictions of an "outworn creed" such as allowed the ancient Greeks access to Proteus and Triton. When one has lost track of the argument it is often best to go back to school; and throughout European history this has often meant learning again to read the Greeks.

Part of this book's purpose is to become reacquainted with certain Greek words surrounding the sacred, in the hope of finding some of them not altogether outworn; but since our general sense of human origins has in the past century been pushed back from the ancient Mediterranean to the apes on the African savannah, our search for the true story of man's relations with the gods should probably begin there. So I believe in any case, and also that the reasons for going so far back are a good deal more compelling than the undoubted pleasures of tourism. The modern religion of getting and spending (which encourages us to forget our previous affiliations) manages almost to conceal (while it actually exacerbates) a spiritual confusion that may without exaggeration be called an identity crisis: modern man no longer knows who he is, and this is largely because he has forgotten where he comes from; and just as a neurotic individual can be strengthened by retrieving some repressed or disavowed aspect of his past, so can we all, both individually and collectively, be strengthened by remembering our sense of the sacred and the animal powers from which that sense arises.

The case for believing this is enhanced when one remembers that the sacred animal powers were (and are) above all concerned with the management of sex and violence, two things we have been mismanaging for some time. The consequent damage is everywhere apparent—in the banality of politics, in the acrimony released by the feminist debate, in the arts and sciences where nihilism is widespread, and in the surreptitious worship of the bomb. The seriousness of the crisis confronts us daily, with messages from a planet increasingly polluted and violent, calling us urgently to mend our ways. Freud was surely right in thinking our troubles stem chiefly from sex and violence, but surely wrong not to notice that primitive man's religious approach to these matters was often more effective and also more fun than is our secularism.

That there is a religious dimension to the present global crisis is suggested by the word "pollution," which is in fact one of the oldest religious terms in the lexicon. And yet the word "pollution" owes its current revival to the scientists and not to the religionists; moreover, most of these scientists have little idea where the word originated or how the religious mind understood it. This state of affairs nicely symbolizes aspects of the identity crisis that this book addresses. The voice of authority in our culture is unquestionably the voice of science, and yet that voice is still unable (and often unwilling) to master those parts of speech (many of which are locked up in old dictionaries) without which no utterance can be fully human, no author authoritative. The evidence is increasingly accumulating to suggest that the occidental experiment in secular scientism over the past four centuries has involved the suppression of certain vital processes of a more or less religious nature, and that this is becoming intolerable. Thus when the word "pollution" comes to scientific lips, with no memory of its former life, we may have a nice instance of what Freud called "the return of the repressed." In this case, remembrance of the former life is crucial, for pollutions both ecological and religious have much to do with the mismanagement of sex and violence; and until ecological language realizes that the problems it addresses are ultimately religious ones, it will be less than fully empowered.

This is most apparent in the worst of our pollutions, the nuclear bomb: the desire (disowned of course) to nuke the planet is but the tumorous extension of the old sacrilegious dream of making war on the gods, the desire "to become as one of us" as Yahwe puts it in Genesis (3:22). In primitive terms this means producing a phallus sufficiently potent in its erection to beat down the gates of heaven. This would be a perfectly acceptable theme for carnival hijinks (one can imagine the parade bearing the ogre with an endless dong made out of *papier-mâché*); but having forgotten how seriously important to our sanity are the playful fantasies ritualized in carnival time, we have (obscurely, to be sure) instructed our priests to construct *the real thing*, in official time, and hide it in the temple; and this they have done. Until we can in sufficient numbers learn to tell the story in this way, which is how any moderately intelligent primitive would tell it, we have no hope of grasping the enormity of its insanity. The recent thawing of the Cold War provides an excellent opportunity to begin.

To put all this a little more quietly, the answer to our identity crisis and the planetary problems it has generated is to heal the rift that opened in the Western soul some 400 years ago when science and religion went their separate ways. Luckily, for the hour is growing late, such a reconciliation seems conceivable to some. On the recent humanizing of the sciences one thinks of the developments outlined in Fritjof Capra's *Turning Point* (1982), which we shall consider in Chapter 1. On the religious side the development is longer and more complex. If one sees the rift at its theoretical worst when the Romantic poets abandoned a culture whose scientific materialism called for the liquidation of cultural memory as an arbiter of value, the nineteenth century subsequently threw up several developments to counteract such amnesia. One thinks not only of primitive tendencies in the arts, nineteenth-century ethnography, and psycho-analysis, but the geology of Sir Charles Lyell and the biology of Charles Darwin. More recently, the confluence of philosophy, anthropology, mythology, psychoanalysis, feminism, and literary crit-icism in what has been called "discourse theory" is attempting to get behind the various intellectual specialisms that have so fragmented our thinking over the past century.

Although these theorists are usually too abstract for my taste, this book is comparably interdisciplinary, and it inscribes itself in the general endeavor to build a true science of man, a serious anthropology, in the belief that the groundwork for such construction was laid in the "materialist" nineteenth century—by the open-mindedness of ethnographers in their collection of data, by the irrationalist skepticism of Nietzsche, by the psychological insight of Freud and Jung, and above all by the evolutionary theory of Darwin, which offered us compelling grounds for rethinking our origins. Though I frequently disagree with Lévi-Strauss, I share his hope and belief that there is such a thing as "the primitive mind," which can and should be known.

What unites the three master poets of the twentieth century, Yeats, Eliot, and Pound, is their belief that modern man must return to the mythic voice if he is to heal the divisions in his soul. Despite their various achievements in this regard, it is a massive undertaking, and still lies before us: centuries of rational habits of mind remain deeply engrained, leading us to mistrust and resist what we are disposed to hear (sometimes correctly) as the Siren songs of the mythological. In retrospect it appears that all three poets (Pound particularly) went at the matter too vigorously, hastened unslowly, and underestimated their own implication in the *fin de siècle* decadence they were trying to oppose. Another way of putting this is to say that all three were a little contemptuous of their fellow man, and a little negligent of the need to stay in touch with him. Contemplating this, it occurred to me some years ago that before we can expect much more serious mythic *poetry*, we need more of the *prophecy* that is its essential precondition: we should be looking for John the Baptist, not Jesus.

In other words, more work needs to be done on the foundations, on preparing the mind for a new (very old) way of thinking; and this involves, above all, taking account of the fact (which all three poets scorned) that the modern mind is still profoundly scientific in its allegiance, and that any move back to the mythological will have to address that allegiance and obtain its permission. As a contribution to this undertaking, I originally thought of writing a somewhat Jungian essay on the mythological mind that prevailed before the rational procedures inaugurated by Plato. I soon realized, however, that the mythic too has an important prehistory that has to be known, and so I was driven back to the apes on the African savannah. Thus we need mythology to illuminate philosophy and psychology, and anthropology to illuminate mythology. The further back I went, the simpler and more physical the language became, and it occurred to me, as it has to many others, that here we may indeed find an antidote to the bewildering abstractions of the modern tongue. But though it would be fair to say that my dominant concern in this book is with language, with finding words both simple and searching enough to illuminate our first and last things, I am also trying to tell a story.

The story begins with the arboreal monkey evolving into the chimpanzee. Here is the animal base from which all man's higher activities arise. Many readers will be astonished to discover how much we knew of love and war before we learned to talk. When we stood up and moved from the forests onto the savannah we became both more violent and, necessarily, more preoccupied with nurturing the young. To move simultaneously toward violence and domesticity put an obvious strain on the mind, and what we now know as the sex war was underway. Our desires to make both love and war were clarified on the dancing ground where divinity was discovered. As he danced for the buffalo, and as his dance *became* the buffalo, primitive man discovered those powers of representation that underlie sympathetic magic and the ideas of totemism and pollution.

The more or less cheerful tale of how we moved from monkey to man on the savannah is told in Chapters 2 and 3. But then one day, as all the saddening stories agree, something happened: the apple was eaten, innocence was lost, and we discovered the limitless anarchy that comes loose when sex and violence become truly human (which is to say, god-haunted). This is the Fall, and the version of it most of us know best is recorded in Chapters 3 and 4 of Genesis. Although these stories seem to me almost preternaturally accurate in most respects, we are no longer desert bedouin, have different narrative expectations, and moreover have access to certain information these bedouin seem to have forgotten when composing their tales. Not only do I think that the apple-god we ate was occupying a human body at the time, but also that the impulse to eat him came among us while we were dancing. Although these "events" cannot be at all accurately dated, I find some plausibility in linking them with the domestication of fire, around 50,000 B.C.

For a revision of Genesis to be at all compelling to the modern mind, it must do justice to the best that has been thought by our scientists (both natural and social) about the moment of intersection between mammal and man; and this takes up most of Chapter 4, which concludes Part I, the more or less scientific section of the book concerned with human evolution. Part II examines the measures taken by paleolithic man to live with the loss of his innocence, the cultural moves he made to protect himself from further exposure to that sacred monster that had originally tempted him ecstatically into cannibalism and worse. The word I use for these measures is "lawlines," and in the beginning this is literally what they are, lines drawn in the mind and on the dancing ground to regulate the flow of energies no longer governed by the codes of primate instinct. What is being sought in these chapters is effectively the grammar of primitive experience, the ways in which magic, myth, and ritual were used to allow us to talk to the gods without being swallowed by them.

Although these three chapters (5–7) are the least chronological in the book, they do attempt to progress from the simple to the complex. Thus Chapter 5 begins in the timeless mists of the paleolithic hunt, and Chapter 7 (which concentrates on sacrifice, the central mystery of all religions) ends with Isis and Osiris, who lead us through the perplexing darkness of the neolithic revolution and into the light of what we have for some time agreed to call "civilization." It is perhaps worth mentioning here that although much of the discussion in Part II may seem to be of a psychological, even psychoanalytic, complexion, I do constantly try to allow the primitive to stand its ground (to keep its otherness other) and not to be swallowed in modern imaginings.

Part II is not only less chronological than I would wish, but also less empirical, and I should say why. It is concerned not simply with the primitive grammar of the sacred (about which anthropologists have gathered empirical testimony) but with the process whereby that grammar evolved into the language used by "historical" (or "scriptural") man who emerges at Sumer about 3000 B.C. We are more than somewhat in the dark regarding the process of this evolution, and have to cobble the story together from both ends, as it were. Chapters 5–7 for the most part approach this dark age from the primitive end, whereas the Appendix, by examining some very old words from the Greek lexicon, attempts to reconstruct the religious experience that lies behind them. Etymology is one of our chief resources for excavating in this darkness, and the Appendix can most profitably be read in conjunction with these chapters.

The overall progression of the book is from the African savannah up to Egypt and the Near East, and then to ancient Greece where it concludes. But though this northerly progress of the human story was in obvious ways progressive, in religious terms there was a falling off; and Part III is concerned, as its title indicates, with "Occlusions of the Sacred." By looking at four major texts from the early days of civilization, all of which lament a lost contact with the gods, I attempt to indicate what is primarily being lost by patriarchal man in his epic endeavors to kill Death with his sword: the feminine touch, then as now our chief stay against violence. The melancholy movement of this section is arrested in the finale, where we go looking somewhat playfully for the lost magics of the Cretan Bull. Although he seems to have escaped us, his secrets lie buried no deeper than human forgetfulness, and we could find him if we try.

2

This book is much concerned with beginnings, with how we once began and how we may begin again; and since introductions are warm-ups, often awkward attempts to establish and delimit the relevant playground for the game to follow, I shall now sketch a rough map of the terrain we shall begin to explore in Chapter 1; and since crude maps are the most useful kind when in a strange land (or in the beginning), as Ludwig Wittgenstein reminds us, I shall take this opportunity to be very crude indeed.

Body and soul. The world's body (which used to be called *res extensa,* the extended thing) is the visible material stuff "out there" that seems to be just waiting for us to push it around. One of the reasons we call primitive man a child is that he tended to use magic in his attempts to push it around, though he was also in fact quite impressive with science and technology—(there are 200 species of edible plants in the African Bushman's botany book, and even with today's clever tools I would not like to be asked to organize a Lascaux cave-painting expedition). Still, it must be said that we are infinitely better at science and technology than was primitive man, and this has everything to do with our having suppressed our magical instincts.

The world's soul is composed of all those powers that seem to move invisibly and immaterially, "in the wind" as it were. It is insufficiently recognized that the words for wind, soul, and breath commingle in virtually every language,[1] which is one reason why I have chosen the very old Greek word for wind, *pneuma* (pronounced as in "pneumonia"), to designate the mystery of invisible soul-power (and I attempt to show how the wind blows through the soul of ancient Greece in the Appendix). Is the soul a thing? I call it a mystery because we still don't know much about it. We tend to think of it as a thing, but it is more like a no-thing. Aristotle, trying to think the unthinkable, came up with "unmoved mover" as a description of the cosmic wind-generator, which at least does some justice to our sense of a thinginess that issues in movement. Thus what moves the visible world-body, indeed pushes it around, is the invisible world-soul, which is wind, which is *pneuma,* which is divinity, which is God.

Unlike us, primitive man was not disposed to separate his own soul from the world-soul. Soul is soul, invisible power that moves in the wind, so how can it be chopped up and compartmentalized? (I think there is much to be said for such primitive stupidity, as shall become clear in due course.) Of course men everywhere and always have wanted to ask of this mysterious divinity who it is and what it wants. The answer heard by the Jews, profound in this as in so many matters, is *"ehyeh asher ehyeh,"* "I am that I am" (Exodus 3:14), which the scholars now think better translated as "I will be what I will be" (the importance of *movement* coming clear in the revised version). Sensing a Zen-like difficulty of paradox and tautology in this response, the plain man (and this book longs for the plain man) will be happier with another line from the Bible that says that divine *pneuma* "bloweth where it listeth" (John 3:8), and for listeth read lusteth, which is to say *pneuma* desires, or simply *is* desire; and it is fair to say that whatever *pneuma* wants, *pneuma* gets.

Thunderstorms, earthquakes, volcanoes and the like, are mysterious wants that still tease the mind (and devastate the cosmos), but we really wake up for the wants that get issued through the human body; and these rarely appear without ambivalence and contradiction. Is it me or some demon that wants to break into that woman's body? What for? My teeth grind my food: when does a kiss become a bite, and when does a bite lose its ingestive goal and stand clear as the desire to mutilate? And how are all three related to the word I sometimes speak instead? And is it me doing this, or is it the wind blowing through me? And why? These are some of our first religious questions, for which there are no certain answers, and they lie at the heart of this study.

There are no certain answers to these questions because the world-soul blows in the invisible wind, unlike the world-body which seems to lie before us in the sunshine. The simple proof of this is in the library: under "science" you will find a number of books which will indicate that we have the world-body pretty much "locked in," as we used to say in the early days of space shots and computer terminals; or perhaps one should say "locked up" or even "locked out." Under philosophy, theology, poetry, psychology, anthropology, etc., however, you will find that the question of human desire is just as baffling today as primitive man knew it to be. Freud (not to mention a host of lesser Freuds) deeply wanted his books on human desire to get into the science section, but alas, not so; and one of the heartening signs as we move toward the end of this our second post-Christological millennium is that more and more people are cheerfully admitting "Not so."

I am being crude of course, but the distinction I'm after is both crude and crucial. Science *does* take a hand in (declares an interest in, hence fictionalizes or constructs) the knowledge it gathers of the world-body, as we shall see at considerable length in Chapter 1, but it nonetheless *does* on the whole subdue its material (at whatever cost); and each scientific theory is an improvement on its predecessor. Science works because the body in question is visibly *there*, to confirm or falsify (register its compliance with) the present theory about how best to push it around. The arts, on the other hand, are fictional or constructive through and through, and do not progress as science does. Since the invisible soul of desire is not palpably *there* to confirm or falsify our naming of its parts, not only must we darkly imagine those names, but our imaginings are to a disturbing extent self-certifying, particularly when ritually enforced in a coherent religion: "Right you are if you think you are," as Pirandello said. Thus myth is not only less accurate than science in significant ways, but under ritual auspices a good deal more tyrannical. This potential tyranny of the fictive is often poorly understood these days, as most of us take our mythic instruction from novels we read in solitude, and many of these books make some effort to "deconstruct" themselves, i.e., subvert their own authority to name the parts of desire.

Which is to say, we take little mythic instruction. The self-deconstructing novel may be good for a laugh or a sub-Zen reminder of the void, but its fastidious refusal of authorial authority at best illuminates and at worst exacerbates our mythic muddle. We seem to be forgetting (what our forebears clearly knew) that the winds of *pneuma* call upon us to name the parts of desire as best we can. We cannot refuse this call because Mother Nature in her wisdom (or unwisdom) unlocked the instinctual primate codes by which when we were apes we used to navigate the seas of desire. A good myth or poem stands in for these codes, addresses our appetitive anarchies, and offers safe conduct to some life-enhancing energy by giving it a name; and a bad one does the opposite, "binding with briars my joys and desires." But in the *absence* of an authoritative myth or poem, the lights simply go out and the soul is closed down: no name, no game. In other words, we *have* to play; and if we refuse, our robotic bodies are simply wired up by this week's television commercials.

Could it be that the seeming certainties of science and the delusive promise of its protecting care have rendered us unwilling to shoulder the risks involved in authorizing our desires? If so the irony is considerable, for even now our science of the world-body is not only admitting its inability to govern the world-soul, but is itself calling out for governance: our relations with Mother Nature have gone wrong (the Ozone hole is gaping, CO_2 emissions are rising), and it will take more than a poem or two to get them right. This is another reason for consulting primitive man, for he not only kept in close touch with Mother Nature, but did so through the application of startlingly strong mythic medicine.

Without preempting the arguments to be engaged subsequently, we can say a little more about myth versus science (or rather "myth/ritual" versus science, since myth draws much of its power from ritual). I have suggested that it is a good deal easier both in principle and in practice to develop techniques for mastering the world-body than the world-soul, not only because the soul is a genuine antagonist that *will* not be mastered, but also because its invisibility means we must make do with far less of the empirical feedback that is the secret of science's success with the world-body. In its attempts to summon and clarify the world-soul, myth/ritual relies heavily on what might be described as "feed-forward," a dancing pantomime or verbal formula that seeks to *invoke* the relevant spirits, inviting them to manifest themselves in the space-time we provide; that is to say, myth/ritual relies on *magic,* that process whereby the wished-for thing is made credibly (and incredibly) to appear before us through the metaphors and symbols that "give to airy nothing a local habitation and a name."[2] But science, having progressed by eschewing the magical as primitive and childish, has tempted us also to forgo the magical in our pursuit of the world-soul. This simply cannot be done: if you want to traffic with the invisible, you *have* to use magic. Because we have forgotten this, particularly since the Renaissance, we are in many respects more ignorant of *pneuma*'s desires than were our primitive forebears.

I oversimplify too much: myth/ritual is also nourished by feedback, as science is by feed-forward, which is to say that these two modes of knowing and manipulating overlap to some extent. This overlap is explored in Chapter 1, where I have chosen the word "fiction" to designate the "made-up" elements in both myth and scientific hypothesis. To see that fiction is inescapable is to see (among other things) that we could profitably renew our acquaintance with certain aspects of magical enchantment without offending our sacred obligations to the gods of science. These gods are in any case becoming more liberal, since subatomic physics has decided that matter, the world-body, *res extensa,* is a fiction we can now do without. This is quite a good joke: when a physicist says that matter doesn't exist, and is *really* just a misleading epiphany of the energy gods, he has almost come full circle, very close to the primitive animist who knows that everything is alive, and derives its liveliness from the winds of *pneuma* that blow through it. I will suggest in Chapter 1 that this joke is reasonably innocuous as long as we remember that plain men need plain talk, particularly when it comes to the gods; and just as we will go on speaking meaningfully of "sunrise" and "sunset," so will we go on distinguishing between the world-soul and the world-body: the world as we *see* it makes certain fictional demands on human language that we neglect at our peril.

This discussion is becoming dangerously uncrude. Let us now take a brief look at the figure who is the real hero of this book, the shaman or myth-making poet. Compared to the sober (?) scientist with his tidy mathematical traps, he looks rather like a loony fisherman casting into the wind with what we may as well call *symbols,* in Jung's sense of "the best possible expression of a relatively *unknown* fact." Such symbols or metaphors are drawn to some extent from what Lévi-Strauss has helpfully described as *bricolage,* odds and ends gathered from coincidence and the wood lot out back; that is to say, those who would fish the wind *bricolent* their bait out of worms that live locally, and hence there are as many "sciences" of human desire as there are human habitats producing dreamy fishermen. This whole process is rendered less whimsical (for primitives obviously and for us less obviously) by the rituals that bind fisherman, bait, and fish (?) into agreed procedures. Whether or not there are common threads or themes (Jung's archetypes) that run through all these different ways of fishing is a question that haunts Lévi-Strauss, and this book as well.

Enough of this metaphor. Man fishes for the logic of human desire with myth and ritual: the primitive knows this, even Plato still knew this (whenever he has something important to say about being human he slides helplessly—and happily—into mythic mode), and scientismic man tends to forget this, and when he does he builds prisons that try to catch the wind; and here *we* are, almost post-scientismic, remembering that they had it right in the old days, ah the wind, *felix culpa* and the dreadful freedom of being human. I say "dreadful" not only because this is the freedom to play a game that was always dangerous and in the end must be lost, but also because right now, as the millennium draws in, we are being asked to turn off the television, remember all we have forgotten of the holy game of poker, and play a hard card *right now.* To do this will not be easy: Mother Nature is ill and we don't care; and instead of serious poker the game we dream about looks more like bridge, with all of us holding the dummy's hand.

If modern man is alienated man, troubled by the distance between himself and the gods or reality, we are by and large postmodern, aimlessly adrift on the tides of indifference and puzzled by an excess of toys in the playpen (not to mention the monstrous phallic toy hidden in the closet). But though the distance back seems formidable, the alienated space we must abolish was spun in neurosis, and neurosis can be dispelled in the wind, magically indeed, if you get the formula right. The card table still stands in the front room, and if we don't return to it the game will simply go by default; and the last hand, played somewhat absentmindedly by our fathers and grandfathers, will stand with our fingerprints appended thereto. Less apocalyptically, though the game was always dangerous, it is also supposed to be fun. The principal objective of mythic play was always the permission to live life more abundantly, and as I read the historical evidence, it succeeds more often than not. But lest the reader suspect from the breezy tone of this opening song that I think I have the answers to modern alienation, which I will ceremoniously unfold in Chapter 8, let me assure him/her this is not so. I think these old stories are interesting in themselves, and call upon us to find them quite pertinent to the present distress; but what we should make of them can only be decided if and when we agree to show up.

3

> There is more ado to interpret interpretations than to interpret the things, and more books upon books than upon all other subjects. We do nothing but comment upon one another.
>
> —Michel de Montaigne

Let us, without abandoning crudity, try a more scholarly approach. In the eighteenth century Giambattista Vico turned his mind to the study of history, and came up with one of the great "unlocking" perceptions: in the beginning we are ruled by the gods (theocracy), then by the nobles (aristocracy), and then we are ruled by the people (democracy), *and at each stage of this development our language conceives the world differently*; and when this process is complete (when democracy discovers its anarchic objectives), there is a return (*ricorso*) to the beginning and the whole cycle runs through again. The master Vico-ite of our time is Professor Northrop Frye, and since he was my first and most influential teacher, it is hardly surprising that I am still more or less a Vico-ite too (at least in linguistic matters).[3]

The first stage covers primitive man and ends somewhere in the background of Homer (where this book concludes); and its language is mythical or metaphorical, which is to say its words are thought to be alive, magically participating in the life they represent, capable indeed of summoning into our presence the powers they name. The second stage begins with Plato and ends in the eighteenth century (Kant its last giant), and its language is conceptual or metonymic (for which word we are indebted to Roman Jakobson). The metaphor is essentially magical, claiming to *be* what it calls forth ("A garden enclosed is my sister, my spouse") whereas the metonym aspires only to stand in for the absent thing it designates. Whereas the language of myth is concrete, physical, of the body, the language of conceptual propositions (and mathematics) is abstract and reflective, a notation not thought to be in itself real but capable of discerning analogies or ghostly paradigms of the god who has withdrawn (absconded is too strong a word) from his creation. The metonymic mind is typically concerned with the sub-stantial, literally "that which stands beneath the appearance of things," and sub-stance is to be met up with (analogically) in the under-standing. If the god of myth is a musician (a song and dance man originally) the god of metonymy is a mathematician and a philosopher. But music is intrinsically the baffling borderline case, since however metonymic its structuring principles, its mysterious immateriality *means* metaphor: it must always finally *be* what it represents. Bach's organ fugues, for example, are among the last triumphs of the metonymic mind, rational quasi-mathematical structures that analogize the mind of God; and yet in their moments of sublime dissonance, who would deny the move into metaphor? Something comes into the church and shudders the backbone.

The third stage (an elaboration of the metonymic) is dominated by the language of empirical science, where reality is thought to be "out there," declaring itself to the senses. The idea of God is declared meaningless, and the task of words is simply to match themselves up to the things they find. Needless to say, the three stages overlap and interpenetrate a good deal: even today some people think they have met an aristocrat, some poets or musicians think they have met a god, and science is beginning to confess its unempirical tendencies. Such overlap breeds confusion, of course, as was evident in the recent controversy over the people's right to burn the American flag in public places. The Supreme Court decided that the flag is more of a Protestant metonym than a primitive metaphor, and this decision, whatever its legal wisdom, dismayed not only uneducated jingoists but a good many thoughtful people as well.

Lest some readers are becoming alarmed, I should quickly say that the word metonymy does not occur once in the text of this book. I mention it here because it updates and corroborates Vico's insight, and helps us to appreciate two important implications of seeing things in this way. The first is that although a concern with divinity may be a constant in human affairs (the most empirical scientist will be "devoted" to Beethoven), the mode of addressing it is not. This means that although the rigorous rationalism of Thomas Aquinas (metonymist par excellence) will not help many modern readers to clarify and deepen their intimations of immortality, this is not in itself to say he got it wrong, nor that he got it right and we have lost it, but only that he got it *different*. The second point is the cyclical one: having exhausted the riches of the metonymic dispensation (and the simple descriptions of empirical science) we are almost ready once again for myth and metaphor, the *presence* of divinity, "becoming the music while the music lasts," as T. S. Eliot almost said.

This was perceived first and best by Wordsworth, who was in my view not only the major poet of the nineteenth century, but also one of its most intelligent men. Though still a metonymist in many respects (admiring Newton, for example), he was also subject, as was no other Romantic poet, to the radically primitive, the presence of divinity:

> Points have we all of us within our souls
> Where all stand single; this I feel, and make
> Breathings for incommunicable powers.
> —*Prelude*, Book 3

These are extraordinary lines, awkward, stumbling, earmarked for derision in smart London: "*Points* within our souls on which we *stand,* Mr. Wordsworth? Cumbersome stuff, Mr. Wordsworth, back to Cumberland with you." The "points" do seem bizarre at first, as if appealing to Newton to hold him as the wind carries him into strangeness; and yet metonymically speaking, they arguably stand quite well. The nineteenth-century soul, after all, is a place within the body that cannot be placed; and so mathematical points, locations without extension, may fittingly identify the regions within this regionless region where the soul may rise in significant singleness.

"This I feel" at first appears to be an egregious interruption, but in fact earns its keep by both announcing a new direction (the heart not the head, farewell metonymy) and enforcing a silence in which the breathings can become audible. I would go further: although "this I feel" presents itself as a halting qualification, even a worry about the merely personal, it is also paradoxically what authorizes the outrageous move into metaphor that follows it. (The modern tone? Perhaps it is: one thinks of the stunning announcement that opens Rousseau's *Confessions*: "Je sens mon coeur et je connais les hommes.")* To "make breathings" is necessarily a move into the darkness of the radically metaphorical, and any attempt to visualize it will produce banality and farce—the image of a carpenter drilling portholes in some obscure structure so that the wind can blow in and out. But if we close our eyes and *listen,* it hangs together quite perfectly, and may even remind us of some childhood afternoon spent in the waving branches of a wind-tossed tree.

To speak thus candidly and thingily of matters that, as he has just said in the previous line, lie on the whole "far hidden from the reach of words," is singular indeed, such a departure from the prevailing decorums of metonymy that both in his day and still in ours, Wordsworth was and is usually derided as impossibly old-fashioned. The truth of the matter, however, is that he is so radically new (in his oldness) that we still on the whole can't keep up with him. At the heart of this mystery is his belief, which brings him nearer the primitive dancing ground than any other modern poet, that the way to make breathings is to stop talking, and if you do *that* (self-cancellation for the poet), the words (or the music) may come of themselves, unbidden, unforced, and deposit themselves as real presences in the silent spaces you have cleared for them. So certain

*"I feel my heart and know mankind."

is Wordsworth of the metamorphic power that he persuades us the breathings have been made by the words on the page.

Enough of mysticism and the return to primitive metaphor. As if all this were not sufficient load for three lines to carry, there is yet another theme, and it bears upon our present undertaking. Look again at the run of seven plurals in the first two lines that shrink into the singularity of "all stand single." Bizarre? For non-Wordsworthians let me offer a subtextual gloss: the man who wrote this had recently returned from France, almost crazed by the desolate perception of what the September Massacres had made of the ardent ecstasies in which the Revolution had begun. Imagine him saying this: "These breathings I have known walking alone in the Lake District, and yet they paradoxically reveal the powers that unite 'all of us.' Such powers, as my poem indicates some thirty lines before the present passage, were originally revealed to 'the first men, earth's first inhabitants,' when they were gathered together on the dancing ground. But alas, such things 'may in these tutor'd days no more be seen with undisorder'd sight.' I know this now because I went to France in the hope that the ecstasies I once knew alone could be risked there by all of us together in the name of brotherhood. I have returned home severely chastened, and again I walk alone, but in the troubled hope and faith that moments of mystical solitude may still be a pledge and a promise of our communion with others."

But are they? This is one of Wordsworth's major dilemmas, and its bearing on the lines I have cited is clearly indicated in the ones that haltingly succeed it. And it is our dilemma too, for though we all long to allow the incommunicable powers to enter and bind us together, our most profound experiences are also usually solitary, made possible by the *absence* of others. The call of primitive ecstasy is the call of the wild; and for modern man, as my generation was reminded in the sixties, it ends in tears. We are still not ready for it; and yet it remains the dream we deeply dream.

4

Since this book clearly believes that a reacquaintance with our primitive selves can make us *more* human rather than *less,* it had better recognize the obvious objection to such a proposal: that both Nazism and (more complicatedly) Stalinism were infected with primitive dreams, and hence the Romantic longing for a return to the original thing has been decisively proscribed in our time.[4] My answer to this is that the primitive elements in both "religions" were decadent or kitsch, and that the monstrous perversions in both cases manifest the pressing importance of our primitive reeducation rather than render it taboo. The great authority on this matter, as on so many others, is Friedrich Nietzsche.

As a young man he rapturously heard the call of the wild in Wagner's music, and his contribution (aged twenty-six) to the primitivizing renaissance in Germany was *The Birth of Tragedy from the Spirit of Music,* an essay on the Greek gods Apollo and Dionysus (which still stands, despite its febrile prose and excessive devotion to *Kultur,* as a minor masterpiece). Soon after this, however, Nietzsche smelled a rat, as not only German nationalism but the racist dream of Aryan purity began to befoul the 1870s of Bismarck's Reich. Dionysus renovated was not to be trusted: in the foreground, of course, anti-Semitism (infecting his erstwhile friend Wagner along with others who he had hoped were made of sterner stuff), but more ominously prophetic of future disaster to his ear was the decadence he increasingly discerned in the music swelling out of Wagnerian Bayreuth. Why more ominous than anti-Semitic speech? Because he knew, as Plato and Aristotle knew before him, that music makes claims upon and gives expression to profounder energies than words can ever reach; which is to say, it is our most powerful magic, for good and for ill. (This truth, self-evident to any primitive, has almost been forgotten in today's noisy world, which is yet another indication of our need to return to first and last things.)[5]

What did Nietzsche hear? Vulgarity, first of all, glaringly apparent to any ear even moderately chastened by the development of Western music from plainsong to Beethoven. This gives a clue not only to the ungoverned nature of the energies but also to what Nietzsche called the "pose" of Wagner's theater, its camp and its kitsch. Subtending all his specific objections is the simple perception that all good music dances, Wagner's doesn't, and hence it "makes sick":

> Richard Wagner wanted a different kind of movement; he overthrew the *physiological presupposition* of previous music [my emphasis]. Swimming, floating—no longer walking and dancing . . . [Wagner's] "infinite melody" seeks deliberately to break all evenness of time and force and even scorns it occasionally; the wealth of its invention lies precisely in that which to an older ear sounds like a rhythmic paradox and blasphemy. The imitation or domination of such a taste would result in a danger to music which cannot be exaggerated: the complete degeneration of rhythmic feeling, chaos in place of rhythm.*

Among the many important things being said here is that when music gives up its "physiological presupposition," its somatic rhythms, the emotions it conjures are no longer channeled through and harnessed by the enacting human body (which is therefore allowed to wander unmonitored into camp and kitsch). Our clinical adjective for such a breakage is "schizoid," and I believe I can hear it foreshadowed in late Beethoven; in the Ninth Symphony clamorously, in the pastiche of the *Missa Solemnis* anguishingly, and in the discarnating last quartets sublimely.[6] There is a momentous issue involved here: one might call it the latest version of the Prometheus story, modern man's project of escaping his body. Instead of being chained to a rock, the supremely gifted and intelligent Beethoven had his hearing taken away (at once a release from, and a solitary confinement to, the body); and his enraged defiance issued in a breathtaking mixture of bombast, chaos, and

---

*From *Nietzsche Contra Wagner* in Kaufmann (1954), p. 666. Baudelaire's ear, that of a poet, was even more acutely offended: he heard in Wagner's music "the ultimate scream of a soul driven to its utmost limits." Baudelaire was also the man who said "The devil's last trick is to convince you he doesn't exist."

preternatural beauty. He is the great modern Lucifer, and anyone who thinks his story merely Viennese or merely German or merely musical should read again Wordsworth's prophetic warning about the dangerous "application of gross and violent stimulants" to the mind: Wordsworth heard the rumors of violence and decadence without having to listen to Beethoven.[7]

I digress, though not really, since one of this book's major purposes is to commend the concreteness of the primitive imagination as an antidote to the bodilessness of modern abstraction. But whether or not I am right about Beethoven, Nietzsche's case against Wagner does seem to me unassailable, and one should hear it in the background of the famous line from Zarathustra (which appears as epigraph to this book's Chapter 4), "Never trust a god who doesn't dance." Wagner, to his credit, finally realized that the Dionysus set loose in his music was being hijacked by evil demons and had to be crucified in *Parsifal*; but the damage had been done, the proverbial genie was out of the bottle.*

To say that Wagner's music is anti-Semitic is a nonsense, but to say the so-called primitive gods it invokes were still on stage in the 1930s is, I submit, to speak meaningfully. To speak meaningfully of Nazism is no easy task (truly the banality of evil in our time, as Hannah Arendt has taught us) and so I shall be brief. What is immediately striking about the newsreels of Hitler's rallies (and the Leni Riefenstahl film, *Triumph of the Will*) is that despite Albert Speer's Art Deco flair, the theater of King Rat was astonishingly kitsch, Punch and Judy stuff, the badness of bad carnival, which nonetheless tolerated Wagner's *Meistersinger* (his *healthiest* piece!) on the Riefenstahl soundtrack.[8] And the question of how Weimar Germany could have mistaken such revelry (revery?) for revolution

---

*Could it have been otherwise? Nietzsche's beloved composer was Mozart, and the search for healthy gods in the Revolutionary era is clearly begun in Mozart's *Magic Flute*. Sarastro's great arias indicate that Father's voice can still be heard after the parricide. Why did we not build on that? Why indeed. With no disrespect to Beethoven, and the almost inconceivable rhythmic genius of his early music, we must go back and look for Sarastro, to see if he cannot be persuaded to address the anger of his queen, *die Königin der Nacht*, Mother Night.

can be much clarified by first asking a larger question of the nineteenth century: how was the spirit of Western music emptied of its priceless treasures and rendered diabolical in less than a hundred years? This is finally a religious question, which certainly involves the French Revolution, and we have hardly begun to ask it. The Germans, as masters of the music since the late seventeenth century and hosts to Hitler, have been elected and appointed chief witnesses in the case. But Britain, though her theater was less decadent and her dancing more robust, also loved Wagner; and the French loved him even more. However one plays the game of "It couldn't have happened here" or "It couldn't have happened to me," it also could have.

The shadow this casts over enterprises like the present one is deeply disturbing. However one estimates the prophetic significance of Wagner's music, the element of decadent primitivism in the totalitarian insanity is undeniable. The evil that overcame both the Russians and the Germans included a schizophrenic dream of Aztec sacrifice: though the blood surely flowed into some weird fantasy of the body politic, no altars were built for the offering, and no one was there.

Those who ignore history are doomed to repeat it; and though I believe some of our decadence has been purged in the bloodbaths of this century, and though the recent dismantling of the Russian horror is immensely heartening, and though I would think primitivism one of our mandatory subjects even in the absence of good news, I also think we are still ill; and hence that any strange figure who might tempt us with a serious tom-tom today or tomorrow will be some relation of the Pied Piper. We must learn to trust ourselves again: we must learn to dance again soon or the game will escape us; but we are not yet fit. The law must be repaired. In the beginning is plainsong.

As the body of this book will make clear, I have no doubt about the magical power of the arts in the shaping of human utterance; and since music is the most magical of these (particularly for modern man), it should provide deeper insights into the soul than language can.[9] Thus my musical examples are offered here not as metonyms (analogies or illustrations) but metaphors, *actual* expressions of the Romantic soul of bourgeois Europe. My rough sketch of this soul may be concluded by briefly considering Beethoven's last piano sonata (Opus 111). This piece is a wonder of sanity regained, also a prophecy: after some initial argument melody returns gracefully to its home in the human body, and the syncopated rhythms point amiably and unmistakably forward to ragtime and the jazz age. As he leaves the stage, this last of the European grandmasters quietly announces that he has concluded (consummated and killed) a musical life that had begun in medieval plainsong. As Vico would say, it was time for a *ricorso* to primitive beginnings, and Beethoven tells us here that we should look for it not in Wagner's Europe but in the southern states of America, where the chanting equivalent of monastic plainsong would be the Negro "holler" that had come from West Africa. Whereas most nineteenth-century music (post-Beethoven) seems to me only somewhat slandered by Ezra Pound's description of it as "steam ascending from a morass," the jazz that evolved from holler and folk music has housed as best it could the wandering soul of the twentieth century, and I know of little genuinely life-enhancing music from our time that is not jazz-based. But whereas European music took centuries to reach its discarnating conclusions and postmortem "savage torpor," time moves more quickly in the American Age, and our jazz had already become significantly disembodied by the 1930s. This melancholy fact makes me think of something Yeats said when contemplating the vacuous decadence of poetry and drama in the latter nineteenth century (and his remarks apply equally well to its music):

> All the arts when young and happy are but the point of the spear whose handle is our daily life. When they grow old and unhappy, they perfect themselves away from life, and life, seeing that they are sufficient to themselves, forgets them.[10]

Although much of our jazz became old and unhappy some time ago, leaving us once again spiritually adrift, with "no direction home" in important respects, its origins offer most of us a more accessible meditation "in the meantime" than does plainsong. In the beginning is the holler.

5

> I speak truth, not so much as I would but as much as I dare; and I dare a little the more, as I grow older.
>
> —Michel de Montaigne

While Europe at home in the mid-nineteenth century was getting ready for Wagner, abroad it was despoiling *real* primitives, often with a viciousness worthy of Odysseus's raid on Polyphemos (a discussion of which dominates this book's concluding chapter). And just as Odysseus's violence was increased by envy born of admiration, so was ours then.

These facts are particularly painful to Americans; for though we were Europeans abroad at that time, we were Americans at home, and our sinful deeds were not only committed at home and hence refused to be hidden (out of sight, out of mind), but were committed upon peoples also trying to be at home in the place that we were. What is even worse, the Indians had in obvious ways a better title to the land than we did. The full horror of what was done only becomes apparent in retrospect, of course, for many a grizzled cavalryman saw the Indians as only a kind of buffalo, dangerous animals that had to be cleared if the land was to be settled. Such "mis-taking" of the quarry comes naturally to the hunter, whether modern or paleolithic, as we shall see in Chapter 5.

And yet even at the time we also admired both the Red man and the Black man, and this admiration is still encoded in our speech and in our dreams. In the nineteenth century it usually found oblique expression (my grandfather and his pals, for example, *obsessed* with fine horses on the North Dakota border of the Sioux country), but in the twentieth the secret is out. I have already alluded to the importance for all of us of the jazz that evolved chiefly from the Negro work song and religious gathering; and anyone who might disclaim acquaintance with such disorganized music could be reminded that whatever musicality there might be in his daily speech is undoubtedly jazz-sprung. But for a simpler example, consider the irony of this: the only serious kneeling done by me and my pals when we were young was in the bottom of a canoe, in order to become Indians, and none of us doubted the importance of the undertaking. As the famous speech by Chief Seattle (some of which can be found on the epigraph page) would suggest, much of what we know of natural piety we learned from them.[11]

In due course I learned to kneel in the Anglican church, and though I can hardly bear the barbarous changes recently inflicted on its liturgy, I remain grateful for the learning in at least two respects that relate to the present enterprise. First of all, the sins of the fathers *are* visited upon the children, at the very least in the form of bad dreams; as Chief Seattle says, "The dead are not altogether powerless." Part of what makes us white folks still resist the reclamation of our primitive selves (whether we be American or European) is the fear that we may bump into the angry ghost of some colored "savage" and have to call him brother. The only way to unlock this fear is to ask for forgiveness (which involves not only recognizing what *was* done, but also what is still being done, for the story is not over).

The myth of Jesus Christ is particularly well suited for such an undertaking, as it seizes upon the hatred we feel in the presence of a stranger whom we darkly suspect to be somehow superior to ourselves. Such hatred becomes poisonously dissembled and disowned if the stranger's superiority calls upon us not only for respect but also for *gratitude*. Is this not apt? My own case is particularly clear, not only because of what I still remember of canoeing in North Ontario as a boy, but I often wonder what would have become of me without the warmth of my "Black mammy" in Evanston, Illinois; and yet as I have tried to indicate, the matter stands similarly, however abstractly, for all of us.

Like all powerful myths, the Christian one does not confine its gift to those who can bear its ritual upon their bodies; which is to say that we need not have learned to kneel when we were young in order to find the story of Jesus *actually* of use when addressing the tangle of our hatreds and our guilts. And yet such youthful training is undoubtedly a help; as this book tries to demonstrate, ritual runs on automatic pilot and myth without ritual runs on half-power at best. I am reminded of this whenever in a strange town or village my steps are drawn to the church, an empty building that nonetheless welcomes and still seems to promise ecumenically that if we could sort out our bodies again, and find some appropriate ritual to make it so, we could address the pleasure and pain of being together.

Such thoughts, though they feel quite contemporary, are by no means new. Look again at the opening chapters of *Moby Dick,* the wonderful play between Ishmael and black Queequeg, rolling amorously between the dour Presbyterian chapel and the offering of burned biscuit to the cannibal gods in their bedroom fireplace. "But what is worship?" as Ishmael plaintively asks (twice). Though quintessence of negritude from across the seas, Queequeg is also an Indian when he smokes his tomahawk peace pipe; and though Ishmael fares better with the cannibal biscuit than Queequeg does in the Presbyterian chapel (where people tend to sit by themselves), together they dream the dream of an ampler form of worship in which animal power and angelic aspiration may be gathered in a single party. As a result of this, Ishmael feels the lifting of some ancestral curse: "No more my splintered heart and maddened hand were turned against the wolfish world."

Of course this was scandalous stuff in 1850, which is why Melville camps the whole thing up in blackface; and yet he wasn't fooling at all. The matter continues to stand with us.

ORIGINS *of the* SACRED

PART ONE

ORIGINS OF THE SACRED:

The Evolution of Man in Nature

1 ▪ PERCEIVING THE WORLD:
Science Versus Mythology

There was a muddy centre before we breathed.
There was a myth before the myth began,
Venerable and articulate and complete.

From this the poem springs: that we live in a place
That is not our own and, much more, not ourselves,
And hard it is in spite of blazoned days.

—Wallace Stevens, "Notes Towards a Supreme Fiction"

Every culture finds its charter—its rules and identity—in the stories it tells of its beginnings. Genesis did this for us until, as religious belief began to fail in the West, we increasingly looked to science to find out who we were and where we came from. This long and complicated process culminated with the publication of Darwin's *The Origin of Species* in 1859, which was widely thought to sound the death knell of Christianity. But can science replace religion? Can its stories replace the old mythologies? Yes and no is my answer: it can tell us much of how in fact we began, but it needs help from mythology to tell us how to begin. Since this book is to some extent an exercise in reconciliation, an attempt to enlist science in the cause of mythology and vice versa, some preliminary discussion of the conflict between them is appropriate.

Beginnings are mysterious, not least because they are hard to find; and often, just as one thinks one has found the spot, antecedent traces appear, spoor receding even further into woodland darkness. But when one comes to the point where no further antecedent traces appear, one has reached the edge of the known world, an edge that itself cannot be known. Thus the idea of beginning involves the intersection of the known with the unknown, of being with nonbeing: something begins only where nothing ends, and this nothing can prove so daunting that many philosophers (including the scientific materialists) have tried to do away with it.[1]

Science, to put it bluntly, is uneasy with beginnings. Mythology, on the contrary, is concerned above all with what happened "in the beginning," as we shall see in subsequent chapters. Its signature is "Once upon a time," and its characteristic way of bridging the gap between nonbeing and being is to imagine gods and goddesses to step over it. But it differs most importantly from science in that its explanatory account of how we began is also a prescriptive account of how subsequent beginnings (which renew the cosmos) should proceed; the Last Supper, for example, tells us not only how the Christian era began but how its energies can be periodically renewed in a communion meal that commemorates and thus recalls its inception. Modern poets such as Wallace Stevens have inherited from the myth makers of old the disposition to supply the perennial human need for once-upon-a-time stories that also inform our own beginnings, but they realize that such stories must on the whole do without the gods and goddesses of old, about whom we have become skeptical. Without such figures the gap between being and nonbeing is difficult to bridge, and this is one reason why serious modern poetry is both rare and obscure.

In the justly celebrated Stevens poem cited above, the "venerable myth" before mythology is what survives of the mythic enterprise even in a demythologized age, man's inescapable need for a story that will tell him where to begin and legitimize his desire to do so. What Stevens sees, in the absence of gods and goddesses, is that we must "live in a place that is not our own," and this means recognizing the shadow of nonbeing that both threatens and structures our days in the sun. To speak of this shadow is to speak of what is and is not there, which we may as well call a "fiction," as Stevens does, as opposed to a "fact," which is simply there. Facts, as simple presences, can stand on their own, but make no *human* sense until woven into fictions or stories that relate the facts to each other and to what is absent. An older way of putting this is to say that life takes on meaning and value in the light of death: thus to realize we die is "hard," as the poem puts it, but it also *makes* us hard—for good and for ill—by disposing us to construct a culture ("blazoned days") that can transcend and hence defy our mortality. Such blazoning of our fictions begins in a blaze of energy that hardens toward sclerosis as we gradually turn away from the "muddy centre" that cradles and kills us. As the culture sets, it hardens the arteries by insulating us from any vivid perception of mortality.

Modern poetics are abstract and Stevens is not an easy poet. In this chapter I shall try to identify some aspects of the scientific contribution to the hardening of Western arteries since the Renaissance, and also to suggest that although science can tell us many things about how we began, it cannot tell us how or where to begin or end, and if we ask it to do this, we run into trouble. This latter point can be briefly glimpsed by considering, in very general terms, the contrasting case of primitive man: in order to instigate a coherent narrative action he needs the gods' permission, which means that the particular time and place must be consecrated, separated off from the surrounding chaos of endless time and space, into which to wander is to die. In a simple sense he lives in a remarkably "closed" world: within the zone of consecration he is free to do only what the gods of that time and place permit. The invisible framework, ritually established, allows him to begin and constrains what he does.[2]

Although manifestly unprimitive in many ways, medieval space was also remarkably closed (look at the maps and paintings), and actions were remarkably ritualized.[3] The signal achievement of modern science was to abolish the invisible framework sustained by Christian theology and effectively "deconsecrate" both space and time. In the physics of Galileo and Newton both space and time become infinite and eternal, without beginnings or endings, and no units of either are privileged; i.e., no unit of space or time is more real or significant than any other. Also no *less* real: if orderly space and time stretch everywhere, there is no such thing as chaos (except perhaps in the mind), which means we can dispense with the fearful business of asking the gods to consecrate (i.e., keep from chaos) our projects: an unspooky universe has no interest in when or where we do what.

Such an opening up of the cosmos was immensely liberating of course, but also disturbing to the narrative mind seeking a context of limitation for the human story—(an early example is Milton in *Lycidas*, more than somewhat at sea in the vastness of the new space). If restrictions on our movements are no longer perceived to be built into the structure of the cosmos, we shall be guided only by our Protestant conscience; and this, as Milton also saw, would not ultimately be equal to the task. Once the shadow of nonbeing no longer hedges our every beginning, we are encouraged to forget that we owe the gods a death, and after the manic excitement of this subsides, we discover not only the nightmare of insatiable appetite but also the banality of all beginnings—if "anything goes," then nothing need do. The difficulty of living in unconsecrated or deregulated space and time is nowhere more searchingly described than in The Book of Ecclesiastes, where the poet knows that "To every thing there is a season, and a time to every purpose under heaven," but also that when heaven ceases to stand over us, both "things" and "purposes" are displaced, and in the end "desire shall fail."

Much of Ecclesiastes seems to address our present condition directly, which would suggest both that our problems of living in unconsecrated space and time are not unique and also that they have become widely apparent. However one assesses the historical "villainy" of science in this matter, what is undeniable is that it is the scientists who are now calling us back to order. It is the biologists and the ecologists who are telling us that there is indeed a context of limitation in which the human story unfolds, and furthermore it is built into the structure of the cosmos. Its name is Mother Nature, and she is alive and not well; moreover if we do not soon agree to curb some of our appetites, particularly in relation to CO_2 emissions, she will become seriously ill. The primitive mind would find this story instantly recognizable: mankind has turned ungratefully upon the mother goddess (in some mistaken attempt to get free) and is polluting her with its waste, farting in her face. Could it be that the primitive mind is at ease with certain home truths that we have forgotten?

In any case there is undeniable trouble in the ecosphere, and thus the shadow of nonbeing is returning to the human story once again. The ancient religious word "pollution" has become central to scientific discourse, and one can even discern the outlines of a goddess whose blessing or permission we require for our human projects. It is the beginning of a beginning, and there is a nice irony in the sense that science seems now to be restoring to us what it dismantled in the Renaissance. But since it cannot actually *tell* us to begin, only what will happen if we do not, the ecologists need some help from another, older kind of discourse, the fictions of mythology or religion. Can the facts of science be reconciled with the fictions of the mythopoeic in a story that tells us not only how we began but how we may begin again, and renew the cosmos?

Often the best way of getting out of some tangle is by remembering how you got into it, and what follows is offered as a contribution to that undertaking.

2

Scientific materialism arose in the seventeenth century as the champion of fact and the enemy of fiction (though, as we shall see, science cannot do without fiction, in fact). Not only were all stories that begin "In the beginning" deemed frivolous, but, as I shall argue presently, the shadow of nonbeing was entirely removed from the Cartesian-Newtonian idea of the cosmos as a machine in perpetual motion.[4] In the terms of Stevens's poem, fictions remain "supreme" only so long as they remain in touch with the emptiness that hedges birth and death, by no means an easy task. What we would now call the fictions of scientific materialism fall well short of the supreme, being the products of "reason's click-clack" (Stevens again). The dire effects of this imaginative impoverishment were accurately foreseen by Jonathan Swift, science's first and ablest critic, though he was more or less ignored as a madman.

But there are grounds for believing that the tyranny of scientific materialism is now coming to an end. This idea is ably expounded by Fritjof Capra in *The Turning Point* (1982), which lucidly summarizes the tale that began, as Yeats put it, on the morning Descartes decided he could think better by staying in bed than by getting out of it. Capra is himself a distinguished physicist, which is important not only because subatomic particles and nucleic acids are beyond the layman's grasp, but also because in a scientific age, only scientists will have the authority effectively to challenge prevailing orthodoxy and invite us all, as Yeats might have said, to get out of bed again.

For present purposes, a brief discussion of modern science must suffice. The first and perhaps most important point to make is that science in the modern sense arose in the Renaissance along with the "parvenu Machiavel," a man impatient to be free of the old-fashioned Christian theology in order to pursue power of every kind. What the new science offered him was power, unfettered by responsibility, to explore and exploit Mother Nature; and he eagerly accepted. To realize this one need only consult Francis Bacon's *Advancement of Learning* (1604), the great advertisement for the new science, which abounds in macho images of penetration and mastery: witchy Nature (manifestly feminine to the Renaissance mind) must be "hounded in her wanderings," "bound into service," and even "put on the rack and tortured for her secrets."[5] Even allowing for the witch-craze of the period, by the wing of whose madness Bacon was touched, this language is shocking; and it registers, with astonishing candor, unseemly appetites and a brutalizing tendency at the heart of the scientific urge—what one might call its besetting sins. Needless to say, Christian theology was well aware of these sins, as Marlowe indicated in 1592 when he offered us a gluttonous *Doctor Faustus* who "surfeits on cursèd necromancy." But as Marlowe's play also indicates, theology was at that time losing its power to make the culture disapprove of such unbridled appetite. Necromancy, redefined and smartly dressed as science, was becoming respectable—not only because Christian authority was in confusion and decline, but because Nature, in the

Christian view, was more like a whore and a witch than a virtuous lady, and hence she merited little protection in any case; indeed her devilry might even be chastened and subdued under the scientific whip. It is because she was at best an unruly wench that Bacon (who certainly thought himself a Christian) could speak so candidly of mastering her.

Such cavalier talk was gradually replaced by the voice of Puritan sobriety, which suggested that the scientist was more like a monk than a rake, a seeker of truth not power, the facts of God that are concealed and betrayed in man's fictions. Like a good surgeon, the scientist is utterly unaroused by the bodies he handles, and indeed the only thing he feels passionately about is the need to remain strictly dispassionate once he enters the lab. This view of the virtuous scientist had become established even by the early eighteenth century, the time of Swift: how else explain why he couched his major criticisms of science in the fantastical terms of *Gulliver's Travels*? Today the official view is still that the knowledge science seeks is of the dispassionate and not the carnal kind; and yet the evidence everywhere of Nature's violated body suggests this is not altogether so, and that Bacon's metaphors told important truths that have been subsequently lost in fogs of mystification and self-deception.

The sexual metaphor seems to me decidedly useful, particularly in our sex-obsessed age; but there is a simpler and cruder story to tell. Like the magicians who preceded them (and whom they resemble more than one might think), scientists have always dreamed of stealing the thunderbolt of Zeus, a definitive raid upon the heavens. Prometheus the fire-thief is the culture-hero of science, and the appalling punishment he incurred is usually dismissed as mere spiteful nastiness on the part of tyrannous Father. Such hubris is breathtaking; and yet the fire-theft appears truly petty when compared with the medieval discovery of gunpowder. Surely *this* would dispose the culture to read the Prometheus story with a little more intelligence!

Not at all: on the contrary, the discovery of gunpowder made men realize that if they were not to be outgunned by the enemy they must understand *precisely* the motion of moving bodies; and so the science of ballistics was given priority funding from the national treasuries, as it were. It is lamentably little-known that the impulse behind the great strides made in Renaissance physics came from this quarter. The greatest of these ballisticians was, by a nice congruence, *il signor* Galileo, of sainted memory, the father of modern science. There is more than a little irony in the fact that before he turned his hand to constructing a telescope in order to confirm the Copernican hunch, he did absolutely brilliant work on the laws of motion; that is to say, before he took on the tyrannous Church Fathers and cleared astronomical space so that scientific man could find his humble place in the cosmos, Galileo proved himself a Promethean wizard at the thunderbolt mathematics. What immortalized his *Discourses* of 1609 was the idea that behind the mysteries of acceleration lay the law of inertia: all things being equal, a moving body will move for ever. (Note the abstraction here: things in fact are not equal on planet earth, because of friction, etc., and so moving bodies tend to stop.) Classical dynamics were perfected in Newton's four laws of motion: if inertia reigns, and action = reaction, and the world's energy remains constant, then not only is death neither here nor there, but motion itself is never decisive, a kind of illusion. The space through which these bodies move, so chastening in its abysmal vastness to the medieval mind, becomes orderly, almost domesticated, when colonized by the law of gravity. The apple that notoriously hit Newton on the head one afternoon (as he dozed in a Cambridge college garden) bore no malice but was in fact obeying a law ordained by planetary motion and the alternation of the tides. By *abstracting* himself utterly from the relatively "closed" garden world in which the event took place, he managed to locate its source in a benignly impersonal god far away.

As a result of Newton's discovery the cosmos itself became unfrightening, regulated, unhedged by chaos; and time, *edax rerum*, or "the eater of things" to the ancients, was seen to be ultimately unreal, or strictly speaking, "reversible." The initially calming effects of this settlement are everywhere apparent in the confident achievements of eighteenth-century culture. Since then, although there have been a few attempts to find irreversible time (e.g., entropy in the nineteenth century, and certain aspects of "big bang" cosmology in the twentieth) the laws of the conservation of energy seem to be holding on, just. All very well, one might think, and yet not so; for what begins as calming often ends up as boring. Time is measured by movement, and movement is the signature of the gods (as discussed in the Appendix): if all three are ultimately unreal, then life is endless bar billiards, in which case the ultimate challenge is how to end it; which brings us back to thunderbolt thinking, the hallmark of physics.[6]

If it is true that the bottom line in what used to be called "natural philosophy" has always been the search for the thunderbolt, it is also true that it has always been thought tasteless to point this out—so much so that when Einstein, last of the great thunderbolt mathematicians, was shown what he had done he was first thunderstruck and then genuinely contrite.* And yet Einstein was by any standards an intelligent man, thoughtful and well-read. Could he *really* have forgotten about the thunderbolt? Yes, but only if the mind of science had become so separated and abstracted from its body and the body politic as to be effectively schizoid. That this might indeed be the case was thoroughly understood by Swift in *Gulliver's Travels,* but the matter had become so sensitive by 1726 that he knew he must proceed carefully on the thunderbolt question if he wanted to keep any scientific readers at all. Thus we find two extended passages on the depravity of gunpowder (whose first contriver must have been "some evil genius, enemy to mankind," p. 133), rocks and excrement are thrown about somewhat ballistically, and there is even a contrivance for squashing unruly cities, but in all this no mention of the scientist; and when Swift finally comes to list the abstract inanities of science, thunderbolt longing is carefully omitted. Despite this fastidiousness, and despite Swift's being the great wit of his age, his book was briefly the talk of the town and then made its way to the nursery.[7]

---

*"If only I had known, I should have become a watchmaker," he said (in the *New Statesman*, April 16, 1965).

Still, he did not labor in vain. In the past hundred years or so a good deal of energy has been expended by the culture at large in combatting the notion of a world in which time does not matter. These efforts, necessarily fragmentary in a science-dominated age, might be collected under the (somewhat unsatisfactory) heading of "existentialism"; and their effects, despite the fragmentation, have not been negligible. But even more significant, and insufficiently recognized until recently, is that in the middle of the nineteenth century a *scientist* emerged with a metaphysic to challenge and civilize the "timelessness" of post-Galilean physics. In the evolutionary biology of Charles Darwin not only does time matter (and the pun is intended), but the space that physics has geometrized into blankness comes alive again as it should to the human eye, as a realm wondrously moved by events both unique and contingently caused. Such is the sanity, and indeed timeliness, of Darwin's idea, that one can arguably already see signs of its pressing for an "evolutionary physics."[8] Be that as it may, by offering itself as a powerful example of "good science," it lifts the taboo that inhibits us from seeing examples of "bad science" in various quarters, and enables us to speak of them without the Swiftian indirection.

3

Let us return to quieter ground. Some idea of the important and puzzling ambiguities surrounding the "interest" science takes in Nature may be gathered by considering its relation to the hand. Science's "good hand," as it were, is the one that led us out of the medieval monastery, where hands were folded in prayer, and did not dare (or did not deign) to touch the body of this witchy wench. This good hand, by returning us to the earth that bears us, delivered us from the paranoia that inevitably besets the alienated and the disdainful. Our reward for daring and deigning to touch again the body that nurtures us, was, as mytho-logic would suggest, powers undreamed of in scholastic theology. This is literally so: the extraordinary powerfulness of modern science arises from the fact that its thinking about Nature, unlike that of theology, is not only unconstrained by taboo, but is conjoined with and shaped by an experimental method that touches, orders, and manipulates the body in question.

And yet this experimental touching and manipulating in deconsecrated space and time is also what calls forth the bad hand, the predatory claw that grabs and violates. Just as carnal knowledge explores the borderline between the nurturing hand that cradles and protects and the predatory hand that violates, so too does scientific knowledge. This ambiguity of the hand, so central to human experience, is a source both of endless adventure and endless confusion in human affairs. Its confusing aspect reappears in another version of the scientific story, in which we are asked to see the scientist *either* as the unarmed pilgrim who walks out into Nature's plenitudes to see what he can gather from the world to which he essentially belongs, *or* as the alienated intellectual who, in Yeats's reconstruction, chooses to do his thinking in bed so as not to be distracted by the senses. "Which one is it?" we are tempted to ask, in some exasperation: and the reply is "Both: you must live with the ambiguity." Heaven knows it is not easy, as we shall see presently when we come to consider the most important and ambiguous scientist of the nineteenth century, Charles Darwin. But the important point here, and it is crucial, is that those medieval hands folded in prayer knew something that science first ignored and then forgot: any hand that is not sometimes folded in prayer will in the end turn into the predatory claw.

The hand also helps to illuminate the simplest criticism of science, which almost everyone has heard of, that it is somehow "reductive," that "we murder to dissect." What is it that science reduces? Mankind, in a word, and with it the kindness of Nature, the song of kinship that sings throughout creation and binds us all, one to another. The hearing and singing of this song have traditionally been the poet's and the shaman's responsibility; and the scientist, for his purposes, ignores it. This would be tolerable if only the scientist did not exceed his brief and suggest (either implicitly or explicitly) that such singing is beside the point—or, even worse, that it muddies the waters of truth. To put it crudely, science finds its power in *abstraction,* in ignoring certain aspects of what we perceive in order to concentrate on certain others; and the overall effect of this is to make life seem smaller, cheaper, and nastier than we know it to be.

The matter is, needless to say, by no means so simple as I am suggesting, but this is not a book about the philosophy of science, and so I will continue to simplify. The damaging abstractions of science arose in the Renaissance, when it became experimental and mathematical, when its reductive hand entered into its meditations. The science of ancient Greece is comparatively nonreductive because it speculates, classifies, and on the whole keeps its hands to itself.* The best account I have read of this and the "fall" into modern science is Jack Lindsay's *Blast Power and Ballistics* (1974), particularly his description of the difference between the "pious" mathematics of Kepler and the "blasphemous" mathematics of Galileo, an account that emphasizes the reductiveness of Galileo's abstractions. The comparison of Kepler and Galileo (contemporaries working in the same field) illustrates the difficulty of generalizing about reductiveness in science, and yet for present purposes we must. When speaking against science in this chapter, I have in mind chiefly the impure aspects of applied sciences such as physics and chemistry, where the experimental hand is most active. The historical sciences, such as geology, concerned with taxonomy not power, are indeed aspects of "natural philosophy" as the pre-Socratics would have understood it, relatively benign if not downright virtuous.

Some sense of these differences can be gathered by considering the man who is by all accounts much the best of our contemporary writers on matters scientific, the somewhat pre-Socratic Stephen Jay Gould. What distinguishes his prose, apart from its prodigious

---

*Norman Mailer makes this point with admirable crudity: "It was not the original desire of science to convert nature, rather to reveal it. Faust was still unborn when Aristotle undertook his pioneer investigations" (*Cannibals and Christians,* p. 245).

learning, is his vivid sense not only of the serious playfulness of Mother Nature as she plots and unplots her evolutionary moves, but also of the scientist's constant duty to resist his occupational disease of reductiveness. It seems to me altogether likely that Gould's admirable prose is connected to his somewhat pre-Socratic specialism, paleontology, that very pure, virtually nonexperimental science given to the classification of ancient parts, a meditation, in the broadest sense, on history. A paleontologist needs a good eye, a quiet hand, and thoughtfulness: all of these distinguish Gould's writing.*

4

The problem of reductiveness and the ambiguous scientific hand, nicely encapsulated in Wordsworth's "We murder to dissect," was in fact being literally explored in a thriving aspect of late sixteenth-century science, the dissection of human corpses. To the primitive mind, a dead body is full of dangerous magic, not to be touched without ritual precaution. This was still true for the medieval Christian, and the rituals of laying-out and burial both protected the living and enhanced the possibility of resurrection for the dead. The soul was undeniably *in* the body, but so too was devilry, as the chaotic mess of guts and smell would suggest. Thus the inside of the body—particularly the dead body—if not taboo in the primitive sense, was at least unmapped and dangerous.[9]

If anatomical knowledge was to progress, this belief had to be shifted, and it was chiefly done by the major philosopher of the scientific dispensation (himself something of an anatomist), René Descartes. To say "I think therefore I am" is to say (among other

*See, for example, the prologue to his *Flamingo's Smile* (1985). One might also suggest that to write as cheerfully as Gould does, one needs a clear conscience. Not only is paleontology unimplicated in thunderbolt aspiration, but its large perspectives keep it uninfected by the urgencies of our time. Some years ago a mathematician told me that the only scientists writing pretty equations were the astrophysicists. Gould's second love, since childhood, has been astronomy.

things) that my being is in my thinking, hence not in my body, which may then appear as an unspooky machine whose workings we may liberally explore. But of course it cannot be this simple: despite the incalculable alleviation of human suffering made possible by the knowing hand of the anatomist, vestiges of our primitive suspicion that such knowledge may be to some extent forbidden continue to haunt us. Not only are we uneasy about the excitement possibly felt by the one who wields the knife (the analogy with morbid sexuality), but once the body is desacralized, how are we to draw the line between legitimate and illegitimate entry? Despite four centuries of surgical triumph on an increasingly secularized body, we are still troubled by such matters as abortion, heart transplants, *in vitro* fertilization, genetic engineering, and so on.

Some sense of the ambiguities surrounding the surgical hand can

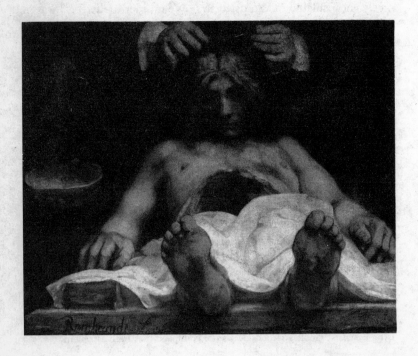

be gathered by looking at Rembrandt's famous *Anatomy Lessons* of 1632 and 1656. In both cases one's first impression is of horror: these bodies are being tortured. Is this impression altogether mistaken? Both bodies belonged to executed criminals, as was frequently the case in those days. Furthermore, the dissections commemorated by these paintings were an annual event in Amsterdam, performed in a theater before a paying audience, and this "ritual" was followed by a feast. What, one wonders, was the public paying to see? And what was the feast celebrating? Some new extension to "the long arm of the law"? Perhaps.[10]

What is acutely disturbing in this detail from the 1656 painting is the *liveliness* of the corpse: the body is half sitting up, the hands are semi-flexed as relaxed hands naturally are, and the feet seem not only sentient but almost close enough to touch. Both hands and feet lead us to the eyes, which may be admonishing us from the shadows. It is only after registering these perceptions that we take in the hole where the guts used to be, and then notice that this barber is not cutting hair but taking the brain to bits, and will discard them in the attendant cup, which is in fact the man's cranium that has just been sawn off. What is both alluring and dreadful is that the body is both intact and utterly violated. What if it were to get up from the table? What if those feet were to break through the membrane of the canvas and walk again?

Sir Joshua Reynolds (in 1781) was surely not the first to find this body reminding him of Mantegna's Christ; and yet even he—no fool by any standards—failed to think through the story. If a common criminal (a petty thief in fact, Joris Fonteyn by name) has thus become the Christ crucified, and lively enough to haunt us still, does this not suggest that Professor Deyman (the anatomist-barber) is standing in for the desires we all carry to despoil the body of innocence and beauty? What Reynolds could not see—and he a painter—also escaped the doctors who commissioned the work; and so a subversive masterpiece was quietly inserted into European history. It hung proudly for generations in the Surgeons' Guildhall at Amsterdam.

The question of when life begins is to some extent a religious one, and hence it perplexes modern science, both with regard to amino acids and the womb: so too is the question of when it ends, that is, when a body ceases to "belong" to its previous occupant and hence is no longer appropriately called "his." The primitive and religious answer is that bodies are a gift from the gods that must in turn be given back when the occupant yields up his interest; hence the mutilation of corpses (as we shall see with regard to Homeric Hektor) is *prima facie* sacrilegious, an attack on the gods' domain. The way to recall this perception, even to secular man undisturbed by Jesus, is to render the dead body, for all its ghastly pallor, undeniably alive; and this Rembrandt does. Just as Bacon's unguarded prose can remind us of certain aggressive energies no longer obviously displayed in scientific endeavor, so Rembrandt can illuminate what still shadows the surgical hand. Beginnings are almost always explicit.[11]

5

Not unrelated to the ambiguous scientific hand and the problem of reductiveness is the more abstract question of the scientific preference, endorsed and to some extent inspired by Puritanism, for fact over fiction. No one can fail to be impressed by Bacon's critique of medieval scholasticism and its unempirical theorizing, those fictional webs spun in minds that read old books and never went for a walk in the woods to consult Mother Nature herself. Indeed what is scientific humility if not this reverence for fact, open-mindedness before the evidence? The short answer to this complex question is, again, "yes but no," and it was first and best unraveled by Swift in *The Battle of the Books* (1704), which answers Bacon by detecting a kind of spidery pride and self-aggrandizement at the heart of scientific humility—what Swift perceived as a web-spinning fictional element. Since those early days science has moved further and further from the sensible world of so-called facts and into the lab where virtually immaterial entities like quarks are caught in webs of mathematics, which would seem *prima facie* to bolster Swift's argument.[12]

For present purposes this complex question need not be engaged, and yet if we are to appreciate the extent to which science *did* deliver us from the confined and confining fictions of medieval theology into the open sunshine of Nature's democracies, we do need a working distinction between fact and fiction. We might begin with a metaphor: if we think of facts as simple presences that stand intelligibly on their own, they bring to mind the plain-spoken and plainly dressed yeoman farmer, who labors the earth with his hands, lives without frills, and is beholden to no man. Fictions, on the other hand, "add to" the facts by relating them to one another and to invisible entities (often ancestral) that somehow give them meaning and value; and this brings to mind the aristocrat, whose hands are delicate, whose speech is subtle if not deceitful, whose clothes seek to embellish his body, and whose claim to being more important (even more real) than the yeoman farmer has a good deal to do with the invisible, the ancestral, and an alliance with the clergy. Both the French and the American revolutions announced our growing preference for the yeoman farmer over the aristocrat (and the poet who might be his servant); and science as champion of the facts became, along with capitalism, the "religion" of democratic man in the nineteenth and twentieth centuries. In the circumstances, it is not easy to speak up on behalf of fictions, which to many no longer even seem aristocratic but merely long-haired, foppish, dreamy, and decadent.

But it must be done. If fictions are to be rehabilitated, the first order of business is to dissociate them from the memory of a malignant aristocracy (and a decadent poetry) and to suggest that certain services provided by aristocracies remain valuable in democratic eras; we need poetic fictions to teach the scientific hand how to pray. Second, we must consult the wise men of long ago to be reminded that fictions are not necessarily untruthful—quite the contrary; Aristotle, for example (no enemy to science, by the way) says that poetry is *more* truthful than history because it is *less* encumbered with facts.[13] And third, we must realize that not only is the distinction between fact and fiction by no means absolute, but that science is more involved with fiction than its "ideological" advocates would allow.

The fictional element in science is the constructing of hypotheses, models, and theories, those immaterial, ideational, mental structures that enable the facts to be perceived in relation to each other. Although scientific theories differ from religious myths in certain obvious ways, they also share important common features, as we shall see presently. The question of where facts end and fictions begin is one of philosophy's perennials: the hardheaded and tough-minded (often called realists or materialists) say that facts are somehow "given" and can be known in the mind uncluttered by the preconceptions of fiction; whereas the tender-minded (often called idealists) point out that the line between fact and fiction is difficult to draw, as is nicely indicated by their almost sharing a common etymology (from Latin *facere* = to make) and by such words as "factitious," which means "untrue."[14] Idealists believe that there is no such thing as the innocent eye: all of our perceptions are shaped (not to say corrupted) by the spectacles we wear, and all of our facts, made not given, remain unintelligible until coherently clothed in fiction. Needless to say, the tendencies of this book are idealist, and as we shall see presently, such tendencies are becoming increasingly respectable again, even in science.

The central importance of fictions, though not of prayer, is certainly appreciated, perhaps even too much, in the contemporary theories of culture that have evolved from the linguistic thinking of such as Ludwig Wittgenstein, Ferdinand de Saussure, and Claude Lévi-Strauss. These structuralist theories see man above all as the *story-telling* animal, the one who is called upon to *make* sense of his world. There is almost certainly a world "out there," but what we *make* of it has everything to do with our language and the stories it composes. Such making is the essence of fiction, which one might call the construction of culture. Traditional cultures manifestly differ in the way they construe themselves, but all are built upon fictive ground, stories whose arbitrary or invented beginnings are generally masked and transformed into absolute divine *fiat* by religious ceremony and ritual. In this way the central facts of a culture's experience are valued. The myths (and rituals) that tell a man who he is and what he values compose his religion (from Latin *re-ligere* = to bind back): they bind him back through memory to the divine ancestors who call upon him to act and think in certain ways. Although these myths do not carry the signature of what we nowadays call an author, this paradoxically is part of what makes them authoritative: were they "merely" the product of one man's mind, they might be interesting, even instructive tales, but would lack the largeness to speak to and for everyone, to authorize (from *augere* = to increase) a general prosperity. When a culture loses its authorized version, the body politic fragments, and its spiritual prosperity withers into individualism, solipsism and despair, afflictions all too well known in our time.

What mainly keeps our culture from mythic bankruptcy is our faith in science, and yet as mythic structures go, science is anomalous. Although it agrees with other mythologies in claiming to tell us the truth about our world, and indeed in playing down the element of personal authority, its stories identify our central facts without telling us how to value them. Indeed science brandishes its abhorrence of value judgments as its principal virtue, which it calls "objectivity" (though, as we have just seen, a reading of Bacon suggests that certain strong desires lurk beneath such objectivity). Traditional or religious cultures, which value their facts, are always ultimately tied to geography: the divine ancestors came down from that mountain over there, bearing the tablets of the law, and their authority is sustained by the local priesthood. Scientific culture, however, claims to be universal, tied to no locality: its laws, descriptive not prescriptive, inhere in the nature of things, everywhere the same. Instead of rituals it conducts experiments, in which its truths are made manifest, and these can be conducted any place, any time, by any one—utterly democratic. Thus the great strength of a scientific story (e.g., that falling bodies accelerate at 32 feet per second per second) is that it needs no priestly voice in a ritual context to tell it. The story tells itself, and its writ runs everywhere from China to Peru—and that's a fact. But as the logicians have been pointing out for some time, no amount of knowledge about the *facts* in one's premises will enable one to say anything about their *value* in the conclusion. By cleansing its spectacles of moralistic mumbo jumbo, science has vastly increased our perception of and power over the facts; but to value them we still must listen for poetic inspiration or the voice of God, just as man always has, and this task is made no easier by the scientist saying such talk is mumbo jumbo. Indeed this task is made much more difficult: under the scientific dispensation our ears have been stopped up, our moral and religious faculties atrophied, and our hands rendered incapable of prayer. Because of this stupefaction we have become, from time to time, vulnerable to infection by lurid fantasies of salvation. Hitler is much the worst example, and the general loss of nerve consequent upon this pollution of the European heartland is still everywhere apparent. One of its effects is to drive us ever further into the church of science, even as we increasingly realize that science is as much a part of the problem as of the solution.

A scientific "fact" might be called a tale without a teller. We believe Einstein's stories not because he tells them while dressed in a purple robe, but because $E = MC^2$ looks good on everyone's slide rule. This "democratic" simplicity, objectivity, and universality are science's great strength, but also its great weakness. A tale without a teller has no author, is not authorized, lacks authority: like a foundling in our midst it stands unconnected to us, without relation, unpredictable. Not named within the circle of our human bonds, this foundling may be monstrous. Who was to say $E = MC^2$ would turn into an atomic bomb? Certainly not Einstein, the unfathering father, full of remorse. What makes this story monstrous is that it tells us where to find power, but is silent about when and where to use it. This silence, which claims to be high-minded, in fact allows unspeakable desires to slip from the shadows. Like a violent, psychotic child, this equation carries power without either self-control or the restraining hand of its father's law. Such power is intrinsically chaotic.

Not unlike the violent child, science finds its power in simple-mindedness: by abstracting from its consideration all matters of morality and value, it gains access to the engine room of planet earth, an access forbidden to pre-scientific man by religious scruple, father's restraining hand. When fire breaks out, the scientist scratches his head in boyish puzzlement and asks the politician or the soldier to deal with it. All this is not new: the medieval theologians understood perfectly well the dangers implicit in Faustus's lust for "cursèd necromancy." They knew that he would gain power and lose his soul. Now that the nuclear bomb and other pollutions of the planet have made this clear even to the man in the street, the Western mind may at last be ready to reconsider its pact with the devil.

A tale without a teller either tells itself or does not get told. $E = MC^2$ is a mathematical story, conveyed by numbers not words, numbers moreover that are unintelligible to almost all of us—that is, utterly *un*democratic. Even to the initiate these numbers speak only of power, and say nothing of its use and abuse. Such numbers are inhuman in their abstraction, their carelessness, their lack of context. Until they are subsumed within a larger story that governs their use, they promise only unauthorized violence. The primitive mind, hedged in by fears of the invisible powers, would distrust a tale without a teller; and rightly so, for power unharnessed by responsibility is power that will shortly run amok, the devil's work, as a Christian would say. Moreover, scientific stories only *seem* to be tales without tellers, for there is a scientific priesthood, of sorts, that both controls access to experimental equipment (necessary even to watch a falling pebble accelerate at 32 ft./sec.^{2}) and passes judgment (in learned journals etc.) upon the acceptability of new hypotheses. All one need do to discover this priesthood is try to gain access to a laboratory to test a hypothesis subversive of received wisdom: doors have been known to slam under such provocation.

The mark of a seriously empowered priesthood is that it convincingly denies having any political interest (in the broadest sense), any fish to fry: its regulations and procedures are god-given, or in secular times, dictated by reason. Thus science was at its most powerful as religion or ideology when it convincingly denied having any, when its claims to "objectivity" were accepted in every quarter, as was the case, arguably, in the nineteenth century. Now that these claims are being questioned, from within and without, it is safe to say that the ideological power of science is less than it was. When it comes to be widely seen as simply one human enterprise among others, with no heavenly charter and no claims upon absolute truth and virtue, the world will breathe easier.

My argument is becoming rather complicated. I am suggesting that scientific tales lack "proper" tellers but actually carry concealed and hence improper ones. The problem may be somewhat clarified if we look at Einstein's story, $E = MC^2$, and imagine ourselves trying to tell it to some amiable Bushman here on a visit. It says that "In the beginning" this pebble in my hand (M for mass) lived free and easy as a bundle of energy (E), and then one day along came Father and the forces of orderliness, constraining it into dreary pebblehood. In time the scientific fraternity arrived and said: "Wouldn't it be fun and even possibly virtuous to liberate this pebble and restore the innocent freedom it enjoyed before the Fall?" A pretty enough tale until one looks at C^2, where C is the speed of light, a mere 186,000 miles per second. Square that and M for mass moves into next week: you have a massive nuclear explosion on your hands. [15]

$E = MC^2$ would appear to awaken us from the endless ticktock of Newton's perpetual motion machine, characterized by William Blake as "single vision and Newton's sleep"; but in major respects it drives that sleep into coma. Whereas Blake's version of anti-Newtonian energy is "eternal delight" because it comes "from the body," which provides it with a "bound or outward circumference," Einstein's is eternal despair because it is boundless, groundless, and disembodied. [16] Whereas Blake (not unlike the Bushman) would call us into a world moved by human imagination in time, Einstein's geometry takes us out into schizoid space, a deepness of sleep from which no innocent apple could bonk the Newtonian head into gravitational dreams on a Cambridge afternoon. A sleep that is dreamless may be catatonic: Einstein's nonchalant silence concerning who these E gods may be, and how their unimaginable fury is to be propitiated, deeply disturbs our unsleeping primitive Bushman; and when we tell him that this story came from the heart of a Europe that, having more or less shot up Bushman culture, was about to consume much of its own absentmindedly in the most appalling war ever fought, he simply shakes his head in utter dismay.

When he retrieves his good humor, he offers to tell us an old tale from southern Africa. There once was a man given a magically beautiful wife on the condition that he never open without her permission the little basket that was her one treasured possession. When one day curiosity finally prevailed, he opened the lid, found nothing inside, and laughed a good deal at the whole silly business; whereupon his magical wife vanished into the sunset. She left him not because he broke his promise but because he found the basket empty: in fact it contained all the beautiful things of the sky whereby their earthly life was to be enriched.[17]

One might suggest, not altogether facetiously, that the next day the deserted husband emigrated to Europe and became a scientist. This is not altogether fair because science too has its fictions, but they are on the whole anti-basket in tendency. Curiosity and skepticism are not, as in this tale, the source of desolation, but the road to freedom, according to scientific belief; and people treasuring empty baskets are particularly attractive targets for our demystifying laughter. The promise of science has always been to replace the insubstantial dream of beauty with a full basket of power; and $E = MC^2$, its crowning achievement, discovers not only endless power but a kind of beauty too, it seems, both in conception (according to the mathematicians) and in the delivery (Dr. Oppenheimer was moved to quote from the Bhagavad-Gita at the atomic bomb's unveiling in the New Mexican desert). But what if access to such terrible beauty is granted only to those who have laughed off the magical wife and the comfort she might bring, as Goethe's story of Faustus attests? The sexual symbolism of the wife's empty basket makes the point tellingly. After pondering this for a while I looked up and saw that our amiable Bushman visitor had left us, perhaps justly; or perhaps he merely sensed that these stories have brought us to the edge of the argument between beauty and power, a complex matter best left until later.

The myths that compose the religious and political structure of every culture are tales of power, how it is to be found and where it is to be used. They are told by those in authority, in a voice that calls upon and recalls those ancestors and gods who called us forth in the beginning. If we are to repair what one might call the "narrative dislocations" in our scientific culture, we must put ourselves back to school with our forebears, to recall the myths that legitimize our existence and tell us how to live with godly power. We know a great many of Nature's secrets—too many, undoubtedly—but can value very little with certainty. Our facts cry out for fictional order, stories that tell us what to make of them, but we seem to have forgotten how the thing is done. In order to remember we must retrieve our faith in another kind of knowledge, a knowledge that knows what to make of the knowledge science provides. At the heart of such knowledge is the capacity to hear those stories (as our forefathers did) that call us to take our place in Nature, that begin in the beginning.

Our task may be compared to the one Milton set himself, trying to recover Christian authority in the face of the burgeoning natural sciences. But whereas his problem was to reconcile Christian and Greek mythology (by absorbing the latter into the former) and find no conflict with science, ours is somewhat different. Our new mythology, like the scientific one it will emend and replace, must be positively planetary in its tolerance, and yet adamant in its insistence on respect for Mother Nature. For this we must return to our origins on the African savannah, to retrieve a sense of our common heritage, the debt we all owe for the gift of life. A daunting task, certainly, but we do have a signal advantage over Milton: whereas science in his day was full of the unstoppable brashness of youth, in ours it is old enough to recognize the follies, both witting and unwitting, that have been committed in its name. The planet is now in imminent danger of destruction, and this, our great despair, is also our best hope. Allusion to Milton reminds us that, as with him, the task before us is both religious and political, the two necessarily intertwined. The secular (or liberal) notion of politics that has prevailed since the eighteenth century—that of trade-offs and adjustments between various interest groups—is simply not robust enough to address the crisis.

The scientific myth must be recognized as one that calls forth a clever but schizoid child whose refusal to concern himself with the moral law surreptitiously licenses his lust for power. To do this we need a story arraigning both Faustus and Frankenstein; in which the mythic Father reappears (after some considerable absence) in order to identify and call in the child's anarchic appetites, and the Mother to identify the horrors of monstrous creation in the lab. The hand of science, like all human hands, must be recognized as *both* nurturing *and* predatory, and the predatory hand must be restrained by laws and prayers to which the heart bears allegiance. To talk this way tends to make liberal intellectuals nervous (intimations of crypto-fascism) but it cannot be helped. The child cannot be identified as wayward and asked to grow up until the outraged voices of the parents can be heard once again. Until then, antinuclear movements and the like will go on being stalled in their failure to appear as anything more than just another "interest group" emerging from the sibling squabble.

6

Thus far I have been putting the case against science as religion, often called "scientism." The argument is as old as science itself, and until now its exponents, such as Lewis Mumford (*Technics and Civilization*, 1934) and Henry Adams (*The Education of Henry Adams*, 1918) have been as voices crying in the wilderness against the march of empire. But this is no longer so: there are grounds for believing that the cultural prestige of scientific materialism, its "religious" hegemony, is lessening as the Western mind shifts its allegiance from Cartesian mechanism to the ecological. This idea is ably expounded by Capra in *The Turning Point* (1982) and I do not propose to summarize it here. One part of the argument, however, does bear upon our concerns, and shall detain us briefly; and that is the shift in theoretical physics from materialism to idealism. In quantum theory the basic constituents of the Cartesian mentality (call it scientific materialism) are subverted, inverted, and even possibly perverted; for in quantum theory the intellectual "posture" around which the prestige of science has accumulated for four centuries has been revealed to be just that—a posture, materialism, one position among the many possible ones from which reality can be addressed, and not an altogether pretty one at that. It is a nice irony that such subversion should come from the scientists themselves, and at a moment when they were thinking not of reforming their ways but only of writing new equations. On reflection this seems perfectly in order: the prestige of science is arguably so great in our time that only scientists could undermine it, and of course they would not do so on purpose.

Whether or not quantum theory will significantly civilize the physicists (as Capra believes), it has at least, by shifting the scientific posture toward idealism, enabled us to see the preceding Cartesian one (which still holds sway in most quarters) as a historical phenomenon, a *Weltanschauung* that prevailed over certain minds for a certain time, with good and bad effects. Thus in addition to "The Myth of the Good Scientist," which has solemnly prevailed for so long, we can now also enjoy its shadowy complement, "The Myth of the Bad Scientist." Taken together, and judiciously mixed, these stories reveal a scientist whose formidable magic has both helped and hurt us, and whose newly acquired modesty will enable him both to practice a more humane science and share the stage with other, older figures of authority—the poet, the shaman, the master of the music. This is unequivocally good news, and it means that books such as this one may be taken seriously.

The Myth of the Good Scientist began in the Renaissance but did not fully ripen until the mid-nineteenth century, when the doctrine of scientific materialism established a "religious" hold on the culture. The story runs briefly as follows: reality is composed only of matter in motion, and only scientists are capable of understanding it, because they are plain men, with no ax to grind, who discover the objective facts in the lab by suppressing their subjective prejudices and fantasies in the almost monastic rigor of experiment. Such men are indeed the true leaders of the culture: unlike poets and politicians who deal in rhetoric, dreams, and prejudice (often for their own profit) scientists renounce all private and egotistical interest as they submit themselves to the facts as given, armed only with "clear and distinct ideas" as Descartes said, sufficient theory (not fiction) to make the facts visible. As with the monks and mystics before them, the reward for such selfless activity is the rapture of discovery, the contemplation of reality; and the truths they discover, available to all, may indeed be utilized in a democratic society for the well-being of all—an obvious example is Joseph Lister's discoveries concerning hygiene and infection, whose effects upon society were truly magical. Scientific discoveries can also be put to bad use of course, but this is a problem for the politician not the scientist. It would, for example, be highly undemocratic for a scientist to rule out research on nuclear fission or genetic engineering because it might be misused. Such matters, of concern to all, should be decided by all in a political forum.

This is a powerful story, and it has prevailed in the West until quite recently without much challenge from its brotherly complement, The Myth of the Bad Scientist. The Bad Scientist begins, as we have seen, with Marlowe's Faustus and Bacon's macho Machiavel, lusting for power and control. This story, well aired by such masters of forthright English prose as Bacon and Swift, was increasingly buried and suppressed as science grew solemnly respectable in the eighteenth and nineteenth centuries and gave birth to scientism. Thus the engines of destruction almost lasciviously imagined by Leonardo in his scientific fantasies are certainly not discernible in Newton's utterly sober and almost bourgeois notion of energy as simply the capacity to work; and of course the idea of the young buck Science having his way with Dame Nature, that unruly wench, soon enough became a joke in very poor taste.

The combination of nuclear bombs, pollution, and quantum mechanics in our century has changed all that, and The Myth of the Bad Scientist, in an updated and more lurid version, is now available again, even to the man in the street. This story suggests that shadowing the scientific saint, call him Dr. Jekyll, is a sinner called Hyde, looking for carnal knowledge not the other kind, and whose sexual fantasies run even to necrophilia. He dreams of dominating his girl in the lab, where her resistance can be overcome by a shot of anesthesia. In fact he *wants* her etherized upon a table, for there she yields even her most inaccessible secrets to his unchallenged curiosity. Needless to say, such treatment wears her out and wears her down, and she is no longer as pretty as she was. But she's not dead yet, and luckily for all of us the word about Hyde seems to be getting around: we may be able to reach him soon.

But in order to reach him we must first of all *know he's there*; and that remains very difficult. Walk into any lab by day and you will meet the good Dr. Jekyll—bespectacled, soft-spoken, clean, kindly, a pillar of the community. Suggest to him that his lab is sometimes taken over in the night by something nasty, a *doppelganger* for which he is moreover ultimately responsible, and he will call you a raving lunatic and ring for the police. So much good has come from the lab, and for so long, that it has become a kind of temple in our time, and our time is short on temples; and if you tell a man his temple is bedevilled, you can expect a noisy reply.

Still it must be done, and the conditions for doing it are growing favorable. To translate this story from myth into epistemology involves suggesting a kind of corruption implicit in the Cartesian mind's relation to its objects, a corruption stemming from abstraction, mechanization, and a consequent misattribution of passivity (or indifference) to both knower and known, a process that ends in the schizoid denial of violence. Such an epistemological argument should persuade the mind to abandon what the myth moves the heart to abhor. Taken together they can help us to remember that Nature is indeed the Eternal Feminine that we hold in common, and that she has almost been exhausted by the violence of Hyde, which Jekyll must now acknowledge and recall. In the place of macho man whom Bacon introduced, we must call upon our feminine side, and learn to approach the lady with gentleness.

And each other, of course: it goes without saying. It is worth mentioning here that although I have been stressing our oppression of Nature, urban man these days knows and dreams much more of oppressing his fellow man, usually in some back room, with subtle instruments. Hence it seems altogether appropriate that a remarkably successful recent version of The Myth of the Bad Scientist focuses on the "scientific" methods we use to dominate our deviant fellow citizens. In *Discipline and Punish*, Michel Foucault (1977) has done the culture a major service by showing that the principal modern methods for controlling, subjugating, humiliating, and torturing recalcitrant citizens have to do with "knowing" them in certain ways. What he does not go on to say, strangely enough, is that these methods are extensions, adaptations, and perversions of the methods science has perfected for knowing Nature in the lab. The French word *"surveillance,"* Foucault's central notion, has a richness English cannot match, but it gathers the ideas of guarding, overseeing, snooping, restraining, and controlling. Whence *surveillance* if not the badlands of science? One can only assume that some combination of reticence, timidity, and vestigial Cartesian deference led Foucault effectively to indict the enemy without naming him. In any case his book has sold well, deservedly so; and part of what has made such a success possible is that the culture is no longer in thrall to Cartesian mechanism. We are paranoid because the culture is paranoid, and vice versa: a liberating perception. Sympathy for the more abstract sufferings of Mother Nature is manifestly more difficult to arouse; but as more and more acid rain kills more and more trees, more and more people will wake up—unless, of course, the thought-police insist on more anesthetic.

7

If quantum theory and the shift from Cartesianism help us to appreciate The Myth of the Bad Scientist, they also point up the role of fiction in science. Central to the ideological strength of scientific materialism in the nineteenth century was the insistence that science (unlike religion and poetry and metaphysics) contains no element of fiction, but rather is a technique whereby Nature is induced simply to reveal herself in facticity. Thus whereas pre-scientific man had to make do with fictional gods and magical mumbo jumbo, scientific man is a grown-up who lives with the truth. This of course is nonsense: modern science is not the revelation to end all revelations, merely the one that has prevailed over Western man in the past four centuries. It proceeds through the construction of hypotheses, inductive leaps that make connections hitherto undreamed of. Scientific breakthroughs, like poetic masterpieces, tend to arise in the middle of the night, in dreams, and the genius appointed to transcribe them tends to have no idea where they came from.[18] Like poems or Greek myths, the "models" of reality made by scientists offer new ways of seeing, of organizing experience, and they retain their authority only as long as the relevant experts think they do: indeed, old-fashioned theories are even less admired than old-fashioned poems. This point about the tentative nature of scientific models (and our tendency to forget it) is made with admirable clarity by R. W. Braithwaite in *Scientific Explanation* (1963):

> The last trace of the old hard massy atom has disappeared; but it lies latent whenever a model is used. Thinking of scientific theories by means of models is always *as-if* thinking. . . . The price of the employment of models is eternal vigilance. (p. 93)

In short, the scientist with his model weaves a fictional web not altogether unlike the poet's, a crucial point in the argument against scientific hegemony in cultural matters; and though the philosophers have known this for some time, the movement of modern physics back to idealism in quantum mechanics is making this clear to any interested layman. Thus, for example, not only do we find the physicist Werner Heisenberg asserting that the perceiver modifies the perceived, but that the idea of matter itself has more or less disappeared:

> On this point modern physics has definitely decided for Plato. For the smallest units of matter are, in fact, not physical objects in the ordinary sense of the word; they are forms, structures, or—in Plato's sense—Ideas, which can be unambiguously spoken of only in the language of mathematics.[19]

Elsewhere he notes that "what we observe is not nature itself, but nature exposed to our questioning." If this is so, it may be that we question her badly, in which case it may also be that she responds badly in turn. In any case, remarks such as these by Heisenberg utterly rule out the idea of science as simple empiricism, the plain man standing open-eyed and without preconception before the evidence of Nature. It is quite clear that in particle physics man brings at least as many laws to Nature as he discovers there; and as he soberly denies the reality of matter, he sounds as intriguingly outrageous as any poet, philosopher, or shaman in full flight.

Consider, for example, how things stand with the smaller subatomic particles such as the somewhat fictional and much-mistaken quark: not only are its movements so dizzy and febrile that it cannot be observed without being distorted, nor can its next moves be predicted with any accuracy, but what causes its motion seems to be so unlike the satisfying clunk of one billiard ball on another that physicists such as David Bohm are shelving the old notion of causality as contiguous impulse and speaking instead of almost unimaginable "nonlocal connections." In short, the simple world of predictable stresses and strains that Newton invited us to live in now seems to be an illusion we sensibly adopt in order to stay sane, but underneath it all the woodwork is crawling with unpredictability: an impeccably "religious" view, with which any sober primitive would agree. Consider also the work being done in what has been fetchingly but misleadingly called "chaos theory," which is prepared to consider that massive events like hurricanes may originate in the almost indiscernible flickering of a butterfly's wings. Until recently such a fanciful idea might have been thought appropriate for a poetical meditation on time and the mysterious "divinity that shapes our ends," but no matter for the scientific mind to address.[20]

Even though physics is now moving away from materialism back to a kind of idealism, the virus of scientism is still very much alive and well; hence something more must be said about scientific fictions, how they do and do not resemble the unscientific kind. Physicists are not embarrassed to admit that they have two theories about the cosmos, general relativity and quantum theory, and that "time" is thought to behave rather differently in each. They can live with this because a scientific theory is only and always a working hypothesis, which stands only so long as it gives an adequate account of its field. As such it is a fiction that, like a Greek myth, seeks to make sense of the unintelligible, and it cheerfully stands aside when someone comes up with a better story.[21]

A scientific theory differs from a Greek myth in principally two ways. First, as Georges de Buffon said, it interrogates the how and not the why of things (hence the idea of its being value-free): thus it tells us how waves are transmitted through the water, not why the sea-god Poseidon gets angry. Second, because of its experimental nature, its practical moment, its "handling" of its material, it is so formulated as to be universally confirmed or falsified, as no Greek myth can ever be, with the result that it "works" in the sense of delivering power to its user as no myth does. But power corrupts, as the saying goes, and scientific theory corrupts the mind chiefly through its abstraction, as I have insisted throughout this chapter. Such abstraction, the decision to ignore certain aspects of experience in order to concentrate on certain others, may seem harmless enough (even rather beautiful) when it ignores the tediousness of sublunary friction in order to perceive the law of inertia. But when one sees contemporary physicists playing games on their linear accelerators, one becomes distinctly uneasy. Quite apart from the vast expense involved in constructing these cosmic pinball machines, one notices that their abstraction from merely mortal conditions encourages the fiction of safe, indeed playful, nuclear explosions; which is to say that even now when Einstein's monster is on the loose, physicists choose, for their purposes, to ignore what the Greeks profoundly knew, that Poseidon gets *angry*.

The battle between Poseidon and the scientist for the allegiance of modern man, though probably won by Newton, did not become apparent until Kant and the more thoughtful Romantics made a last stand for what one might call "the mythological mind." By the mid-nineteenth century, when Darwin published *The Origin of Species,* the problem became fairly generally noticed. If evolution is blind, cried Samuel Butler, the gods are dead and Darwin their executioner. Darwin's work profoundly dismayed the Victorian religious sensibility, not only because it challenged Christian orthodoxy but also because the idea that life evolves haphazardly, by means of random mutations, seemed to give aid and comfort to the advocates of scientific materialism, as in fact it surely did, and indeed Darwin intended it to do so. And yet, although his work arguably represents the high-water mark in the fortunes of scientific materialism, dealing the *coup de grâce* to an exhausted religious fiction and delivering us over to randomness and the chimpanzees, it can also be seen as the major component in a new (very old) dispensation, a pantheism returning us from the Victorian grotesque to the bosom of Mother Nature and our fellowship with the animal kingdom. Darwin's enthusiasm for the radically primitive forms of Nature is abundantly evident in his early writing from the *Beagle* voyage, notably on the Galapagos islands, where amid spooky volcanic craters he would pick up "ugly" 15-pound lizards by the tail to see if they might bite him, and cheerfully cavorted with 200-pound "antideluvian" tortoises, riding on their backs.[22]

Much more fun than difficult young ladies in civilized frocks. Some years later Karl Marx, drawn to a different version of the primitive, was pleased to think of himself as "the Darwin of sociology." Marx in fact wanted to dedicate *Das Kapital* to Darwin, who politely refused on the grounds that certain subversive aspects of his own work had already sufficiently troubled his wife and such other authorities as he cherished. The chief troublemaker was, of course, the idea of random mutation: first came the idea of evolution itself, knocking out the father god of Genesis and his six-day creation, leaving only Mother Nature in the pantheon; and then came the idea that she operates through random mutations, which seemed to turn her into a blind amorphous monster, flailing stupidly in the dark, and only occasionally getting it right. This left us altogether alone in a monstrous world of chance.

A chilling enough story, particularly if one is prone, as so many Victorians were, to religious despair; or indeed to resentment of religiousness, as so many are today. And yet the story needn't be chilling. Consider first of all that the phrase Darwin actually used was "spontaneous variation" not "random mutation": his phrase is much livelier, more like a goddess than a monster from science fiction. "Random mutation," the current jargon, comes from Mendelian genetics, and nicely illustrates the reductive tendencies of the scientific imagination. Darwin, as we shall see, would be both pleased and displeased at the reduction; but the important point is that, even assuming (as for present purposes we must) that such complexities as the human eye could have evolved randomly, there is no matter here for religious despair.

When geneticists speak barbarously of "random mutation," let us cheerfully agree that it is well suited to their purpose, but realize that "spontaneous variation" is better suited to ours, which is to stay in touch with science while retaining an animated, unified sense of that Nature (capital N) that gives us life and calls for our respect and reverence. As our author and authority, Nature is no transcendent deity but rather the life force itself, fully immanent, the pulsing, striving, playful force that throws off forms in such indiscriminate profusion as to seem blind or at least unthinking. Some of what comes up looks good, some bad, some failed, and some beautiful. The archaic Greeks called it *phusis* (which stems from puffing and blowing, as the sound suggests): Henri Bergson called it the *élan vital*. At the heart of such a notion is the idea that life calls to life, that life desires its own increase—a desire that in so many evolutionary stories is artfully gratified. To say that it proceeds through random mutation and the vagaries of weather is an inoffensive description of the "technology" of creation, a scientific fiction or hypothesis that evolutionists find useful. Such talk only becomes offensive when as scientism it dresses up as metaphysical certainty, and claims to know that there can be no authority in this tale told by an idiot and signifying nothing but randomness.

Authorship and authority are the crux of the matter, and much is at stake. If Nature is blind and does not know what she is doing, she is not the author of the evolutionary story, and hence lacks the authority to call upon our reverence. This means that insofar as the tale has an author, it is man the scientist, who pieces it together retrospectively; and to him we ascribe the authority to tell us that there is no Authority, that man is indeed the measure of all things. Some sense of the outrageousness of this idea may be gathered from the fact that our words "author" and "authority" derive from the Latin *augere* = to increase (as discussed in the Appendix); and who is the source of evolutionary increase and hence authority if not Mother Nature? She is also, of course, the author of decrease and extinction, but should this lessen our respect for her authority? On the contrary, surely. But the voice of scientism would have no god but science, to restrict its activities; for if Nature cannot call upon us for reverence, we are free to call upon her with our inquisitive mind, free to handle her deepest secrets in our search for knowledge and power. This we have done, to our cost, despite Goethe's warnings about the Faustian demon of modern science, and despite Wordsworth's eloquent song.

Still, it is never too late to repent, particularly when, as in the case of evolutionary theory, the two sides can be reconciled. Let us assume for present purposes that the case for random mutation is overwhelming: there is nothing here to dismay our natural piety— quite the reverse. What it tells us is that Mother Nature, in her profound and relaxed wisdom, adopts randomness as the means of proposing her story. Like a swarm of bees she throws herself upon the winds of chance, abandoning the known safety of the home place in a gamble for new life. This she does, as the bees do, from a position of strength and abundance, and is not dismayed when the gamble fails, as it often does. All that one needs to appreciate the beauty of such strategy is some sense of the wealth at her disposal—the vast amount of time that does not harry her as it harries mortal man; and for this sense we might profitably look to the poet rather than the scientist—to Yeats, for example, when he says "Only the wasteful virtues earn the sun." But one should also look to the fine prose of Stephen Jay Gould: in his recent and best-selling *Wonderful Life* (1989) he decisively dismantles the widely cherished belief that the story of evolution is an exfoliating "progress" from simple to complex structures culminating in the glory of *Homo sapiens,* and argues persuasively, on the basis of the Burgess fossils, for the central importance of "contingency"; that is to say, had the weather been slightly different, *Homo sapiens* wouldn't have happened at all. And yet this in no way lessens the *wonder* he feels in contemplating the story, nor the "consequent moral responsibility" (p. 291) it inspires in him. I see no reason why, with perhaps a little friendly nudging, he should not join the "broad church" I am proposing.

Many readers will be surprised to discover that the argument over Nature's sacredness is not new, but as old as philosophy itself. The Ionian "scientists" in ancient Greece proposed that we dispense with the primitive fiction of divine creation and see the cosmos as having evolved simply "by necessity" (*ananke*) through the confluence of elemental forces. First Plato then Aristotle spotted the dangers implicit in such a proposal: to say that Nature (*phusis*) evolved through blind and irrational *ananke* is effectively to say it evolved through chance (or as we would say, "randomness"); in which case man's notion of what he should do and value, his world of law and morality (*nomos*), has no divine sanction and is purely conventional, relative, or fictional; and this means that sooner or later someone like Protagoras will arrive to announce that "Man is the measure of all things"; and this will lead, sooner rather than later, to solipsism, nihilism, and moral anarchy. The only way to forestall this, as both Plato and Aristotle recognized, is to insist that within and beyond and behind the seemingly whimsical fatalities of Nature there is a divine power whose purposes, beauty, and urgency call upon us to assist, as best we can, the realization of its intentions (the famous "entelechies" of Aristotle); and what Nature intends, as Aristotle so simply and eloquently argues, is excellence. Thus the constructions of culture, the moral and esthetic laws (*nomoi*) that we fashion and revere, though shot through with human frailty, ignorance, and local variation, are actually fashioned in response to a divine presence always imperfectly known, but *there* to witness and measure the justice in our answer to its call. Plato, the more poetical of the two, finally decided that gods and goddesses are indispensable for securing this perception (see his *Laws*, particularly Book 10). His student Aristotle, more scientist than poet, said that everything in Nature displays its purpose (entelechy) to the degree that it shines forth (*epiphaino*) with its very own specific virtue or excellence (*arete*);

that the divine power intends the realization of such excellence; and calls upon man both to lend a hand and to admire whatever instances of virtuous *arete* he might meet, whether in Nature or among humankind.

I would suggest that our spiritual dilemma is much the same. Most educated Westerners have been persuaded by Darwin to dispense with the primitive notion of something sacred in Nature that calls upon our reverence and legitimizes our cultural aspirations. The moral and esthetic anarchy consequent upon such secular thinking is everywhere apparent. What is to be done? The crucial point in my view is to see that the mental move from a sacred to a secular Nature is a perfectly "natural" one to make, neither fiendishly diabolical on the one hand nor even remotely compelled by "reason" or "logic" on the other: that is to say, it is an *option* (anthropocentric, to be sure), that people from time to time find attractive, and that they then try to justify by dressing it in the more dignified clothing of "reason" or "science." What is so useful about the writings of Plato and Aristotle is that they enable us to see this, to see that Darwin's secular move was essentially similar to the one made by Ionian science, humanly plausible but not compulsory, and one whose ultimate cultural implications are dire. Once a sufficient number of us have seen this, corrective action can easily be taken. Aristotle, being less theological, is probably the more appropriate of the ancients for us to follow, and among modern poets Wallace Stevens is perhaps the best Aristotelian, teaching us to seek the sacred in accurate perceptions of Nature's excellences. Weather gods are the oldest gods, and one might, for example, begin by meditating

> Weather by Franz Hals,
> Brushed up by brushy winds in brushy clouds
> Wetted by blue, colder for white.
> "Notes Towards a Supreme Fiction"

From here one might go a long way. Part of the pleasure in the going will be to discover that Darwin was by no means single-mindedly opposed to the trip, as we shall see presently.[23]

8

If, as I have been suggesting, the problem of our "scientismic" despair is as old as Plato and Aristotle, and its solution not difficult to envisage, why is it that we have not solved it? Why is it that scientism (in evolutionary as in other matters) is still thriving?[24] To explore this would take us too far afield, but the short answer is that "A man hears what he wants to hear and disregards the rest": not only does Faustian man want no check upon his lust for knowledge and power, but he is also seeking to revenge himself upon the gods who have absconded and left him, unauthored and unauthorized, a waif among the galaxies. Because Faustian man still haunts us, the evolutionary text of random mutation can be read today in diametrically opposite ways; either as the triumphant abolition of divinity or as our contemporary perception of Nature's genius. In this case, as so often, you find what you want.

In Victorian times, however, the latter reading was not generally available (despite the kinder phrasing of "spontaneous variation") not only because Christian orthodoxy held the foreground, but because the background had not been sufficiently prepared (despite Goethe and Wordsworth) for the seeds of neo-pantheism or animism to take root; which is to say that Darwin appeared—to himself as well as others—as god-slayer but not also as redeemer of an old religious idea whose time had come around again. But since we can see him as both hero and villain of the piece, we can see both piety and Faustian fury; and indeed Darwin was deeply divided on the fundamental question of authority. In "spontaneous variation" one can see subversion of authority, even anarchy, even nihilism; and yet vestiges of his youthful natural piety are evident throughout *The Origin of Species,* where he extols the wonders of Nature in fine prose with a capital N and makes some apology for the not strictly scientific use of the personification "she." In a significant sense his book can be seen as a rehabilitation (however subconsciously intended) of the ancient mother goddess, the Magna Mater of classical and pre-classical cultures: both the Christian father-god and William Paley's mechanist "watchmaker" god (and indeed the

Victorian paterfamilias who honored them) are displaced by a feminine Nature endlessly prolific, appallingly cruel, and carelessly ruthless in the dispatching of her unsuccessful children. On her days off, however, while sexually selecting, she flaunts her whimsical and esthetic side, as a goddess should. In no way are such things as peacock tails and elk antlers "adaptive," but the girls find 'em pretty, so that's that.[25] All in all, one can see in Darwin's idea of Nature an intriguing amalgam of Inanna, Isis, Demeter, and Kali, the inner circle of Magna Maters.* These goddesses fall in love, give birth, and kill: their matter is mortality, and the earth that bears it. Darwin's rediscovery of them in the evolution of natural species offers to release the scientific mind from the ballooning abstractions of the higher mathematics and return it to earth, in the study of whose history it might even find the invigorating perception of its own finitude (a perception effectively hidden since the promulgation of Newton's perpetual motion machine). His thought offers to release not only the scientific mind, of course, but the modern mind we all more or less inhabit. Consider this entry from his M Notebook (1838): "Origin of man now proved. . . . He who understands baboon would do more towards metaphysics than Locke." This is not only true (providing we spell "proved" with a small "p") but we still read it 150 years on with a virtuous sense of mischievous liberation; which means, among other things, that it still has some liberating to do.

It is for this that Darwin is to be cherished; and yet, since he did it ambiguously, half-reluctantly, even to some extent unintentionally, not only was it ill-perceived at the time, but it continues to puzzle his readers and his followers. Some light may be shed on the matter by casting a psychological eye on his deeply ambivalent attitude toward the feminine. On the one hand, he seems to rehabilitate the mother goddess with his evolutionary theory, and yet on the other,

---

*Inanna is Sumerian, Isis Egyptian, Demeter Greek, and Kali Indian. The first three we shall meet at some length in subsequent chapters. Kali unfortunately falls beyond the scope of this work, but she bears a marked family resemblance to the others.

he seems to kill her off (and indeed theology itself) by randomizing her procedures. Both gestures can be understood as having originated in a desire both to provoke and placate his formidable father; and also in a desire both to venerate and to punish the mother who died when he was a child. The ambivalence is everywhere apparent: in the foreground we admire the patience and the piety of the natural scientist who was repelled by the brutal practices of medical school; and in the background we see a young man obsessed with shooting birds, which would suggest an interest in Nature not altogether benign. As he aged and became contemptuous of religious belief, the poetry and music he used to love began actually to nauseate him. Was this some mutilated part of his feminine self crying out in pain?[26] Bearing in mind that Nature for the thoughtful post-Wordsworthian generation (which includes Darwin) carried such remnants of divinity as were imaginable (the Christian god having been buried *pro tem* in Victorian sanctimony), one can see that by randomizing (and hence apparently de-animating) Nature, Darwin was not only opening her up for untrammeled scientific investigation but was also striking a subtle blow against that Authority by which parents have traditionally constrained and fostered rebel sons.

At the risk of overloading an already complex story, one might add that Darwin's father, an agnostic physician, had, with consummate Victorian hypocrisy, for a time persuaded his feckless son that a career in Holy Orders would be the proper discipline for his unsettled soul: which is to say that the Authority young Charles had to confront was nothing simple, a many-headed monster indeed. And so, although he defied the father's hypocritical clericalism by recalling the Magna Mater, he effectively neutralized this gesture by randomizing her activity, which points toward what Nietzsche would call scientific nihilism, something radical and cold enough to leave both father *and* mother (*and* pious wife) gasping. Unable to meet his astonishingly formidable father head-on (and who can blame him?), he turned to the Mother *qua* Mother Nature (his earthly one having died and thus "randomized" his existence): "If mother is dead let the Mothers die," one can imagine him whispering to his father's ghost, but so quietly that even he could hardly hear it. The nausea and ill-health that plagued him in later life suggest what this subconscious whisper may have cost his sensitive nature in terms of repressed remorse. In this his darker side, not just in the enduring lightness of his fine prose, he still has much to teach us.[27]

9

Well over a century has passed since Darwin's epoch-making book was published, surely almost long enough for us to absorb it correctly; i.e., be admonished by, forgive, and then discard its Faustian fury, while recognizing in evolution the *idée matrice* of our age, a metaphysic upon which scientist and poet can meet, sink their differences, and get on with the urgent task of telling the story of how to save the planet. This work is already well underway, in the name of ecology or oecology, from the Greek *oikos* + *logos,* the rule of the household, aptly inscribed by Gary Snyder as *Earth House Hold.* Darwin's founding influence on this discipline is widely recognized, and the word "ecology" refers to a rich and expanding tapestry of concerns—intellectual, religious, and political.[28] And yet, for all that, the myths of scientism are proving remarkably difficult to shift: we *still* tend to see ourselves as mild-mannered men asking clever questions of the computer rather than idiot children wandering around the school-yard with pockets full of high explosives; and in many quarters the scientist is *still* thought to be a person of unique and peculiar wisdom concerning human affairs.[29] If the culture is to be healed, and time, as they say, is running out, we must find our way back to those stories that call upon us to engage seriously with our violence and our greed. Such stories run in the blood, somewhere below the apartments in which we read the latest novel. They used to be called myths, and they used to make the world go round, by showing us when and where to dance. We could do it again if we tried.

Not the least of our difficulties arose in connection with cultural relativism. As nineteenth-century ethnographers brought more and more of the world's mythologies to light, it became increasingly apparent to the liberal mind not only that the gods are differently apprehended around the world, but that the religious beliefs that myths articulate are a major source of prejudice, fanaticism, and warfare. From here it was but an easy and fateful step to the conclusion that all religious fictions are at best growths and tumors that should be discouraged in the name of tolerance, scientific objectivity, and planetary democracy. To take this step, as Nietzsche understood first and best, is to step into the void; for man is a myth-making animal, and if you take away his gods he will replace them with devils: as Nietzsche put it, "Man would rather have the void for his purpose than be void of purpose." This aphorism wonderfully summarizes and condenses the case against scientism. It reminds us that hands never folded in prayer will be finally grabbed by the spirits of devastation; and it points not only to what the Nazis made of Wagner but also to the less evidently diabolical intentions of a "value-free" science, accurately adumbrated in Mary Shelley's *Franken-stein*: science unfettered by piety breeds monsters that return to plague the head of the inventor. But whereas the fascist monster is by now fairly well known, the monsters of science still have many of us foxed; and without myths to remind us of the moral stupidity of science, planetary prospects are poor.

Cultural relativism, however, can be lived with. What enabled the Greeks to tolerate the temple of Isis down the road from the temple of Demeter was an irony grounded in reverence for Nature, the *phusis* that underlay and underwrote man's various attempts to fashion the gods. If we are to retrieve a comparable irony, we must first retrieve our reverence for Nature—Mother Nature and human nature—on the basis of which our various religious fictions can be compared and evaluated, and our scientific fictions kept humane. Without such a reverence (which so much of our "scientific" culture has undermined in the past century), the planet will yield to our greed and our hatreds. In our reconstructed pantheon a crucial figure will be Charles Darwin, whose work returns us to that touch of Nature that makes the whole world kin. That the Victorians denounced him as the enemy of true religion is an irony and a paradox we should by now be able to appreciate. Natural piety is in itself insufficient of course, for Nature is also "red in tooth and claw," as Tennyson said; and if our hand is not to be infected by Nature's claw, our reverence must be tempered by an appropriate resistance. Unlike our fellow creatures, we need a hand that can both prey and pray. Hands that are folded in prayer not only point to the source of their power, but are closed against undue exposure to it.

Thus the way forward is back: back first of all to Darwin's liberating perception that the chimpanzees are our brothers with much to teach us of that "muddy centre" (as Wallace Stevens puts it) from which we arose to draw our human breath; and then back to the origins of culture where "the myth began," those fictions we must find the courage to breathe again. The courage we find will be of the wrong kind unless it is accompanied by humility, pictured throughout this chapter in the hand that prays; and yet before our hands can be taught again to express the prayers of mind and body, they must be used to reclaim and restrain the modern mind that has wandered so far from lively intercourse with its own mortality. Here is Yeats:

> Hands, do what you're bid:
> Bring the balloon of the mind
> That bellies and drags in the wind
> Into its narrow shed.
>
> *Collected Poems,* p. 175

Gravity is what we lack; and the shedding of hot air will make a start.

If we are to begin again, we must be properly admonished but not disheartened by the dangerousness of the enterprise, to which the wreckage of totalitarian experiments in our century bears witness. In the center of that danger is the waywardness of language itself. The names we distribute in the beginning (tinker, tailor, soldier, sailor) may well compose the fabric of meaning within a culture, but they also create the possibility of mischievous nonsense. Just as clothes are usually "made up" to clarify one's social standing and yet may conceal disfigurement or weapons, so the names we distribute can be misleading (in the simplest sense our John the Smith may be a bastard, not his father's son). Fictions then, which most importantly name our beginnings and assign values to them, also inaugurate possibilities of deceit, pointing thereby to the dangerousness and fragility of culture; and long before philosophers began skeptically scrutinizing the idea of beginnings, primitive man was indicating *his* unease not only by the great importance he ascribed to the elaboration and revision of his nominative fictions, but also by the grave rituals in which he embedded all human commencements.

Though much has changed since then, nothing much has changed. Oblivion reigns in many quarters, but some are still trying to remember the story that begins "In the beginning . . ." The wonders of modern science have enormously extended our knowledge of man's natural background, but also much destroyed our sense of wonder, without which the story makes no human sense. Most damaging here is that tired knowingness that regards all human fiction simply as material for psychoanalysis, demystification, or deconstruction, and has forgotten that a human life is made shapely and given direction only through a song, a dance, a prayer, a curse. Although lip service is widely given to the notion of man as the animal who is called to make sense of his world through the fictions he offers it (in his scientific theories as well as his myths in religion and politics), there is little evidence these days that we truly wish to address the gods with anything but the numbing products of a runaway technology.

And yet, even as the planet wobbles ever more crazily in its elliptic, we must not be distracted. When T. S. Eliot in one of the few great poems of the century, *East Coker*, reminds us that "In my beginning is my end," he is not only recalling us to what has always been man's major meditation, but also pointing to a crucial ambiguity. The end we seek in our beginning is not only the vision of human life we are called upon to realize and protect, but also the death we may properly die. Eliot reminds us that both involve waiting; and even if one thinks circumstance is rendering the first of these projects fantastical (as politics escapes us), the second remains unassailable, quite enough to keep us on course, waiting for the call.

2 ꞏ IN THE BEGINNING:
From Monkey to Man
on the African Savannah

Origin of man now proved. . . . He who
understands baboon would do more
toward metaphysics than Locke.
　　　　　　　—Charles Darwin, 1838

The purpose of this chapter is to provide the reader with a brief
sketch of our monkey prologue, not only because the story is
intrinsically fascinating, but also because it can tell us a good deal
about our human selves: how we began, and to a remarkable extent,
how we still are. The idea that our distant past holds the key to
much in our present has understandably gained in favor as the
authority of Christian teaching on human origins has declined. In
our century both Freud and Jung were drawn back to our "savage"
origins in their attempt to understand the human psyche. Both of
them, moreover, saw the exercise as one of retrieving a lost integrity
by *remembering* things pleasant and unpleasant that the Christian
emphasis upon the spirituality of man, his superiority to the rest of
creation, has led us to forget and deny.

　The idea that learning is remembering is at least as old as Plato's
Meno, but in our post-Christian confusion it has taken on a new
focus and a new urgency. Here is Freud on memory:

　　Since we overcame the error of supposing that the forgetting we
　　are familiar with signified a destruction of the memory trace—that

is, its annihilation—we have inclined to the opposite view, that in mental life nothing which has once been formed can perish—that everything is somehow preserved, and in suitable circumstances (when, for instance, regression goes back far enough) it can once more be brought to light.

—*Civilization and Its Discontents*, p 6.

It is often ignored by those who are made uneasy by the tender-minded Jung that the tough-minded Freud agreed with him that everything we experience, however convincingly repressed or forgotten, is preserved in the memory and can in principle be recovered. Even more important is the idea that the stages of an individual's development may mirror the evolution of mankind ("ontogeny recapitulates phylogeny," as the jargon puts it), and hence our memories may carry some very archaic material indeed.[1]

Such speculation has certainly not been hindered by scientific developments since Freud's death. I will cite only three instances. The first of these is that we are now thought to be much closer to the chimpanzee and gorilla than has hitherto been supposed. The date for the hominid departure from the ape line has been recently moved forward from about twenty million years ago to perhaps as little as six. This makes the chimpanzee more like a brother than a cousin (99 percent of the DNA is common), and removes at a stroke a huge cushion of time during which we as humans might have distanced ourselves comfortably from the apes. Second, we have discovered more about the "limbic" cortex, the old mammalian brain erected upon the rudimentary reptilian "chassis": the limbic governs our instincts and coexists rather uneasily with the clever neocortex that grew around it in the higher primates and man. Not only is this old brain more or less the same in all mammals (obviously a successful design), but in man it often doesn't listen to the newfangled ideas of the neocortex concerning instinctual affairs. According to Arthur Koestler (*The Ghost in the Machine*, 1967), this conflict is responsible for the maladaptive irrationalities that make the human species uniquely dangerous and absurd. If he is right and we go this far back for our violence, it may be worth going back to look for it; that is to say, if our instincts are controlled by a reactionary and rather deaf old brawler, we had better try to understand him, in order both to negotiate changes where we can and also to submit gracefully where we must.

Third is the discovery of DNA itself, the extraordinary amount of information we now know our genes capable of storing and transmitting. Not only does this discovery speak up in general terms for "Nature" in the Nature-nurture debate, but it allows that we may have inherited from grandfather not only his blue eyes and a disposition to speak grammatically but also some remarkably old memories, perhaps of the days when we were hunted by snake or jungle cat, even pterodactyl. This possibility is enhanced by the fact that for all our astonishing penetration of the mysteries of DNA, we still understand remarkably little about how the memory actually works; but it seems increasingly clear that there is more of it than we think.[2] When these matters are set beside the very recent updating of our separation from the apes, we have strong grounds for taking our animality seriously: in each case we find "hard" sciences proposing that our biological past may have a firmer grip upon our present than has been hitherto assumed. Freud would certainly feel pleased, particularly in view of the criticism he endured for his belief that many of our present discontents (pleasures too) stem from the archaic past and must be pursued there.

Some paragraphs after the one I have cited above, Freud rather nervously but admiringly mentions a friend who "through the practices of Yoga" seeks "regressions to primordial states of mind which have long ago been overlaid. He sees in them a physiological basis, as it were, of much of the wisdom of mysticism" (p. 9). I think Freud's friend was talking sense, quite like the primitive shaman who would seek in his trances both to become the lion (in order to acquire the power of the leonine) and also to converse with death; and moreover would see the two to be connected. Freud's nervous admiration of such an "alien" approach to religious experience sounds an uncharacteristic note of humility ("Let me admit once more that it is very difficult for me to work with these almost intangible qualities"), which both mitigates the un-wisdom of much of his writing on the subject and encourages us down the road he did not take. In what follows I commend to the reader nothing as physically disturbing as the "practices of Yoga" but a degree of mental disturbance certainly, enough to consider the possibility that we in the late twentieth century may be sufficiently sophisticated to benefit significantly from "regressions to primordial states of mind."

2

Once upon a time, some ninety million years ago, there was a tree shrew: first of the primates, ancestor of us all, small and mouselike. The major problem in its life was cousin rodent, whose ever-growing teeth dealt more effectively with the tough vegetation, and probably with tree shrews as well. In any case the competition between rodent and primate led to the extinction of several species of primate before the solution was found, in Africa it seems: the primates took to the trees while the rodents held the ground.[3]

In this arboreal exile one can discern the outlines of our first nightmare: a timorous beastie is driven off his land into a new and precarious element by the sound of munching teeth—teeth moreover that munch in the night (for the rodent remained nocturnal while we became daylight creatures). Primates then, though destined one day to dominate the planet, began life rather as wandering Jews, forced by our better-armed cousins to abandon both Mother Earth and Mother Night for a new existence, in which we could both dream of the devil (so like us) who expelled us from our kingdom and also imagine our certain revenge. Primates still fear the rat; and not only the earth but also the night have retained in human annals the ambivalent sense of both home and the terrifying; and the rat himself (like us, not designed to kill, and whose propensity for murder within its own species we share) has retained an allotment of hatred and fear in the human imagination that can only be called irrational. Indeed in Chapter 6 we shall see that the rat was one of the original "creeping things," our first sketch of the devil.

I should emphasize that I am not asserting that we somehow have access to memories of the Original War against the Rodents. We may have, as I shall indicate presently, but for present purposes this is not the primary question. What is at stake is the retrieval of an interesting old story, one that gives a certain "natural" resonance to such ancient notions as paradise, exile, and evil; and the question is whether we humans are entitled to lay claim to such an old story, and be enriched by it. My answer is yes, and I would seek the title deeds not in some hypothetical memory-trace (fetish of a materialist age), but in the fact that from earliest times our shamans and wise men have thought it valuable both to simulate animal states (in poetry and trance) and tell stories of what life was like when we lived in animal form (our theriomorphic phase). Such stories, after centuries of neglect, once again seem important as we listen to the evolutionists tell us we are much closer to the chimpanzee than even Darwin imagined, and the ecologists tell us we have become a disgrace to the animal kingdom.

As can be seen in the Appendix, memory lies at the very heart of human culture: *Mnemosyne* is not only mother of the muses but she may be the original goddess of the *nemos*, the stand of trees that enclosed the first temple. And since it could be said without exaggeration that the present work is inscribed to her memory, it is pleasing to report that scientific materialism is having considerable difficulty in bringing her to book (in "booking" her, as they say at the police station): for all the recent dazzling success with DNA, scientists are still unable and may be *in principle* unable to give a plausible account of how (or indeed whether) memories are stored in the brain; and it may be, as Henri Bergson originally suggested, that memory or habit lies at the heart of Nature as well as culture. The implications of this are momentous: for example, if memories are not etched as physical traces on the brain, there may be more of them than we think.

If memory is not restricted to a physical record of what a living body has experienced, and if, as Rupert Sheldrake (1988) argues, something very like the memory is at work in the evolution of species, then Jung's much-ridiculed notion of a Collective Unconscious, which he describes as "a million-year-old man" in whom the archetypes of human culture and its evolution are stored, immediately ceases to look ridiculous and becomes possible; and a work such as this one, devoted to the retrieval of our formative cultural experience, for the sake of sanity, immediately looks less eccentric.*

In any case, after our difficult start with the rodents, things improved considerably. When the dinosaurs disappeared about sixty-five million years ago, probably as the result of some heavenly disturbance, a great deal of land came free for development, and the age of mammals began. As promising squirrel-like creatures, the primates were ready to go, already developing our major features: eye, hand, and brain.[4] Gradually we turned into monkeys, and these organs developed remarkably, eyes above all. By moving them to the front of the head (like the owl whom we have always admired) we acquired binocular vision, capable of locating objects with great precision and also of seeing them in technicolor (the bright ripe fruit standing out from the unripe green among the leaves). As vision became more important so smell became less, and our muzzles shrank. By shedding our claws and moving the thumb to oppose the four fingers, our paws became hands and feet with extraordinary powers both of locomotion and of grasping objects and manipulating them with precision. As the eye and hand grew smarter, so the brain kept pace, always relatively large for our body size. Indeed eye and hand still provide major metaphors for the acquisition of knowledge—"Do you see what I mean? Can you grasp it?"—and this points accurately to the evolving picture of the brainy primate: not very big, not very fierce, but very fast and extremely in*sight*ful.

Graceful too, an important point to bear in mind, as nowadays the brainy tend to be physically graceless. Anyone who has admired

*One also thinks in this connection of Chomsky's work, which suggests that the acquisition of language involves the releasing of innate capacities, not the inscribing of a *tabula rasa*; i.e., our learning to speak is also a remembering. Furthermore, if the rules of grammar are ultimately the same for all languages, this too speaks for Nature over nurture; and the Tower of Babel story becomes less dismaying, in the sense that at some consoling level it may be true that "The whole earth" is *still* "of one language, and of one speech" (Genesis 11–1).

the seemingly effortless speed and accuracy of monkey movement in the trees cannot doubt that work under such conditions becomes playful: what's more, one may suspect that the playful and the graceful are related to each other, and that wherever they are found, mastery is not far away.

Like many another successful species, the monkeys kept developing larger models, and as they grew bigger they tended to become less agile, increasingly confined to the stout lower branches, until gravity had its way with us, and we came back down to earth once more. On the way from high-flying squirrel to ponderous pongid ape-on-the-ground a momentous development took place, which, like the other two key moments in our movement from monkey to man (upright stance and the big brain), still has the experts puzzled. It is called "brachiation," which means the ability to swing beneath branches by the arms rather than moving on top of them quadrupedally. Our latest guess is that this occurred (probably in Asia) between fifteen to twelve million years ago. What we *know*, however, is that brachiation was utterly, as the evolutionists say, adaptive. All the ape lines that have survived have been brachiators: i.e., all non-brachiating apes have become extinct. Very significant.

The word "ape" is rather confusing. Crudely put, apes are larger, later, and brainier than monkeys, that is, more human. The *Oxford English Dictionary* says "tail-less monkey" and mentions gibbon, orang, chimp, and gorilla, the four brachiating survivors. (The earliest apes, *Aegyptopithecus* ca. 28 million and *Dryopithecus* ca. 20 million, did not brachiate.) A crucial discovery on our way to the updating of our separation from the apes centers on brachiation, and the credit largely goes to Sherwood Washburn's work in the 1960s. Briefly summarized, he (and his pupil Virginia Avis) established that no monkeys brachiate, but all the apes and man do; which leads, by not very tortuous paths that we cannot examine here, to the idea that man and chimpanzee diverged from a common brachiating ancestor as recently as eight to six million years ago, a notion that recent advances in the molecular measurements of DNA is confirming. To move the date of separation forward to six million from the previous figure of twenty million is to move it a long way, and of course the argument has met with considerable resistance, as we "naturally" find such intimacy with the apes disconcerting, if not insulting, though the burden of my argument is that we should, on the contrary, be very pleased to find ourselves less lonely.

The functional point about brachiation is that it enables the relatively heavy ape to negotiate the slender whippy branches to reach the fruit at their tips. Anatomically it straightens the torso and greatly increases the fluency of shoulder and wrist (while also, not unimportantly, preparing the pelvis for the subsequent walking adaptation). The straightening torso, surrounded by articulate shoulders and hands, opens a protected space in front of the eyes where objects may be delicately presented for intimate consideration. It is the creation of this zone of what one might almost call "personal space" that distinguishes ape from non-brachiating monkey in our eyes, leading us instinctively to call the ape our brother and the monkey a distant cousin when, say, we visit them in the zoo. The opening of this intimate space where eye, hand, and brain interact, seems to me full of import for the human story, establishing the physical conditions for thoughtfulness.

But this is to anticipate. Brachiation *begins* as the very opposite of meditation, more like the acquisition of amazing gymnastic skills that will put off the dreadful day when we have to sit down and think about things. And yet brachiation is undoubtedly associated with braininess, as witnessed by the oldest of the surviving apes, the gibbon (ca. twelve to ten million), who is both markedly brainier than the smartest monkey and also the best brachiatior of all the apes. And why is brachiation brainy? Because, as a trip to the zoo will suggest, it is *very* difficult accurately to assess the stability and measure the "distance off" of branches being used to support and propel four limbs moving at speed. Not only difficult but dangerous: whereas a mouse can survive a fall of 1000 feet (quickly reaching its terminal velocity), the densely bodied large primate is ill-designed for falling. Hence our brachiating ancestors *had to pay attention* even on their early-morning stroll through the trees—and even more attention than did the already clever non-brachiating monkeys before them: hence the quantum leap in intelligence represented by the gibbon.[5] And yet, curiously enough, although the importance of brachiation is generally admitted, the experts remain puzzled as to why it occurred. Listen to Gribbin and Cherfas (*The Monkey Puzzle*, 1982), two authors never pleased with puzzlement:

> We don't know why the brachiating apes developed as they did [i.e., brachiated] though we suspect it had something to do with the availability of food, and neither do we know why, of all the dryopithecine lines, only the brachiators survived, but that is what happened. (p. 145)

Such theoretical blankness invites one to have a go.

Big is beautiful to a point, and then it becomes clumsy. Successful monkeys got bigger and brainier as gravity slowed them down and called them back to earth—until the gibbon (or to be exact the gibbon's forebear) breaks the downward drift with a major anatomical shift that not only restores fluency but quite literally flings the whole hominoid question back into the treetops where the first primates had set it forth so many million years before. Gibbons not only inhabit the treetops, the forest canopy, but with elongated arms and hands they fling themselves from branch to branch with such speed and agility that they seem to be flying. Here is grace and mastery at play, as never before or since: the dream of becoming a bird (our oldest dream?) never so nearly realized. Or call it the dream of becoming an angel: retain the mammal form but extend the arms and hands into wings.

At once one sees that brachiation is very brainy indeed: by devising this major anatomical shift the ape managed to retain the evolved grandeur of his bulk and brain while retrieving avian loftiness, king of the castle now in a sense his squirrelly ancestors never knew. And thus a long-standing problem was resolved: for who can doubt that once the primates had settled in to arboreal life their admiration was collected by and fixed upon the birds, whose defiance of gravity still seems magical to our tired eyes.

Fanciful talk? Surely not. Our fellow-feeling for the birds is rooted in the fact that both birds and arboreal primates, because they left the earth where smells linger, relegated the primordial nose and moved predominately into a world of sight and sound. Most of the birds can (like us) distinguish colors, and most of the mammals cannot: whereas when it comes to smelling, the dog does it at least a hundred times better than we do—which, since he's our best friend, gives us something to think about in terms of how at home we ever are on the earth. Thus distanced from our fellow mammals, we were thrown toward some fellowship with the anatomically strange, almost reptilean, birds, whose social and sexual activities, triggered like ours by sight and sound, seem less than strange, almost familiar, to human eyes. And yet such structural similarity only serves to highlight the crucial difference—that birds have wings to outwit the monkey's two major anxieties, snakes and the fear of falling.[6] It is surely not surprising that birds and snakes play such a large part in man's early religious imaginings. The god who would best minister to our monkey memory would be both bird and snake, and his name is Quetzalcoatl, the feathered serpent of the Toltecs.[7]

Monkeys are doubtless sufficiently evolved creatures to be thought capable of admiration, even envy, and they had been watching the birds' effortless motion for some fifty million years before brachiation. Birds defy both gravity and snakes, the monkey's two major problems, which makes them seriously magical. But though we know monkeys to be both playful and mimetic, sober evolutionists do not count such things among the factors that cause evolutionary change. The official Neo-Darwinian line is that changes are random (i.e., accidental mutations), and are then confirmed by proving to be "adaptive," a portmanteau word that declares its origin in the utilitarianism of Darwin's day. If evolution is ultimately random, the gods are whimsical, not significantly involved in writing the script, and this will always certainly please the anticlerical party. Furthermore, one should remember that one of Darwin's mentors was English economist Thomas Malthus, and that the notion of "survival of the fittest" was based upon the assumption of a deadly serious competition for scarce food supplies (an assumption that has recently been challenged). Playfulness was clearly not serious; and not only did Victorian science need sobriety and godlessness to achieve respectability, but the idea of play implies leisure, which is mildly upper class, not quite the thing for either monkeys or primitive man, to set a bad example for the Victorian worker. Today our shibboleths are somewhat different; and just as Marshall Sahlins in *Stone Age Economics* (1974) has dared suggest that primitive man in fact enjoyed a good deal of leisure, so it seems high time evolutionary theory loosened up to the point of admitting that there may be more to "adaptiveness" than the dreary business of getting and spending the food supply, particularly where brainy mammals are concerned.

And of course it does admit this, but it does so in a theory that, until recent advances in genetics, was much ignored, and it still gets rather short shrift among male chauvinist writers. Darwin called it "sexual selection," and devoted a good deal of attention to it in the *The Descent of Man* (1870). Very simply, it is the process whereby unserious, even maladaptive, things such as peacock's tails evolve because females fancy them. Have we not all been dismayed to learn that birdsong is *only* the marking of territory; or that the beauty of the flower is *merely* a ploy to get its seed into circulation? The fact is that beauty has evolved because the Eternal Feminine decrees that prettiness is preferable to ugliness. If this had been widely appreciated by the Victorians, they would have found the idea of evolution much more palatable. As for brachiation, I would say this: to thrive is to be lively, and what can be livelier than a game that is dangerous, skillful, and fun? Brachiation may well have secured easier access to bananas, but the females also found it sexy; and so it was bound to prevail.

The gibbon's life, as one would expect from a playful genius, is remarkably simple in comparison not only with the brainier great apes who succeeded him but also with most of the less brainy monkeys who "preceded" him, such as the baboon, macaque, patas, and langur. According to anthropologists Chance and Jolly (*Social Groups of Monkeys, Apes and Men*, 1970), he spends 85 percent of his time foraging in bands of about four, defending a territory of forty to three hundred acres of treetop he virtually never leaves. The other apes and monkeys favor larger groups (twenty to thirty, though baboons often rise to eighty), considerable time on the ground, and a great deal of social interaction, which means mostly bickering.

Another fascinating and important analogy with the birds can be seen in the fact that like them and unlike the other apes, gibbons are territorial in the classic sense; that is, they tend to marry and occupy territories with small overlap, which they defend largely with ritual display (brachiation and sound); which leads to a life of relatively little violence compared to the chimp, for example, as we shall see. With a band of four you get some scrapping on the territorial borderline but no scheming female assemblies, no thuggish male cohorts, and very little politics: in fact you get mostly brachiation, roomy flights through the treetops. The other thing you get is a good deal of singing: the dawn chorus in a gibbon forest is a high-spirited affair. Darwin (*The Expression of the Emotions in Man and Animals*, 1873) surmises that language originates in the music of courtship, the songs of love, rivalry, and triumph (see p. 87). He notes that many animals take pleasure in the sounds they make, and also that tone, timbre, pitch, and interval are significantly developed. Best of all, gibbons, it seems, produce the diatonic scale of one octave, including the semitones, and their marriage vows are renewed each morning in an operatic duet of some subtlety in which Mrs. Gibbon finds the theme and her husband plays variations on it.

If Darwin is right about language, and I think he is, the gibbon looks very like the lord of the primates—angel, rather, the lord of musical flight. Not only had he the wisdom to stay high and small, protecting his treasured freedoms against the false lure of evolutionary progress into gravid grossness and social complication, but he also found the voice its diatonic home and saw that it was good and stayed there. What's more, the birds had taught him that under certain conditions marriage not only works but maximizes the music, a song we have been trying to remember ever since. On either side of him both "lower" monkeys and "higher" apes drifted down to a life of less (or no) brachiation, social and sexual aggravation, predatorial anxiety, and undiatonic noise. Such a drift was surely a significant fall, and hardly fortunate.[8]

The mundane explanation of the gibbon's singularity would seem to be the food supply. In the treetops the living may be roomy but is not easy, which is what brought the other apes and monkeys down. The dominant view among biologists is that a species will become territorial if it increases their chances of survival, but if not they won't bother. A gibbon territory has just enough food to supply a mating couple and their offspring, who, like young birds, are thrown out at weaning or soon after. Thus territoriality and the almost sexless marriage that goes with it may be the price (or the prize, depending on one's view) for the gibbon's refusal to abandon his brachiating splendor. (The well-fed savannah baboon does not marry, whereas his hard-up desert brother is forced to take a harem, which he constantly harasses.) Is this to say marriage is only for the hungry? Perhaps. Is the gibbon's sex drive so low because his formidable wife wears him out or because brachiating is more fun? One can only speculate. In any case two views may be taken of the gibbon: on the one hand a brachiating junkie who specialized himself out of the evolutionary game, and on the other an aristocrat who found his virtue and accepted certain stringencies in order to keep it rather than adapting to the fashions for bourgeois prosperity.

3

The next of the hominoid apes is the orangutan (Malay for "man of the forest"): although too large for the high-speed life, he remains very much the arboreal brachiator, specializing in slow-motion gymnastics. After him the gorilla, at 600 pounds simply too big to brachiate, the first terrestrial ape. After him comes the common ancestor of man and chimp, a smallish, knuckle-walking brachiator who lived on the borderline between woodland and savannah. The date is probably between eight and six million years ago.

Both gibbon and orangutan are Asian apes (which suggests that brachiation evolved in Asia), whereas both gorilla and chimp are

African. This strangeness has led to the intriguing suggestion of an ape migration from Asia to Africa about eight million years ago.[9] However that may be, it is generally agreed that what brought the apes down was the opening up of the savannah as the lush Miocene forests shrank in the drier conditions of the Pliocene: the major climatic shift was from eight to six million years ago, according to the eminent anthropologist David Pilbeam,[10] and it was during this period that all the big plains animals evolved. Thus it was a plausible time for Australopithicene to bid farewell to brother chimp, stand up straight, and move onto the dangerous savannah.

The problem here is that since we have a fossil gap from eight to four million years, the dating of these events is still (and may remain) open to debate. But for our purposes the "when" is less important than the "why." Crudely put, did we choose to leave or were we pushed? One's answer to this question has crucial implications for the human story, and once again, as with brachiation, the scholars are puzzled. All we know for certain is that the celebrated "Lucy" from Ethiopia (hominid but not our line) was standing erect at 3.8 million years, and that she was, at 70 pounds, both smaller than a chimp and also small-brained (by human standards—less than 400 cubic centimeters). She is the benchmark, as it were, from which we must speculate backward, to construct a plausible picture of what led us to stand up and trade a safe world for a dangerous one.

The orthodox Neo-Darwinian line is that species diverge gradually when some geographical barrier divides a hitherto unified population into differing habitats. In this case a group of proto-chimps could have been denied their forest cover and forced onto the savannah by geological change. Adriaan Kortlandt believed this as recently as 1972 (*New Perspectives on Ape and Human Evolution*). On the other hand, it may be more interesting. First of all, unless the barrier appeared very suddenly there would have been time for some territorial scrapping among the borderline troups to decide who should give up their tree cover, the weak or the strong. Second, bipedal stance, in the words of anthropologist Owen Lovejoy, "is an absolutely enormous anatomical change," not for the faint-hearted.[11] What's more, we now believe there to have been at least four species of Australopithicene hominids sharing the same patch of East Africa about four million years ago, and this puzzles the Neo-Darwinian assumption that slightly divergent species cannot coexist without the strong eliminating the weak. Without going into the complex controversy over "punctuated" evolution and sympatric speciation, we can say that, once again, a crucial step in the human story is still less than clear; and that speculation from the layman is therefore allowed.

What *is* clear is that forests were shrinking in the dessicating conditions of the Pliocene, and there was an evolutionary scramble to fill the ecological niches opening up on the savannah—more game on the run, to tempt the hunter. And we have recently learned that chimpanzees in the wild *enjoy* both their weekly hunting expeditions and the aggressive patrolling of their perimeters. The chimp is the only hunting ape, and he does it for fun and not from need; i.e., he *chooses* to do so. And if he chooses to do it today, our ancestors in that other day may have seen the savannah as more like an exciting challenge than a dreadful exile when they made their momentous decision to move onto it. What's more, Kortlandt (1972) has established that present-day savannah-dwelling chimps are both better organized and better fighters than their forest brethren, which may mean that this was true in the beginning. From all this it would seem reasonable to suggest that long ago when it came time for deciding who was to leave the safety of the trees, it was the small, brave, clever, nasty, and adventurous who set forth rather than the weak and the timid who were pushed.

An academic point one might think, and yet the implications are important. To say that we backed onto the savannah (because of either a geographical barrier or being pushed) is to say that we were the reluctant hunters, and hence that our past six million years have been less violent than if we had chosen the savannah. Furthermore, it is consonant with (even perhaps implicitly favors) the view that the move into bipedalism and toward the carnivorous was a bad day for the planet, unnatural, and therefore not our fault; i.e., it was thrust upon us, did not flow from the instinctual repertoire that was already within us. To say this seems to me pernicious: a dire day it may have been, but to deny that it was *our* day sounds ominously like the invocation of that fatal human propensity—Rousseau its modern master—for believing that our faults lie not in ourselves but in our horoscopes, our rulers, our technology, our culture, whatever. The copyright for the reply to this thought is held by Shakespeare:

> Men at some time are masters of their fates:
> The fault, dear Brutus, is not in our stars,
> But in ourselves, that we are underlings.
> *Julius Caesar* I–2

Brachiation was a necessary anatomical prologue to bipedalism; and just as I have suggested that easier access to bananas is an insufficient account of the former, so I would suggest that shrinking forests is an insufficient account of the latter. To each I would add the simian specialties of curiosity, playfulness, and adventurousness. And just as hands are the focus of brachiation, so are they of bipedalism: for in standing up, our flattening feet lost speed, balance, and tree-climbing ability, but our hands were now freed from assisting locomotion (the "knuckle-walking" of the apes) to hold and carry food and weapons. Darwin believed this; and also that the weapon-bearing hand allowed us to shrink our canine teeth. Also the eye: when we walk tall we can see over the high grass of the savannah, taking in a larger world. To lose both canine dagger and the refuge of the trees means that we must learn to stand and face the predators with sticks in our hands. To coordinate this busy world of eye and hand, our clever brain is called upon to develop new skills. As with brachiation, a significant improvement for eye, hand, and brain, the major triad of primate virtues.

Bipedalism thus concludes the story of primate exile to the trees by returning us to the ground with our three specialisms formidably enriched. Not only must the rodents who banished us beware, but we are now almost ready to take on all comers. Our love affair with the birds is over but not forgotten, as we have left the gibbon in the treetops to testify. The gradual growth in size from shrew to monkey to ape indicates that the pull of the other pole, wealthy Mother

Earth, had her way with us and called us back. The extraordinarily ambivalent event in the middle was brachiation: it brought us lower, enabling the bulky ape to move certainly below uncertain branches, and began the anatomical changes that bipedalism would complete; and at the same time it offered us a chance to arrest the downward drift and return to the heights of innocence with the gibbon.

4

Having emerged onto the savannah we were by no means immediately transformed into mighty hunters. The basket was what we carried, to gather nuts and berries and insects and foliage: there is not much evidence of *serious* hunting until about 2.5 million years ago. Our slow habituation to the carnivorous diet came doubtless through an unheroic snatching of the small and weakened animals we met. But what must be emphasized is that we were doubtless drawn to the animals from the outset. Jane Goodall's chimps in the Gombe reserve go hunting successfully about twice a month, and they get very excited.[12] So let's say we began with three successful expeditions a month, and on up from there; and that what drew us to the animals we hunted was not simply hunger or blood lust but something both simpler and more complex: fun. How do we know? We don't; but we were the hunting proto-chimps, and hence Goodall's evidence is the best we have. Why is it the best? Because in most respects the chimp is closer to us than to the other primates, and because he has doubtless changed less than we have since the days when we shared a common ancestor.[13]

Before pushing our speculative raft into the largely uncharted waters of hominid man's early days, we must thoroughly mark the shore we are leaving; and this means a close look at the chimpanzee, his hunting and aggression above all. Jane Goodall's admirable book *The Chimpanzees of Gombe* (1986), a large and masterly summary of her twenty-five years in Tanzania, provides shocking evidence to suggest that we humans come by our intraspecific violence honestly.

Her chimps not only occasionally cannibalize the infant chimps they kill, but one troup was observed to wage a genocidal war on its neighbor, killing all its males over a three-year period. How can this be?

The explanation must begin with hunting. Unlike the carnivorous predators, the chimp is not designed for hunting: no claws, unspectacular canines, and most important, no instinctive definition of proper prey. This means that not only is he a grossly inelegant killer but his hunting behaviors are unstable, having been recently cobbled together in the neocortex from his aggressive repertoire and his sense of play. Fully half the kills at Gombe are colobus monkeys: the rest are bushbuck, baboon, and bushpig.[14] In almost every case the prey is an infant snatched from its mother. Killing is by biting into the head or neck, flailing on a rock, stomping, disemboweling, or dismemberment. The colobus is usually bitten in the head, as the brains are almost always consumed first. In this case death comes quickly and relatively cleanly: with the other techniques death can be slow, the spectacle messy and disgusting, the prey half-eaten before it dies.

With infants the blood and the brains are eaten first; with larger prey the viscera go first, probably because the skull is too hard for the brain bite (which is difficult to administer even on a young animal). Once the skull is opened, the brain case is swabbed out with a finger or a leaf. The brains are clearly the delicacy, often reserved for the killer if he is high-ranking. In any case the prey will be intensely fought over, with politics to the fore: the high-ranking grab, the low-ranking beg, and the opportunists snatch and run to a nearby tree to eat in peace. The male chimp is demonstrably more aggressive than the female, more skilled with weapons, and hunts more often; but given this, the females are surprisingly keen. Scavenging, the eating of carrion, is extremely rare: only ten instances have been observed at Gombe.

Well, at least they draw the line at scavenging. Even so, chimp violence is a nasty business, as Jonathan Swift was one of the first to intuit. What makes it worse is the pandemonium that tends to infect the chimps on such occasions, as it does on the occasion of

serious displays of hostility within the troup itself: a contagion of
screaming, biting, defecating, groveling, touching, mounting, and
embracing—surely the origins of what the Greeks would call the
Dionysiac frenzy.[15] Such behavior seems decidedly out of line with
the subtlety, delicacy, refinement, and affection that characterize so
much of the chimp's existence.

Should we call it madness? Perhaps we should. The more one
learns of these amazing creatures, the more one is struck by the
discontinuity between the subtle complexity of their quiet transactions and the crude confusion of their noisy ones. One even thinks
of Dr. Jekyll and Mr. Hyde—and the word schizoid comes to mind.
And indeed it is this discontinuity that disturbs one's ethological
sensibility, not the tearing of flesh: after all, the lioness also takes
the weakling and eviscerates him, but her behavior is graceful and
all of a piece, almost musical; and so we venerate the lioness.

With the chimp even relatively minor ritual displays of aggression from some ruffled male often seem to overheat both actors and
audience—leading to a mild frenzy of excitement, fear and loathing,
gestures of submission, appeals for reassurance. It is as if chimp
subtlety calls forth and is paid for by chimp crudity, as if such a
brain cannot equably master both refinement and violence. This
impression, which I frankly offer as an esthetic judgment, a piece of
drama criticism as it were, finds some corroboration in what we have
recently discovered about the brain.

The chimp's basic emotional life is governed, as is the case with
all mammals, by the limbic cortex, the "old" brain. What makes
him such an astonishingly inventive piece of work, however, is his
rapidly evolving neocortex, which specializes in what Aristotle
would have called practical reason, judgment, and decision. Unfortunately, the overlap between the two brains is not altogether
seamless, the chain of command not altogether clear; so that certain
neocortical projects may be resisted in the limbic lobe, which is, in
the words of the anatomist Paul Broca, "structurally primitive
compared to the neocortex."[16] To put it simply, the eternal themes
of hunger and sex and fight and flight are deeply engraved in the old
limbic codes or instincts that the *arriviste* neocortex is concerned to

elaborate, challenge, and supplant: one imagines an old-fashioned country squire of few words challenged by a polysyllabic progressive from the university. In view of this cerebral conflict, is it any wonder that the chimp overheats, particularly when one remembers that his old man was raised as a vegetarian?

On the question of brain evolution, the work of anatomist Paul MacLean is suggestive. His research has led him to isolate within the old brain a reptilean core, which he calls the "R-complex." In this core he locates the instinctual programs of sex and aggression, and also, more interestingly, the ritual behavior by which they are defused in both monkey and man; for example, the pseudo-sexual mounting of a submissive monkey by a dominant one. As this reptilean core was gradually surrounded by the limbic cortex, behavior became less programmed, more intelligent, and above all, bathed in emotion. The reptile, it seems, is indeed cold-blooded, and the emotions invented by the mammals in the nurturing of their young are administered from the limbic lobe. Thus when monkeys defuse an aggressive situation through ritual mounting, they are "cooling it" by recourse to reptilean tactics administered from the R-complex. According to MacLean (*A Triune Concept of the Brain and Behavior*, 1973), these two brains, together with the neocortex, effectively give us three separate mentalities, three ways of ordering space and time and the events within them, which our "triune" brain is charged with integrating. Needless to say, it does not always succeed. As he puts it, "Speaking allegorically of these three brains within a brain, we might imagine that when the psychiatrist bids the patient to lie on the couch, he is asking him to stretch out alongside a horse and a crocodile."

Although MacLean's mechanistic approach to the brain already seems rather old-fashioned to a number of biologists, his basic ideas do illuminate the question of chimpanzee aggression for the layman. Not only must the chimp, like all mammals, seek to override excess emotion with ritual cool from what MacLean calls the R-complex, but he is also learning to *decide* when and where to strike on the basis of complex information from his relatively new and massive neocortex. When one adds to this the fact that as an omnivore he has no relaxed and well-established predatory instincts to call on, it is small wonder that he tends to overheat in moments of serious aggression, be they inter- or intraspecific. Nor is it surprising that at Gombe the "cool" chimps tend to be dominant: grace under pressure was always important, the more so when it is in short supply.[17]

Because Konrad Lorenz's seminal work *On Aggression* (1966) has enjoyed a relatively large readership, it is fairly well known that throughout the animal kingdom intraspecific aggression is usually defused by instinctive rituals of attack and submission. The well-armed devise rituals that avoid the use of their weapons: thus the males of many poisonous snakes will wrestle at mating time, and not bite. But since even the unarmed do themselves no evolutionary good by intraspecific assault and battery, they too play the game: thus the common lizard fights a chivalrous duel in which each in turn offers the neck for biting until one of them recognizes superior mandibles and retires.[18] The celebrated exceptions are the rat, the lion, the hyena, and the wolf, who will sometimes fall without inhibition upon conspecifics (members of the same species) of another group—and the neighbor becomes prey. Living socially, which means defending a territory together against strangers, may well be the beginning of culture, but it also seems to be the beginning of big trouble.

The beginning perhaps, but it doesn't become noxious until we get to the chimpanzee—and even then, it must be said, the taxing question is "How noxious?" and the answer is not yet clear, nor is it likely to become so, given the difficulty of studying these threatened creatures in the wild. What we do know is that the chimp is the most violent of primates, and though well provided with ritual fuses, he rather frequently blows these fuses and inflicts wounds or death (or wounds leading to death) either on his own troup or on his neighbors. For a gloss of my "rather frequently" I can only refer the reader to Goodall's Gombe book, as the factors involved are certainly complex. What can be said here is that only two long-term studies of wild chimps have been undertaken, at Gombe for twenty-five years, and at Mahale in Uganda for nineteen: both have witnessed one genocidal war each, and both have witnessed cannibalism of infants, both within and without the troup.

Again, why? The brain's the thing: not only because of the "triune" instabilities already mentioned, but because clever gets bored, and bored gets inventive, inventing not only extremely complex political plots on the domestic front, but also, quite simply, *hunting*. The devil finds work for idle hands? Something like that.

Among predators, hunting is for food, "professional" work, though also certainly fun—dogs wag their tails, and lions have been photographed effectively smiling:[19] indeed one might even say fun *because* it's professional, nothing (as a rule) to be afraid of or to get angry about. Imagine the non-predatorial chimp, having mastered the banana, watching the lion at work and deciding the lion has *class*—we still think so—and putting himself to school. In the end, because he's so clever, he becomes quite accomplished: impressive feats of cooperative stalking are recorded by Goodall. But though the chimp certainly enjoys his hunting, leonine grace at the death eludes him: it takes millions of years to become a professional.

The killing of prey deeply excites the chimp. This excitement is never without fear, even if the prey is only a baby colobus—*not* because the colobus is dangerous, but because the performance is somewhat unscripted, the procedure undictated, the activity even perhaps a touch forbidden? No, not yet; but strange certainly, and strange fruit is exciting. Most importantly perhaps, in the absence of fangs and claws the killing of even a baby colobus will require the production of considerable violence, and violence for the unarmed means rage, and rage is *par excellence* the emotion that moves into the unknown, the uncontrollable; and so when the moment comes it lacks decorum, and in fact it often looks like bloody mayhem.

Unsurprisingly, most of the chimp's so-called hunting gestures are adapted from his repertoire of domestic aggression, the charging displays and so forth that he uses in his daily politics. The grammar of these domestic gestures is, as one would imagine, more orderly and predictable, but once again, what impresses is the degree of invention and strangeness. The classic example of this at Gombe was provided by Mike, the chimp who became alpha male by devising a display in which he banged old kerosene cans together with such *brio* that everyone thought it was Zeus himself. (And if that story fails to impress, consider the youngster Figan who was observed alone in the bushes practicing with Mike's kerosene cans, and doubtless dreaming of kingship.)

The word that is called for here is "imagination," undoubtedly, and it stands with the chimps as a major source of both our weal and our woe. As the neocortex grows, so does the ability to imagine life being arranged differently, and this will mean both new forms of grooming and new forms of aggression. As the ancients knew, and many of us prefer to forget, the energies for love and war lie side by side.

5

The story I have been sketching at this point in the argument comes to this: it is the chimp's cleverness that leads him (through boredom) to being the most aggressive (as well as the most affectionate) of the nonhuman primates in his domestic relations, *and also* to the adoption of hunting, *and also* to the sometime practice of cannibalism and fratricide. Does warfare come from hunting? Common sense would say so, but this has been questioned recently in the study of seemingly pacific paleolithic hunters, notably the Bushmen, the Eskimo, the Pygmies, and the Hadza of Tanzania. Each of these, however, are now living in reduced circumstances, and almost certainly practiced warfare in their heyday. The evidence is convincingly summarized in Eibl-Eibesfeldt's *The Biology of Peace and War* (1979). What is at stake here is ultimately Rousseau's noble savage, the peaceful paleolithic that knew no warfare until the neolithic and the domestication of animals. This notion has always struck me as both ideologically noxious and inherently implausible. To have a war you need not covet your neighbor's ass nor even his goods: his wife and above all his *territory* will suffice. What is remarkable about Goodall's work is that it indicates that even the chimps know this.

That animal is territorial who defends a feeding range against the intrusion of conspecific strangers. Primates with large home ranges, such as baboons, are not thought territorial in that they neither monitor nor mark their boundaries, offer no vocal displays on the border, and will often give way at the approach of a neighboring troup known to be dominant. Territorial primates, on the other hand, such as the gibbon, howler, and vervet, occupy smaller ranges (with small overlap) whose borders they police with noisy displays but little violence. Aggression is doubtless involved in defining boundaries at the outset, but once established they remain fairly stable. In between these two comes the violent chimp, whom Goodall classifies as "quasi-territorial" for three main reasons.

First of all, the territorial move about their ranges almost without exception in stable groups, and thus encounters on the borderline tend to become symmetrical, balanced, and hence easily ritualized. The spotted hyena, on the other hand, whose patrols vary in size, will, when the odds are good, invade the neighboring range with intent to kill. Tense with fear and excitement, the male chimp goes on patrol about once every four days, in gangs of varying sizes, often accompanied by estrus females. As with the lethal hyena, if this band should meet a neighboring chimp patrol on the borderline, and the odds look good, they will invade and do battle. Goodall's second reason is that the truly territorial usually have a small overlap of "no-man's-land," and are very unwilling to fight on foreign soil as they will almost certainly lose. The chimps, on the contrary, run large overlaps and will expend considerable energy to arrange encounters within them. The third reason, most important, is that their violence is extreme. Whereas the territorial animal enjoys *chasing* the invader back home, the chimp (like the hyena and the lion) enjoys *catching* him, whether in the overlap or on foreign soil; and when he catches him, the assault may well continue until the enemy is mortally wounded and left to die.

Even this brief summary will suffice to indicate that the chimp has modified the rules of territoriality in order to satisfy what we may as well call his bloodlust. (The baboon, with his fearsome canines and military discipline, looks mild by comparison.)[20] But if bloodlust is satisfied in skirmishing, warfare calls for dominion, the desire for the annexation of territory; and this indeed is what seems to be at the root of the three-year war among the Gombe chimps—for at the end of it the vanquished males had died, their females and their territory absorbed by the victors. The war at Mahale lasted for ten years, but was in other respects remarkably similar. It has been urged by those of the pacific tendency that these wars were to some extent "unnatural" since the chimps involved had been ecologically disturbed by being supplied with bananas; and yet even though there is widespread agreement that such provisioning had *some* effect on the Gombe chimps, precipitating considerable hijinks at the banana station, I have nowhere seen it suggested that bananas were either the necessary or sufficient condition of the violence.[21] This question of ecological disturbance was uppermost in Michael Ghiglieri's mind while he spent two difficult years tracking unprovisioned chimps in Uganda. By the end of his stay he was convinced that his undisturbed chimps were indeed walking on the wild side: "The males here in Kibale Forest behaved with such solidarity toward one another as to appear prepared for war at any time" (*East of the Mountains of the Moon*, 1988, p. 258).

These reports from Gombe, Mahale, and Kibale cut through a welter of endless academic disputes with startling simplicity. The question of whether hunting is both a necessary and sufficient condition of warfare is rendered truly "academic," and Freud's gloomy (and unpopular) speculations about our aggressive instincts seem more than vindicated. We can now say, with some assurance, that quite apart from the violent stimulus of the savannah, hominid man was disposed to spend some time seriously scrapping with his neighboring tribe or troup, shedding blood and looking to improve his territorial assets, women and children, and the food to feed them. Big is beautiful, not only genetically but politically: the desire *to be more*, utterly central to the emergence of religious ideas (as we shall see in Chapter 4) is there in the beginning.

Of course evolutionary thinking has always countenanced competition, both for the ecological niche and among conspecific rivals for the best grazing. What is quite new is the idea that by the time of the chimpanzee, such competition was already looking much like war as we know it. And the fact that at both Gombe and Mahale it was undertaken for fun and for profit refutes the idea that war arises with scarcity: the best grazing is always scarce if you actually enjoy fighting for it. To say that the chimp will occasionally go to "war" is to say that he is sometimes a social predator, like the lion and the hyena, capable of classifying his conspecifics as prey. What makes the Gombe story truly horrifying is that the war was in effect a civil war: the two troups had originally been united, and so the murderers were in fact stomping their former friends. And just as I suggested earlier that the chimp's large brain is responsible for his adopting predatorial ways, the expanding brain will remain crucial as early man moves onto the savannah; not only for the refinement of weaponry and gladiatorial prowess, but for the acquisition of those cooperative skills that make any hunting pack so formidable. However disagreeable, the evidence is fairly clear that the human brain began its prodigious expansion at the same time as we became serious hunters, about 2.5 million years ago.[22]

Finally, we must briefly consider the hideous question of chimp murder: what light does it shed on Abel and Cain? Most of the descriptions suggest that an attack on the enemy continues until it stops moving, whereupon, unlike the prey animal which is eaten, it is abandoned, usually to die of its wounds. Goodall's observers insist that such attacks are *murderous*, seeking not surrender but stillness.[23] What *can* they be after? They themselves seem not to know, for some time later the warriors will return, either that day or the next, to see if the body is still there; and if so they poke it, prod it, stomp it, and groom it. In effect they will interrogate the corpse, and this, surely, is the dawning intimation of mortality. Soon enough, one feels, they will find some ritual gesture appropriate.[24]

Of course, one has to interrogate the corpse only if one does not eat it, and since infants who are killed in the process of attacking a female are frequently eaten (at least partially), one assumes that the problem here is in some cases technological—an adult body is very difficult to dismember without tools. Indeed, one of Goodall's adult chimps, expiring with a burst of blood from the mouth and nose, was immediately leapt on by his thirsty assailant. The conspecific who is killed but not eaten is "prey-that-is-not-prey," a nonsense, an anomaly, a contradiction, a problem, and finally a mystery. In other words, cannibalism is in a sense "natural," certainly not world-shattering: only murder, wherein a conspecific is first reclassified as prey (in order to unleash the lethal attack) and then "un-preyed" as a corpse, can provoke in the mind the unintelligible idea of "he that was and is not," and so bring death into the world. This distinction is absolutely crucial. For a chimp to kill and eat another chimp, or to kill and abandon one as technologically inaccessible, or to kill an "enemy" female's child in order to expedite her recruitment for breeding purposes, is extremely unpleasant but relatively straightforward. But to kill, abandon, return, poke, and *think* is quite literally mind-blowing. If we are to interpret the two wars (of three and ten years duration) as sustained strategies of territorial and reproductive expansion, as surely we must, they presuppose the idea of gradually eliminating the enemy males; i.e., the idea, however dimly perceived, of murder—the very idea we see the chimps wrestling with as they prod and poke a corpse. And once the idea of murder arises to stand proud, the social predator who occasionally kills neighboring conspecifics is almost ready to consider killing *one of his own.*

In conclusion I would say this: that the idea of death comes to the chimp in puzzlement as he prods his victim's corpse, and that this puzzlement will in due course break open the world of hominid man in the most profound way possible. But such a breaking is fearfully exciting as well as terrifying, not only a breaking but an opening, *the* opening indeed, toward the beginnings of human perplexity. In all the instances of both chimp cannibalism and murder that I have read about, there is no trace of remorse, not even when "Passion" killed and ate the infants of her own troup-mates. Such violence, as I have said, is by no means routine, but neither does it constitute a *monstrous* perversion of chimpanzee nature. What it does indicate is that the primate codes that forbid intraspecific violence, defusing it through rituals of dominance and submission, are destabilized in the inventive complexity of the chimpanzee neocortex (as in our own).

These instinctual codes (call them taboos), laid down in simpler mammalian days, tend to crack under the pressures generated by the adoption of hunting and territorial games. As the story moves forward from chimpanzee to man the hunter, this tendency to crack will increase; but so too of course will our capacity for remorse, and a great deal of our newly found hominid intelligence will be devoted to the devising of rituals for the repair and maintenance of our taboos against inappropriate violence.

Much of the trouble began because we are naturally unarmed. Had we carried poison sacks as the snake does, or even the fearsome canine of the baboon, Mother Nature in her evolutionary wisdom would not have allowed her best brain-child to tamper so freely with the intraspecific taboos. What allowed our "unnatural" development, so to speak, was the mild exterior concealing a uniquely lethal brain. (Is it surprising that "deceit" has always been one of our major meditations?) By the time that brain began to offset the lost canine with the fashioning of serious weapons, it was far too late to recall the freedoms granted on the savannah; and man was left with a unique policing problem, which he hasn't managed very well, as any history book will attest.

The important contribution of weaponry to human darkness was noticed early on: there are numerous myths to indicate that the discovery of metallurgy in the blacksmith's forging fire was a particularly bad day for mankind.[25] Although I agree with this, and the subject is a fascinating one, it lies just beyond the bounds I have set for this book. Luckily, the subject is not essential to my argument: which is that our boundless capacity for destruction was "created" back on the savannah when the burgeoning neocortex applied for permission to unlock the instinctual codes forbidding intraspecific violence. Of course the subsequent development of metallurgy (particularly the smelting of iron) vastly increased both the efficiency and the maddening abstraction of our mutilating powers; but the whole sad story of weaponry became possible (I will not say "necessary") on the day the first brainy chimpanzee picked up a stick or a stone to bash his neighbor.

6

Freud was not the first to notice that we dream chiefly of sex and violence, and that the two are significantly related. A nice illustration of their proximity is that female chimps are often uncertain which of the two an aroused male has in mind. Similarly, an appeasement ritual practiced by both male and female involves "presenting" the hind quarters to an angry superior for simulated copulation; which suggests that "being fucked" is isomorphic and comparable with "being beaten" (a suggestion the Dutch root of our word "fuck" does indeed confirm). Despite such ambiguity, sex among the chimpanzees seems on the whole to be a pleasant, albeit perfunctory affair. Rape is rare, and females often solicit sex, which would suggest they enjoy it.[26]

The estrus cycle of the female lasts for thirty-six days. During fourteen of these her genitals are flat, as a rule sexually uninteresting and uninterested. For at least ten of the other twenty-two, as she moves from tumescence through ovulation to detumescence, she is more or less promiscuously available to all comers (except her sons, who seem to know that it is bad form to tamper with one's birthplace—though hard-line scientists would speak only of the genetic wisdom of outbreeding in this case).[27] As her genital swelling increases, the dominant males will try to prevent the subdominants from mounting her, and on the day of ovulation the alpha male will try to keep her to himself. In this way Mother Nature declares her interest in the transmission of the best warrior genes. Some chimp females (about 20 percent in an eight-year study at Gombe) form "consortships," becoming (for a month or so) the exclusive sexual resort of some male. There may be an element of coercion here but not a great deal, as the bark of an outraged estrus female will bring the other males running.

Sex appeal seems to vary: Flo, a popular Gombe female, was observed coupling fifty times in a day, though the average would be more like thirty. Such promiscuity makes heavy demands on the male genitals, which are relatively huge compared to those of the gorilla. How much of all this activity is actually enjoyed is not altogether clear, although the male performance can be distinctly rough and unfriendly, occasionally savage (as the similarity between his sexual and charging displays would suggest). And if one can readily imagine a degree of intimidation in the female experience, one can also imagine the hapless male caught in the vicinity of an estrus female and obliged by his monstrous equipment to interrupt his snooze and do his duty. On the whole, however, Goodall reckons that sex is usually pleasing to both partners, and one sees no reason to doubt this.

Significantly, the estrus female remains sexually swollen far longer than she need do for the purpose of conception, which would suggest that sexual activity is generally "adaptive," in the interests of chimp evolution. Ah, but which particular interests? As described in the literature, chimp sex seems a rather aggressive business, *yang* not *yin*, a schooling for war not tenderness. And yet, as Blake said, the fool who persists in his folly may become wise; for as Goodall points out (*Gombe*, p. 485), the female bonobo chimp remains partially swollen *all the year round,* and bonobo sexuality is distinctly civilized: sex may be initiated by either male or female, affiliative bonds are high, food is shared, even *beds* are sometimes shared, and dominance rivalry among the males is low. Most importantly, copulation is ventral (face to face) whereas the chimp mounts from the rear. From all this nothing certain can be inferred; but the case of the bonobo does at least indicate that the opening of the sexual season *can* soothe the savage breast. Is this what happened among our hominid forebears, who unleashed upon the world the perpetually fanciable female? Yes and no will be my answer, though we can only speculate. The crucial factor seems to me to be the ventral position, call it Pandora's box, comparable in importance to the chimp discovery of murder, whose implications are endless. But there, we have almost come to human affairs, time for this chapter to end.

3 ▪ MALE VERSUS FEMALE:
The Paleolithic Beginnings of Love and War

I found that ivory image there
Dancing with her chosen youth,
But when he wound her coal-black hair
As though to strangle her, no scream
Or bodily movement did I dare,
Eyes under eyelids did so gleam;
Love is like the lion's tooth.

When she, and though some said she played
I said that she had danced heart's truth,
Drew a knife to strike him dead,
I could but leave him to his fate;
For no matter what is said
They had all that had their hate;
Love is like the lion's tooth.

Did he die or did she die?
Seemed to die or died they both?
God be with the times when I
Cared not a thraneen for what chanced
So that I had the limbs to try
Such a dance as there was danced—
Love is like the lion's tooth.

—W. B. Yeats

Once upon a time (about 6 million years ago) some apes stood up and left the African forest to live on the savannah. There were many changes made. Some of them we know about, many of them we don't. The story we tell of this time begins with the ability to stand up, arguably the biggest change of all, which we accomplished in about one million years; but why we did it nobody really knows, and perhaps never will. (The eminent anthropologist David Pilbeam remains impressively agnostic.)

What we do know is that human feet can neither run very fast nor climb trees very well; so that in standing up we were taking a stand, though against what predatory opposition is not altogether clear. As we gave up our speed we also gave up our canine teeth (which in the male chimp are one-and-a-half times longer than in the female, hence for fighting, not eating). To give up our one poor natural weapon at such a critical moment would suggest we carried a stick in our hands, both to harass our predators as we moved through the open and to pursue our domestic quarrels back home in the campsite. The renunciation of speed, tree shelter, and formidable canines might also suggest that the world we stood up in wasn't all that dangerous, which is but one of the attractions of zoologist Sir Alister Hardy's idea that we may have spent a good deal of time in the early days camped by the waterside, swimming and fishing. But however mild our opening chapters may have been, there is little doubt that by about 2.5 million years ago things were heating up considerably.

Literally. By this time serious drought had set in, and the East African Rift Valley, where most of our early fossils come from, was turning from lush parkland to wilderness. Ecological pressure was widely felt, and many gentle browsers were displaced by clever migrating grazers. Were we too almost displaced? Perhaps. In any case the going certainly got tough, and however unnecessary our hunting expeditions may have been before, they now surely became serious: one animal carcass is worth a great many berries to a troup of hungry humanoids, and the earliest evidence of competent hunting and butchering comes from Kenya at about 2.5 million. It would be strange if such a time of ecological stress did not significantly "advance" the human story, and it is now generally agreed that *Homo habilis,* whose earliest recovered fossil from the

Rift Valley is at two million years, is the first human properly so called. He made stone tools, probably spoke a little (according to Leakey), and had a brain twice the size of Ethiopian Lucy's, forged no doubt in the heat of the Pleistocene drought. It looks as if *habilis* was the real leap forward (the French expert Yves Coppens thinks so), and that from him the brain went on growing fast but more or less equably through *erectus* at 1.5 million years ago, *neanderthalis* at 100,000, and *sapiens* at 40,000. We find domesticated fire (in China) at 500,000, huts (in France) at 400,000, slaughtered elephants (in Spain) at 300,000, bear cults and human burial among the Neanderthal in Switzerland and elsewhere from about 80,000.

So much for the broad outline. Our interest, however, as in the previous chapter, is in love and war, the main avenues to the sacred; and since our discussion of the chimpanzees concentrated on war, let us begin this time with love, both for the sake of balance and because, though the chimp may have invented war, we probably invented love—at least as it is practiced between consenting adults. What there is of love in the chimpanzee troup is mother love, the impressively strong bond between mother and child that can endure well past childhood. What there is of durable friendship is intermale: but since it is always hedged by political considerations, and hence subject to tactical cancellation, one is reluctant to speak of male *bonding*. Beyond these two serious forms of relationship there is a great deal of playfulness and affection, chiefly expressed through grooming. But as for durable affiliative bonds between adult male and female, that we do not find.

The human female changed all that. First and most importantly, she abandoned the estrus cycle, sequestered her ovulation, and became easily able to have sex at any time instead of only on ten days out of every thirty-six. Second, she moved her vagina forward so that the male (whose penis became further elongated) could readily enter from the front. Third, for no milky reason she vastly increased the size of her breasts, shed her body hair, and, along with the male, acquired eyes that dilate when sexually aroused. Why should she do these things? The answer usually given is that the feckless males, high on hunting and wanderlust, would otherwise stay out all night and bring home no bacon. This seems to me basically correct, but its important implications are frequently underrated. If we are to appreciate these, we must return briefly to the simian world to sketch a background.

To the militaristic baboons, notably, as their disciplined existence on the savannah is closer in important respects to what ours must have been than that of the individualistic chimps in the forest.[1] Our genes place us much closer to the chimpanzee, but since he stayed in the forest and we did not, we can learn much of our past from the common baboons and macaques who, like us, chose to dwell more or less in the open. The baboon faces such predators as lions, leopards, cheetahs, hyenas, wild dogs, and raptorial birds. No lion will attack them on the savannah because an organized troup of baboons (of, usually, about forty to eighty members) is simply too much hassle. What enables them to protect themselves so impressively is social cohesion, mediated through eye contact from alpha male to dominants to subdominants, a chain of orientation and command whereby the lower ranks attend upon the higher. The females and their young cluster near the boss males in the middle of the formation, with the young and subdominant males circling as outriders on the periphery. Remarkably enough, baboon males have been known to *sacrifice* themselves in the troup's defense (unheard of in chimp land). The price they pay for acquiring this discipline is harsh, what we would call prolonged initiation rites: young males do a lot of hard traveling on the solitary margins of the troup before they may acquire subdominant status and access to the females. Many of them die in the process. Lionel Tiger (*The Imperial Animal*, 1974) cites one estimate that 80 percent of primate males do not reach maturity. Baboons and macaques run in what are called multimale troups, in which the boss males (themselves ranked on the basis of strength and subtlety) will usually be outnumbered by the adult females by about four to one; that is to say, three out of four males either don't make it or get delayed. Thus the rites of passage to adulthood are both prolonged and extremely severe for the male baboon, which makes it less than astonishing that the human male is still obsessed with the games that determine his rank order.

Female baboons and macaques, by contrast, have a quiet run in the middle of the troup until estrus marks their passage into adulthood. They inherit social position from their mothers, significantly enough to justify our speaking of female "lineages," stretching back as far as four generations, and maybe more. As with any aristocracy, these lineages provide alliances, clan gatherings, mild incest avoidance, and various kinds of privilege over their inferiors. To be *de bonne famille* is of permanent value to the female, and this shows up in her young son as both confidence and a head start in the long quest for dominance. Jane Austen, with her fine eye for the nuances of class distinctions, would almost feel at home here; and these lineages, so astonishing in their serious subtlety, form the basis of the matrilineal kinship systems that figure so importantly in primitive culture.

The female baboon is half the size of the male, with canines one quarter the length, and hence she is not designed for fighting. Inheriting her social position from her mother, all she needs in order to acquire full citizenship is a fruitful womb. While the males burn testosterone and file their teeth (and die), she has the young to nourish and play with, and her world, as Tiger (1974) suggests, is realistic in a sense that his is symbolic; for while her attention is principally focused on things as they are, his is absorbed in a theater full of signs and codes where an invisible thing called status is being constantly negotiated. And yet, although his theater of dominance rituals distracts him from the play of things as they are, it is by no means simply footling; for it sustains the law that in moments of danger saves the troup from disintegration. Needless to say, such sacrifice of quotidian pleasure in the service of an abstract order of perpetual preparedness against the enemy's appearance hardly appeals to our modern anti-militaristic sensibility; but though we can't *like* the male baboon's world, it may be that we should respect it more than we do. In any case, one can see in it an ethological origin for the widespread belief that the masculine mind is more abstract than the feminine; and one can also see the outlines of a certain argument about culture (which shall concern us presently): the god-haunted male insisting on ritual ablutions to stave off the devil while his frivolous wife is content simply to sit down and have an apple for breakfast.

Did we become very baboon-like in our early savannah days? Probably, though our large brain would have made us, like chimp and gorilla, more playful, imaginative, and inventive—and also somewhat resentful of the discipline required by savannah life. Anthropologists Chance and Jolly (*Social Groups of Monkeys, Apes and Men*, 1970) distinguish between the hedonic and the agonistic modes in their classification of social primates, with baboons the most agonistic, whereas we, like the chimps and gorillas, would have inclined to the hedonic. In the hedonic mode, male rank order is significantly determined by charisma as well as aggression (one thinks of Mike and his kerosene cans) and this leads to more open, flexible communication within the troup. Attention is "polydyadic," which means that it shifts easily among the troup members, whereas in the agonistic mode one attends fairly constantly to one's immediate superior.[2] Although the hedonic-agonistic distinction seems to me a useful one, it can be misleading; for example, the male baboon seems to be fonder of infants than is the male chimp. The tempting generalization would be to say that early man was predominantly hedonic in the campsite and agonistic when hunting or on the move.

Although the structure of dominance is similar in baboon and chimp, the chimp's day is notably less socialized. Indeed, relative to all the other social primates, the chimp both desires and easily achieves a striking amount of privacy.[3] The male, both young and adult, is more gregarious than the female, and he prefers male company; but after leaving his mother's side at about eight years (having been weaned at four), he will consistently spend much of his day alone, exploring his green world. The adult female tends to be alone with her children, except when estrus makes her sociable. What she has instead of society is kinship, and the bond between mother and adult daughter is stronger than any male friendship. Among the males, unfriendly encounters outnumber friendly ones.

They move about a good deal in gangs, and young males typically begin their quest for status by picking on an adult female. Females are less aggressive than males, and spend less time dominating their inferiors, which they tend to do with a beady eye rather than a charging display. As they grow old both male and female become more solitary. Goodall suggests that the freedom enjoyed by both sexes to choose their paths through the day reduces the stress of social contact. Half a chimp's waking hours are spent in foraging, and about 13 percent in moving around: males typically travel 4.9 kilometers daily, females 3. When evening falls, everyone chooses a nearby tree and builds a nest in its lower branches; and the day's dispersion is collected in the gathering darkness as a chorus of drumming and hooting calls from tree to tree, informing the forest and whoever else that all is well, unified once again.[4]

2

When we left this green world for the savannah, not only did we "baboonify" to some extent our social arrangements, but we also modified our bodies. The acquisition of bipedal stance has already been discussed. The second major change was the huge growth of the brain, and this was made possible (along with a number of other changes including the relocated vagina) by a process called "neoteny," one of Nature's more intriguing mutations whereby a species is allowed to become sexually mature but in other respects remains anatomically arrested at the fetal stage. By this process we became the apes who stay forever young, which is why the chimp's face looks so old to us. More importantly, it enabled our brains to increase relative to body weight, and to go on growing for years after birth inside a soft, incompletely ossified skull. In a sense we are born prematurely, which is why we remain helpless and vulnerable far longer than ape babies do. It is also why, for better and for worse, we never grow up.[5]

Such brains come expensive, and it was the woman who paid, frequently with her life, in childbirth. Less dramatically, not only did she become a less efficient walker as she broadened her pelvis to give us passage, but she had to give up the wandering life she had enjoyed as a protochimp in order to mind the children. Home was no longer a range she could amble through (and occasionally hunt) but a place of fairly fixed address, from which she could forage for nuts and berries while the men were free to go further afield in search of game. As to who was actually the breadwinner, Richard Lee's recent study of the Kalahari Bushmen found the labor about equally divided, with meat preferred to vegetables and comprising about a third of the diet.[6] While this has significantly sobered the Tarzanist faction, one should remember that in early days the savannah was teeming with wildlife, which moreover had no reason to fear the newly upright ape. It was not until relatively recently that weapons became sufficiently lethal to inflict the wholesale slaughter of species that we find in the fossil records (particularly striking in North America). Throughout the planet, sooner or later, the hunters have always overhunted their game, and so it is hardly surprising that today's primitive remnants, usually on marginal land like the Kalahari Bushmen, eat so little meat. Further evidence for early meat-eating has recently come from the biochemists: without fire for cooking (until fifty thousand years ago in Africa), it would have been difficult otherwise to find sufficient protein and fatty acids to feed our growing brain.

The argument will doubtless continue. But bearing in mind the chimp's inordinate excitement in devouring his prey, and the other factors we have noted concerning our upright move on to the savannah, some version of what Robert Ardrey has called "the hunting hypothesis" seems compelling. If we accept it, one of the first things we see is an inequitable division of labor and fun along gender lines—serious sexism clearly begins here. The men go out and see the world, the women stay close to home and mind the children. The men gather confidence as their bonding and hunting skills improve while the women, appointing juvenile baby-sitters so that they can forage locally, are physically constrained and never free from predatorial anxiety. Not only do the men have more fun, but when they return with the kill, the women have only their vegetables to offer in exchange, which they must supplement with respectful applause for the male performance. And if, in these opening rounds of the sex war, the women are disposed to complain, male muscle will remind them where the power lies; and if the nagging continues, the men will threaten simply to leave them to the leopards and not come back at all.

It doesn't take much imagination to see that woman had to come up with something fairly significant; and so she did. She invented love. By means of the anatomical changes mentioned earlier, she changed sex from a ten-second jump and a shriek into something altogether formidable. But before we speculate about how love might have altered our early days on the savannah, let us briefly consider pair-bonding, a much less daunting subject. Pair-bonding is rare among primates, but occurs frequently among territorial species (such as birds) where the young cannot be adequately nurtured by the mother alone. In other words, it is the invention of economic necessity. In every case the young are reared in one place, a nest or a lair, and usually the male's commitment is primarily to his territory and only secondarily to his mate, to whom he becomes bonded in a triumph or courtship ceremony. Most of these bonds are dissolved when the young are fledged. In some mammals, such as the gibbon and the beaver, male dominance is slight or nonexistent.

Such ethological evidence seems to fit the human case quite well. Our children are inordinately helpless (and for a long time) when compared with the young of other species, and this plus the dangerous savannah would have called for male participation in their nurturing. Since as a wealthy social primate the human male would have been loath to give up his freedoms, extensive anatomical and sexual modifications were offered as part of the deal, but even so he remains less than totally convinced. As with the gibbon and the beaver, the change seems to have been in the direction of parity between the sexes. And as with the other primate bands, the females would have frequently outnumbered the males, which would have meant harems for the dominant males.

Suppose then that we assume evolutionary pressure for the natural selection of pair-bonding among early hominids on the savannah.

The obstacles were formidable. Not only were we promiscuous primates, and only quasi-territorial, but we were rapidly becoming creatures who *chose* our social arrangements rather than had them selected for us by Mother Nature. Briefly put, pair-bonding may well have been the best of all possible ideas, but it was deeply flawed. And several million years on, it remains deeply flawed: all human societies practice some form of marriage, but all also have difficulty making it work. It seems fair to say that without the sexual modifications noted above, marriage didn't have a chance. What remains genuinely difficult is to assess with any precision what effects these modifications had.

3

Let us consider, somewhat digressively, what the sociobiologists call "the desire for reproductive success." Among promiscuous non-marrying animals, such as the chimps, competition for access to an estrus female on the day of ovulation is considerable, and will generally be won by the alpha male. Of course he doesn't "know" he wants a baby, but in some sense he knows perfectly well: his instincts have been honed by natural selection to want her on the day, though if you ask him why, he would look blank. This problem is made no easier by the fact that evolutionists speak (in shorthand, of course) of his "desire" for reproductive success. Among territorial creatures this "desire" in the male is even more impressive: consider, for example, the swallow who tracks his wife on her pregnable days with that miraculous wingtip-to-wingtip flight in order to forestall cuckolding. Of course the swallow doesn't know what he's doing either—nor does Mother Nature: only we "scientists" are allowed to know. Still, common sense is bound to observe that if the male swallow doesn't know what he's doing, the play of Nature is a truly dumb show, and since we know it isn't, we can say that evolutionary theory has, for its purposes, a rather restricted understanding of knowledge.[7]

This dumb desire for reproductive success also works in reverse, of course: the bird that discovers the cuckoo's egg in its nest will throw it out: the ewe, sufficiently aroused, will batter the orphan lamb to death; and not only lions but certain monkeys will practice infanticide when they take over foreign females, in order to waste no time on another's progeny. Is there no way we can say such creatures "know" what they are doing without offending the goddess of random mutation? I suggest that there is, that there are two kinds of knowing—practical and theoretical, instinctive and learned, intuitive and conceptual—and that although this distinction is no longer registered in English, it is still retained in French (*connaître* as opposed to *savoir*) and in German (*kennen* as opposed to *wissen*). Such practical knowing is conative and usually nonverbal, has more to do with touch and smell than sight, and is epitomized in what our language still just about registers as "carnal knowledge," the doing not the reading of instruction manuals ("And Joseph knew not his wife . . ."). In short, it is the way we knew the world before the neocortex began unbolting our instincts and pushing us toward the partiality of language, that tool whereby our experience can be not only mediated but replaced by symbols. One might further suggest that it is the way we knew—and know—the world before we began—and begin—to talk too much, read too many books, build too many machines, and abolish the family.*

---

*A brief digression on the kenning of sheep. In my first years of shepherding I was outraged by refractory ewes who sometimes refused to accept an orphan lamb or even one of their own (which can arise from an unsettled or difficult birth). The traditional techniques for persuasion begin with deceiving mother's nose, by smearing the lamb with her afterbirth, or with perfume or whiskey, or by dressing the orphan in the pelt of the foster mother's dead lamb; and one must then physically restrain her to enable the lamb to suck. "You will thank me for this in the end" we say to mother, but it can be unpleasant and tiring work, and some ewes will hold out forever. In time the shepherd learns to know when to give in and give up—"Thy will be done"—and the making of this decision is a fine archetypal instance of the making of culture; for it involves deciding how far we may legitimately interrupt the course of Nature in the pursuit of our desire for increase. This proximity to first and last things is part of the reason why shepherding has always been associated with religiousness.

I might add that such resistance in the ewe is about imprinting and has nothing to do with their widely supposed "stupidity." Stupidity can only be defined as a

Returning to our problem of reproductive success, we can borrow from the Scots and say the swallow *kens* his wife very well, both in the nest and on the dangerous wingtip days; and that such knowing tends to disconcert the intellectual, who has always been disposed to degrade it, not least because it is the very opposite of dispassionate. It is the desire that runs in the blood, that instinctively or intuitively knows what to do (as ken relates to both kin and can). It is the knowledge (*connaissance*) that is also desire (*conatus*) to be "born together" (*connaître*), i.e., to be one, to be kin, to be conjoined. In short, the word looks quite like what French philosopher Henri Bergson called the "life force" (*élan vital*), and it will do almost perfectly for the swallow who gracefully knows and wants and is able to be one with his mate for the purposes of life more abundant.

That such a basic notion (indeed is it not *the* basic notion?) should have almost disappeared from our language poses an eloquent reproach to our alienated modern mentality, and part of this book's purpose is to advocate its restoration. I mention it here because of our need at this point to illuminate somewhat the "desire for reproductive success" as it addresses early man on the savannah. Just

---

failure to thrive within one's ecological niche, which makes the sheep one of God's least stupid creatures, and modern man the most. (Another stupid one is the seemingly clever goat, who deforested the ancient Mediterranean, and so of course we call the mischievous goat clever, like us. I used to keep goats.) Most of what looks like sheep stupidity to the human eye arises from the "untextualized" awkwardness with which they shy from the touch of man, a predator not in the neighborhood when their flight responses were being perfected by natural selection.

The ewe is in fact a superb mother, having to distinguish on slender evidence between "to care" and "not to care," and the bond (olfactory and aural) between mother and lamb must be made firmly and quickly, particularly in the wild. The reverse side of her ruthless refusals is absolute commitment to her lambs at foot, which she nonetheless normally bestows in a remarkably relaxed fashion; and yet I have heard no sadder sound than that of a mother bereft of her newly born lambs and not seized for fostering. If left alone to register her bereavement, the sound she makes is not altogether unlike the howling of a wolf, and yet the mouth remains almost closed, so the sound is not given up or out, nor is the wound that it retains. It is the open-mouthed sound in the wolf howl that registers ecstatic compliance with the night, and this is absent from the ewe's moan. It is a sound she makes on no other occasion, and I imagine neolithic man was instructed by it as he shaped the lamentations that we shall try to recall in later chapters.

as the swallow kens his wife and the danger of being cuckolded, so, we may assume, does early man. But whereas the female chimp proclaims her day of ovulation by maximal swelling, menstrual woman takes it inside and "sequesters" it, as the saying goes. At once man's policing problems are vastly increased. Or are they? Sensitive women, even today, can "ken" their ovulation, and so it is quite possible that in the old days, with less neocortical suppression of smell and touch, they kenned it as well; and so did their men.

Anthropologists labored long under the delusion that men remained ignorant of their contribution to baby-making until about 10,000 B.C., when the neolithic domestication of animals brought them the *Wissenschaft* to put two and two together. This, of course, is to forget *Kennerschaft* and the connoisseuring swallow's flight. What I would say is that we kenned the matter as best we could until our language became sufficiently evolved for us to tell a story about it (the beginnings of *Wissenschaft*); and the story we told may well have been like the one Ashley Montague (1974) found among the Australian aborigines: that the woman cannot conceive until the penis has opened a passage for the spirit baby to enter.[8]

One notices that such a story constitutes a remarkable loss of the swallow's accuracy; and one is tempted to observe that Mother Nature's *kennen* knows its stuff rather better than man's *wissen,* and moreover that the general loss of instinctual and intuitive certainty about our world as the expanding neocortex unlocked our instincts is one of the important falls from grace into fumbling that our mythologies lament. Man, as the generalized ape, pays a price for his evolutionary virtue of extreme adaptability. At this point it is worth recalling our discussion of brain evolution in the previous chapter. When archaic instincts are unlocked and overridden by the expanding neocortex, they do not simply die; rather like old soldiers, as the saying goes, they fade away, ghostly paradigms awaiting the chance to make some kind of comeback, in the theater of dreams most obviously. (Other obvious theaters are hypnotism and certain forms of madness.) The subliminal place in the mind where these ghostly paradigms reside is a region that Freud has taught us to call the unconscious, to whose liberation we are all devoted, and it comes as no surprise to discover from empirical surveys that we do in fact dream mostly about sex and violence, our old and troubled instincts. (Some Englishmen still refer to their genital member as "my old man.")

4

Returning now to the question of reproduction on the savannah, we can say that the male's kenning of ovulation gradually faded into the stories of *Wissenschaft,* which told him that and why he wanted progeny. During this time, vestiges of his relegated instinctual certainty would appear in his dreams to shape and confuse these stories. On this matter two other points are pertinent. First, as promiscuous quasi-chimps we probably kenned ovulation far less fiercely than pair-bonded creatures do: the females advertised it quite clearly, and alpha male usually provided the significant seed. Furthermore, since the males took little responsibility for nurturing the young, who in a sense belonged to all, the whole issue was less pressing. To put it more exactly, kenning for cuckoldry and ovulation seems to be the speciality of the pair-bonding male who defends a territory and helps feed the young; and early man was neither strictly territorial nor strictly pair-bonded. When one adds to this the second point, the human sequestering of ovulation, it becomes clear that the confusion must have been considerable and that the gents didna ken the ladies all that well.

Why did Mother Nature add sequestered ovulation to our other anxieties? One can only speculate, but it seems probable that, along with the open sexual season and the ventral position, it increased female power. As man gradually moves from the certainties of *kennen* to the imaginings of *wissen,* his reproductive instinct will become troubled. A matter that never before called for thinking now increasingly does. A matter that Nature had settled for us must now, to some extent, be settled by ourselves. Sequestered ovulation makes it more difficult. The man may even worry that his role is supernumerary (the worry is still, after all, very much with us). Such worry, along with the exciting possibility of ventral sex tonight, will make him not just an assiduous policeman but more attentive to his wife and the babes, as if such attention might minister to his doubts. He will begin to discern the possibility of his mortality. He is almost ready to fall in love.

But we are still not quite ready to watch him do it. First we must look briefly again at the question of pair-bonding, to see what it might tell us from the outside, as it were, about early man's reluctance to marry. Briefly put, the question is this: since the gibbon appears undersexed (as do many pair-bonders) and yet seems happily married, is there any reason to think that man needed bribing with woman's new sexual gear to get him to settle down? Does not such a suggestion tell us more about our own sex-obsessed age than about early days on the savannah? My answer to this is that yes, man *did* need bribing, and that our sex-obsessed age has nothing to apologize for in this area, which makes a nice change.

Throughout creation, the male needs to be coerced into child-rearing. The gibbon analogy is misleading for the simple reason that, as we saw in Chapter 2, like other pair-bonders he marries and territorializes for economic reasons. In order to remain a gibbon brachiating in the forest canopy he must do as he does. Man's case is considerably different. The food supply varies from lush to sparse, but in either case it calls for the formation of cooperative hunting bands, not individual territories. Infant nurture *does* call for a male contribution, but we don't know how loudly, and moreover this call must make itself heard over the well-established hum of quasi-chimp promiscuity, which one imagines being reinforced by male-bonding in the hunting bands: thus we are a long way from the elegant simplicity of the male who marries his territory and then attracts a female onto it (though such simplicity has remained a masculine dream down to the present). And finally, when the males *did* begin bonding with the females, they probably began with harems for the lords and celibacy for the commoners: sharing the wealth, in this as in other cases, probably called for a revolution. Thus we can say that pair-bonding was Mother Nature's ready remedy for the human dilemma, but the anomalies were such that some special sweeteners and a good deal of time were required to make it stick; and even so, it sticks with difficulty.

The ethological picture is roughly this: the very well-fed can afford promiscuity (like the chimps), the moderately hard-up haremize (like the desert baboon), and the very hard-up marry (like the gibbon and most birds). Man as quasi-chimp is promiscuous, probably haremizes in hominid days, and ends up, according to an exhaustive survey of the ethnographic record, as a pair-bonder with pronounced polygynous tendencies (i.e., more than one wife when he can afford it).[9] The question of the "revolutionary" move from harems to exogamous marriage is fraught with difficulty, and can be left until the next chapter; but we have already noticed various factors that will be pressing on the dominant males to distribute the women more widely:

a) the infant need for male nurture;

b) the complexities of meat-sharing and bartering for vegetables;

c) the tendency for weapons to be even then the "great equalizer" would lesson alpha's authority and hence his ability to sequester a couple of reserve females (already in short supply) in a campsite pullulating with randiness;

d) the gradual expansion of lust into love.

In the end, as we shall see, distribution will prevail; but I suggest we imagine the opening scenes being played out between the dominant males and the leading lights of their harems.

5

And so to love. The scene we must imagine is complex, indeed it is almost human. The men go hunting by day, where they both compete and cooperate under increasingly violent conditions; i.e., both the weaponry and the game are growing more dangerous. By night they return with their kill, which they are learning to share with the women and children (as no other primate does); and they are learning to *cleave* to the women and children. Let us imagine the campsite growing quiet as dusk settles over the last ululations from the dancing ground: peace, full bellies, and a starlit night: time for the men to consult their almost-conscious desire for reproductive success. What *then?*

When man was invited to look his woman in the eye and lie upon her much extended breast and be enfolded, not only was he being both delivered from the anxiety and distracted from the pleasure of hunting with the boys, but taken back to when he lay upon her breast as a suckling child, and she was all the world to him. Such magical retrieval of primordial unity was both real and unreal; for though he could get there, he couldn't stay there long, and would fall away. And when he mounted her not as child but as hunter closing on his prey, something similar happened: the most astonishing kill imaginable was questioned by the prey's immediate escape and the hunter's shrinking into helplessness and depletion—a child again.

In both cases the man is mocked. As the woman bears the world upon her back, the man-child seeking to return is reminded of a paradise lost, and the hunter learns that even in his moment of glory he remains a child. On the one hand you can't go home again and on the other you can't ever leave—an aspect of the double bind. Both thoughts lead to death: if paradise is lost you are not what you were, and such change involves mortality—to glimpse the child one is no longer is also to glimpse the corpse one will become; and if your finest moment is an illusion that leaves you dispossessed and weak as a child, you are a tree too weak to stand. *Post coitum omne animal tristum est* said the preacher ("After intercourse all animals are sad"), and he was a man. (What the lady preacher said we haven't been told.)*

---

*The preacher may have been a gorilla. Like us, he often prefers the ventral position and can spend up to fifteen minutes getting there. Like us too, he seems to be aware of others' suffering and to carry some melancholy sense that the world is out of joint, either that he has squandered his birthright or that the gods have plotted against him. Some males even seem to choose not to breed, and mortality among unmated males is high. It may be that the gorilla's extraordinary sensitivity

The nineteenth century provided two notable essays on the origins of marriage. Johann Bachofen, one of Nietzsche's early gurus, was a Swiss bachelor who reckoned, largely from reading Herodotus, that primitive women were formidable creatures who installed monogamy in order to stop being swamped about in the hunter-warrior's orgy. This sounds a little feverish to the modern ear, and in any case we now know that even the female chimp can refuse a male she doesn't fancy, though she rarely does this, and so the idea of perpetual and debilitating promiscuity among the early humans is unlikely. The second essay is from Friedrich Engels, whose *Origins of the Family,* drawing on the work of American ethnologist Lewis Morgan, comes much nearer the mark. He suggests that the story begins with Nature bonding the mothers and children, and the men bonding the body politic. This corresponds well enough with contemporary primate studies, which find female lineages and the mother-child bond ubiquitous, but the males, though often fond of the young, never paternal. The young belong to the female, and the male belongs to . . . Where *does* he belong? It is an important question.

If one thinks of the mothers and children as constituting a nucleus, with dominant males at the center and subdominants circling the circumference—which is the actual pattern of land-based monkey troups—the problem becomes clear. The man consorts with the women, tolerates the children, fraternizes and fights with the other men, and encounters what lies beyond the tribal circle. One might say he can go anywhere but belongs nowhere, and if he belongs to anything, he belongs to "the tribe." "What's that?" a female might ask him one day, "I've never seen it." "It's the whole thing" he replies, "invisible certainly, everything and nothing. I've just discovered it while standing in the center of the circle"; and

to failure derives from some recent awareness of his ecological doom, which he finds confirmed in the arms of his lady gorilla. On the other hand, it could be that one day in the dim past he stumbled upon love, and its dreadful lessons turned him into a philosopher who despaired of evolution: which left the unphilosophical chimp and the quasi-philosophical human to continue the story. [10]

soon enough he will tell her that it is collected in the sacred body of an animal, which will one day be called a totem. She will scratch her head in skeptical wonderment and return to realistic matters, reminding us of the origins of this conversation in the male baboon's attachment to a symbolic theater of dominance rituals.

The question of male abstraction versus female empathy is worth pausing over. As well as the male primate's constant concern with "invisible" rank order there is the simpler matter of the value placed on distance from others in an aggressive world. Not only do dominant male chimps and baboons protect themselves from their inferiors with a zone of "personal space" that they vigorously enforce, but the dangers of predators and the hunt indicate very early the desirability of open space and weapons that will kill at a distance. Thus for millions of years the male has been taught to desire separateness and be wary of proximity and touching. Maternity, by contrast, requires tolerance of continual invasion of one's space and body. Estrus females usually copulate thirty times a day, and in childbirth a part of the mother's body seems to come loose: she must then share her personal space for years with the little one who comes to eat and play with her. Modern mothers often find this a good deal more oppressive to their sense of personal integrity than did their primate forebears.

Despite (and because of) his wariness about touching, the hominid male's abstraction and mobility probably made him more susceptible to the magic of erotic love. Since his identity is more open to question than the female's (not least because he vigorously defines and defends the contours of his body, a prologue to paranoia), he is both more driven and more free to explore the question, and also more disturbed by the answers he might find. A lord of the tribe he may be, able to move without restrictions and command a larger personal space than even the highest-ranking female, but lords are lords only as long as everyone agrees they are; and since one can detect elements of self-doubt even in the chimp (his rather feverish charging displays), imagine early man drumming his chest before his recently promoted and somewhat skeptical women—those women who whisper to him in the night that he is child, worm, and emperor of ice cream. No wonder he kept coming back for more: "Perhaps tonight my emperor will stand, and will not melt."

Love's discovery thus opened a nightly theater of dream and dominance rituals to rival and complicate the one that prevailed by day. Woman's power was greatly enhanced. Having been downgraded by the move onto the savannah and the exigent demands of rearing human children, she was back in contention. What was ultimately at issue between male and female can be readily gathered in the image we have already considered, the pull between the still center and the moving circle around it. Woman held the center, as in due course the hearth would hold the fire: the hearth's prologue lay between her legs, as central a hold as may be, the first of all our rooms, both vacuous and the source of life's renewal, both radically finite and endless. Also both dangerous and mysterious: as the brain and its cranial casing expanded, the experience of childbirth became utterly perilous for the mother, and when successful, grounds for general celebration. Thus the center centered. On the circle's circumference moves the man who comes and goes, crossing and thereby defining its bounding line as he is drawn out to dangerous adventure and in to the nurturing center. One would imagine this to be the pattern we would take up when we begin to explore the body politic on the dancing ground; and this is indeed the case with the African !Kung, as old as any dancers we know. One can see in this pattern of male and female an apt illustration of the old and much-disparaged saying "Woman is, man does"; and one can imagine that whereas her first anxiety was of abandonment, his was of imprisonment.

And yet she too would have feared imprisonment. The female chimp is excited by the violence of hunting and does enjoy her daily perambulations: hence early woman almost certainly felt housebound. This would have set her dreaming of the dangerous savannah, dreams that would have been both gratified and frustrated by the hunter in her arms; for he was both her ticket to ride out and her jailer, just as she was both his prey and his nemesis. And as the one who possibly touched her womb, he might be either her redeemer or the tomb of every hope. What Yeats called love's "contrapuntal serpent" (and the psychologists call ambivalence) could doubtless be heard hissing from the outset.

6

Discussions of the sex war are frequently vitiated by crude and lazy thinking that makes binary lists of masculine and feminine attributes and then forgets that, as Jung reminds us, the male has his feminine side and the female her masculine. A good way of avoiding such crudeness is to speak not of masculine and feminine but of *yang* and *yin,* those ancient Chinese terms that gather and conjoin the world's divisions. The human mind has always been disposed to think its binary thoughts in terms of gender (and for good reason, I think) and yet the descriptive simplicity this provides can easily degenerate into prescriptive rigidity. The Chinese terms both cancel and preserve the gendering tendency, and remind us that there is no *yin* without *yang,* and that an excess of one always calls for redress from the other.

The present question of female-center and male-margin, stillness and movement, is a case in point, and is best seen as a dialogue between *yin* and *yang.* The *yin*-center *is* feminine, was originally colonized by the females, and was both desired and resisted by the males. And yet this desire and resistance in the male was also the expression of his own *yin,* his feminine side. And so with the male margin and the females, *mutatus mutandis.* To lose sight of such complexity is to lose quite a lot, a fall into what Blake called "single vision and Newton's sleep." Having said this, we can go on to observe that ultimately, in neolithic times, the center would prevail; not only rooms and houses and pots and granaries, but *temples* would be built to house the *yin*-feminine mysteries. This is *not* to say that the females ruled. History offers us several rumors of Amazon tribes thought to dwell just over the horizon of the known world, but it is generally agreed that no serious evidence of matriarchy has ever been found, either paleolithic or neolithic.[11]

In any case, during the several million paleolithic years of migrant/nomadic hunting and gathering that preceded the neolithic, it seems reasonable to believe that man and his *yang*-mysteries held off the challenge of woman and hers. The main reason for this is that the world of male dominance was there first, inherited from the apes, deeply imprinted in the instincts, and adapted to a dangerous world. Not only would the discovery of love have been a slow business, but it depends upon the ability to believe one's dreams, and for this one needs not only a large brain but some agility with symbols. Furthermore, the theater of love constitutes a *threat* to male power (as all the world's mythologies testify), and one should never forget the importance of man's strong right arm in defending his interests, particularly in early days. Finally, since this is ultimately a struggle between movement and rest, we should remember what extraordinarily nomadic creatures we still are. Not only did we probably set out from Africa to walk all over the planet a hundred thousand years ago, but even in historical times there has been a great deal of migration. Gypsies still seem romantic, and the flight of the bird still moves us.*

7

Not far from the well-known adage "All's fair in love and war" is the less well-known but widely held belief that men are generally more disposed to "play by the rules" than are women. If this is so, why? The usual explanation points out that hunters follow set sequences, under patriarchy boys handle sharp tools and play more games at school than girls do, and that success in the work place comes from observing the rules or conventions of the local game; whereas female success in the getting and nurturing of infants calls on other talents. What's more, when the rule-making male wants a serious innings

---

*The African walkabout hypothesis (dubbed "Out of Africa" in the schools) has been recently challenged by the notion of "multi-regional" emergence, but seems to be holding its ground reasonably well.

with his anarchic instincts, he declares war on his neighbor, thereby legitimizing a good deal of mayhem without disturbing his sense of himself as "one who reveres the law"; and of course when it comes to sex, promiscuity in the married male has rarely been much punished through the ages, which further encourages the male to overestimate his readiness to be rule-bound.

To this list I would add another less obvious factor that nonetheless emerges fairly clearly on the savannah. We have noticed the male baboon's concern with the "invisible" structure of male dominance, which he fleshes out with various rituals, and also the makings of an identity crisis for early man on the savannah with regard to his place in the eternal circle. If we put these together we can see a basis not only for the male disposition toward the colonizing of abstract realms but also toward the invention of various games for the answering of the who-am-I question. As we have noticed, woman has both children and kinship before the man does, which might lead us to suspect that even when he gets them, they are less certain possessions. (Hence, in some measure, the elaborate constructions of the kinship networks studied by ethnologists, cats' cradles to keep away the dark.) Beyond kinship, of course, lie the complexities of myth and ritual, and here again I suspect the men will be more disposed than the women to believe in the invisible realities attested therein.

The feminists I have asked about the female disposition to "move the goalposts" have on the whole agreed it exists, pointed out that the law has historically been a fiction in the service of male interests (hence the male is even further disposed to overrate its importance), and that the virtuous aspect of female "lawlessness" is in its realism and flexibility, its ability to quickly sense when some conventional procedure is obstructing the life force rather than allowing it to flourish. Thus man the ritualist, woman the pragmatist. What is interesting about this gendering proposal is that in *yin/yang* terms it reads man-*yin*, woman-*yang*; which is to say it has both operating out of their "shadow" sides. *Yang* is the aggressive energy that initiates, breaks, and changes a pattern, and stands forth clearly (its original meaning is "banners waving in the sun"), whereas *yin* is the submissive energy that yields to and completes the *yang* initiative, conserves a pattern, and stands obscurely for that which is concealed (its original meaning is "cloudy or overcast").[12] Thus, to initiate law and ritual is *yang/yin* (the yanging of yin, so to speak) but the keeping of it is *yin* and the breaking of it *yang*. I suspect that a good deal of contemporary male outrage at the female view of goalposts originates in shock and dismay at such role reversal, the women poaching on our *yang* preserve and abusing our *yin* constancies. "A taste of your own medicine, and high time too" is the obvious reply, just before the music gets drowned out in shouting. Gender generalizing is tricky work, and the ancient Chinese ordered these things rather better than we do. I suggest that all concerned should spend more time browsing in the *I Ching*.

8

It is important to distinguish between pair-bonding and love, even though in practice it is difficult for us to do so. Pair-bonding is one of Nature's evolutionary strategies, adopted under duress when the going is tough. Love, as I have briefly sketched it, is something so subtly insane that only humans are clever enough to fall into it. Pair-bonding is about feeding the young: love is about something else—after all, mother chimp nurtures her young perfectly well without it, and the human male is still having difficulty with the fiction of paternity. And yet, though theoretically separable, we can see them beginning to interact in the ventrally disposed bonobo chimp, and hence imagine them actually coming together on the savannah, where love is the lure that moves the male toward something like pair-bonding, which will lead him ultimately to speak of "his" children. I put it this way for several reasons: first, the hominid move onto the savannah was all in his favor. The young had always been her problem, and his major instincts were pulling him the other way, toward hunting and politics with his pals. In order to make him accept some responsibility for her and the kids, something more than his already troubled urge toward paternity was needed, and needed quickly. She, on the contrary, was bound quite simply to her children, and she needed him for them. Evolution offered her love as a means of getting him, and she took it, which is not to say that she liked it (though she probably did). But he *had* to like it, or else he would have been even more feckless and fond of his pals than history has indicated he was and is—and we would not be here to tell the tale. To see the sequence in this way illuminates not only why Mother Nature took less care in arranging for the female orgasm than the male, but also why love has been widely thought to be a card dealt by woman and played by and for man: *l'homme propose, la femme dispose.* It also suggests why man's allegiance has always been divided between household and the world that lies beyond it. Very simply, the pair-bond was a crisis measure that never had time to set; and the annals of love record the slippage.

If, as I have suggested, woman was the major player, however mixed her motives, how was man persuaded? Partly, one assumes, by the sense that bonding was the most efficient way of dealing with both child-nurture and his desire for reproductive success; but partly also, surely, because of love. One of the things love seeks is a return to our first world of playful safety and trust and intimacy. Since that was a world we knew on one breast and one breast only, it makes sense to seek its retrieval under similarly exclusive conditions. If one remembers that mammals warmed up the cold-blooded reptilean world by nurturing their young, then human love can be seen as an attempt to rekindle those fires in the no-longer-young through recapitulation. And just as the infants of many species are bonded to their mothers by the experience of visual, auditory, or olfactory "imprinting," one may imagine something similar in the case of love—occurring through the eyes, probably, as the poets suggest. Not only is the eye our most expressive (hence individual) feature, but staring is a prelude to war (hence taboo) with everyone except mother and lover, in which case the eye dilates and melts and promises union.[13]

Strong stuff, one might think, and yet it had to be strong to override our promiscuous primate instincts, which are still, needless to say, very much with us. The children doubtless also helped to cement the adult pair-bond, not only because the male would have gradually learned to mother the young somewhat, but also because of the dreams he was dreaming in the theater of love. If, as I have suggested, love leads him to a paradise lost, and ultimately thereby to the idea that he will die, this will arouse in him a concern for the future, what may succeed him, and indeed how he may succeed himself. Not only in general terms does the child bear the promise of time future, but just as the male may imagine himself dying sexually (in the "little death" of orgasm) so he may imagine the child as the fruit of his sacrifice, and ultimately himself reborn, immortal. The wombless male needs such ideas in a way the female does not, the connection (both physical and metaphysical) to her children being of all things the most indubitable.

The male's problematic connection to his children brings us back to the difficult question of how and when his desire for progeny became conscious. As he grew more thoughtful under the conditions of sequestered ovulation, what was an instinctive kenning gradually became a troubled and darksome imagining. He kens his woman (somewhat) and cares for her children, but are they *his*? They are and are not. Such profound ambiguity doubtless focused his mind admirably, not only informing some of his strongest and most important dreams but also making him dance attendance upon his woman's mystery. But it is not simply a matter of an ancient instinct "coming loose," as it were, and looking for accommodation. Once the theater of love has opened, the idea of death will begin to trouble the male mind, and the need to be associated with the powers of regeneration will grow apace. In addition to his own death, of course, is the anxiety doubtless provoked by his spilling of blood in the hunt and the occasional war (as we shall see presently). All in all, the problem of paternity deserves to be placed at the very forefront of what one might call the "cultural anxiety" of early man, where indeed it remains to this day.

To say that love was in the beginning more important to the male than to the female is not to say that she was unmoved, and merely exploiting cynically the power it brought her. The gender difference would make her less readily imagine the retrieval of childhood simplicity in his arms (she could do this better with her own child);

and yet, what he lacked as mother surrogate he made up in strength, the amazing safety she could find in his embrace. For her the day was doubtless dangerous enough to make this quite significant. In addition to his strength he brought her traces of the world beyond domesticity—the magic of travel, the adventure of things unknown; and she was his prey, the animal he lovingly killed (or killingly loved); and she was the mother whose child he was hoping to find once again. Most importantly, I suspect, she was drawn to him to help her bear the lethal mystery of her womb, the appalling fact that her day of major triumph ended so often in hideous death. All this is not nothing; and yet neither does it seem as significant to her world as the dreams her love could awaken in his. Could it be that love not only began unequally, but remains so, and for the simplest of biological reasons? If its primitive origin lies, as I have suggested, in the dream of retrieving union with the mother, and if it arises similarly in us, as psychoanalysis believes, this manifestly suits the male better than the female. Quite apart from the possibility that he may usually receive preferential treatment at the breast, when the time comes for falling in love he faces the relatively straightforward task of seeking an improved version of the mother he left some time ago, whereas she must renounce (while also retaining) a homosexual bond and resurrect it as best she can in the opposite sex. It seems to me a profoundly unfair aspect of biological destiny, for which we have all been paying throughout human history. Be that as it may, the dimorphism in sexual development seems still to be with us, despite all the apparent changes in circumstance: man's continuing puzzlement with women in love in the twentieth century was memorably identified by Freud when he plaintively asked, "But what does woman *want?*" The short answer to this in a culture that abhors the feminine is "She wants to be a man": for the long answer some patience may be needed.

Finally, amid all this talk of love one should not forget about hatred, its constant companion; nor indeed that, as the ancient folk song puts it, "When love grows old, she waxeth cold." The gist of my argument in this section has been that the goddess of Love (yes, she *is* feminine) came to disrupt and enrich our lives very early on, much earlier than we commonly suppose, and that her coming was responsible for significant changes in the way we lived. If I have understated the negative aspects of love's comedy, both our promiscuous resistance to love's confinements and the ever-active demons of deceit, jealousy, and boredom, it has been to keep the narrative line as simple as possible. Such negations, though essential to the novelist, may be justly neglected in a brief discussion such as this one, for they complicate but do not alter the basic themes. In any case, we shall meet them in due course.

As coda to this section, a word about the disreputable nature of my love story. I should plainly state that in all the evolutionary and ethnological literature I have read, few voices speak up for love at this stage in the proceedings.[14] Although I find this bizarre, it certainly gives me pause; on the other hand it is well known that ethnologists, and scientists generally, are made uneasy by love-talk, and the traditional male bias of these disciplines makes it no easier. In any case let me freely admit that I am here *speculating* about the early love story, and the only things that might look like *evidence* for my proposals are a) the remarkable anatomical changes associated with the ventral position, which invite us to see in the sexual civility of the ventralizing bonobo chimp an evolutionary sketch for hominid man; and b) the remarkable analogies between hunting and sexuality, which would, I think, have amplified for early man and woman the thrillingness of each. We shall explore these analogies briefly at the end of this chapter, and at more length in Chapter 5.

9

I suggested in the previous chapter that a crucial aspect of brachiation was "the straightening torso, surrounded by articulate shoulders and hands, which opens a protected space in front of the eyes where objects may be delicately presented for intimate consideration." Perhaps the most important of the objects so presented to early man was the face of the lover. As the bonobo chimp may know, when eye meets eye in a loving gaze, the perimeters of the self both melt and discover a mirror in which they find themselves drawn. It is a dawning of self-consciousness. The self only arises for itself when its loss (or metamorphosis) can be contemplated. Thus, the lover's introduction to death and transfiguration is full of food for thought: and since such thoughts arise in the dance of love, they will be intimately related to (as both cause and effect of) our dreams.

What can we know of hominid dreaming? There can scarcely be a more important question for the origins of myth, since mytho-logic *is* dream logic, but as with many important questions, much remains obscure. The simplest thing we know is that reptiles do not dream, whereas mammals do. This suggests that dreaming is concerned with the affective thinking and learning introduced by mammalian life and the limbic lobe of the brain. Babies do a great deal of dreaming, presumably to master the "blooming buzzing confusion" (William James) of their experience. Animals, such as horse foals, that dream more than humans do in the womb, emerge more competent at birth as a result (quickly on their feet to get a drink); which would suggest that "reality testing" in the playful space-time of dreamland not only sorts out what one has done today but prepares for, and even perhaps chooses, what one might do tomorrow. That such playfulness is serious business is indicated by the fact that both animals and humans deprived of dream-sleep tend to become forgetful and unhinged; and conversely, the unhinged tend to dream with urgent vividness. The demons of memory are significantly at work, not only choosing important material to be stored in the long-term memory, but also probably running some very old movies: even the tough-minded Darwin thought the disposition of children to dream of monsters involved archaic memories, of the time when we were much afflicted with reptiles.[15] Perhaps the major point in this list is the first one: dreaming arises in mammals who, unlike the reptiles, nurture their young and thereby introduce emotion and learning to the world. Crudely put, when as mammals we gave up the almost robotic instinctual life of the reptiles, we began the gradual process of modifying the "push-button" instincts of fight and flight with information we absorbed from mother and the environment. Recent research suggests that such information gains access to the long-term memory by being repetitively "dreamed in" through what Jonathan Winsom has called "neural gates" in the hippocampus. Such theorizing is quite compatible with the fact that our human dreams are indeed chiefly concerned with the ghosts of semi-retired instincts, those things we used to do automatically but now must submit somewhat to the tribunal of our culture, or conscience, located in the memory. May I kill this pest? May I leap on that woman? Check with the memory bank, and do it quickly. Thus the dream, like the myth and ritual in which we "dream awake," is above all the theater where facts are valued, where desire would find its form, where the ambiguities of culture are transmitted, and where instinct ("stereotyped behavior" in Tinbergen's [1951] useful phrase) gets defined and refined. This is implicitly recognized in the psychoanalytic commonplace that we dream insistently of sex and violence, those facts most difficult to value, where desire is shrouded in psychic and social inhibition, and where the ghosts of archaic instinct fly in the night.[16]

More light has recently been shed on dreaming by the ascription of differential functioning to the brain's right and left hemispheres. On this theory, the right is *yin*-intuitive (concerned with pattern recognition, music, holistic thought, and 3-D vision), whereas the left is *yang*-rational (concerned with reading, writing, speaking, and mathematics). The left processes information sequentially, the right simultaneously, several inputs at once. It has been suggested that originally—tens of millions of years ago—the two worked in parallel, like our eyes and our ears; but as the neocortex grew, the left began to specialize in the new mentality. The left also controls the right side of the body, and the apparently universal human preference for the right over the left (*sinister* in Latin) may be an elementary gesture of piety, verbal man recognizing the gods who have delivered him from the kingdom of dreams. Perhaps the simplest way of sensing the difference between the two is with marijuana, which enhances our musical perception and sense of the connectedness of things while macerating the words that might report such experience: clearly a suppression of the left hemisphere.

It seems appropriate to our computer age that the engineers working on artificial intelligence can elicit marvels of rationality from their robots, but have difficulty with 3-D vision and pattern recognition: the right hemisphere is apparently resisting their schemes. Dreaming is also predominantly right hemisphere, as it deals with images not words, and with pattern recognition not logical sequences. Works of poetry and mythology are clearly coproductions, verbal attempts to translate the ineffable stuff that dreams are made of. And just as the left hemisphere has superseded the right in the evolution of man, so has rational discourse superseded the archaic modes of mythology, poetry, and music in the history of culture. Freud certainly exacerbated this dismal progress with his notorious distinction between two kinds of human thinking, which he called "the primary and secondary processes." The first, (right hemisphere) he labeled childish, primitive, and neurotic, the second (left), rational and realistic. This central aspect of his thought still needs denouncing, as it continues to impress people who should know better.

However useful one may find the right/left classification as a mapping of *yin/yang* in the mind, one must beware letting its tidy and materialist tendencies reduce the irreducible complexity of mental life to mere physiology. Human memory, for example, as we saw in Chapter 2, is resisting attempts to locate it as physical traces in the brain, and memory is absolutely central to the life of the mind. One must also beware the tidy generalizations that left/right thinking can encourage: thus, for example, although intuitive (imagistic, poetical) modalities in the mind clearly precede rational ones in several senses, both grew together in the huge expansion of the human neocortex. Not only do chimpanzees not walk around in a dream: man dreams a lot harder. Though our verbal powers can and perhaps must oppose our dreams in certain ways, they also make them possible: they license our dangerous travels by night with the promise of making sense in the morning. Conversely, our travels in the dream-time help to keep our language clear (as the unhinging of the dream-deprived would suggest). Recent research indicates that without dreams our thinking condenses and implodes, trying to say several things at once: in effect the dream spills over into waking life, and we "dream awake" in the bad sense, as schizophrenics do. Thus, dreaming in its proper context is a kind of licensed madness that ensures sanity. The suppression of such madness produces insanity. Primitive myth/ritual should be understood as the socially licensed attempt to clarify, interpret, and detoxify the nightly mad excursion into the dream-time: it is what chiefly selects from the "blooming buzzing confusion" of primitive experience those images deemed significant enough to be in turn dreamed into the long-term memory for instinctual reference. Although ultimately playful, such work is an utterly serious aspect of the human undertaking; and when a culture forgets this aspect of the human contract with the gods, and suppresses its dreams, as ours does, it too goes crazy.

With this brief sketch of the dream-time, let us return to early man falling in love on the savannah. Could he have done it before he learned to speak? My tentative answer is yes. As the cortex grew, his dreams would have become more vivid (replacing old instincts with the totems and taboos of culture), and his rational powers would have increased as well. One could imagine that just at the moment before speech arrived his dreams may have been difficult to bear, to disentangle from his waking life. One could even imagine that this difficulty had more than a little to do with his finding his voice. But once he did find it (let us say two million years ago), his dream life would have become truly significant and he could have afforded to fall seriously in love. That said, let us remember that this is to some extent an academic point. The ventral position and the open sexual season were substantial evolutionary moves devised to meet a crisis that, as we believe, antedated the discovery of speech by perhaps three or four million years. And there is nothing to suggest that preverbal man was not a sufficiently accomplished dreamer to gaze into the eyes of his beloved on the dancing ground and find the contours of the self both magically dissolved and outlined for the first time. If the chimp can discover mortality by murdering a rival, early man (following the bonobo) can certainly do so by silently falling in love. The point in either case, and it is certainly contentious, is that both love and murder came to us much earlier than we have supposed, and came before language did. Needless to say, both experiences were much deepened by the words that could name them, and the dreams those words could license.

10

Since the major concern of this chapter has been with the original imbalance between the sexes and the extent to which this imbalance may have been reduced by the loving pair-bond, it seems appropriate to conclude such speculation with some attempt to test it empirically. The earliest significant body of evidence we have of how paleolithic man saw the world is the cave painting of southern Europe from about 15,000 B.C. To look briefly at it now does mean getting ahead of ourselves somewhat, as in the next chapter we must return to the savannah to think about our first gods; but the leap will not, I hope, be unduly disorienting, and may be justified by the fact that these paintings, in the opinion of their most eminent student, André Leroi-Gourhan, are principally concerned with the matters we have been discussing here.

A leap, however, *is* involved, and a not inconsiderable one at that, because we have been discussing love between man and woman, and the paintings discuss the gods. Can the one pass intelligibly into the other? My reply is yes, and that brief reflection can indicate this to be so. It is a commonplace that theology begins with the awareness of death, and this comes to mankind, as I have argued, through sex and violence, love and murder. What is essentially involved in both love and religion is the repairing of unities broken by experience, and beyond that the retrieval of a Unity both all-encompassing and sempiternal. The reader may have already noticed that my discussion of love has been presented in terms quasi-religious at least, and this may be thought anachronistic: how can we be religious about love before we have even discovered the gods? My reply, admittedly contentious, is that it is precisely at that moment, *before* the gods, when we will be most "religious" about love; in a word, love discovers theology (as Christianity still supposes). Put another way, before the mind has grown sufficiently abstract to imagine divinities, love alone must minister to the fear of death. Its inadequacy in this regard must surely have been a principal stimulus to the development of religious imagination, as we shall consider in a later chapter. In any case it seems altogether plausible to suggest that as divinity takes root in human imagining, through the hunt, the religious pressure on love will ease, and it may be allowed to appear in almost "human" dimensions. Thus can one imagine love's absolute centrality to early man, and its gradual attenuation as divinity is discovered; until by the time of the Ice-Age painters the central dramas involve transactions with the theriomorphic gods. The theme is constant, the setting evolves.

Having said that love—and subsequently theology—begins in the attempt to retrieve the security and delight first tasted at mother's breast, I should perhaps also stress that this in no way implies that such activities are *merely* childish or "regressive," as the Freudians suggested. Freud's attempt to debunk both love and religious feeling by pointing to their undignified origins in infantile experience was not only wicked in its nihilism ("If I must live without love or God, so must you") but plainly irrational in its illogicality. His crime against logic is called the genetic fallacy, the absurd suggestion that any process that begins in helplessness and squalor cannot grow beyond it: thus, the fact that our first intimations of love and worship come to us (like so much else) from our parents does not mean that our subsequent adult attempts to pursue these dreams are necessarily neurotic and cowardly evasions of reality. The antidote to Freud is Wordsworth:

> not in utter nakedness
> But trailing clouds of glory do we come
> From God, who is our home:
> Heaven lies about us in our infancy!
> "Immortality Ode"

To calm this down for the skeptical contemporary mind, one might say that the adult task is not to abandon one's infantile desires but so to clothe and transform them through art and religion that they may again be housed, and paradise perhaps regained, in such a way that life is lived *more* abundantly, not less. If this is not the cultural task, what is it? To say that it is very difficult, or even that most attempts are regressive failures of the kind Freud identifies, is no argument against the enterprise. Growing up was always difficult.

11

Although the caves of southern Europe were decorated with a remarkable consistency of theme over a period of about twenty thousand years, the great painting was done in the Magdalenian epoch (about 15 to 10,000 B.C.), particularly in the middle of it, when a warming climate called forth a luxuriousness and amplitude of style much nearer our own taste than are the abstractions of ancient Egypt with which art history traditionally begins. It was at this period that the artists left the sunlit entrances and crawled with their blubber lamps deep into the darkness to paint their master-pieces on the walls of the large inner sanctuaries. In the huge cave complexes that compose these cathedrals of the paleolithic, the furthest sanctuaries are more than a kilometer from the entrance, and the journey, frequently precipitous, often involves crawling on all fours through extremely narrow passageways. Even today with good torches and no danger of getting lost in the labyrinthine maze of alleys and dead ends, the journey unsettles all but the utterly insensitive. Imagine how it would have struck the Magdalenian youth when, as is probable, he was sent down to be lost and found there, initiated into the mysteries of life and death.[17]

The idea of an underground labyrinth, in the depths of which cosmic power is concealed and disclosed, is familiar to us from Greek mythology (notably the Cretan labyrinth of the Minotaur)—an intes-tinal maze that leads to belly or womb, where life is replenished and extinguished. The motif is still with us today, in the stoutly defended Colorado mountain where we have buried our control center for nuclear war. In the large central sanctuaries of the Magdalenian caves, one finds symbols and paintings of animals in which, according to Leroi-

Gourhan, the female principle is being attended by the male. At the cave entrances, in the corridors, and in the furthest "back-cave" shrines, masculine symbols prevail. He suggests that this may be because the caves themselves are obviously feminine (*Treasures of Prehistoric Art*, p. 174). The overall impression is of a harmonious balance between masculine and feminine.

His general thesis, which he expounds convincingly over five hundred pages of astonishingly detailed text, is that for thousands of years the grammar of Ice-Age religious art remains constant, and that its message is the simple one shared by all the world's profoundest poems: that harmony (or reality) involves the conjunction of opposites, *yin* and *yang,* feminine and masculine (or as the Oriental masters of such poems would learn to say, the seeming opposition and necessary separation of contraries is an illusion shattered by the mystical mind in its moment of self-canceling wisdom). I find it deeply consoling to think that at this, our first major opportunity to say our piece and have it recorded, we more or less got it right.

The feminine or *yin* animals are the bison (above all), the ox, and sometimes the hind. The masculine or *yang* animals are the horse (above all), the ibex, the cervids, the felines, the bear, and the mammoth. The abstract symbols, which evolved originally from vulva and phallus, include ovals, triangles, and quadrangles for the feminine; dots, dashes, hooked and barbed lines for the masculine.[18] Human figures are rare—more male than female—and rendered abstractly (stick drawings). They tend to be bent forward, as in the dancing "cakewalk," with arms raised in what is usually interpreted as a gesture of invocation. Such meager abstraction in the human world contrasts strikingly with the wonderfully animated realism of the animal painting, which tells us clearly that the life being worshiped here is animal not human, the religion theriomorphic.[19]

As to what rites were performed in this religion, the caves are almost silent. The mutilation of certain images suggests they may have been ritually stabbed, perhaps the young hunter making his first kill. This gains plausibility from the fact that slaughtered animals on the walls always "appear singly within a group of intact animals" (Leroi-Gourhan, p. 181), which might suggest to the young hunter that Mother Nature is strong enough to bear his violence. This is in turn substantiated by a number of paintings that alone appear to be telling a story: according to Leroi-Gourhan they "make up almost all the narrative 'scenes' known to Paleolithic art" (p. 130).

The name he gives to this narrative is "the wounded man theme," and its depiction on cave walls is "very familiar indeed . . . a theme known from the Solutrean to the Middle Magdalenian (p. 316)," i.e., from about 17 to 11,000 B.C. Briefly put, the male who wounds the female, with either spear or phallus, is himself wounded. To hunt the bison or the human female—whose vulva both looks and bleeds like a wound—is a dangerous undertaking, in which the hunter may himself be wounded, physically or spiritually. And yet such woundings can be not only survived but should perhaps be seen as fruitful; for does not the wounded bison nourish the stomach just as the bleeding vulva nourishes new life? Thus to hunger (for meat or for sex) is to wound, to kill and be killed, and from such death life is renewed. What enabled Leroi-Gourhan to crack the code of this story was discovering the equivalence of wound and vulva signs, and also realizing that the spears impaling the bisons were not actually spears but male symbols. From this he inferred that "it is highly probable that Paleolithic men were expressing something like 'spear is to penis' as 'wound is to vulva' (p. 173). He goes on to say:

> Taken as symbols of sexual union and death, the spear and the wound would then be integrated into a cycle of life's renewal, the actors in which would form two parallel and complementary series: man/horse/spear, and woman/bison/ wound. (p. 174)

The most eloquent depiction of the wounded man theme is in the shaft or crypt of Lascaux. In this much-discussed painting a bison (female) has been pierced by a line (or spear) very near the vulva and her intestines hang beneath her belly like a bag. Lying apparently rigid on his back beside her is an ithyphallic (i.e., sexually erect)

man with the head of a bird. Nearby stands a staff with a bird on top, and further off (perhaps unrelated) a rhinoceros is exiting stage left (trailing some male dots once interpreted as turds). The bison, wounded but apparently unhurt, looks at the man, flat on his back but also apparently unhurt. What is going on?

Birds are everywhere associated with shamanism in the paleolithic—one thinks of the splendidly owl-eyed Sorcerer of Trois Frères—and the bird-headed man with the bird-headed wand makes good sense when seen as a shaman entranced, bad sense when seen (as he often is) as a hunter wounded.[20] Not only does he bear no wound (indeed potency of the blood moves within him) but the stillness of the composition suggests its subject is vision not violence. What has flattened him is not the bison's horn but the vision of life's woundings, and his erection promises that the cycles of such wounding, properly understood, are not only bearable but the source of life's power. The bison's wound is comparably ambiguous: not only does the broken line "pierce" her (if it does) from a position no hunter could easily manage, but she appears undismayed and her intestinal "bag" makes one think of an udder or even the membrane bag in which mammals are born. In any case its firm outline does not suggest the chaotic spillage of her life, and together with her massive shoulders and sturdy legs seems to be saying, "There is more to me than your thin instruments can worry." The rhinoceros and the dots may or may not be related to this scene, but as masculine symbols are quite at home in such a back-cave area.

What distinguishes this painting, and some others, from crude renderings of the wounded-man theme, in which hunter and beast are simply opposed, is the ambiguous depiction of the wounds. By placing the male wound in shaman rather than hunter, the story is no longer confined simply to the physical luck of the hunt, but moves out to include the metaphysical or spiritual wound (the beginnings of remorse) man opens himself to whenever he inflicts violence upon the feminine, either sexually or in the hunt. By presenting the bison so that she appears at once wounded, gravid, and indifferent, the painting suggests that such violence is indeed destructive, but that it can be borne (pun intended) even perhaps forgiven (notice the nodding horns) in a world that piously dreams of such bison abundance as one finds on the inner sanctuary walls at Lascaux.

This painting is unquestionably the finest of all the presentations of the wounded-man theme, a theme that, as we have seen, is central to Magdalenian man and constitutes virtually his only narrative subject. And just as it may be seen to culminate and resolve the Magdalenian meditation on violence, so it points forward to subsequent shamanic developments: the bird-topped wand will lead to the magical wand of Hermes, and the man who acquires power and wholeness by being wounded will lead to the hermaphroditic shaman who acquires access to the feminine through the undergoing of violence, a tradition that culminates in Christ. It seems appropriate that such a significant painting should be found in one of the most splendid of the paleolithic cathedrals, and in an obscure chamber whose pattern of use and decoration suggests to Dr. A. Laming-Emperaire (1959) (the other major authority on cave art) that "the place was particularly sacred or important." What does seem odd to me is that neither of these cautious scholars allow themselves much room to speculate on the meanings of this painting, despite their being the ones to have uncoded the overall grammar of paleolithic painting. My interpretation is based upon and does no violence to Leroi-Gourhan: but it must be said that he neither calls the bird-man a shaman nor does he speculate upon the implications of ithyphallic wounding.[21]

12

What makes the European caves so thrilling is not just the beauty of the painting but the sense that here, over a period of several thousand years, the paleolithic dream-time was elaborated with a consistency and splendor that qualifies it as one of the world's great religions. By this I mean it easily transcended its probable origins in sympathetic magic; that is to say, although some of the paintings (the "slaughtered" animals) look like technology for the hunter (picture the animal, stab it, and this will bring you luck tomorrow), the bulk of them were aiming far higher—to dream the dream of cosmic energy, and through art, myth, and ritual, find man's place and make it so.

But what, if anything, may we infer from it concerning male-female relations in the early savannah days? Strictly speaking, of course, nothing at all; and yet what is astonishing about this culture, which doubtless hunted a good deal more than it gathered, is the gravity it ascribes to the eternal feminine—the masculine undoubtedly does, but the feminine even more unquestionably *is*. (One thinks in this regard of such imposing female figurines as the famous "Venus of Laussel.") The second astonishing thing is that the wounded man theme, as I have argued, suggests a highly evolved sense of the violence that is inflicted by *yang*-masculine upon *yin*-feminine, and of the means whereby reparation, even forgiveness, may be envisaged. Both of these notions indicate that the *yin*-feminine attributes were taken remarkably seriously by the Ice-Age hunters.

On the other hand, we are dealing here with a religion of theriomorphic (animal) gods, and it might seem inappropriate to infer much from it concerning Ice-Age sexual relations, let alone to leap back to pre-theological days on the savannah. This seems to me an important point, and though early man's move into theology will concern us in the next chapter, something can be said here. Briefly, the chimp has a remarkably sophisticated sense of himself and a great interest in personal relations, but a very hazy sense of the gods. I imagine this to be true of early man as well, and that his dreams of both killing and making love would have begun in highly

personal terms. Only by infinitely slow degrees would his symbolizing brain have abstracted these activities into transactions with the
gods. By the time we get to the Ice-Age, this process has advanced
so far that the human figure is barely represented (love is certainly
not mentioned) and energy has been altogether assimilated by the
animal gods. And yet it seems to me that this theologizing process
does not fundamentally alter the terms in which the problem of
violence presents itself to the Stone-Age mind; which is why we can
hope to gather something about our early days from the earliest
coherent paleolithic evidence we have, the Ice-Age cave paintings. If
it be urged that these paintings never mention copulation, I would
simply reply that neither does Chapter three of Genesis.

My argument is essentially a simple one: Ice-Age painting suggests
a remarkable sensitivity to the problem of violence, both predatory and
sexual, in which the wounder risks being wounded, the killer killed,
and yet redeemed. Where could this sensitivity have originated? The
story I have told in this chapter suggests that the hunter found it in
love, that predatory embrace that both kills the predator and promises
renewal, in which the hunter is gathered. It is the obvious answer, and
there is no reason to suppose man did not find it early on. What makes
us resist it, in my view, is our stereotyped image of the cave man as a
rude crude thug who drags his woman by the hair. Thug he
undoubtedly was, in certain moods, but he was also the proto-chimp's
offspring; and the chimp, though the inventor of murder, is a creature
given daily to the most subtle and tender transactions.

In conclusion, a very old Greek myth recounted by Hesiod may
be cited in support of my proposals. In the beginning, the sky-god
Ouranos covered the earth-goddess Gaia, and tyrannized, endlessly;
until one night at Gaia's bidding, son Kronos emasculated father *in
flagrante* with a sickle (made from Gaia's original hunk of iron) and
threw his father's severed genitals into the sea. Some of the paternal
blood entered Gaia's womb and produced the Furies, while from the
sea sprang Aphrodite. Thus the movement of history—call it
savannah life—begins in violence, weaponry, and female retribution, the confusion of father's hunting law; and the hopes of
reparation are vested in love.

4 ˈ ON THE DANCING GROUND:
Divinity Discovered and Innocence Lost

Never trust a god who doesn't dance.
—Nietzsche

The devil has the best musick.
—Milton

In keeping with the tendency of the book thus far, the reader might expect me to suggest that the religious life was not a human invention but was in fact discovered by the chimpanzees; and so I shall. What I have in mind is the wonderful raindance described by Jane Goodall in her early book, *In the Shadow of Man*. Astonishing as it may seem, she actually saw four males responding to the outbreak of a particularly heavy thunderstorm by charging up and down a hillside at Gombe, tearing off tree branches and hooting wildly. This continued through twenty minutes of thunder, lightning, and downpour, and was witnessed by a congregation of females and youngsters who had climbed into the trees nearby to watch. The old joke that religion began with man shaking his fist at the heavens is thus not far wide of the mark.

The principal gods in historical cultures, such as Zeus and Yahwe, originated as weather gods, and the storm is an appropriate vehicle for divinity on several counts: it arises from nowhere and prevails everywhere, its source is invisible and yet its designated effects are palpable, and it manifests a quite astonishing power to move and disrupt the pattern of things as they are into a new arrangement—all in all, a plausible origin for the high winds of *pneuma.* One might further note that the storm's power is both real and symbolic: the thunder and lightning boom and flash theatrically, but the wind and the rain make the chimp actually cold, and the "thunderbolt" snaps a large tree as if it were a matchstick. As if in response to this, the chimp both booms and flashes and actually damages some trees. The storm has provoked in him the notion of an almost-present adversary who is, at least on this occasion, to be defied. It is a striking illustration both of the chimp's courage and of his powers of symbolization.

How are we to understand this defiance? The answer is to be found in those charging displays by which the male chimp routinely intimidates those who would oppose him. When one watches one of these, two features are salient: first of all, as with displaying creatures of all sorts, the charging chimp seeks to make himself larger, to *increase* himself, most obviously by the erection of his body hair, or as in canines, the hackles. Second, one notices an element of contagion: not only do his hooting and thrashing and stomping seem to feed upon themselves in the building of his frenzy, but those nearby seem to catch the mood, to become infected or possessed by the power that is infecting or possessing him. Under such conditions the group seems to dilate: one has the impression that it has *increased,* that its power, its substance, has *become more,* even as the creatures run amok. It is as if the raging power that runs among them creates, beyond the foreground chaos, some kind of unification in the amplitude of sound and movement. On reflection this makes sense: in self-abandonment the self is abandoned, which is to say the perimeters of self and other are disregarded, and one feels oneself expand even as the sense of self is fading away. At this level the ecstasy of violence is not significantly different from the ecstasy of sex, and the two come together in the Dionysian orgy, which in Nietzsche's view was the first major fixture of the religious life. "Orgy," like "orgasm," derives from the Greek *orgao*=to swell, become excited.

But this is to anticipate. At the moment we are looking only at the crude prologue to Dionysus in what one might call, not inaccurately, instances of pan-demonium in the chimpanzee troup.

The crucial point is that both charging display and raindance should be seen as a kind of theatrical performance that plays upon the illusion of increased power, from bristling hair up through the contagion of violence to the edges of ecstasy. Even on this primitive stage the question of illusion and reality is puzzling: when does the illusion of power become the real thing? One can imagine a performer replying, "Here is a play whose subject is my invocation of power: if you are insufficiently impressed and intimidated I shall cross the footlights and bang you on the head"; and as we saw in Chapter 2, the line separating the stage from the audience is a thin one at the best of times, and frequently crossed.

The other word that comes to mind in this context is ritual. For the ethologist, animal aggression is "ritualized" when it is programmed (textualized, one might say) in a set sequence of movements that conveys as clearly as possible how formidable the aggressor is, and what the cost of not believing his display might be. For the student of man and his religions, ritual is more serious than theater to the extent that it is less playful, claiming actually to *be* what it represents. Both the rain dance and the routine charging display are rituals en route to improvised theater. They originate in a program of aggression, and yet the set sequence of movements is subject both to the inventiveness of the chimp's imagination and to his loss of self-control. But the important thing to notice here is that the symbolic element, the element of mimesis, of make-believe, in the chimp's aggressive display is both symbolic and real: it both is and is not what it represents. Such complex communication we usually associate with the arts and religion of "cultured" man; but no, it starts here, before language, and this means that henceforth we must keep one eye on the poetical even as the other stays sensibly on the matter of anthropology.

Returning to the raindance, what we can now see is a serious play devoted to the conjuring of increased power through contagion in the players in order to defy a formidable adversary both ubiquitous and not altogether perceivable. At once we notice something new: contagion is moving not only through the chimps but is coming to them from the sky. The storm is not only their adversary but their partner in a dance devoted to some extensive version of abandonment, what Yeats would call "the delirium of the brave." All it lacks in order really to justify the word "dance" is an element of rhythm and harmony. This element, though never recorded at Gombe, was observed by Wolfgang Köhler in his pioneering chimp study of 1916:

> The whole group of chimpanzees sometimes combined in more elaborate motion-patterns. For instance, two would wrestle and tumble near a post: soon their movement would become more regular and tend to describe a circle round the post as a center. One after another, the rest of the group approach, join the two, and finally march in an orderly fashion round and round the post. The character of their movements changes; they no longer walk, they trot, and as a rule with special emphasis on one foot, while the other steps lightly, thus a rough approximate rhythm develops, and they tend to "keep time" with one another. . . .

"It seems to me extraordinary," Köhler concludes, "that there should arise quite spontaneously, among chimpanzees, anything that so strongly suggested the dancing of some primitive tribes."[1]

2

There is also a quiet prologue to the dance, and it emerges on those wonderful occasions, briefly described earlier, when the fading light of evening calls upon the whole chimpanzee troup, each sequestered in his tree, to drum in the darkness—the wood resounding each to each and all to the all-embracing night, as it isolates and enfolds them. To ponder this stirs us deeply, as if a door were opening to allow us back into our first world, something precious. And indeed brief reflection proves this to be actually so: not only do the African Bantu also drum in the darkness, but we can follow the line all the way down, through the Catholic Vespers and Angelus to the Protestant Evensong and "Taps" on the army bugle, prayers at bedtime to "protect us from the perils and dangers of this night." It feels exactly right, and astonishing to think it comes from that far back.

But surely the chimps can't be *praying?* No, but nor are they merely warning off predators, for the chorus of drumming and hooting sounds somewhat softly on the night: these animals, after all, are going to sleep. What they are addressing, as they lie in their nests, is above all the darkness descending; and the anxiety it arouses is consoled both by the sounds of self-assertion—"Here I am, in good heart"—and the sense of others not far: distant enough to inflict no presence, near enough to amplify and confirm my world. One can imagine a nascent interest in esthetics here, as pleasure is taken in the shaping of hoots and drumbeats both to challenge and commingle with the general song.

Of course the skeptics will urge that there is no question of addressing the sky at such moments, and the chimps are addressing only the predators, themselves, and each other. Such skepticism, as is so often the case, cannot be argued away but only invited to look again and consider that things may indeed be as they appear to be: the chimps *are* looking at the darkening sky, which has not only triggered this performance but is the medium through which their messages to predators, selves, and each other are mingled. What's more, one's ear tells one that this is indeed a chorus, and that the chimp is capable of perceiving this; and that for this to happen, the sounds must be addressing something sufficiently abstract and amorphous to reflect and engender the idea of "the troop as a whole"—to wit, the darkness descending. As with the raindance spectators in the trees, there is sufficient leisure (i.e., release from the obligation to respond to signals given) to make room for the perception of a signal, both serious and playful, sent to everything and nothing, everywhere and nowhere—the sky in fact.

From this signal emerges both the experience of the troup as unified substance and the sky as ubiquitous animation—a preliminary sketch of divinity. Some will say that the chimp's brain is insufficiently large for such thoughts, which must await, say, *Homo habilis* and rudimentary language at the two-million marker. They may be right, though I doubt it; but since the matter cannot be proven one way or another, the best one can do is make the case for such perceptions being plausibly chimpanzoid (or at least early hominid) and leave it to the reader to put his date on it.

An important part of the case is to emphasize that both perceptions arise in the euphoria such music induces: as in the charging displays from which these concerts derive, energy moves contagiously through the assembled in such a way as to suggest not only that "We are one" but "There is more of us: we have become larger." We may as well call this magic, the beginnings of magic: a spell, a charm, an incantation, a state of mind in which things seem unaccountably to unite and expand *instanter*, an improvement that will subsequently disperse. (The analogy with sex is notable: perhaps we should call sex "natural magic," progenitor of the cultural kind.) In the raindance the experience of magical increase is on the violent side, whereas in the evening chorus it arises soothingly, a kind of mellow hum on which we happily float into sleep.

As with the raindance, one imagines the sound arising in defiance of the sky, but then this defiance gradually melts into the hymn that mimes the darkness in which we are gathered—just as the raindance ends in the ecstasy of becoming the thunder. Thus, in both cases self-assertion leads from defiance toward ecstatic identification with the sky (in darkness and in light), a union that causes awareness of self to recede before and mingle with a growing sense of tribal totality—a moving spirit of contagious amplification. Again, in both cases all (or nearly all) are involved, and we can discern (particularly in the raindance) the pattern of chorus and principal dancers; and finally, both performances are constructed from symbolic materials with considerable scope for esthetic emendation. Almost operatic, we are in the foothills of art.

3

From here to the prospect of hominid dancing is not far. At the center of the campsite, which will become the hearth, the ceremonial meeting place, the threshing floor, and finally the agora, is the dancing ground, where in the evenings we often gather in a circle for a little drumming and hooting. It all began one day when a few of us felt the good vibes of mild contagion as we joined hands and stomped in unison. With every beat we grew and we grew, until we spread most everywhere. By now we have a perfectly serviceable drum, which we made by stretching animal hide over a hollow log; and though our singing is still nowhere near the gibbon's, it is certainly better than the chimp's. Antiphonal dialectic is beginning to emerge as we find that the secret of song and dance composition is in the movement back and forth from conjunction to opposition, from harmony to strife. We also notice the emergence of solo work from the ensemble (or *tutti*, as musical notation puts it).

The emergence of the solo is worth pausing over, a difficult moment, as the dance is fundamentally given over to the experience of unity in contagion, however much we may pull against each other within it. Moreover, as we shall see presently, the oppressiveness of alpha male has been particularly hard to bear recently, fomenting in us dire thoughts of rebellion. Hence when he breaks away from the circumference into the center of the circle to perform his solo (for it is he who does this), we are half-disposed to feel the magic die, and our eyes cry "show-off" as we watch him leap before us. This means, at the very least, that he'd better be good; and the circle, as he surges, tightens round his leaping, a mouth to crunch him should he stumble. Alphas, of course, are made of sterner stuff than the rest of us, and if our man is on form, his grace under pressure will astonish us all. At this temperature the dancing is terrific.

Let us look more closely. I suggested in the last chapter that in the beginning the men would dance in a circle around the women in recognition of the actual pattern of land-based monkey troups; and this indeed is what the !Kung do. But I imagine in those "progressive" tribes, where the first murmurings of women's liberation were heard, that this would lead, in due course, to dances in which all the adults, men and women, would unite on the circumference to address together the center of emptiness, both in recognition of tribal totality and to see if there was not something beyond all of us here, centering the dance. (Male chauvinists who think I am at this point cravenly capitulating to feminist importunity should simply imagine a proto-religious "warrior" dance from which the women are excluded; and good luck to them.) The dancing circle stomps in unison: even though one or other voice may distinguish itself (as in the evening chorus of the chimps), this is basically plainsong, we have no leader. We leave the center empty, like the evening sky, and into this potent emptiness our dancing is directed, unself-conscious, mirrorless, questioning. The circle is charmed because it encloses emptiness. The emptiness is charged not only because we have constructed it by joining hands and gazing inward, but also because it is what our dancing bodies address. As undifferentiated unity it both symbolizes ourselves, the tribal body magically unified, and also that other thing, not ourselves, the spirit that unites and augments us in contagious ecstasy—or does not. If the dance "works," if the mysterious *pneuma* rises and moves among us, it arises within the space that separates and unites us, in answer to our conjuring, our invocation. Like the wind and the rain and the evening darkness, the spirit of the dance comes invisibly from nowhere; but in the dance it is a nowhere that we may have constructed, somewhere, by joining hands in a circle.

And thus when alpha-male dares to leap into this magical space, he becomes (or is possessed by) the spirit while the music lasts. This is most disturbing. As alpha show-off he has broken the spell of our ecstatic unity, and reminded us of quotidian political realities (for we remember that in land-based monkey troups alpha-male moves at the very center of the troup); but as incarnation of *pneuma*, alpha-dancer becomes the dance itself, which may at any moment strike us down and yet is also the very source and proof of our unity, our vigor and our luck. The enormity of this is both fascinating and repulsive; and therefore should he stumble, we'll have him in a flash. The enormity of it also foreshadows a development of comparable significance in the ancient Greek Festival of Dionysus: when the "protagonist" emerges there from the eternal circle of the choric dance, something momentous is beginning; the dithyrambic is giving birth to the drama, the god incarnate is calling us into history. I shall say something about the religious origins of Greek tragedy in Chapter 7, but the reader will already have realized that we are dealing here with its prologue on the African savannah.

4

The next question we must ask is, "When alpha leaps into the center, who is he leaping for? Whose spirit does he incarnate? What does his dancing look like?" The answer, simple enough really, is "the buffalo." Of course he may in fact have begun with something less daunting like the eland, but I choose the buffalo on mythic grounds: not only was his cousin the bull the principal god of the neolithic, but he dominates those movies set on the American plains where most of us as children first meet the paleolithic. Also, not unimportant, the African buffalo is formidably fierce: the Bushmen, for example, find the lion easier prey.

As prologue to this, we must imagine primitive man, time out of mind, admiring the appalling efficiency of a pack of hunting dogs or hyenas as it closes on its prey: ah, to be seized by such power! And then to seize it! Less viciously, imagine him taking to the trees as majestic herds of buffalo, wildebeeste, eland, springbok, and elephant thunder by. Such thunder is almost as amazing as the thunderstorm, more so in the sense that the power becomes visibly incarnate. What makes a herd at speed so thrilling (even to our jaded palates today) is not just the beauty or the surging power but the sense that this amorphous body, this seething mass of unintelligibly pounding hooves, seems out of control, its direction unpredictable. Not only do the hooves represent the most convincing death imaginable (a stomping beyond dismemberment), but their tumult represents the power of chaos. Both in themselves and with regard to anything they might meet, they seem absolutely committed to the abolition of contour. What's more, the elements of playfulness, contagion, and increase also seem present: a gathering herd attracts its outriders, the animals seem to gather energy and size from those around them, and the man in the tree is comparably infected: his spirits rise as his pulse races. The whole tribe has been thrilled from time to time by the rush of the buffalo herd (though the youngsters are simply terrified); but alpha is deeply interested. Indeed he spends so much time up in the trees trying to get close to them that some of us think he may be almost sufficiently dreamy and negligent for us to make our move and overthrow him.

Back at the campsite, life has become both more orderly and more dangerous since chimpanzee days in the forest—more orderly because more dangerous. Alpha rules until he is overthrown, and when that happens he is usually killed. Since we now carry weapons, we can no longer afford the luxury of the charging display: our instinct for the occasional bout of frenzied self-abandonment is confined to the dancing ground, and we find that what the dance may lack in actual fear and loathing is more than offset by the pleasures we discover in rhythm and song. Although the dance occasionally breaks up in violence, it usually leads us in the direction of sex.

And thus it is that one evening after getting close to a particularly stunning herd of buffalo, alpha makes *his* move, and leaps into the center of the dance. Why must it be alpha? Because only he will be bold and brave enough to be drawn to the buffalo, closer and closer; to defy the unwritten rules of the dance by breaking into the center; and above all, to dare imitate the movements of divinity. As our best hunter he is already more animal than man; not only strength, speed, and agility, but uncanny powers of tracking, of anticipation, of *imitation*. And as our brainy and imaginative leader, he has realized that the buffalo dance will be even more astonishing and intimidating than were Mike's kerosene cans. In sum, for anyone but alpha to dare all this would immediately provoke alpha's wrath and a terrible beating—unless of course the upstart were to prevail, in which case he would become the new alpha. Either way alpha does the dance.

Here we must once again entertain the skeptic who will say that all this is sounding like some feverish nineteenth-century poem; and that just as there are skeptics today there were skeptics then, who thought dancing was less real than hunting, and hence the dancing imitation of the buffalo was not such an act of daring. To this the answer is "yes but no": yes in that the pull between real and ideal, hunting and dancing, is always with us; and yes in that some irony is detectable even in chimpanzee charging displays (their "theatrical" element); and hence yes we may assume some element of make-believe from the outset: but no in that make-believe is also serious (if you doubt that, trying interrupting a child absorbed in playfulness); and no in that the dancing ground is the theater for ritualized aggression, which in those days was not at all funny (though jokes would be developing offstage); and no in that the discovery of divinity was of all things the unfunniest, for primitive man was capable (as children still are) of being frightened to death. As to the innocuousness of imitation, not at all: from earliest days the best of all chimpanzee games involve the young imitating the grown-ups; but though this is great fun it is also the high road to learning and development, to becoming what we are not (and essentially are). We become what we become by doing what we do, and *mimesis* lies at the heart of this simple mystery.

Thus when alpha imitates the buffalo it really *is* an act of daring, which our already existent sense of dramatic irony registers both as something like youthful play and *the thing itself*, incarnation of *pneuma*. Anyone unmoved by the dance may consult his neighbors later and be told that yes, in that intoxicated time and space, it really happened. In order to mock, one would need to have the experience of divinity located elsewhere; and this, on the day of its discovery, by definition one does not have. And clearly, the more we dance, the more ritualized it becomes, and the less room there is for ironic subversion.

As I said earlier, alpha's leap into the solo constitutes a quantum leap for the dance itself: our tame round robin now becomes truly antiphonal, and the dialectic of energies, one against all, all against one, expansion, contraction, love and hatred, grows truly fierce. Not only can we explore the body politic with astonishing presumption, but the dance also enables us to participate in the buffalo's divine frenzy without becoming intolerably infected by it. What is dangerous and electrifying in both the chimpanzee charging display and the thundering herd is that the energy released therein is unpredictable, out of control. Because the dancing ground is both real and unreal, actual and symbolic, it enables us to invoke the energy, and then before it becomes truly frenzied send it off again, thereby releasing us from its spell: as the Christian *Nunc Dimittis* says, "O Lord, now lettest thou thy servant depart in peace." What is involved here, which our recently acquired weaponry makes us appreciate keenly, is the ambiguous nature of divine energy: a certain amount of it is life-enhancing, and a little bit more is lethal. This ambiguity will set us in due course to imagine divinity as something that "pollutes" the person in contact with it unless his exposure is regulated by the laws of taboo. It is worth noting that these laws, which invoke and dispel divinity, and which properly absorb a good deal of the anthropologist's attention, are originally esthetic: what protects us from overexposure to divine energy on the dancing ground are the lines drawn upon it, the rules of the dance, the shape it takes.

Ah, but these lines will soon enough prove unable to contain the energies released within them: there is too much at stake. When alpha leaps for the center his political power doubles in one roll: he is now both king *and* chief-priest, having just invented shamanism. This is infuriating, since, for reasons largely to do with the women (which we shall examine in a moment), we have been looking lately for ways of *reducing* his power; which of course he sensed, and so intensified his researches into buffalo magic.

Look at him now as he mimes the buffalo. He does it so well, under the intense pressure of our eyes and limbs, and yes, the sustaining thump of our feet as we beat out the rhythm against the drum. He does it so well that he really does *become* the buffalo (thereby inventing sympathetic magic); and as the mystery of this transfiguration is borne in upon us we are drawn even closer to him. And then something truly astonishing may happen. Since poetry does this sort of thing better than prose, let us call upon Coleridge to help us through it:

> And all should cry, Beware! Beware!
> His flashing eyes, his floating hair!

> Weave a circle round him thrice,
> And close your eyes in holy dread,
> For he on honey-dew hath fed
> And drunk the milk of Paradise.
>   "Kubla Khan"

As our magic circle is woven ever more tightly round him, the spirit of the buffalo suddenly leaps the gap and infects us; and when the stomping finally stops, alpha's body is torn in pieces. Perhaps he stumbled first, perhaps not. In any case we eat him, then and there, all of us, raging for the buffalo version of honey dew and the milk of paradise. Remorse can wait for tomorrow.

5

Thus our first experience of holy communion. Before we can explore its religious dimension, however, we must call a "time-out" and engage, albeit perfunctorily, with the mainstream of anthropological thinking in our century; for our story intersects with another one, secular but absolutely crucial for human evolution, called "The Instituting of Exogamy," which literally means "marrying out." The move into exogamy was momentous for human affairs because it ordained that henceforth breeding females be assigned by *rules* rather than simply snatched by the powerful. The best account of exogamy's origins, in my view, is the one Freud gives in *Totem and Taboo,* and in what remains of this chapter I shall outline it, suggest some modifications, and further propose that in fact the two stories coincide; i.e., that exogamy was discovered in the aftermath of our catastrophic collision with alpha-shaman on the dancing ground. Regrettably, this will involve leaping over some fairly dense abstractions, for which I apologize, but it cannot be helped.

The reader will remember that in hard-living baboon troups, males live dangerously and hence are regularly outnumbered three to one by the females, and sometimes by as much as nine to one. Also, because of the dangerous predators, their society is much more hierarchically stratified and given over to dominance displays than are the more easygoing chimps. And so, when the living is not easy we find baboon harems in the desert; that is, the dominant males monopolize several females, and the young subdominants have none. This creates much tension in baboon land—as it does among the harem-keeping gorillas.[2]

It is commonly assumed by students of hominid man that we baboonified ourselves considerably during our early testing time on the savannah; and this probably meant harems for the lords, and nothing for the commoners. As conditions improved, however, and the male-female ratio evened out, and the young hunters grew increasingly competent and bold, and the women were capable of doing it *any* time, one imagines the pressure rising considerably on the lords to share the wealth.

Whether or not all or most hominid bands were haremized in early days cannot be known. But Fox argues in *The Red Lamp of Incest* (1980) that whatever the local variations may have been, the following structural features were almost certainly universal:

a) a fundamental division between the dominant and the peripheral males;

b) access to the breeding females controlled by the dominant males;

c) peripheral males having to work their way in to the dominant center and access to the females by one means or another: many failing.

Fox comes to these conclusions after exhaustively reviewing both the primatological and anthropological evidence, and I find his arguments convincing.

The huge question that has fascinated anthropologists throughout this century is, "What happened then?" How did we shift from hominid harems to the arrangements almost universally adopted by primitive humans, matrilineal kinship networks built upon exogamy in accordance with the incest taboo—in a word, the rule of law. To many minds this looks very like the origin of culture: not only is it a huge leap for man to make, but its universality cries out for an evolutionary explanation. To leap so far man must have been in deep trouble: some kind of catastrophe? What is it that everywhere happens "in the beginning" to call forth such a universal response?

Ah, but who says the response is universal? Surely once we move into the world of kinship and exogamy we stop evolving as a species and start elaborating the unique cultures that manifest human diversity? Yes and no, say the anthropologists and evolutionary biologists: there is enough common ground among human societies to justify the search for what one might call "cultural universals." *All* cultures classify their kin; that is, devise rules to govern breeding relationships, and these rules arise to replace the sheer power struggle whereby the older hominid males controlled the younger by controlling their access to the females. Thus the disposition to kinship has been selected for human evolution, bred into the genes to emend and replace the breeding instincts of our pongid forebears. This, very simply, is the argument that has exercised the best anthropological minds, from Frazer and Freud down to Lévi-Strauss. As visiting philosopher, my concern is only to summarize their thoughts, cast my vote for Freud, and suggest that the religious dimension has been sorely underrated by all of them.

6

When Sir James Frazer produced four volumes on *Totemism and Exogamy* in 1910, Freud pondered them deeply and produced a little masterpiece in 1913 called *Totem and Taboo,* which proposed, among other things, a cannibal meal not unlike the one I have just outlined. *Totem and Taboo* has been much disparaged over the years (by Lévi-Strauss for one), but it has found a distinguished ally recently in the anthropologist Robin Fox. His impressive book, *The Red Lamp of Incest*, patiently sifts the arguments and cites the evidence: any reader troubled by my summary breeziness will find all the background and bibliography he needs in Fox.[3]

The tangle of problems that Freud addresses in *Totem and Taboo* may be broken down under four headings:

1. The political problem: How did the young males persuade the old to share the females? Revolution?
2. Whence exogamy and the incest taboo?
3. What is the function of totemism?
4. Are we talking about myth or history?

Let us take them in turn. The political problem comes first, not only because it looks backward to the apes, but because it is the simplest. On this matter Freud takes his cue from Darwin and J. J. Atkinson, who proposed that the young males must have united to kill the horde patriarch in order to gain access to his females. (Freud adds to this that they would then go on to eat him, an idea we can defer for the moment.) Must the revolution have been bloody? Fox thinks so, and I agree, simply because the change involved is *enormous*. Also, to take exogamy as the *outcome* of quiet negotiation rather than its *origin* simply throws the problem back a stage, into the darkness. But the crucial point is that we are dealing here not with a *coup d'état*, whereby one group of tyrants is replaced by another, but with genuine revolution, whereby age-old patterns of dominance are replaced by something altogether new. One cannot imagine the boss males being simply *cajoled* into giving up such a major manifestation of their political power.

Second is the question of exogamy and incest. Why is it that as a result of this revolution (whether quiet or bloody), humans everywhere make more or less complicated rules enforcing and/or outlawing certain breeding relationships? Lévi-Strauss in *Elementary Structures of Kinship* (1969) refuses to speculate about some possible revolution and begins with what we know, exogamy as the first and brilliant composition of man the classifying animal, who divides his world into "us and them" and then negotiates exchanges between the two, exchanges that, like gifts, enrich the exchangers with bonds of alliance and communication in the broadest sense. There is much to be said for the tidiness of Lévi-Strauss's approach, and it has many adherents. Freud, on the contrary, like Darwin before him, felt that exogamy, a crucial event in human evolution, calls for an evolutionary explanation, however difficult and necessarily speculative the search might prove to be.

Central to his account is totemism, a word taken from the Ojibwa in North Ontario, referring to the widespread primitive practice of identifying a clan with an animal (or a plant) understood to be the clan's original ancestor, and hence not to be eaten by clan members except on ceremonial occasions. The importance of the totem meal to the development of Jewish religion was bravely and brilliantly noticed by Robertson Smith (1889) almost at the cost of his academic job, and the significance of totemism generally became apparent in the classic study of the paleolithic, Spencer and Gillen's *The Northern Tribes of Central Australia*, (1904). The bearing of totemism on Freud's story is this: having killed and eaten our patriarch, remorse leads us to unite as a clan around some totem (who stands in for the devoured patriarch we guiltily wish to forget) and renounce our sexual claim upon his (now our) women. These women (our kin) we offer as wives to another clan in exchange for theirs (thus incest becomes taboo); and we ritually remember this appalling day of alpha slaughter whenever we ceremonially devour our otherwise taboo totem animal. Lévi-Strauss in *Totemism* (1964) objects to this part of the story by pointing out that totemism is by no means universal among primitives, some totems are inedible, and so forth. Robin Fox retorts, correctly in my view, that edible totems are sufficiently widespread to be compelling. We shall return to this.

The fourth question is myth versus history. Are we talking about catastrophic events that actually took place in hominid evolution and then became wired as archetypes in to the phyletic memories of mankind (Jung's Collective Unconscious) or are we merely telling "just so" stories to amuse and console our ignorance? Crudely speaking, Lévi-Strauss says the latter, while Freud, Fox, and myself say the former. But the matter is complex: Freud in *Totem and Taboo*, understandably anxious to be scientifically respectable, writes his book in sober ethnographical prose until he comes to the central events, whereupon he shifts abruptly to mythic mode: "One day, the brothers who had been driven out came together, killed and devoured their father. . . ." (p. 141). This shift into "Once upon a time . . . " has been noted and denounced by his critics, and indeed Freud half-anticipates the outcry with an apology in a footnote. And indeed some apology *is* appropriate, at least for the speed with which he nervously steams past such apocalyptic matters. If the once and for all Father-Feast does not call for slow motion, what does? The mythic mode, however, is another matter, *in principle* correct in my view, though it will take a while to say why. It is as if Freud's fine instincts are pushing him into myth while his "scientific" super ego is objecting up above, and the result is a somewhat hasty pudding.

In what sense might the mythic mode be appropriate to the recounting of these events? First of all, let us be clear that what is being proposed by Freud (and Fox and myself) is a real event in human evolution, the violent birthing of exogamous marriage; that is, there is a logic in human affairs that calls for an actual parricidal catastrophe, in the wake of which totemism and the incest taboo establish the structures of matrilineal kinship for the human mind.[4] We must imagine this cannibal meal being actually eaten by the, say, ten bands of hominids roaming the African savannah in the year dot. Of these, say five break up in psychic and political confusion, wandering away into madness, death, and perhaps assimilation by the other five, which succeed (perhaps only after repeating the experience several times) in establishing the kinship structures that both prevent the recurrence of the parricidal meal and enable us to half-remember its terrible beauty on ceremonial occasions. Thus the parricidal story is both about *what happened* to our forebears in historical time, and *what happens* to us all in mythic time when we ritually remember these events and the energies that call them forth.

But if the story takes place in mythic time, need it also have taken place in historical time? When we say "Once upon a time" are we not implicitly conceding that the "once" is neither here nor there, a fiction indeed, and that it neither matters nor can we know if there ever was a once? At the very end of *Totem and Taboo* (pp. 159–60), Freud considers this to be possible but unlikely, agreeing with Goethe that deeds come before words; and so do I.

Two further points. Like all major myths, this one still hums in the bloodstream, calling us to call it our own. Thus it is mythic in the honorific sense that we think of it as a narrative necessity, flowing *ab intra*, from the terms set upon the human condition, rather than as a contingent historical fact, determined *ab extra*. And finally, in my version it is mythic in a literal sense, in that it takes place on the dancing ground where mythic time originates. Modern Darwinians speak of patterns of thought being selected for human evolution, just as patterns of muscles were: and I would propose this piece of "mythic history" as one such pattern, by no means the least important.[5]

At this point some readers may still be feeling that it is ethnocentric if not imperialistic to impose this story on human evolution everywhere, a kind of mandatory freak-out on the road to culture. After all, cultures vary enormously in the way they play about with the incest taboo, with totemism, and with kinship structures; and many of them seem to carry no memories of chewing up Father. What profiteth a man to escape the strictures of scientific materialism only to fall into a new set? To fully engage these objections would involve restating the arguments made with care and intelligence by Fox (1980). What can be said here, however, are two things: first of all, the simple point that cultures evolve under local conditions, have been doing so for a long time, and hence it should not be surprising if some have forgotten (or altered) their totemism, and few have held on to their primordial memories with the single-minded intensity of the Jews (an intensity that, needless to say, lies at the heart of Jewish genius). After all, we must remember the psychological factor in the story: to eat alpha-shaman *is* the abomination, which we then (variously) deny, forget, half-remember, disguise, etc., in our approaches to totemism. In the circumstances, what is surprising is not that some weird tribe should totemize the mosquito (doubtless for its prolific properties), but that *any* should have the courage (or the folly) to totemize a venerated "ancestral" animal whom they taboo and then ceremonially devour once a year.[6]

The second point is more complex: Mary Douglas in *Natural*

Symbols (1970) has proposed an ingenious scheme for classifying cultures in terms of the seriousness with which they draw lines to protect their purity from the pollutions of trespass. At one extreme we find the Jews, much concerned with pollution, guilt, totemism, and violent blood sacrifice. At the other extreme we find such people as the Pygmies, mellow and laid-back African hunters whose idea of theology is to get a little stoned, do a little dance, and sing to the "*molimo*" who keeps their forest humming. How did the Pygmies lose their "seriousness"? Imagine the day, back then on the savannah, when a particularly wise and hippified shaman arose to collect a new tribe from the shambles of a particularly botched parricidal meal. With a vow of "Never again" he led them off to a nomadic life in the forests of the Congo, and told them stories that emphasized the beauties of their green haven, its tall trees, and the banalities of power, politics, and shamanism. One might be forgiven for thinking such people blest, even when, inevitably, they were bullied by their neighbors; but history's verdict is that they have been passed over, and so we cannot here follow them further.

We cannot because this book is concerned with the story that led from primitive Africa into history (via the Jews, the Greeks, et al.) to us. But what is it that decides whether a culture will insulate itself from history (like the Pygmies) or make it (like the Jews)? It may have more than a little to do with their response to the parricidal meal that begins human history. Thus the Pygmies say "What brings history on stage is an overdose of *pneuma*. We have had a taste of history, can tell that it will not work, and so forget it. We will repair to the forest, with no alpha, minimal structures, and a mythology that will seek to prevent history from bothering us again."

The Jews, on the other hand, say "We have tasted history, its terrible beauty, and so must remember this day in case history chooses to return and disrupt us again"; and their myths and rituals ensure that it does. Such wild speculation is thoroughly unscholarly, of course, but speculation is occasionally for fun. In any case, we of today, having supped full of *pneuma*'s historical irruptions, are disposed to admire what looks like the Pygmies' sage refusal. They have not managed to return to the garden, of course, but they seem to have given it a very good try.

7

So much, then, for a necessarily brief outline of the Darwinian-Freudian-Foxian root-stock on to which I would graft the story of alpha-shaman. The next question that must be addressed is "Why combine the two stories? Why not leave the cannibal meal to institute exogamy, complex enough, heaven knows, and deal with alpha-shaman somewhat later, and less luridly?" The simple answer to this, already intimated, is that the dancing ground is the natural and indeed the only plausible place for such an unnatural act to occur. To see if this may be so, let us run through the slides again, taking on some extra ballast from Freud and Frazer as we go.

We noted in previous chapters that the divinity of alpha chimp and alpha baboon is hedged not only by the strong right arm but also by complex patterns of deference; that is to say, we all hate to be bossed around, and yet we all dearly love a lord. We dream of toppling him and cringe at the thought. Such a mixture of love and hatred (which Freud calls "ambivalence" and identifies as the source of neurosis) showed up early and clearly in the human record, as Frazer illustrates again and again with his wonderful tales of sacred kings who were both worshipped and defiled, first absolutely cossetted then absolutely dismembered. One thinks, too, of the ritual rending of sacred Dionysus. Here, it seems, we really acted out our dreams of love-hatred. These tales inspire much of Freud's best writing in *Totem and Taboo* on the psychology of ambivalence.

With some sense of this ambivalence, imagine the dreams that afflict us nightly on the savannah. Now that we are all armed, alpha lies within the reach of all, his authority balanced on some perhaps still metaphorical knife-edge. And yet because the thing is so easily done, perhaps *was* done a while back when some crazy, low-ranking malcontent crept up on alpha in the dark and all hell broke loose in a general carve-up, our prohibitions against such violence have been doubled and redoubled: which in turn exacerbates desire, and so on. But it is not just that we fear the chaos of violence, its bloody contagion: we also *venerate* alpha, without whom we would have no luck in the hunt, nor with predators, nor with that tribe to the south that is leaning on our hunting territory. And this is not to mention the thunderstorms, when he masterfully takes charge and inspires us to defy the emptiness instead of leaving us to cower beneath the trees.

In sum, the ambivalence level is high: which is to say, in Freud's definition, we are very neurotic. Under such circumstances, is his idea of a political plot among the unempowered a plausible one? I say very unlikely. First of all, neurosis makes bad politics, and we would have to be quite cool on the day. Second, the very idea of such Machiavellian plotting so early on sounds a little modern. More importantly, to then go on and eat the corpse (a "rational" move to make sure of alpha's power) sounds distinctly newfangled. Here is Freud: "Cannibal savages as they were, it goes without saying that they devoured their victim as well as killing him." (p. 142)

One's nostrils twitch: very often when "it goes without saying," it almost certainly doesn't. And "cannibal savages" is a strange mouthful, to be sure: a taste for raw brains we doubtless shared with the chimps, but "cannibal savages," whoever they are, we certainly were not; and to propose the tearing and eating of alpha's body as if it were merely an item on the agenda is simply looney. Moreover, if it *were* merely such an item, almost routine, it would not produce the remorse and guilt Freud's story requires. In short, this simply won't do. In those early days not only were we not complacently cannibalistic, but our taste for raw brains was utterly terrifying, our prohibitions against *intra*-tribal ingestion absolute. Freud has at this point gone blank on the very complexities of patriarchal ambivalence that in this book he teaches us to appreciate.

When a master stumbles, it is almost always significant. My suggestion is this: because the issue was not just revolt but profound revolution, Freud realized that murder was not enough. After all, plots and *coups d'état* among the dominants occur frequently in the monkey world, and deposed alphas often go to the bottom of the pole, or wander away, permanently maimed. For one of these to die while being deposed would not be world-shattering. But what we need in order to break the dominants and institute exogamy is *precisely* something world-shattering. Freud secretly knew that the shattering of worlds is a religious experience, but since his career was dedicated to the debunking of such experience, and this made him a little nervous, he brusquely threw us a cannibal meal as if it were a usual fixture on the political menu; and then he hurried on, hoping no one would notice the lacuna.

The story of alpha-shaman addresses this lacuna. Nobody shatters a world "on purpose." To shatter a world, to break it beyond repair so that it must be *reconstructed,* we must be beyond ourselves, more or less delirious; and this happens only on the dancing ground. When alpha-shaman brings us the buffalo, he brings us not only a quantum leap in our imagination of the dismembering powers, but by incarnating them he becomes sufficiently "other," alien indeed, not only to override our taboo against alpha-violence but to release the consuming mandible passion. And *that* is what shatters the world. On a less delirious note, he also allows the women to participate, whereas Freud's story leaves them absolutely out of it. Are we to imagine the women hanging on the periphery, begging for a scrap of their erstwhile master? Very implausible. What we do know about ritual sacrificial dismemberments among primitives (such as the Greek *Bouphonia* to be discussed in Chapter 7) is that they require the participation of *everyone*—the guilt must be shared by all. What's more, if with Freud we imagine the murder as politically plotted, the women would probably hear about it (remember those lineages!) and be opposed. After all, they are geared to select alpha's genes, which they all enjoy under harem conditions, and civil war is bad for the children.

A not unrelated objection, technical but important, concerns the size of what Darwin called "the patriarchal horde," which Freud assumes to be an extended family under one father. Of course we cannot *know*, but I am persuaded by Lionel Tiger in *Men in Groups* (1969) and Robin Fox that the hunting pack of about a dozen males (plus females and children) was the probable unit, which might suggest a triumvirate of alpha plus two dominants holding off nine subdominant and adolescent outriders. Thus nine must kill and eat three in order to get the women: the politics grow positively byzantine. My version resolves this problem by isolating alpha *qua* shaman and relegating politics: *pneuma* has come among us and we unite in ecstatic seizure.

Let us look again at the scene of the crime. The crucial weakness in Freud's account is that the killing of alpha cannot be construed as world-shattering; but the dismembering of alpha-shaman can. Alphas are violently deposed when their powers fail, and are succeeded by the next alpha. But who will step forward over alpha-shaman's bones into the center of the circle? *No one*: each will know what fate awaits him, and sooner rather than later. The violent deposition of alpha when his powers fail is almost a natural event, like supersedure of the queen in a beehive; but we have just killed alpha-shaman *at the peak of his powers*, and then we tore him in pieces, just like a pack of hunting dogs, or hyenas, and then we ate him. But worse, far worse, is that in some profound sense we have destroyed and consumed *ourselves*, since in his prime alpha-shaman gathers and collects all our power and all our luck. And thus our world is truly shattered.

8

It would be irresponsible to conclude this part of the argument without nodding at least perfunctorily in the direction of Lévi-Strauss, the major opponent. Though undeniably the Big Man of postwar anthropology, he appears rather bizarre to Anglo-American eyes in his seemingly empirical disdain for the empirical. On the one hand, he helpfully indicates where Freud went wrong on important points (such as his overrating of the incest taboo), but then goes on to deplore the whole business of asking what happened in prehistorical time. All we can know, says he, is that the human mind everywhere classifies its kin and construes its experience through binary oppositions, and if we can know how it does *that*, we can know the human mind. The myths we study show us the mind playfully at work upon its own calculus: any attempt to relate them to *something outside* the mind, a life lived in joy and sorrow perhaps, is misguided. And as to those passionate and catastrophic events that may (or may not) have kick-started the brain into the constructions of culture, they are quite simply beyond us, and the desire to reach them is *un peu vulgaire.* Thus the ghost of Descartes still moves upon French waters, cleverly disguised in empirical modesty. I find this aspect of Lévi-Strass so wayward as to merit no detailed reply: it seems to me to have derailed a good deal of his monumental enterprise. In some regards, however, his thinking is undoubtedly brilliant, and we shall meet him again in the next chapter.[7]

In a sense, however, my detailed reply to Lévi-Strauss and the know-nothing party is the story I have just told. Is it myth or is it history? they might ask. It is both, I reply. Did every hominid band in the line of human descent eat the cannibal meal? Perhaps, but not necessarily. Here is a possible exception: imagine a large and thuggish band, good at hunting, bad at dancing, decidedly into sex and violence. Weak alpha, almost *primus inter pares,* strong cohort of subdominants, occasional orgies at night when some of the women take on the whole platoon. Bloodshed becomes almost routine, and perhaps two alphas in a row (plus their favorite females) get bumped off and their bodies mutilated. We are sadly approaching Charles Manson country, the band is weakening and crazy. Just before they collapse in confusion, a lunatic shaman expelled from a neighboring tribe wanders in with stories that soothe and settle their paranoid agitation. Bit by bit they work it out, stories and totem rituals that enable them to survive; but they never look good.

Let us then say that *most* of the surviving hominids ate the meal, and those that danced the best and tore the hardest were probably the first to come up with the totemized and exogamic solutions to prevent recurrence of the catastrophe. But even so, it would have taken more than a weekend; and this points to the irreducibly mythic element. We can know nothing of the incoherent process of trial, error, and near-miss, of dismemberings botched and bungled, by which we actually moved into the light of human coherence; nor can we know, in any empirical sense whatsoever, that the dominant form the drama actually took was the dismembering of alpha-shaman on the dancing ground. *But we do not need to know this*: what we do need is a story both coherent and concise, a fiction as defined in Chapter 1, which accommodates what little we *do* know and speaks plausibly of human beginnings. On this matter Aristotle remains the great authority:

> The poet's function is to describe, not the thing that has happened, but a kind of thing that might happen, i.e., what is possible as being probable or necessary. The distinction between historian and poet . . . consists really in this, that the one describes the thing that has been, and the other a kind of thing that might be. Hence poetry is something more philosophic and of graver import than history, since its statements are of the nature rather of universals, whereas those of history are singulars.
>
> *Poetics* 1451

Note well that the key to gravity here is in the slide from possible to probable to necessary. I am offering the story of alpha-shaman not as historically singular (though it might be) but as poetically universal; and if it is genuinely *"possible,"* i.e., true to the structural essentials, its being is probable or necessary. Three centuries later, Sallust somewhat coarsened Aristotle when he said that myth consists in things that never happened but always are. This plays too crudely with the idea of being, in my view, and for present purposes gives too much away to the scoffers. Aristotle's formulation keeps "being" as the mysterious bridge between happening and not-happening, a masterpiece of boldness and delicacy from this wisest of tough-minded philosophers. But enough of this for the moment: to persist in it would take us into the impossible tangles of "the incarnate spirit," and we have a story to tell.

9

Before proceeding with the story of alpha-shaman, it may be helpful to summarize the main points of our somewhat abstract but necessary excursion into the origins of kinship and exogamy. This is a book about divinity, and the idea of alpha-shaman's buffalo dance as a necessary aspect of its evolution is my discovery (or invention, if you will) based upon, among other things, a long acquaintance with Greek tragedy. Freud's book is principally about the violent origins of kinship in sexual politics. Although his book was written almost eighty years ago, in major respects it is wearing remarkably well, according to Professor Fox's review of the vast amount of data that has accrued since then. I have chosen to combine the two stories because, although it complicates the exegesis, it simplifies the narrative and makes it more plausible. By adding the dancing shaman to Freud's patriarch, I do not alter the terms in which the profound question of exogamy's origin is debated by anthropologists. What does alter is the focus of the story, from sexual politics to religious ecstasy; and this seems to me both to make the story more plausible and to correct an imbalance (call it a "prejudice against irrationality") that has characterized anthropology throughout this century, an imbalance at its worst in Lévi-Strauss. I shall now go on to suggest that the eating of alpha-shaman was, in its *religious* implications for human culture, as decisive an event as was the instituting of exogamy.

Let us return yet again to the scene of the crime. The hangover on the morning after this worst of all bad trips was prodigious. I have already indicated that our mixed feelings about alpha-shaman had, before the event, reached such a degree of ambivalence as to take us into the foothills of collective psychosis; and for a sense of this I urge the reader to consult *Totem and Taboo*, which in this respect still seems word-perfect. What it invaluably provides is a sense of the continuity of the love-hate we have always felt toward our authority figures. Ambivalence and its neurosis begin here (and in the ventral position, of course) and nothing much has changed: we can empathize altogether.

But since I have suggested we now think of alpha also as shaman, the cannibal meal is a good deal more disturbing than even Freud indicates; for not only have we abolished tyranny (for the first and not the last time) but we have also undergone our first introduction to the gods incarnate, as violent and disabling an introduction as may be. A huge concentration of neurotic energy has been released, and we are left bewildered, dismayed, remorseful, pleased; rocking in the arms of our first collective nervous breakdown.

Perhaps after the cannibal meal more violence was done, other scores settled: perhaps not. Perhaps in several instances the tribe dispersed, demoralized; or cobbled some makeshift arrangements that held it together until the next time, or the time after that; or until some predators (animal or human) completed the confusion. But we needn't try to imagine the chaotic aftermath. Suffice it to say that it was our first and worst breakdown: worst because we understood so little (and hence were disposed to deny) what we had done; and also because we had no ritual resources to repair the damage; and also because we had to think up some profoundly new way of dealing with our sexual and shamanic affairs. That so many mythologies record the world beginning in violence, often in the sacrifice or self-sacrifice of a god, bears witness to the enduring memory of these times.

How did we resolve the problems of sex and shamanism? The pieces of the sexual puzzle have now been assembled, and we can recapitulate. At the center is the open season for the females, which together with the ventral position will be making everyone (but particularly the younger folk) a good deal lustier than before. Add to this the sequestering of ovulation, and you have a full-time policing problem for the dominant males as they try to "ken" their breeding females. Add to this the probability that the females are pressing for more help in the nurturing of infants, a better deal in the exchange of vegetables for meat, and more say in the selection of breeding partners—not to mention less draconian punishments for those caught having a bit on the side. Add to this the increasingly violent tenor of our days, as we hunt larger game with better weapons and find deep satisfaction in the spilling of blood. And add to this, finally, the rumor that falling in love is even better than those hallucinogenic mushrooms we sometimes find by the river-bank, something we *all* ought to try.

The answer to this list of pressures and petitions is exogamy, as we have seen. The varieties of kinship system seem endless and impenetrable to the layman, but the crux of the matter is that henceforth breeding females will be allocated on the basis of *rules* rather than the dominant snatch-and-grab. Young males will henceforth acquire access to the breeding pool through orderly and usually painful rites of initiation rather than by fighting their way in. As regards the older dominant males, they have not been dispossessed—are they ever?—but they have been forced both to share the wealth and abide by the rule of law. The position of the females has been enhanced since martrilineal networks of kinship are woven through them—one might even suggest that kinship insti-tutionalizes the power they discover in love. And policing the whole system, however it may be arranged, is the incest taboo, the rudiments of which we inherit from our primate nature, and which proclaims to all mankind henceforth and forever that certain kinds of breeding relationships are prohibited. This, along with the prohibition against illegitimate bloodshed (the cannibal taboo we shall consider in the next chapter), forms the legal basis of the culture that rises from the ashes of the cannibal meal—sex and violence still riding together.

And what of shaman? What happened to him after we ate him? How did we prevent a recurrence of those dreadful events on the dancing ground? The answer is simple, and yet ultimately just as momentous as the instituting of exogamy: we made a rule that henceforth alpha and shaman must never be the same person. This sounds sensible, another rule to add to the list of breeding rules, but far from momentous; and yet, as I shall argue, the splitting of these roles opened a rift in the human psyche that we have been trying ever since to repair.

To say that shaman first appears in the buffalo dance is, of course, a schematic or mythic simplification of a process that begins, not in the chimpanzee raindance, but in the charging displays whereby alpha chimp routinely impresses, excites, and intimidates his troup-mates. We have already noted the theatrical, symbolical, make-believe element in these displays, which in the raindance is beginning to engage with what man will subsequently call divinity or *pneuma*. Another word for it, just this side of divinity, is *luck* (often called *mana* or *baraka* in anthropological literature). When alpha defies the heavens, we all cheer up, our spirits rise, and this rise gives us the courage (literally heart, therefore blood) to meet the danger and see it through. This process, already magical, becomes even more so when alpha, standing stock-still in the approach to a dangerous animal, can inspire us to do likewise: his very presence almost guarantees our success. He becomes the token, the bearer, of our collective power, our luck. Of course as individuals we each have our own access to these powers, which we try in sex, for example, and other dangers met alone in the dark. But in the truly serious collective experiences, when we face cataclysm in the hunt, the war, the storm or the drought, he is the one that counts, his presence all-important. With him we shall prevail: without him, we shall surely fail. He not only carries our luck, but in a sense he *is* us; for, as we have seen, not only did he introduce us to the invisible "blood-raising" powers that make us more than we were, but these are the very powers that through contagion give us the sense of being united in one body. From here to Frazer's sacred kings at the dawn of history, whose bodies are virtually nothing but the vessels that bear their culture's luck, seems hardly any distance at all.[8]

Thus it is that well before shaman's appearance in the buffalo dance, our world is by no means simply secular—quite the reverse. Look at the high points: charging displays, violence, thunderstorms, the evening chorus, the dancing ground, and the mysterious traveling we undergo in the ventral position (again the blood rising in a kind of contagion that makes us for a while more than we were)—all of them running with *pneuma*. What's more, they are not only the high points in our lives but the most important ones—exciting, bewildering, magical, terrifying, decisive, lethal. We are, strange as it may seem, not very far from the world of Thales in which "Everything is full of gods."

10

The usual name for this mentality is animism, and by common consent it animates every primitive mind. It locates the power and reality of things not in their manifest thinginess but in the invisible spirit (*anima*—wind, breath, soul) that lies behind, beneath, or above them. Get control of *that* and you are in control . . . Imagine the mist of animism slowly descending upon the chimpanzoid pragmatism of hominid man, the confusion and heated "philosophizing" that doubtless accompanied it. As we have already noticed, skepticism, not unlike poverty, is always with us, and there were surely a number of scoffers. But animism held all the heavy cards, irresistible in the end. And there was no hurry.

To put it simply, the animist believes that every object he encounters is alive just as he is, and hence is capable of actually *encountering* him, for good or for ill. Some years ago the theologian Martin Buber wrote an influential book called *I and Thou,* which distinguishes between the I-thou relationship in which two people face each other in all their human unpredictability, and the I-it relationship in which man operates upon objects in the light of the scientific laws (such as gravity) that control and predict their behavior. To turn a "thou" into an "it" is to break the Kantian moral law and deaden the universe. Buber's book, ultimately an existentialist plea for keeping some religious wonder alive against the dehumanizing tendencies of the scientific mentality, can also be seen, more simply, as a plea for a judicious retrieval of primitive animism; for in the beginning *everything* a primitive meets is a thou, susceptible to *pneuma,* and the it-world is beyond his ken. I say "in the beginning" advisedly here, for though this is true in principle, in practice such all-pervasive anxiety would paralyze him utterly.

Every intelligent animal is a practicing animist until he learns better. The young puppy on the lawn who chases and cringes and barks at the paper bag that is blowing in the wind is definitely in the grips of an I-thou; and when he becomes more experienced he will know that paper bags are not really alive or in fact animated. So with the chimp and hominid man. What I am suggesting here is that the discovery of *pneuma* as the abstract invisible power that governs everything will shake all the accumulated "scientific" expertise of early man (such as the ability to estimate whether this tree branch will hold his weight: "It will as long as no one has put a hex on it," he will have to say). But again, the word is "shake" not "break": the skeptics in those philosophical discussions around the campfire will point out that if we adopt the animist view we will become not insane, but rather like little children again, even puppy dogs, and the hostile pro-science tribe to the south will have us for breakfast; and he will be right.

The difference between man and the puppy dog is that whereas the dog "learns better," we cannot altogether do so. At the heart of our fall from animal grace into the difficulties of being human is a kind of irredeemable childishness: once our eyes have been opened to the darkness of *pneuma* that forever threatens to infect us, they must remain open, and blinking. This opening is the child's stare of wonder and fear, and though our adult task will be to reduce our helplessness through a judicious acquisition of scientific objectivity, we must not be tempted to overreach ourselves and think that *pneuma*'s darkness can be altogether illuminated and hence mastered. Such overreaching would close the child's eye that must remain forever open, and thus we would lose both our delight in Nature's wondrous movement and also our properly fearful respect for her inalienable power to call forth our irrational energies. The fall into history is paradoxical in many ways, not the least of which is that our assumption of adult responsibility includes the discovery and mandatory retention of a childish dependency undreamed of by the chimpanzees.

That said, it seems reasonable to suggest that the adoption of animism would have been disturbing and disequilibrating for early man, but not disabling; and furthermore, that the degree of disturbance in any particular tribe would be directly proportional to its animistic disposition. There are two obvious implications: firstly, the more "religious" a tribe, the more urgently it will develop and practice magical techniques for propitiating, invoking, and controlling the powers of *pneuma*; and second, the more it will hearken to its dreams.

The matter of dreaming is important. It is fairly well known that even in ancient Egypt and Greece, where the mastery of astronomical mathematics was astonishing, pharaohs and other men of substance would retire when in trouble to sacred compounds in the hope of a dream to direct their actions. Were these men wrong, "primitive" in the bad sense? I say no, and that we are wrong to think so. First of all, *serious* dreams are much more deeply impressive than most of our waking experience, and hence common sense would suggest that they matter. And second, who among us has not had a portentous dream at a time of crisis, one that told truly of the state we were in, and therefore offered, however obscurely, to clarify our confusion? It is only our scientismic belief about the unreal "subjectivity" of dreams that prevents our agreeing with primitive man that *pneuma* occasionally offers us glimpses of how it is stirring our depths with the energies of love and war. The pharaohs could agree to this without offending their reverence for astronomical mathematics: why can't we?

We shall return to these matters in Chapter 6, but I have moved into somewhat rhetorical mode because the issue of animism is a contentious one. The pro-science, anti-primitive lobby points to animism as a farrago of childish and neurotic superstition we have mercifully outgrown. Those of us who, in several disciplines, wish to limit the sway of the scientific I-it by a judicious retrieval of primitivism, must reply carefully: yes, animism *does* tend to encourage the neurotic and the superstitious, particularly in the beginning, but it also brings us priceless gifts that many today have lost: first, the awareness that Nature is alive and calls upon us to respond to its liveliness; and second, that no amount of celestial mathematics will alter the fact that our depths are in darkness, subject to unpredictable movements we can at best partially understand. The challenge posed by the animistic mentality is, as ever, to separate the good from the bad.

11

Let us return to the story. The disturbing adoption of the animistic metaphysic leads us to combat its potential tyranny with what the ethnologists call "sympathetic magic." I suggested earlier that such magic originates in the mimetic play of children, and it comes of age in the buffalo dance: if I can become my father by miming his movements, it will one day occur to me that such transformation may be more widely available, even interspecific. We might say that buffalo *pneuma* (or *anima*), which rides in the wind (*pneuma*), alights when it finds the buffalo shape: a sufficiently expert *representation* will lure it down, much as game can be lured by expert hootings. And when it enters alpha-shaman on the dancing ground, it really does so: he is possessed by the buffalo until the dance subsides.

Such activity is manifestly fraught with danger: a little bit of buffalo is life-enhancing, and a little bit more is lethal. How are we to regulate these infusions of *pneuma?* The answer lies on the dancing ground, those lines drawn in and around the dance that may govern the coming and going of buffalo *pneuma*—in a word, ritual. Sympathetic magic lies at the heart of both religion and science for the primitive mind, as we shall see in Chapter 6; but enough has been said here to indicate that its dangerous discovery will require brave and careful management on the part of shaman, whose powers vis-à-vis the hunters will grow as the mind moves ever deeper into animistic practices.

But why must alpha-shaman be split in two? The first answer is political: the reply to tyranny is always the division of powers. The second answer, more important, is religious: to prevent recurrence of the dismembering orgy. The reasoning here is straightforward:

a) Shaman's job is to incarnate *pneuma* on the dancing ground.

b) Such incarnation tends to arouse in us the intolerably orgiastic energy, for we fear and desire it even more than we do the discarnate thunderstorm.

c) Alpha is already the object of our ambivalent love-hatred, because he is the most real (the word means royal).[9] This means that, dancing aside, we already dream about eating him.

d) Alpha, the most real, is therefore the worst candidate for shaman: the best would be his antithesis, the most *unreal*.

e) How do you make a man really unreal? You kill him and then bring him back to life.

f) If shaman can have already been dismembered and magically reconstituted by the gods, he can conduct the dismembering *pneuma* into our midst without being torn apart by it; nor shall our teeth be tempted, for his flesh doubtless tastes of something else.

g) The paradox is perfect: at his most lively he is most dead—a lightning rod, in fact.

Is this what happened? The evidence is in favor. *Shamanism: Archaic Techniques of Ecstasy* by Mircea Eliade (1964) is the definitive work, some 600 pages long, and he concludes that shamans everywhere are initiated into their calling by means of ecstatic dream-trances in which they die and are resurrected. The preferred method involves the tearing away of the flesh, then the shaman contemplates his own skeleton, and then his organs are replaced, sometimes with jewels.

12

Our decision to split alpha-shaman in two also has an internal logic, as it were, for the two sides of this composite creature would soon pull in opposite directions. Alpha is alpha above all for his hunting skills: our superb animal, he is not only strong, fast, and fine-nosed, but utterly intelligent. Shaman, on the other hand, is something of a dreamer: fascinated by the buffalo, he has also been seen poking into beehives, of all things; and, less attractively, hunkered over rotting corpses, watching the maggots twist and turn. And whereas alpha is, as alphas are, a man of few words, shaman does tend, as evening draws in, to tell stories, some of them bearing little relation to what we did today.

The crux of this matter, as the reader will have noticed a few pages back, is in *representation*. Once alpha-shaman intuits that there is a kind of power to be sought in simulation, a power quite unlike that of the hunt, his days are numbered: he will dance the dance, we will eat him, and then we will split him in two.

Henceforth the two powers will grow apart, in opposition. Alpha will become a man of even fewer words, thickening and thuggening as he sharpens his tools in the evening light, less than best pleased to see the women and children listening to shaman's stories. Shaman, for his part, is in a sense number two, though in another sense he is nothing at all. At first he seems to be a match for alpha, and together they may run the show (much as squire and priest ran the English parish, time out of mind); but their alliance is intrinsically unstable. One day shaman will say "I bring you the best of the buffalo in the buffalo dance: I do it beautifully. What you do in the hunt tomorrow is messy and crude, rather vulgar." And the women, mischievously, will be disposed to agree.

The split that is opening up here will lead to the arguments that have principally engaged us ever since—between the doer and the thinker, the soldier and the poet-priest, the real and the ideal; and it will lead to the dream of their reunion, as in the god Apollo, who cleaves to both lyre *and* bow. The tension between these two will be felt as an undercurrent running through the rest of this book. At this point I might simply mention that at the mythic center of virtually every culture is the story of the hero, and the hero looks like alpha-shaman, who may save both himself and us by refusing to be split in two. The hero story is the subject of Joseph Campbell's best book, *The Hero with a Thousand Faces* (1968), in which (following Otto Rank) he attempts a synoptic survey of the world's cultures in order to extract a universal tale. It runs roughly as follows: heroic alpha-shaman goes out to meet the predatorial danger, which takes him down into death to face the abysmal dragons of dismemberment. He returns reborn and slightly altered, with a tale to tell of how both the lust for killing and the fear of dying may be transformed into energies that are life-enhancing rather than life-denying. At this point in the story, things tend to go wrong: we listen, do not listen, someone forgets . . . something intervenes—perhaps it's alpha sharpening up his tools, ancestral voices prophesying war. In the end we're back to where we were, before the magical voyage offered us salvation: alpha here and shaman there, not hearing each other.

Which leaves us only to wonder which one gets the pretty women. Did you know that Desdemona loved Othello for the stories that he told her? It's in the book, as Casey Stengel used to say: you can look it up.

13

Philosophical coda. The reader will have gathered that in this chapter I have offered a version of the origins of the distinctly human, and that it is quite similar to the Fall as envisaged in chapters 3 and 4 of Genesis. Man's concern with his origins is, was, and ever shall be absolute; and this is as it should be, because so much of how we think we should proceed today and tomorrow depends on where we think we came from. It is a structural necessity that all stories have to begin with a bang or a bump, *ex nihilo,* and this disconcerting fact is reflected in every myth of human origins, for all are constrained to say "One day something happened, and man appeared." Much of my argument thus far has tried to soften this bump by indicating that many things we usually think distinctly human can in fact be found among the chimpanzees; but narrative necessity has caught up with me, and forced my hand.

Like all good origin stories, Genesis begins with a fall from grace; from innocence to experience, from purity to sinfulness, from modesty to greed, from proper food to improper food, from ignorance to knowledge (via curiosity), and from being at home in eternity to being alienated in history. Ethnologists uneasy with the theological would say "from animal to man, from instinct to law, from Nature to culture," but the rhythm remains the same. All of these themes are registered in this chapter. In Genesis, we were having fun in the garden until one of our games got out of hand, and suddenly everything changed: we crossed a line whose gravity we could not possibly have appreciated until it was too late, and there was no going back. Unfair? Certainly, if you think there is an old man up there who owes us justice and should stick to the rules.

On this point my admiration for Genesis, otherwise almost boundless, draws back; for Genesis *does* suggest that we were warned, by a benevolent lord who seemed to be keeping an orderly garden; and even though Genesis 4, Genesis 11, and The Book of Job (to name only three) quite properly withdraw this suggestion, the damage done is considerable, and we have paid dearly for it ever since in terms of unspecifiable feelings of guilt. My version does, I think, steer clear of this, as any responsible treatment of the fall from instinctual innocence must do: alpha-shaman knows the buffalo are dangerous, but only a wimp would accuse him of hubris, and besides, our political restiveness was effectively challenging him to come up with something more impressive than he already had in his bag of tricks. And when we got carried away on the dancing ground, we were seized by nothing more mysterious or diabolical than the old hunting repertoire, and the line we crossed was simply the one that separates art from life, somewhat obscure even in settled weather. And just as Adam and Eve, being somewhat uneducated in the mytho-logical, did not fully realize that in eating from God's tree they were eating his body, so on the dancing ground we had no time to wonder if the body we tore was *pneuma* incarnate.

But it did change everything. What we discovered above all was that the old instinctual arrangements would no longer see us through. We had then to sit down and *think* about the enemy within and make laws to govern his appearance. The snake is an appropriate symbol for this figure, having been traditionally associated with the earth, with hiddenness, with knowledge, with eros, and with lethal violence. He reveals to us heretofore hidden energies, unsuspected powers (the knowledge that we are both good and evil); but since the other tree (which furnishes immortality) is out of reach, we must seek ourselves for the knowledge of how to control these energies. And since we are merely mortal, the laws we devise will never quite suffice, and will stand forever in need of improvement. The word for this is history.

Part of what still commends Genesis to our attention is its

insistence that the distinctively human begins with *knowledge*; for this accords reasonably well with the modern belief in "consciousness" or "self-consciousness" as our distinctive feature. Though not enamored of these terms, I readily admit that my story locates the devil in the neocortical expansion that unlocked our instinctual primate codes and opened the door to what the moralists call "free will," the philosophers "rationality" or "irrationality," the poets "imagination," the psychologists "consciousness," and so forth. What is important in all of them is to cleave to the paradox the snake so nicely symbolizes: we became free enough to be enslaved by passion, rational enough to be utterly irrational, imaginative enough to invent heaven *and* hell, and conscious enough to lose touch with our unconscious. Whereas the animal's life is guarded by an instinctive wariness, we are both terrified and stupefied as we take on the foreknowledge of death; for it both delivers us into morbid fearfulness *and* awakens the hope that death can be denied, in ecstatic experience and in the constructions of culture. In short, the Fall was not altogether Fortunate. That said, I am happy to concede that the "bump" that marks the feast of alpha-shaman is the recognition that henceforth and forever we shall die (though try not to) and must "consciously" make laws that will regulate our actions and our thoughts.*

Even though Genesis 3 never mentions sex, no one disputes that much of the knowledge we acquired from the tree-snake was of the carnal kind; and indeed the most widespread criticism of Genesis 3 is that the sexual factor is both overdone and heaped upon the woman. We shall consider this question in Chapter 8, but it could be urged that the present tale is somewhat deficient in the sexual connection. It is in the background, manifestly, and foregrounded insofar as the hunting ecstasy that overpowers us is clearly infused with erotic energy; but it certainly does not obtrude. Instead of the

---

*I concede this despite my belief that chimpanzees are "self-conscious" in certain respects, because even if they are, they do not "consciously" legislate; and hence culture *is* distinct from Nature, and so the mythological mind may continue to tell its stories.

sexual separation of Adam from Eve we find the alienation of alpha from shaman, a more mental or spiritualized depiction of the historical conflict between *yang* and *yin*. This might be thought more appropriate to twentieth-century concerns, or it might be thought typically evasive.[10]

Enough of this. Having reached the threshold of human history (by which I mean the origins of culture) we must now relinquish, or at least severely curtail, our grand ambitions to tell *the* story of mankind's evolution as it appears to the modern mind. The next three chapters will focus on major aspects of our attempts to recover from the fall of alpha-shaman; and though I shall try to keep the discussion as elementary and universal as possible, historical particulars will increasingly emerge, until the final chapter settles upon a number of specific literary texts. Such a fall into contingency is implied by the tale this chapter tells: what may redeem it is the ancient faith that universals may sometimes be discerned through particulars properly perceived.

PART TWO

ILLUMINATIONS OF THE SACRED:

The Lawlines of Culture

5 ⏐ DANGEROUS ECSTASIES:
The Call to Ritual Drama

The law is a wall.
—Heraclitus

Something there is that doesn't love a wall,
That wants it down.
—Robert Frost

The explosions of Chapter 4 have left us with a good deal of clearing up to do; indeed, so momentous was that buffalo dance, heaving so much of the human story into view, that we shall be lucky to have gathered the major strands together before the book ends. In any case, the more or less simple narrative we have been pursuing thus far must now be abandoned, and henceforth we shall be leaping from flower to flower, in the hope that by the end an intelligible picture will have emerged—no ill-considered collage but something strongly sinewed in the cubist style. The present chapter will focus on four major and related avenues to sacred ecstasy: hunting, war and cannibalism, beauty, and erotic love. In these one may discern the lineaments of *yin* and *yang*: hunting (and war) is mostly *yang,* the opening to beauty is mostly *yin,* and loving is a mixture of the two. What will unify the discussion is the general question of how the ecstasies that *pneuma* calls forth, and that overflowed so disastrously in the cannibal meal, were harnessed and regulated.

The word I have chosen for the measures we took in this regard is "lawlines," and we have met them already, in their origin on the dancing ground, where they measure the movements that both arouse and contain the energies of *pneuma*. Greek *nomos* comes very near the notion, for it means both "law" and "melody," the line that keeps the energies of the music within bounds. More generally, lawlines are boundaries drawn in the mind, or on the world, that channel the flow of emotion and separate things that become dangerous when mixed or juxtaposed. These lines constitute our map of the cosmos, the frame of things that keeps us from chaos, the way of our going. Like the Chinese *Tao,* they identify the path along which our life must move if the conflicting energies of *yin* and *yang* are to be harmoniously composed. Like all figures of authority, however, the lawlines call forth our ambivalence: if "the law is a wall," as Heraclitus says, prime symbol of what sustains our well-being, we also agree with Robert Frost when he says "something there is that doesn't love a wall."

Although the development of law codes and courts comes fairly late in the human story, the idea of lawfulness, of order, is as old as may be, virtually synonymous with the idea of cosmos itself, and nicely abbreviated in the adage "A place for everything, and everything in its place."[1] Its complement, needless to say, is chaos, to which we return when things are significantly displaced. As the Appendix indicates, this primordial idea of proper placement lies in the background of historical notions of the law: Greek *nomos* is originally "allotted pasture," and the Latin *lex* (like English "law") has to do with laying things down in the proper time and place. In order for things to be properly laid down, they must first be measured, laid out, separated from chaos: "Measurement began our might" sang Yeats in vatic mood, and in the background of this splendor we discern the *neuron* as humble line, thread, or cord, used to tie things into coherent bundles and to measure distances. In most primitive cultures a knotted line will magically bind one's adversary (lovers still "tie the knot") and the most celebrated instance of this in Western culture is the life-line spun, measured, and woven into a net by the Three Fates in Greek mythology. The knotted lines (or *peirata*) that compose this net are so fine as to be invisible but they are incredibly strong, and when cast like a hunting net over an individual, lay down or set forth his destiny, the way of his going. Since he cannot perceive these lines without prophetic powers, he will from time to time bump into them, trying to cross uncrossable lines, seeking what is not his portion; until the net finally closes around him, producing its last gift, his death. Not unlike the *peirata* are the Druidic ley-lines, the Chinese dragon-paths, and the Australian songlines, all of which attempt to discover lines of concentrated power in the earth, pneumatic pathways that are life-enhancing if properly traveled, bad luck if improperly crossed (the notion of crossing, as the word "transgression" would suggest, is implicitly antagonistic). They linger on in the childhood game many of us played running home from school: "Step on the crack and you break your mother's back." Whether or not such mappings made good science (electromagnetic fields of morphic resonance we ken no more?) is not my concern (though the skeptics must pause over the inscrutable dragon-paths of Chinese acupuncture): I mention them only because they are, like the lawlines of this chapter, instances of the cosmogonic enterprise— "good to think," as Lévi-Strauss would say.

Since the search for lawlines will take us some distance from everyday matters of fact into the world of dream and magic, let us begin with the most elementary form of the religious life, the ritualization of the hunt (and the war party that would sometimes emerge from it), and preface our discussion with a brief look at such empirical evidence as there is about these matters in the earliest days. Needless to say, it does not amount to much, but as a background against which to set one's meditations, one could do worse than consider Darwin's remark (in *The Descent of Man*) that "No country abounds in a greater degree with dangerous beasts than Southern Africa." In addition to the predators we have already mentioned, recent speculation has suggested that a leopardlike cat called *Dinofelis* may have been a specialist killer of large primates such as ourselves, which would have provided a clear focus for our nightmares, an early sketch of the devil, and a pressing incentive for the improvement of our hunting skills. As regards war, the remarkable number of hominid fossils found with skulls broken so that the brains could be extracted suggests that we retained our chimpanzee taste for this delicacy and practiced a good deal of cannibalism. On a larger scale, the extinction of our three relatively brainless australopithecine cousins (*afarensis, africanus,* and *robustus*) remains a mystery, as does the much more recent disappearance of the by-no-means brainless Neanderthal man when *Homo sapiens* arrived some forty thousand years ago. The answer may lie in a cannibal stew.

As regards hunting, it is important to remember that chimpanzees do not like scavenging. Unlike the truly professional predators, who often don't mind if someone else does their work for them, chimps only want to eat meat that they have killed; which is to say that the spilling of the blood is part of the meal. To put it the other way, hunting is only partly about eating. The other part, call it bloodlust, is about the gods, and will concern us presently. It is noteworthy that our human disdain for scavengers (such as the jackal and the hyena) is not only in some degree "religious," but like so much else that we take to be human, does not originate with us.

On the other hand what *does* originate with us is the sharing of the kill. Among the chimps, as we have seen, the kill is usually somewhat distributed, but this is an unruly, even chaotic affair. As early man's kills got larger and more distant from the home-base, the need to transport and distribute them equably would have become imperative (particularly as we became increasingly well-armed). Among contemporary primitives the distribution of the carcass tends to be an intricate and solemn affair, from which one can infer a good deal about their social relations—the Bushmen have been observed extracting no less than sixty different portions from one butchering. Indeed it could be argued that in such division one sees the rudiments of law, the origins of culture.

Evidence of serious hunting and simple stone tools appear with *Homo habilis* around 2.5 million, and the stylish Acheulian hand-ax appears at 1.5 million. What is astonishing about this tool is not only its prettiness but that it remains more or less the same until 200,000 in Africa, 100,000 in Europe. It would seem that we found the Platonic Form of the handax on our first try, as well as the important truth that useful things should also be beautiful. The biological base for our love of beauty lies in what the evolutionists call sexual selection, that process whereby the pretty ones tend to have more reproductive success than the ugly. The poets have always known that the gods are pleased by beautiful things, and we shall consider this matter in the chapter's latter sections.

These abstractions may be given some focus by a brief sketch of the remnants of a very old hunting and gathering culture, the much-studied and much-admired Bushmen (or !Kung) from the African Kalahari.[2] The hunter-gatherer group consists of about thirty individuals, six families. The pattern of life is nomadic for most of the year with an annual festival, where many bands gather, usually in the dry season around the water holes. Such festivals provide, along with much dancing and story telling, the opportunity for marriages, disputes, and new alliances: fission and fusion among the various bands. The preferred way of resolving disputes is by talking them to death, sometimes at great length. They do not wage war, but this is almost certainly because they lack manpower in their straitened circumstances: they certainly fought bravely in the past, against both black and white intruders. Both men and women work a two- or three-day week at hunting and gathering, and a great deal of time is spent socializing. There is an almost totemic reverence for the eland, which is hunted with poisoned arrows, and almost two hundred species of plants are gathered by these expert botanists. Although food is not as plentiful as it was, and indeed some studies suggest seasonal undernourishment, there is still game in the Kalahari, and a large animal will feed a band for three weeks. Predators include the lion, the leopard, and the hyena.

!Kung society is remarkably equitable and democratic, no trace of alpha-male. The women give birth every four years, in somewhat ritual solitude, whereupon they wean the previous child, who has been much-loved (by Western standards) and seems to be the stronger for it. Although the society is admirably gentle in various ways, wife-beating occurs, and the homicide rate compares with that of most American cities. The central importance of love is beautifully registered in what Van der Post calls their "Song of the

Wind and the Rain," where the woman's longing for the rainy season (upon which survival depends) is sung as a love-call to her absent hunter.[3] The culture's amazing rapport with an inhospitable Nature is celebrated in music and story, and also in the graceful paintings that decorated their caves when the culture was still robust. Perhaps most impressive to Western eyes is how they thrive on little and share what they have, a sharing ritually enforced and commended in the distribution of food. Their easygoing approach to time and labor has distracted many from the fact that they have been losing a serious war of attrition against white men, black men, and climate for well over a century; and though they live nonchalantly, they live right on the edge of the impossible. "Lived," I should say, for the recent terrible drought (1980–88) has devastated their numbers and almost certainly forced the last of the "wild" ones in from the bush to drink the white man's water. Another little candle, crucial to human hopefulness, seems to have gone out. And yet, even if we must henceforth speak of them in the past tense, they may still live on in our remembrance; and in this we are fortunate, for there is much they could teach us if we were disposed to learn.

HUNTING

Let us now try to imagine a hunting party in the very early days. In the simplest sense we are out for treasure, to increase our substance; and indeed as the pack moves out to stalk the quarry we may see fear and anxiety in the hunters' eyes, a wish that there were more of us to face the danger. This wish for increase is perhaps exacerbated by the need for stealth, contraction, camouflage, to make ourselves smaller. But once the quarry is engaged, the opposite magic is immediately invoked: we must become more, raise the blood, release the violence and resolve into one body to subdue the body that opposes us. Our war-whoops both advertise and establish the flow of *pneuma* that binds us together. It is not altogether unlike the dance; or should one say the dance is like the hunt? I suggest we refuse the question and simply say they resemble each other; thus we would dance into *pneuma* even if we didn't hunt into it, and vice versa. In fact we do both, which means that the two clarify and reinforce each other.

The point, in any case, is that hunting does not arise from the seriousness of need but, like the dance, from play. The omnivore chimps go hunting for fun and for mayhem, and the simple proof of this is that *they do not scavenge,* by which I mean they do not eat carrion, but only meat they have killed themselves. At Gombe they hunt about once a week, as we have seen, which is a measure of the surplus aggression they have "on hand." The word I have used to describe their non-ingestive desires in the hunt is "bloodlust," and the human disdain for scavengers proves us to be of their party. This point about scavenging is very important, and has been somewhat muddled in recent years by certain proponents of the anti-Tarzan faction who suggest that early man learned from professional predators like the lion and the hyena that scavenging was the easy way to a meal, and hence that to speak of Man the Mighty Hunter is a load of sexist nonsense.[4] I think they are wrong: if the chimp doesn't scavenge, and the human disdain for scavengers is universal, it looks as if we are talking about a fairly old instinct. While I think it quite certain that early man scavenged when hungry, I also think it quite certain he did it reluctantly and more or less shame-facedly. *Why* this should be so seems to me a mystery of considerable significance, which lies near the heart of our religious origins and has to do with mutilation. To say that the chimp is unmoved by the already dead *may* be quite straightforward, a matter of proper food classification for the aspiring carnivore; but when it comes to early man, it becomes appropriate to speak of something like a taboo against food unearned by the ecstatic exertions of killing.[5]

In any case if, for both chimp and human, meat is palatable only when warmed up by the exertions of killing, then in Lévi-Straussian mode we could regard these exertions as a kind of archaic "cooking," an activity that makes the food fit for consumption. By calling up *pneuma* in the chase, the animal becomes more nourishing. The blood we raise and risk is mingled with that of our prey, whom we seem to be courting in a dance of death. By being carried into a dangerous zone of risk and unpredictability, and by offering ourselves to the Luck of the day, we may rightfully take possession of this foreign body, and make it part of ourselves. Moreover, if we succeed, it is not we ourselves but Luck that has prevailed, which we shall learn to call the bounty of the gods. The animals we catch are both the spoils of war, in that we have despoiled them, and treasure, a gift of the gods, *pneuma,* life more abundant. It is no wonder that from earliest times we have discerned the analogy between the chase of the hunt and the chase of love.

As the hunting party moves out silently in search of its quarry, the mind is tuned to the animal in question. In order to make him come we think about him, and as our thoughts turn to him we may feel ourselves turning *into* him somewhat, imitating his walk, his call, or his manner of tracking spoor. This one might call "anticipatory merging" with the prey, and is very likely an ancient instinct that evolution has preserved because it makes for good hunting— even today's human hunter still feels traces of it.[6] This uncanny business of merging is also, as the words "make him come" above would suggest, a likely source for the discovery of sympathetic magic, a suggestion that gains plausibility from the fact that primitive hunting expeditions are often preceded by dances designed to invoke the spirit of the animal in question. Among the Mandan Indians of America, for example, George Catlin (*North American Indians,* 1844) witnessed a buffalo dance in which the hunters wore buffalo masks to "make him come" (their words), followed by a hunt in which they set off disguised in buffalo skins.[7] By thus magically "turning into" the quarry in advance, the hunter is less daunted by the moment of truth when he must embrace, rend, and consume his adversary: the stranger has become less strange, one has staked a claim.

When this moment of truth comes, the blood that we have raised in the pursuit will, with luck, be spilled only by the animal we kill, and we may drink it then and there, not only to prevent its congealing but also in grateful recognition of the Power that has strengthened and united us—(some echo of this even today in the initiatory "blooding" of a new member of the fox hunt).[8] Indeed it will occur to us soon enough that the power of *pneuma* is actually *in* the blood: what makes us think this is that we see the blood symbolize, in the simplest way, the power we feel rising formlessly and invisibly within both us and the animal we chase, a power that both unites the pack in full cry and connects it to the animal it seeks. In the moment of mutilating triumph the blood appears, the sign, nay epiphany, of death and of life renewed. The reverence for blood is universal among primitive peoples, and even the sophisticated Greeks believed there was no magic more lethal than bull's blood, absolutely taboo. (Appropriately enough, Bull's Blood is now the name of a reasonably good red wine, on sale at discerning wine shops everywhere.)[9]

Often the animal that we kill is beautiful—an eland, say—noble, graceful, proud, a proper object of admiration, emulation, even veneration; and it will occur to us that this animal and its energy are in fact what have collected, focused, united, and increased our own—echoes here of alpha-shaman and the buffalo dance. This impression is confirmed in the sharing of its blood, and subsequently when its meat is shared and eaten together in the campsite, where our bodies are *actually* increased by the weight of its nourishment. Thus we are led to identify with the animal, both when alive and dead, and to find in its scattered body (first dismembered and then masticated) ourselves magically gathered, incorporated. By killing and consuming it we have gained access to the magic of *pneuma,* which not only enlivens us but confers identity upon our collective self, creating a sense of "the tribe." If we find ourselves in the eland, we may think of it as "our" animal, our patron saint, even our ancestor, who sends aspects of his magically self-renewing body to feed us. Such thinking will ultimately lead to the idea of totemism, which rightly fascinated ethnologists early in this century but which has latterly been demoted in some circles to the minor leagues of kinship classification, largely because of the imposing intellect of Lévi-Strauss. Despite this demotion, one can see in the "totem" animal an important early study of the god who sacrifices himself for his people.

However we construe our relationship to our prey, it must be seen as a gift, precipitation of *pneuma*; and as we increasingly ritualize the killing and the eating, we find these ritual forms consecrate two of our most important laws: first of distribution, that each in his separateness be given his portion, and second, that what we legitimately consume is animal not human flesh—traces of alpha-shaman again. So important is this second law that we find even so late a figure as Aristotle saying that cannibalism is the defining feature of barbarism. These laws may be seen both to embody *pneuma* and save us from its excesses. The flesh and blood manifestly contain it and also were seized in violence. On the other hand, the law of distribution returns us from pneumatic unity to our separate selves (while again uniting us *quietly* in the flesh we eat together) and the cannibal taboo reminds us where an excess of *pneuma* can lead and thereby condones the violence we *have* unleashed. Thus *pneuma* is *harnessed* by the lawlines of the hunt, which enable us to ride right up to the edge of liveliness without crossing the line into chaos.

As these aspects of the hunt are gradually elaborated into ceremonial rites, an idea of the utmost importance is being gradually engraved in the human imagination: that what enriches and unites us is the gift of life, violently taken, a gift that somehow enriches us without impoverishing the divinity that gives. If, in the hunt, divinity (a vague word to substantiate the pneumatic powers) cheerfully amputates a part of itself for our benefit, is this not our first experience of sacrifice, a self-wounding that mysteriously enhances? To see if this may be so, let us look again at what seems to be happening. First of all, it is important to realize (though this is slightly to get ahead of ourselves) that as the primitive mind began to imagine divinities, the animals that run in the wild were all seen as aspects of a divine body (called by the earliest Greeks, for example, Mountain Mother or *potnia theron,* Lady of the Wild Things); and so the idea of auto-amputation is not bizarre. What's more, such divinities had amazing powers of self-regeneration (not unlike the Nature goddess of Darwinian evolution) and so the possibility of cheerful self-amputation is equally not bizarre. In the hunt we move into the unknown and meet *pneuma* in the orgiastic amplitudes of violence, where the distinctions between hunter and hunted, pleasure and pain, life and death, seem to dissolve in the flow of blood that manifests the ecstasy connecting each to all. (The analogy with sexual ecstasy is obvious.) When we return to ourselves (ecstasy is from the Greek *ekstasis* which literally means "standing outside oneself"), we not only have the prize to prove we were not dreaming but we feel remarkably good: not only about ourselves and each other (fraternal aggression mysteriously vanished) but about the divinity that portions out our Luck and Unluck. There can be no question in our mind that both the encounter with divinity and the gift that remains its token were freely given. If this were not so, why is it that we feel so good? Indeed it would be fair to say that to encounter *pneuma* in the hunt is to encounter the superabundant.[10] If this is so, if divinity shows itself to us in a gift whose painful death is a sign of divine pleasure and whose loss is a sign of gain, then this may also be how we show ourselves to divinity (the idea of reciprocity arises naturally since we become identified with divinity while the ecstasy lasts). Thus, for example, to cut off my index finger and offer it as a gift to divinity (as the Crow Indians do), a gift that enriches me and whose pain manifests a deeper pleasure, may be a sign of courage (which is heart, which is blood) but more importantly is a sign that *pneuma* runs within me, does not disdain me, and will favor me with its power and its Luck. Such giving originates in the ecstasy of self-abandonment, and only in its decadence will it appear as guilty self-mutilation or a calculated *quid pro quo.* Its proper name is *sacrifice,* and though it takes myriad forms, often breathtakingly difficult to construe, and sometimes quite simply insane, its significant presence in every culture known to man nominates it, in my opinion, as *the* elementary form of the religious life. To sacrifice means literally to make sacred, and our first way of doing this was to tear living flesh until the blood flowed. Our second way was to do something metaphorically similar in the sexual embrace. Though we are not quite ready to address the sacrificial *per se,* I mention it here because it originates in the shadow of our oldest rites, those of hunting, rites that evolved slowly but surely from the day we left the chimpanzees some six million years ago in order to pursue the carnivorous mysteries.

If on a good day the hunt proclaims the coherence of culture (in whose shadows we can discern the sacrificial abyss), what happens on a bad day, when the hunt is unlucky, the wrong blood is spilled, and one of our hunters is dead? Such a day is a very important one to consider, for it raises, in a subtler and more disturbing way than does the case of straightforward murder, the problem of intra-tribal or "endemic" violence. After all, we have a strict taboo against lethal fighting, and when it gets broken, we take appropriate measures to restore order. But when the hunt goes astray, the *pneuma* we have called up has somehow turned against us: our most excellent and habitual game has turned to nightmare, and everything is called into question. As such it will stand as the archetype of the violence that boomerangs, that mysteriously gets misdirected and mistakes its quarry, threatening to infect us all. To consider this difficult question, however briefly, will involve some leaping forward into Greek mythology, which I hope will not be disconcerting.

The reader will recall how messy, crude, chaotic, and even disgusting is the pandemoniac violence of a chimp kill; and one can safely assume that the human kill would have been almost as chaotic for a very long time—the pleasingly abstract bow and arrow, after all, was not discovered until very recently, about 13,000 B.C. Thus what made the hunt dangerous was not just the possibility that the prey would become the predator and take one of us with him, but that in the pandemoniac thrashing of bodies we would stomp one of our own party, perhaps even "accidentally-on-purpose," subconsciously settling some score. In short, on a bad day the quarry is mistaken.

To lose a hunter we can ill afford is sad enough: to lose one mistakenly, by our own hands, is profoundly disturbing; and the hunt would sometimes end in lamentation instead of celebration, in loss instead of increase. Instead of receiving a gift, we gave up one of our own: the difficult idea of gift as sacrifice, and sacrifice as gift, is not far off. The myths that track these memories, such as those of Adonis and Osiris being torn by the boar, register not only the two-edged blade of *pneuma*, but also move toward the foothills of human guilt—Osiris is in fact killed twice, the first time by a pack of thugs he thought his friends, the hunter's nightmare indeed. When the hunter is hunted, someone is holding up a mirror in which we can find our own features drawn: not only is there the idea that the animal we hunt may be our brother, in whose death we can see our own figured forth, but when the one we kill is *in fact* our brother we have stumbled upon the idea of murder, and the one we kill may even be ourselves (his corpse pre-figuring our own). Such killing is truly lamentable, and we will return to the dancing ground and wail together, finding some relief in sharing the burden. Ultimately, such lamentation will lead to the notion of reparation, the redemption of violence in gentleness and sexuality, as exemplified in the rites of Adonis, Osiris, Dionysus, and Jesus.[11]

When the hunt miscarries, the women will of course join in the lamentation: but will they *really* join the men? Although no longer allowed to accompany the hunting party, the woman can remember what fun it was in the old days, and she certainly enjoys the taste of the meat that is its prize. And yet because she is no longer allowed to be a hunter too, and because as "professional" nurturer she runs with the hares and not the hounds, she is the "natural" one to develop the critique of hunting; and this will be particularly so when we are not relying on meat for sustenance. Thus when the man returns sorrowing to the campsite, he must address not only the woman whose hunter was killed today, but the whole body of women whose suckling babes bid him ambiguously good-day when he leaves for the hunt: "Is this roulette with *pneuma* really necessary?" their eyes seem to ask. And behind that look is some reference to their hunting analogue, the dangerous moment of childbirth and its monthly bloody reminder. As in the hunt, the woman's moment of truth is a bloodiness that is either the celebration of life enhanced or the lamentation for life violently lost: "But our gamble is necessary," she seems to say. "Is yours?" Moreover the woman knows that when she dies in childbirth (as she often did until quite recently), she is no longer in the birthing squat but on her back and quite defenseless, summoned by the divine presence in a way the hunter never is. Thus when his expedition miscarries he goes to her with a troubled mind, not only because she knows the lamentable more intimately, but also because her sexual magic may offer a better way than hunting does of absorbing and repairing man's violence; hence her accusing eyes may suggest there is a case to answer, one whose regulation may lie within her ken. "We have sacrificed one of our own," says the hunter: "It was a gift to the gods of the hunt, not simply a bloody mistaking." And she looks hard at him, perhaps to say that his theological constructions are only a make-believe mystification of a death uncalled-for.

Rites of lamentation are prominent in primitive cultures, and though they arise "naturally" in response to the deaths by disease and childbirth, their "cultural" edge emerges here, in the experience of violence that mistakes its object, and for which some human and not some god may be responsible. The conflict between the hunter-warrior and the woman who knows his folly (and must underwrite much of its cost) is as profound as any in human affairs, and this can be readily perceived by glancing briefly at a major clutch of Greek myths. Perhaps most important is what Aeschylus made of Homer in the *Oresteia,* but consider also the stories of Oedipus, Attis, Adonis, Actaeon, Hippolytus, and Pentheus. In each of these, the hunter-warrior's violence (loosely construed) boomerangs on those whose sex lives (again, loosely construed) are in some disorder; and in all of them one discerns the idea that violence unregulated by the proper woman's thighs may go astray, provoke the goddess, and lead not only to mistaken killing but self-slaughter. Thus Agamemnon mistakenly hunts a stag of Artemis and is subsequently forced to "hunt" his daughter Iphigenia: Oedipus not only kills the wrong man but then seeks refuge in the wrong woman: Attis castrates himself and bleeds to death for Cybele: Hippolytus mistakes Artemis for Aphrodite and is dashed by his own horses: Actaeon lustfully mistakes Artemis and is then mistakenly torn by his own hounds; and Pentheus is dismembered by his own mother. Adonis, another victim of Aphrodite, may be gored by his own narcissism (a mirror image of Hippolytus?).[12]

Hunting and sexuality are central to most of these stories, and all of them involve the idea of mistaken identity. Although we cannot at this point follow it through to the complex notion, masterfully intimated in such Greek tragedies as *The Oresteia* and *The Bacchae,* that all lethal violence unleashed by man upon man may involve sexual self-deception, we *can* say something more about its hunting origins, and look for it not just in the hunter mistakenly killed, but further back, in the possibility that every *animal* hunted and killed is in a sense mistaken.

Imagine a dying animal, a beautiful eland that has been unbeautifully smashed. Its head lies quietly now, and its gradually glazing eyes regard us as we stand around it in a circle, the blood that moved us gradually ebbing away. The more sensitive among us (not alpha but shaman) may find some reproach in its farewell: "I am not your enemy but like you, brother, a creature who loves and nurtures life, and now I am dying defenseless, my little ones doomed." This is disturbing, for this is not the opponent we excitedly attacked: the enemy has become the mutilated victim, and resembles us too much—the "anticipatory merging" that turned us into the quarry now turns against us. "Who is this animal?" the hunter asks: "I came to kill a dangerous enemy worthy of my fury, but all I see are the mournful eyes of a violated victim, claiming kin. Those eyes will haunt my dreams. Perhaps I have mistaken my quarry."[13]

Something magical and distressing here, the quarry changing its identity in the hunter's violence? One must beware of oversensitizing the paleolithic hunter with too much talk of "mournful eyes," but still, there is something; and this something has its origin both in the feeling of unity that overtakes the pack in full cry and in the anticipatory merging with the prey. It leads, as we have seen, to an almost erotic connection between hunter and hunted. What gets mistaken in these ecstatic moments is indeed the quarry's identity, and the mistake is two-fold: first of all we exaggerate his "otherness," the danger or the insult his freedom constitutes for us; and then, as the dance moves in our favor, we exaggerate his likeness to us, the sense in which the tearing of our teeth will resemble a lover's kiss, a union somewhere beyond violence. Thus Eros and Thanatos (gods of love and death) commingle and confuse. When the fit has passed, both of these perceptions seem mistaken, and the quarry appears as both less other and less like; what I have called, for the sake of brevity, a brother.[14]

Or is it a sister? To put it in terms of *yin* and *yang,* we have attacked the animal's *yang*-hardness with our own, and now our *yin*-softness is admonished by its wounded defenselessness. An image of gang rape? The animal is buggered, fucked over: "buggered" is appropriate here, for we have been drawn to its hardness, to soften it through mutilation.* One thinks of the crypto-homosexual motifs threading through the amazingly sophisticated Greek myths mentioned earlier; and beyond them, of the comparably sophisticated perception, which seems to permeate the cave paintings discussed in Chapter 3, of hunting violence as a more than sexual attack upon the *yin*-feminine. In this nest of complex problems we may find some clue to why the Greeks designated the virgin Artemis as both goddess of the hunt and patroness of childbirth, and why she dominates the myths mentioned above. Sexually unspecific, both a merciless killer and protector of the newly born, she may represent the perception not only that these two are intimately related in the sane mind, but that the hunter's arrows may all too easily be deflected from their proper target by being confused with the analogous arrows of sexual desire.

To conclude, the problems of mistaken identity in the hunt seem distressingly similar to the ones that can arise in sexual relations, where, for example, the woman as beautiful prey may turn either into predator or mutilated victim, and where the prize may feel like so much dead meat in the sadness of the post-coital embrace. But whereas in sex much of the damage may be rectified by fucking less brutally tomorrow night, hunting damage cannot be recalled. If we mistake our quarry, or if one of us is mistaken, there is a corpse to indicate that the thing cannot be undone, and we are left with

---

*Cf. The Greek heroes stabbing the body of Hektor: "See now, Hektor is much softer [*malakoteros*] to handle than he was . . ." (*Iliad:* 22:373). The word soft [*malakos*] has important sexual connotations, as we shall see presently: it is what a woman should be and what a man shamefully becomes when excessively buggered (or stabbed).

much to think about. Needless to say, such "tender-minded" thinking comes later rather than earlier in the evolution of hunting, and even then it will not put us off the game: too much is at stake. But once it does begin to trouble our dreams, our dreams will become truly troubled; for if, in our finest hunting moments, moments of such heartening ecstasy, we may also be admitting our own mortality, in effect signing our own death warrants, then we have discovered paradox and contradiction at the heart of human affairs. In sanguine mode we will say "This is as it should be: what is religious about hunting is that it leads us to remember and accept the violent nature of our condition, that every animal that eats will in turn one day be eaten. The hunt keeps us honest." But if and when our hunting rites miscarry, as they do when the quarry is mistaken (and as they do even more in warfare), we will tend to lose our nerve as the corrosive worm of guilt fixes itself to the mind and stomach; and this will ultimately lead to the religions of lamentation (Christianity above all), in which violence—and even sex sometimes—is renounced. To attempt such renunciation is noble in its high-mindedness, but fraught with the perils of self-deception: "How can you die (or live) if you do not kill?", the primitive hunter would ask; and this seemingly simple-minded question is not nearly so easily answered as many have supposed.

Before leaving this section I propose a briefly digressive leap into the twentieth century to look for Artemis. Although she is the major goddess at play in the Greek myths mentioned above, and though they are major myths by any definition, the ancient Greeks are surprisingly reticent on the subject of Artemis, perhaps because her wisdom had already become too primitive and harsh for them. Originally a bear (sometimes a lioness in the south), her craving for mountains and the moon associate her with the Cretan "Lady of the Wild Things," *potnia theron,* as old a goddess as may be. Her strange commitment to both virginity and violence is nicely figured in the moon, which to the poetic mind has always embodied both inviolable purity and the lunatic tides that pull us into madness and childbirth. Her necklace of bull scrotums is usually registered by polite scholars as extra dugs, and the Olympians tried to make her somewhat decent and respectable by casting her as Apollo's sister (her moon to his sun), but with only moderate success: she remains formidably frightening, best left to those undaunted by the rock and forest darkness of her mountain ranges. One traveler who has sought her there in modern times is Ezra Pound, and he heard her singing this:

> Compleynt, compleynt I hearde upon a day,
> Artemis singing, Artemis, Artemis
> Agaynst Pity lifted her wail:
> Pity causeth the forests to fail,
> Pity slayeth my nymphs,
> Pity spareth so many an evil thing.
> Pity befouleth April,
> Pity is the root and the spring.
> Now if no fayre creature followeth me
> It is on account of Pity,
> It is on account that Pity forbideth them slaye.
> All things are made foul in this season,
> This is the reason, none may seek purity
> Having for foulnesse pity
> And things growne awry;
> No more do my shaftes fly
> To slay. Nothing is now clean slayne
> But rotteth away.
>
> *Canto* **XXX**

These are hard lines indeed, almost unmanageable in the modern mind, and yet their bearing on the present discussion is obvious. What Artemis is lamenting here is a failure in the culture to distinguish between the "clean slayne" and the lamentably mistaken. One of the central tasks in any culture, crucial to its prosperity, is the unleashing of arrows that find their mark (whether literal or metaphorical). With the development of sympathetic imagination, however, man learns not only to empathize with his prey (to see himself in his victim) but to see all killing as an attack upon the nurturing feminine, and hence in a sense mistaken. Such thoughts threaten (in the person of Pity) to disturb his aim; and yet he must find the courage and the clarity to continue, for if his arrows fail to find the proper opening (*kairos*) into death to the new life beyond it, purity and prosperity will yield to "foulness" and "things growne awry." The arrows of his desire, once yielded up to mischievous Pity, are not returned to their quiver as they seem to be, but are absentmindedly and self-destructively unleashed upon the very energies that might direct him through danger to purity ("Pity slayeth my nymphs, Pity spareth so many an evil thing"). As we have seen, the hunter is usually a man; but this is Artemis speaking, which reminds us that her hunt is also a metaphor casting its light on the activities of both male *and* female.

The dilemma envisaged by this poem is inescapable and will not be tidied away: to live is to eat is to mutilate is to fuck is to kill is to die, and the only way to be forgiven for the necessary attack upon the nurturing feminine is through rituals that establish "clean slaying" (as any hunter still knows). A man or a woman without Pity is simply a brute for whom nothing will grow, for "Pity is the root and the spring"; but without clean slaying (in the hunt and in bed) we will no longer be followed by any "fayre creature," will be engulfed by sexual foulness, a decadent Pity, and our violence will escape us. As guardian of this crucial conjunction of *yin* and *yang*, the line between pity and violence, (mercy and justice), Artemis is properly female since, as we have seen, the "pity-full" critique of hunting comes naturally to the child-bearing woman; but she is also properly a virgin so that she may resist in a manly fashion the mischievous Pity that "befouleth April." Thus hardened, she may properly supervise the rigors of childbirth ("the root and the spring"), twin source—along with hunting—of our paleolithic prosperity.

These lines from Pound are not merely medieval pastiche (in response to Chaucer's lament for Pity) but poetry of a very high order; and yet because of his subsequent derangement (anti-Semitic and fascist) they are rarely cited, understandably enough. The matter is difficult and complex: Pound's heroism led him to address (as few did, as indeed few have since done) our decadence in regard to clean slaying; and yet he underestimated his *own* decadence (too many books, not enough rough shooting of an afternoon), and so he at times affected a manly swagger, a mask of ruthlessness every bit as foul as the pity he warns us against here. Thus does he remind us of the truth of Aristole's teaching that "the mean" does not lie easily along the broad highway of moderation, but is of all targets the most difficult to hit.

Having said this, I would also suggest that these lines *are* wonderful (though on the edge of swagger) and do speak meaningfully of Artemis, who is neither a fascist nor an anti-Semite. They also speak significantly to a world in which more and more of us are awakening to the knowledge of ourselves involved with some demon that "causeth the forests to fail." Why not say that Artemis is extremely angry in the twentieth century, and that she unhinged the poet who dared listen so closely to her wail; and that having registered the dangerousness of her person, we might register our gratitude for Pound's daring by cherishing this poem.[15]

Coda: even though the context of this poem has led Pound to concentrate almost exclusively on the monstrous deformations of Pity (which is why it must be cited with care), it is well-enough constructed to illuminate powerfully even such apparently unlikely cases as the annual killing of seal pups in Northern Canada. Like any good hunter, Artemis is in favor of culling excess populations, but she would be disgusted by the seal-hunt on two grounds: first of all, clean slaying seeks purity, which includes grace and beauty, without which "no fayre creature followeth me"—as Pound says elsewhere, "And in thy mind beauty, O Artemis." But the plain fact is that even a brutalized "savage" would feel demeaned at having to walk among these lovely newborn pups and bash their brains out with a club. The second point, more important, is also esthetic but mostly religious (and indeed provides a good instance of their overlap): to thus kill the newly born in the presence of their demented mothers is as stark an outrage of the nurturing feminine as can be found in the blood-boltered annals of hunting. Artemis knows that pity for the young and defenseless "is the root and the spring" of the new life that returns with April, and that her lust for the chase must not trespass upon its ground. To harmonize these two, as the argument of this section has tried to indicate, is not only difficult but of the first importance in any culture, which is why Artemis is such a significant goddess. She it is who must tirelessly seek to reconcile our two hands, the nurturing hand of tendance and the predatory claw that grabs and mutilates. But the smashing of seal pups is of a predatory banality that almost drives her to distraction. That the fundamentally decent Canadians could have been so deaf to her wailing, and that the international community took so long to awaken and implement its objections, is yet another indication of our instinctual disease that still "causeth the forests to fail."*

WAR AND CANNIBALISM

The hunting pack turns easily into the war pack. As we have seen with the chimpanzees, war arises as the hunting of neighboring hunters, whereby conspecifics are classified as prey for the purposes of acquiring more territory and breeding females. Although such acquisitions were sufficiently interesting to make war of some interest throughout our six million postchimpanzoid years, one imagines a quantum leap around 10,000 B.C. with the domestication of animals: the word for war in Sanskrit means "the desire for more cattle." Thus territory, females, and booty are the three rational or secular grounds for warfare, and as such they do not much

---

*After the free-world fur market collapsed in 1987, as a result of international protests, the Canadians stopped killing seal pups. The Norwegians followed suit some time later, though both countries still 'cull' the adults, and that word is contested. The Russians are still killing the pups: if Comrade Gorbachev would now like to join the league of nations, and this is devoutly to be wished, his people must put themselves to school in the open market. Meanwhile, as I write, the free-world price of furs is bullish again and I don't even want to talk about the whales (nor even about the chimps being experimented upon in labs here and there). All of which is to say, the struggle continues: send your donations and prayers to Artemis, care of *Greenpeace,* who keeps an office in most major cities.

concern us. What does concern us is the irrational, religious ground, the desire to meet the gods in the sacrificial tearing of one's own or another's body. Herein lies warfare's heart of darkness, what still makes us so reluctant to give it up. But though we caught a glimpse of the sacrificial rhythm in our discussion of the hunt, we shall not be ready to engage it properly until Chapter 7, and so in this section I shall confine myself to the relatively straightforward question of cannibalism.

Most ethnologists seem curiously reluctant to address this matter. As we have seen, brains are a chimp delicacy, and the frequently broken skulls among hominid fossils suggest that in the beginning we hunted our fellows at least partly in order to eat them. Once we start thinking about divinity and decide that our foe is a mighty warrior, somewhat alpha and hence well endowed with *pneuma,* which moreover is concentrated in, say, the brains, the eye, or the heart, we will make a special meal of his brains or his eye or his heart, to be consumed with due ceremony so that the *pneuma* doesn't spill.

Gradually we will find such practices distasteful. There are three main reasons. The first of these is the problem of mistaken identity just discussed: once we have an imagination sufficiently sympathetic to be disturbed by the way our violence seems to transform an animal into a pathetic mirror-image of our mutilated selves, we will be even more disturbed by the transformation of a mutilated human body we are proposing to eat. The second reason, quite a late one I think, has to do with respecting a corpse's integrity: whereas it may be legitimate, in certain circumstances, to appropriate another's life, the eating of his corpse (even its mutilation, ultimately) is an attempt to appropriate his death as well, bad magic, though as we have just seen, this did not stop the Homeric brutes. The third reason, perhaps the source of the second, is the most important, and probably arises, along with the incest taboo, in the wake of our catastrophic consumption of alpha-shaman: in order to prevent a repetition of *that* meal, we renounce all meals that might resemble it. The reader will recall that the incest taboo is the law that arises to subdue sexual anarchy in the name of orderly kinship. The only other taboo remotely comparable, both in its widespread distribution and seriousness, is the taboo against cannibalism.

On reflection, they go rather well together. One is for sex, the other for violence, our two major problems, our two major avenues to the sacred. Our desire for forbidden sex was not unrelated to the eating of alpha-shaman, and this was our introduction to serious guilt; and guilt calls for penance, for renunciation. The word for "good" in ancient Hebrew (and many other languages) has to do with ripe fruit, and means "good to eat."[16] Original sin is greed, and original greed is ingestive, the taking in of too much meat, either above or below.[17] Through the taboos against incest and cannibalism we undertake to limit our two major appetites, our desires to enter and be entered by other bodies. It is important to notice that each of these desires, at least in fantasy, passes easily into the other, which augments their power and their dangerousness. By restraining both of them we turn over a new leaf, banish the hideous memory of alpha-shaman's orgy, and yet also keep its flame flickering, for mischievous dreams when things get dull. It all adds up.

Since the ideas of both incest and cannibalism are frequently met with horrified fascination, it is worth pointing out that although tabooing them was eminently sensible, an obvious foundation for legality, they are neither our most damaging sins nor does practicing them violate something sacrosanct in our primate nature. What *does* get violated is something sacrosanct in all of our cultures, the very idea of order, our profoundest covenant with divinity, the path we promise not to take, on pain of dire retribution, the return to the chaos of alpha-shaman's corpse; that is to say, these taboos are prime examples of what Lévi-Strauss calls the "good to think."

This notion, together with its complement the "good to eat," is profoundly illuminating in its simplicity. If we say that in the beginning the good = the good to eat, it is clear that after the fall of alpha-shaman we are forced to discover another kind of goodness, viz., the lawlines we establish to regulate our appetites. To transgress these lines will, of course, lead ultimately to bad eating, but the transgression is *itself* a badness, and will be initially registered as a kind of spiritual indigestion, the fearful perception that, quite apart from the physical implications, we have broken the law and are spiritually polluted. Thus two kinds of goodness (deeds which augment our prosperity and the invisible or mental lawlines that foster them), two kinds of badness (that which offends the body and that which offends the mind or soul), and two kinds of pollution (diarrhea and divine retribution). This distinction may seem academic in the early days when all sins are ingestive; but as the culture is elaborated and the range of disorders is extended and complicated, the two orders tend to grow apart and lose touch. Not only can it become difficult to trace the connection between certain laws and the body they claim to regulate, but the weight of moral-religious concern seems to fall disproportionately on the former. Hence the seeming inanity of many taboos in guilt-obsessed cultures.

I shall say more about this presently in connection with "representation"; but at the moment it will suffice to observe that the taboos against incest and cannibalism, though importantly "good to think," are also "good to eat" to the extent that they clearly direct our appetites away from certain excesses. Let us consider these: Robin Fox (1980) has taken a good deal of the steam out of incest by indicating that we don't fancy our siblings very much anyway (propinquity discourages randiness) and that certain primitives tolerate some incestuous sex (but not marriage) without their culture falling to pieces. We saw in Chapter 2 that male chimps don't fancy their mothers, which suggests that the desire is not "natural," which in turn suggests that when it *does* arise, the culture is overheating and we should have a word with mother. The desire for father-daughter incest on the other hand is altogether plausible, since she neither emerged from his belly nor suckled on his breast. What constitutes incest is of course differently defined in different cultures, but it should be obvious to anyone in our own (even without reading Father Freud) that little boys and little girls have love affairs with their parents, and that for these to be consummated, however pleasantly, is extremely bad for the process of emotional weaning, which our overheated nuclear families tend in any case to mismanage.

Cannibalism is not easy to examine since we have so little knowledge of cultures practicing it. Still, it would seem obvious that to cannibalize your foe (unless in dire need of protein) is worse than simply killing him, since it means not only that you recognize no limit on the violence you may practice when aroused by the furies, but also because his kin will be utterly offended, hence certain to seek revenge, and so on until everyone is dead. Discussions of cannibalism have been considerably distorted since the Renaissance by the tendency of the imperialist European powers to exaggerate and even invent instances of man-eating among the primitives they visited and conquered, in order to justify their own often extremely nasty practices.[18] On the other hand, a book appeared some years ago that, after examining the evidence, seeks to suggest that cannibalism is *nothing but* a clever figment of the imperialist imagination, and that mankind has probably never practiced it; which is manifestly loony. There are still a number of American anthropologists seeking to deny our violent origins, in the mistaken belief that they are thereby doing the cause of primitivism some service. In fact such confusion is a prime example of liberalism in its decadence, and it does no one any good.[19]

In any case the question of when the last nasty tribe stopped cannibalizing its enemies is only of marginal importance in the search for an understanding of violence. Less marginal is the question of ritual anthropophagy, where the body is consecrated before it is eaten, and we shall consider this in due course when we come to the scapegoat. What is not marginal at all, however, is to recognize that the truly appalling thing, "the horror," is not cannibalism but war itself; and that the frequent failure of serious thinkers since Aristotle to appreciate this has led to a kind of smugness about radical evil: "Depraved violence is cannibalism, which we taboo, and therefore we are spared the monstrous evil."

It is not so. The monstrous evil lies in war itself, and what makes it the truly horrifying nightmare of history, which our lawlines have proved incapable thus far of containing, is not the cannibal tendencies we seem to have honestly inherited and suppressed without undue hardship, but something at once simpler and more alarming: the ecstasy that arises in the mutilation of flesh. This disturbing matter will detain us in Chapter 7, but we may briefly summarize thus: "He who lives by the sword will die by it," otherwise known as the revenge cycle. At its most basic it says, "If you mutilate one of mine, I will mutilate one of yours"; and this leads, by a logic of perfect insanity, to the preventive holocaust: "In order to prevent your mutilating one of mine, I shall mutilate all of yours." The heaps of corpses that despoil the pages of any history book one opens are the implacably monstrous outgrowths of "an eye for an eye." Such a demented version of booty, sometimes offered (as with the Aztecs' enemies, and somewhat differently, the European Jews) to appease the hunger of a furious god, is proof positive of a paranoid will to live forever. In comparison with these heaps, the occasional cannibal stew, so fervently deplored by all civilized thinkers since Aristotle as *the* sin, looks like an innocent picnic.

BEAUTY

Let us now look to the brighter side. This book is chiefly about "the ecstasies of love and war," but there is a third kind, which both weaves itself into the other two and also stands in its own right: the apprehension of beauty. It is anomalous in being almost wholly benign (taken in moderate doses), and also both aboriginal (the infant charmed by the pretty flower) and utterly sophisticated (the esthete, well past love and war, entranced by the late novels of Henry James). Since the search for a good love and a good war ends so frequently in lamentation and madness, one is tempted to say "Choose beauty"; and yet the wisdom of history seems to suggest that if one is to avoid a sterile estheticism and be truly *nourished* by the beautiful, one must find it somewhere near the tents of love and war. It is a large question: to say that beauty must be paid for in the coin of broken dreams sounds dangerously Calvinistic, but I do think there is more than a little truth in the old French saying "Il faut souffrir pour être beau."* However that may be, the ensuing meditation confines itself to the simple and somewhat Platonic proposition that beauty is experienced as a filling that overflows, and that to be available for this one must in some sense be empty. In view of the aforementioned anomalies of the beautiful, this seems to me a properly primitive approach to the question, and yet I must also admit some dismay at not having been able to book more time, among the exigent alarms and diversions of love and war, for a discussion of the beautiful *per se*.

It is always the case that we find beauty in the creature we fall in love with, and the reader will recall that this conjunction does not originate with us but is built into evolution itself in the dynamics of sexual selection. The beautiful tail of the male peacock evolved for no functional reason but simply because the female peacock found it fetching and so, by degrees, through her choice of mate, she called it forth. And it is safe to say that wherever in Nature one finds the male more prettily decorated than the female, this is the reason: where males compete for the female's favors, the esthetic factor will often decide the issue. In addition to such things as peacock tails and stag antlers, sexual selection can take the credit for the colors and perfumes of flowers and fruits, as well as the beautiful world of birdsong. And on the grand scale, is it not true to say that Mother Nature herself has acquired a good eye? Certainly the picture books I've seen that compare the flora and fauna of the reptilean age with that of the mammals would suggest that on the whole this is so. Big was not beautiful.

The grand scale feels a little giddy, not altogether scientific, but even on the small scale the questions are difficult. How much brain do you need to find something beautiful? Men have killed for beauty, but is the little robin much moved by the nonchalant sweetness of his song? If sexual selection is so damn smart, why has it not applied itself to the human genitalia, our oldest and least prepossessing features? Or has it left them alone precisely because it *is* so damn smart? Such difficulties luckily need not detain us now,

*"To be beautiful, one must suffer."

though the unevolved genitals will distract us soon enough. Suffice it to notice that evolution declares a serious connection between sexual desire and desire for the beautiful, and this thought should inform our present deliberations, not only helping us to understand what desire for the beautiful is *for,* but also to see how it overlaps with the sexual ecstasies that are associated with love.

Once again it is pleasing to notice that yet another of man's "higher" concerns, his love of the beautiful, can be found among the chimpanzees. At Gombe, chimps have frequently been observed drawing near to a particularly splendid waterfall. In due course the chimp becomes more and more aroused, until he is jumping up and down, hooting with pleasure at the wild water. This is remarkable: one thinks immediately of the raindance, but this event is in a way even more astonishing, for the combative element is surely minimal. The wildness in the water has called forth his own: elements of mimicry and sympathetic emulation, a surge of pneumatic inflation, and yes, probably a touch of "I can take you on" (rooted in the charging display), but mostly a delighted dissolution of central control as he abandons himself to a vision of dancing light and a music of sweetness and thunder.[20]

The waterfall is not only beautiful, as flowers and birdsong are beautiful, but it also embodies power and violence. The roaring water crashes upon itself with great force . . . and yet nothing changes, nothing dies: extraordinary violence is unleashed and yet contained, and contained moreover in an experience both awesome and delightful. No wonder such things tend to draw us to them hypnotically, as if all of life's wearying contradictions might be resolved by surrendering to the mystery of such changeless change, harmless harm, and terrible beauty. All in all, the chimpanzee's waterfall is a fine example of *pneuma*'s sublime two-foldness: could one ask for a better beginning to the story of the beautiful?

Let us now draw back from such sublimity into the woodland to consider some quieter aspects of beauty. We have come to a magical clearing: overhead the canopy of greenery delicately encloses a majestic space that is declared and bounded by massive tree trunks, and it reminds us not only of the vaulted tracery that connects the columns in European cathedrals, but further back, of the wooded *nemos* that stands behind the earliest Greek temples. And as we stand astonished in this our African sanctuary, let there also be flowers, birdsong, and a gentle breeze to further enhance our revery.

The first thing to notice about this delightful experience is that it does indeed *fill* us with pleasure: we can almost feel ourselves expand as some mixture of joy and the peace that passeth understanding flows in and over us. Or call it ineffable ambrosia, for though it fills us, we have eaten nothing. In any case, for it to fill us we must have been unfull, or better, unfulfilled, lacking something. And what we lacked was precisely the perfection we now feel, which since time began has been linked to a sense of immortality (*ambrosia* is a Greek word meaning literally "not mortal"). What helps to make this connection is that the experience distracts us from the business at hand (walking through the woods), takes us out of ourselves (a quiet version of *ekstasis*), and thereby seems to stop time, the moving shadow of mortality.

Another way to approach the stopping of time is to say that the unbeautiful thing or person is incomplete, lacking its beauty, and that such beauty may be thought to be not nonexistent but simply absent; and hence that the unbeautiful thing is searching, calling out, for its absented self. To be in such a state, "not lost but requiring" as the poet said, is to be unachieved, unfull, unfulfilled, never altogether present because always somewhat absent, always moving in time between the two, trying to unite them. Or one could simply say that beauty is a wandering goddess, whom mortals try to find. If, miraculously and for a moment, they do, the searching ends as time is stopped in perfection; which is not only why "beauty is truth," but also why "a thing of beauty is a joy forever." Such thinking, undoubtedly primitive, has nonetheless commended itself to such subtle poets as Keats and Mallarmé, which means there is probably something in it.

We also indicate this stopping of time when we say that the experience of beauty *arrests* us, leading us out of the here and now into the world of dream, where kindly spirits may entertain us, or less than kind ones may detain us, entranced forever in a world that is not ours. Thus again the two-foldness of *pneuma*, the dangerousness of dreaming immortality, implicit in the word "arrest." This ambiguity is beautifully caught in Robert Frost's poem "Stopping by Woods on a Snowy Evening," where the poet, deeply filled with pleasure at watching the woods fill up with snow, is shaken from a possibly lethal dream by the harness bells of his horse.

The secret of successful engagements with the beautiful lies in recognizing their evanescence, in knowing when to stop stopping. Since such engagements are often solitary (as we saw with the chimps at the waterfall), there tends to be no one there to call one back if one is out too far or in too deep. (Luckily Frost had his horse for company, and the horse knew the way.) What seems to be involved here is the idea of beauty as a *gift,* which one may treasure for a while, but which must be given back to the mysterious powers that bestowed it. Some sense of this is felt even in the filling: one is disposed immediately to pass it on, spread it around, let it out, as indeed the chimp did. Thus, again the notion that the goddess Beauty is essentially absent (or concealed) and may from time to time shine forth in our presence. The Greek language captures this nicely in the cognate connection between *kalos* = beautiful, subsequently good, and *kalupto* = to cover or conceal. From this derives (among other things) our notion that neither one's beauty nor one's virtue should be flaunted.

The chimp in the presence of beauty only manages to hoot and leap, but in due course we will learn how to sing and dance "The song of the waterfall," in which the energies elicited by the waterfall are composed and sent back to their source: a gift for a gift. The song and dance somehow manage to commemorate the experience, re-create it, reproduce it, bring it to mind even when it is no longer present. This is strong magic indeed, which we will eventually attribute to the dancing Muses, the daughters of Memory who make music. By means of rhythm and harmony we have discovered a way of preserving treasurable moments, of calling them back, and soon enough this notion of recall will merge with that of simply calling forth, and we will say that the song, properly sung, evokes or invokes the spirit of the waterfall. Evocation calls it out from wherever it is housed, and invocation calls it into this place here, which it may fill to plenitude. Thus Wordsworth, whose ears were open to the wonderful, could say of his song sung by the "Solitary Reaper":

> O Listen, for the vale profound
> Is overflowing with the sound.

For the vale (and its visiting poet) to be filled with sound, it (and he) must be suitably empty, which is one reason why monasteries tend to be located in lonely valleys, and why monks must practice an emptying *ascesis* if they are to make themselves susceptible to heavenly music.[21]

The sound flows and overflows, and yet it does nothing of the kind, and this is most mysterious. The water falls and flows into the beholder, and yet nothing changes; and in the tree cathedral some kind of superflux is poured into us, and yet not so: the cathedral remains undiluted, unimpoverished. This means that what gets poured must somehow be superfluous, surplus to requirements, playful not needful, some kind of wealth that can be given without reducing the life of what enriches us. And indeed this seems to be the case with whatever we call beautiful. Birdsong, the simplest and almost certainly our oldest experience of the beautiful, finds much of its magic in our sense of its playful and generous superfluity:

> That all her thoughts may like the linnet be
> And have no business but dispensing round
> Their magnanimities of sound . . . [22]

If business is concerned with grabbing and holding the thing deemed useful, beauty bestows the pricelessly useless, genuine riches. If business proceeds by pushing and shoving, beauty is that which has no designs upon us, and yet seizes us with a grip no businessman knows.

If beauty dispenses a surplus, which nonetheless leaves its contours unaltered, intact, this invisible surplus must lie somewhere behind or within those contours, whence it flows forth in a suffusion that some people experience as a kind of heavenly hum. But if *pneuma* flows through the beautiful, and flows so mysteriously, it may overflow, and not only fill us but drown us in its dream:

> Sublimity seizes us, almost unbearably,
> But our fear turns to wonder
> As it loftily disdains
> To dissolve us utterly.[23]

The paradox of beauty (in its sublime instances) is that it somehow manages both to elicit danger and contain it. This means that when we no longer simply happen upon it as we stroll through the woods, but seek to invoke it through shapes we construct in the campsite, we shall seek to build into those shapes certain lawlines that will govern our exposure to its power.

Perhaps the finest hymn to beauty ever composed is Plato's *Phaedrus,* a work whose subtlety and sophistication have not been equaled in the 2,400 years that have since elapsed, and yet whose primitive credentials are also impeccable. In this dialogue Plato argues that the beautiful is the most venerable of *pneuma*'s gifts because it enters us readily through the eyes, awakening the earth-bound soul to a remembrance of eternal perfection and the desire to become united with it. Any beautiful thing that we come upon, like the waterfall, awakens the soul to some extent, inducing reverence and awe, but the matter becomes truly critical when the beautiful thing is another person with whom we fall in love. Such an awakening carries the soul into ecstasy, a state of divine madness (*mania*) in which the lover is simultaneously filled and emptied by the supernatural power of the god Eros. Possessed by the desire to possess the beloved, the lover must also be possessed: overflowing with some unplaceable potency, he is also parched with longing for what is not his, not him. Such a disturbing confluence of strength and weakness, tenderness and violence, confronts the soul's charioteer with his most exacting challenge: he must somehow control his chariot, the horse of his strength and the horse of his weakness, and reach the proper place. How to possess and be possessed by the beautiful without despoiling and being despoiled by it?

Do we know of a question more profound? I think not. But this discussion of beauty has passed into a discussion of love, which means it is time to move on to the next section. We shall say more of Plato's *Phaedrus* there.

EROTIC LOVE

I suggested in Chapter 3 that we discovered the ecstasies of erotic love long before we began naming the gods; and yet by the time of our earliest (extant) religious statement, on the cave walls of Magdalenian Europe, no lovers figure among the teeming therio-morphic divinities. Beauty, love's inseparable companion, is abundantly present, but love seems to have been banished. We are now in a position to offer an explanation of this anomaly, and it is a simple one: the ecstasies of love were more or less outlawed in the aftermath of alpha-shaman's catastrophe. Having served its evolutionary purpose of helping to establish a favorable climate for tethering our promiscuity, love gradually became too hot to handle, dangerously inflammatory, a part of the problem rather than the solution; and so it was bundled offstage to make way for the orderly reign of kinship. Having revealed its lethal possibilities in contributing to the debacle of alpha-shaman, it was banished to the wings, where, its potency undiminished, even possibly enhanced, it has been forced to lead a somewhat furtive, criminal, mad existence ever since. Beauty, on the contrary, love's child and "onlie begetter," moved center stage, to bear abstractly the religious weight of our relegated love-longing, at least until such relatively recent figures as Plato, and rather differently, Jesus, explored the possibilities of a spiritual reunion.

Could this be so? Unfortunately, there is nothing that might look like evidence for what happened to love in the aftermath of alpha-shaman, and so the best we can do is indicate that such evidence as we *do* have, from the Sumerians on down, does indeed suggest that love is not only strange, but almost as difficult to civilize as war (with which it tends constantly to commingle). This means leaping rather briskly from the prehistoric savannah into the sophisticated "historical" world where things get written down, which I hope the reader will find a pleasant diversion rather than something untoward.

To begin at the end, romantic love as we know it was discovered (or rather remembered) in the courts of late medieval Europe, where it was clearly perceived as implicitly both criminal and mad from the beginning. Troubadour-shaman may sing his love song to madam the queen of an afternoon, but when alpha comes back from the hunt, shaman must immediately pack up his lute if he wants to avoid big trouble. The bourgeois love-ethic we all grew up on, which insistently whispers "love conquers all," tends to make this point difficult for us to grasp.[24]

The troubadours' notion of love as something dangerously deranged can in turn be traced back well beyond Plato to ancient Aphrodite, the goddess whose savage seriousness was so memorably identified by Racine with "C'est Venus, toute entière, à sa proie attachée."* Man in his innocence or his hubris may imagine himself hunting for love, but in fact it is the other way around, though he may frequently remain unaware of this until it is altogether too late.[25] Christianity, of course, had no time at all for Aphrodite; and yet, even though she was truly alien to the still pious mind of the early Renaissance, she was also increasingly at home there, as may be gathered from the fifth canto of Dante's *Inferno,* where the poet is overcome when he perceives her majestic sublimity, its power and its pathos. Unable to countenance what he sees, i.e., unable to credit the idea of this devastating creature being simply mangled and dismissed in the harsh legalities of his Christian theology, and hence unable either to kneel before her or banish her with words of

---

*This line has never been well translated because it is untranslatable. It means something like "Thus Venus, engulfing, teeth fast in her prey."

suitable outrage, he does the only honorable thing, and falls into a dead faint. Thus we witness a moment of supreme irony, when the great Christian poet of the European Renaissance is silenced by a divinity that moves outside his antinomies.

There is fairly good evidence that she was too much for the ancient Greeks as well. First of all, though an extremely ancient goddess, Aphrodite had remarkably few temples in Greece: indeed it was widely felt in those days, since her principal shrine was at Paphos in faraway Cyprus, that she was almost a foreigner. Second, though she certainly made trouble wherever she went (causing the Trojan war, for example), she is portrayed in the myths as being on the whole idle, frivolous, and almost scatterbrained.[26] For a sense of the huge power that the Greeks seem deliberately to have played down with regard to Aphrodite, one must look to Inanna and Ishtar, her Sumerian and Akkadian forebears, those goddesses with little desire for procreation but shameless appetites for sex and violence, the devastations of love and war. These are the oldest of the great urban goddesses (from about 3000 B.C.), and one can imagine the temperate Greek mind deploring their orgiastic proclivities as it sought discreetly to marginalize Aphrodite, tolerating her tenure at Cyprus but resisting her further advance into Greek waters.[27]

One can also imagine the old patriarchs less than best pleased when her principal lover Adonis imported his very popular festival of love and death into the Aegean from Phoenicia in the seventh century B.C. Some indication of their displeasure may be inferred from the fact that although these Phoenician festivals must have been known to both Homer and Hesiod, neither of them even mentions Adonis.[28] But since he suits our purposes rather well, providing a significant illustration of the "outlawing" of love in the ancient world, I shall now tell his story at some length.

Though something of an eclectic upstart in the official Greek pantheon, Adonis's pedigree is in fact as old as can be. It began way back with the neolithic new year's festival, in which as consort (lover and son) to the queen as earth mother, he was actually sacrificed annually to make the crops grow—an unpropitious start for a love story, one might think, but consoling in its suggestion that in death we are gathered to the breast that bears us.[29] By the time of Inanna and Ishtar his name was Dumuzi or Tammuz, and the lady's original concern with fecundity was being overtaken by the more vivid question of love (and the war that seems to follow it everywhere); and thus his annual death came to have more to do with love and love's alarms than with seasonal obligations. And yet it was somehow both, as it still was much later when his name became Adonis, whose annual festival in some places (like Alexandria) was a springtime celebration of fertility, in others (such as Athens) a midsummer lament for the dying vegetation, which involved an orgiastic release of excessive and illicit passion. This strange conjunction of fertile and sterile sexuality can also be seen in the fascinating practice of temple prostitution, which moved eastward from Inanna's Mesopotamia to India, and came westward through Phoenicia and Syrian Heliopolis. When respectable women (not imported slaves) are expected to spend some time in the temple precincts fornicating with whatever strange men may happen to call, is this a matter of degrading sexual pollution or could it be pious sacrifice to the goddess of fertility? Could it be both? It could, but unfortunately we know so little about temple prostitution that one can only speculate.

It is important to notice that even though women were taken more seriously in Sumer than in Greece, both cultures were patriarchal, and yet the myths, whether of Inanna–Dumuzi or Aphrodite–Adonis, agree that the mysteries of sexual power are vested in the feminine: love leads to death, and though the goddesses may lament, it is the gods who die. What's more, the love affair itself is conducted on their terms: *l'homme* may *propose,* but *la femme dispose,* as was the case, I suggested earlier, on the savannah. Thus Aphrodite arranges the incestuous conception of Adonis, abducts and adulterously seduces him, and then when he is killed by Ares the boar husband and sent to console the equally hungry Persephone in Hades, Aphrodite made such a fuss that Zeus allowed her to reclaim him for a third of every year. There is some indication that the uncomplaining Adonis may have found all this female attention rather tiring, for Zeus also specified that he was to spend a third of the year alone, on vacation.

Young, very beautiful, almost effeminate, Adonis looks like a one-track shaman with very little alpha in him; and hence it seems appropriate that he meets his death not in bed, where his magic might protect him, but out hunting, where he was easy meat for Ares the outraged alpha boar. Perhaps what drove him to the woods was the need to escape, for a while at least, the arms of endless Aphrodite, and prove himself not altogether toy-boy.

In any case, the annual festival commemorating his death was held in August in Athens, the hottest days of the year, and women would grow for the occasion little "Gardens of Adonis," vaginal pots in which seeds were first sprouted and watered, and then allowed to roast in the sun. At the end of eight days, these aborted gardens were thrown with lamentation into the sea. Whatever pious connection to fertility may have prevailed elsewhere, the Athenian festival was a mildly scandalous and drunken celebration of passionate sterility. Just as nothing grows in the dog days of summer (when the Greeks, in any case, become a little unhinged), so the desperately beautiful midsummer love is a brief, adulterous, mistimed thing, in which new life cannot be rooted and which leads only to death and lamentation. A vaginal pot may well provoke a burst of energy in the seed, but unless set in the womb such energy will simply burn up and die.[30]

This midsummer orgy may be usefully contrasted with the ancient *Thesmophoria,* the most widespread of Greek festivals, in which married women soberly renewed their vows to earth-bearing Demeter and everything in its season, in the absence of their men folk. In the *Adonia,* unseasoned but spicy license leads to lamentation, whereas in the *Thesmophoria* seasonal fasting and lamentation for the corn goddess lead to *kalligeneia,* fair birth. We are in fact invited to make this comparison by one local version of the myth, which indicates that Adonis's troubles began when his mother conceived him by lusting after her father when she should have been attending the *Thesmophoria* with her mother.[31]

The *Adonia* also bears comparison with the festivals of Dionysus, in which comparably illicit passions were to be kept within bounds through being released in a carnival context. Like Adonis, Dionysus in his wilder manifestations was thought by any civilized Athenian to be a bit foreign, a bit rough, a bit lower-class even, and their carnivals something of a threat to the piety (*eusebia*) that makes for good order. And yet the marginalization of such profound passions was to be challenged in due course by the appearance of Jesus, who strikingly resembles Adonis in certain respects: both have some irregularity in their conception, ambivalent feelings about the women who would claim them, are mischievously killed for boundless love that the fathers deem illicit, subversive, and sterile, and their deaths are lamented annually by the women they forsake. However sterile his gardens may have been, Adonis prepared the ground for Jesus, and what was "foolishness to the Greeks" found its home among them.[32]

And so to homosexuality, central to the development of romantic love. Two factors are dominant here, both related to the patriarchal culture that arose as neolithic farming gave way to the city states of the Near East: first, the increasing importance of military training and war, and second, the sequestration and downgrading of women. The classic text in which we can observe this happening is the Sumerian *The Epic of Gilgamesh* (ca. 2000 B.C.), where the great goddess Ishtar is denounced as a whore and the bond forged between the warrior brothers is both erotic and sentimental. This text, which we shall examine in detail in Chapter 8, was the Mesopotamian "Bible" for well over a thousand years, much as Homer was to the Greeks.

Greek mythology never *explicitly* engages homosexuality,[33] whose origins are and will remain obscure; but the conventional view today agrees with Plato (*Laws,* 636) that it was a military (i.e., Dorian) matter—wrestling in the gymnasium and no women in the barracks. Warriors, though culturally central in obvious ways, are also significantly marginal: as killers and destroyers they legitimize the illicit, and so offer an appropriately marginal home for a love that subverts the fecundities of kinship. And even though, according to the expert Dover (*Greek Homosexuality*, 1978), homosexuality's "social acceptance and artistic exploitation had become widespread by the end of the seventh century B.C." (p. 196), much of what these lovers actually *did* will remain forever veiled in secrecy and tasteful discretion.

Among warriors the love affair tended to arise in the giving of gifts and instruction to a younger by an older man, and the bond of admiration, affection, and loyalty thus formed often endured until death would both seal and undo it on the battlefield. It was widely believed that lovers fought more valiantly than the unbonded, and though there is no evidence that the secretive Spartan army was organized on this basis, the elite "Sacred Band" of the Theban army consisted entirely of paired lovers, and they died to a man resisting Philip II of Macedonia in 338 B.C. As to the extent of sexual contact, such evidence as we have ranges from the extremely spiritual (caressing forbidden) to the extremely physical (protracted ritual subjugation of the younger by the elder).[34]

The eternal problem for sexual penetration, either of the male or the female, is the achievement of equity in the presence of asymmetrical dynamics. We have seen that the presentation of the buttocks is a gesture of submission among monkeys generally, to which one might add that some species produce erections when their territory is threatened by foreigners. The penis as battering ram or sword would seem to be a symbol as old as may be, very difficult to dislodge from the mind. It hangs on in contemporary slang, where to be metaphorically "fucked" or "buggered" indicates the defeat of some enterprise.[35]

There is, of course, a female or *yin* equivalent to the phallic tyranny, for the male can easily feel demeaned in being housed, contained, enveloped, absorbed, hence incarcerated, infantilized and extinguished in the female body. The difference between these two versions of tyranny is that in the latter case, the meanings are supplied by human imagination, not inherited from our primate past. I imagine them arising with the discovery of love on the savannah (as discussed in Chapter 3) and making a quantum leap in neolithic times when the womb as sacred space begins to lead us toward the idea of the temple (to be discussed in Chapter 7). At this point I would say only this: heavenly sex needs little nudging to fall into nightmare, and we should imagine both male and female dreaming of both possibilities from the outset. And whereas the *yin* anxiety is typically of violation, the *yang* is of confinement; which gives us man the rapist and woman the womb-tomb infantilizer. Between these extremities the culture of sexuality must run its course.

I suggested in Chapter 3 that in our earliest days these anxieties could have been neutralized and overcome by males sufficiently self-confident to entertain their own ontological insecurities (and the mystery of childhood memory) between the thighs of women sufficiently secure in their own fecundity to entertain such vulnerability. And in the opening section of this chapter we considered how sexuality may have provided both male and female with intimations of sacrifice, death, and rebirth very like those encountered in the hunt. Such good sex requires a delicate balance, to be sure, perhaps rarely achieved, but *possible*; and possible too in neolithic times when female fecundity was venerated even more. When this balance was not achieved, of course, sexual intercourse would have reverted to its simian significance, a dominance ritual of no great importance that both parties may have more or less enjoyed.

Under patriarchy, however, this balance becomes increasingly difficult to achieve. The women tend to become chattels, sequestered both before and after marriage to keep their loins uncontaminated by the wrong seed. Like the farmers employed by the warrior aristocrats to work the land, they recede patiently to replenish the earth while the warriors get on with the important business of subduing and laying it waste. Under such conditions the warriors naturally turn to each other for erotic play and for the praise the women might now be seriously disposed to withhold; and we run into the same problem we have always had with heterosexuality, how to penetrate another body without degrading it.

Astute and clear-sighted in sexual matters as in so much else, the Greeks met the problem squarely: they neither denied that sexual desire was for penetration, nor did they deny that to be penetrated was demeaning.[36] On the contrary, they emphasized the demeaning aspect well beyond anything one might discern as the "natural" residue of our simian rituals of submission, and they did this for a very simple reason: the manifest need for an ideology of female inferiority to justify and enforce their subjugation. Thus, whereas the penetrative male is active, self-mastering, and hard, the penetrated female is passive, wanton, and soft (*malakos*). These qualities of mind and body are both revealed and fostered in the sexual act, and hence for a man to assume the female position in sexual matters was both to advertise and induce the fatal softness (*malthakia*) and put himself beyond the pale. If all this sounds appallingly crude for such an intelligent people, it must be remembered that we are here outlining the received ideas of a warrior elite. The outlawing of male *malthakia* also transforms it into forbidden fruit, of course, to be explored in the darkness; and it was so explored, unquestionably, though from this distance much must remain obscure.

For a warrior in the warrior culture of Greece to "play the woman" was even worse than actually *being* one, and so they invented a romantic love in which the older lover (*erastes*) yearned to penetrate anally the younger loved-one (*eromenos*) but settled for less—perhaps a kiss, perhaps intercrural intercourse (his penis held between the *eromenos*'s thighs), but perhaps only soft words. The *eromenos* was supposed to remain sexually unaroused by whatever favors he granted his *erastes* (hence hard in his softness); and thus he would remain not only unviolated but might even be thought ennobled by charitably suffering the relief of his lover's distress (*erastes* soft in his slavishness). Thus *erastes* the hard-soft hunter, *eromenos* the soft-hard hunted, seeking an equitable conclusion. All in all, we are not far from the medieval version of courtly love. As with courtly love, however, one wonders about the gap between fact and fiction: how often were the young lads being buggered? Of course we will never know, but the implication, both of Dover's magisterial review and of the Old Comedy's bawdy cynicism, is that the penetrative deed took place more than once in a blue moon.[37]

In Plato's dialogues the argument is taken one stage further and changed utterly. Although the setting is still the upper-class gymnasium, the military theme has receded, and what entrances the lover is not courage or wrestling skill but the beauty that seems to shine through the beloved's body. Thus the soldier makes way for the philosopher. The perception of beauty arouses both the best and the worst of his energies, his noble horse and his ignoble one, and he is driven to touch, enter, possess, despoil, and be possessed by the beloved's body. It is as simple and as endlessly complex as that, and no one has explored the terrible beauty of sexual desire more profoundly than Plato in the *Symposium* and the *Phaedrus*.

The urge to penetrate and explore is the urge to know and command, readily observable in children and animals at play. The suspicion that what lies hidden inside may be the secret source of power over what lies evident outside, is so ancient and widespread that it feels like an instinct. When this instinct is fully aroused in the divine madness mischievously supervised by Eros, the paradoxical proximities of tenderness and violence may drive the lover to desecrate the shrine where he would worship. But if, through some mysterious combination of reverence, self-mastery, and luck, he finds a way into sensual intimacy that can thrive this side of the penetrative conclusion, he may be blest by the greatest of love's gifts, significant access to the divine light that pours from and through the beloved's body. The erotic ecstasy, which consummation abbreviates, concludes, and distorts in ordinary lovers, is at once magically satisfied, frustrated, and kept alive for the philosopher in a vision of how life should and might be—a vision he can then communicate to the beloved, a gift for a gift.

In the *Phaedrus* Plato recognizes that most of us are not up to the higher calling, and offers a limited blessing to those lovers who occasionally submit to "their full desire" so long as "their minds are not wholly set thereupon" (256 c). This is more than he allows either in the earlier *Symposium* or the later *Laws*. But what is truly remarkable in the *Phaedrus* is that even those who would seek the ultimate blessing of wisdom must pass through the divine madness of erotic love. The agonizing temptations of sexuality cannot be avoided by the aspiring philosopher, lover of wisdom, for it is only in renouncing the all-too-human desire to possess and therefore devalue the beauty of the loved-one that the gods allow the chosen few access to the central mystery—that human fulfillment can be possessed only by those who sacrifice their desire to possess it. And this, according to Plato, is the life truly worth living, where the energies for love and war are reconciled at last in the generative perception of beauty.[38]

Once again we have been drawn forward from the savannah into the light of history. It seemed to me a necessary excursus, not only to lend plausibility to my suggestion that love was more or less outlawed by kinship, but also because it was time to adduce more evidence for my strange proposal in Chapter 3 that the ecstasies of love were just as important as those of hunting to our religious development. When I say that love was "outlawed" by kinship, I mainly mean "recognized as without the law," more or less unsusceptible of governance by the lawlines, subversive, *dangerous*. Needless to say, the rule of kinship also makes adultery a punishable offense in most cultures; and even though the ecstasies of love are better entertained in the myths of Inanna and Dumuzi than in those of Venus and Adonis, both males are more boys than men, and it would be rash to suppose that the Sumerians, among whom even a barren womb was grounds for divorce, viewed adulterous liaisons with indulgence.

Before going on to look briefly at kinship, however, we must consider one objection to my argument about love; and it concerns the gradual neglect of magical fecundity by the old neolithic earth mother as she turns into the glamorous Inanna who paints her fingernails for love (and on from her to warriors wrestling in the gymnasium). Surely, one might argue, this development indicates that love is not very old but very new, a discovery and an indulgence of those sophisticated town dwellers whose technological mastery of Nature had freed them from the primitive's perennial anxiety about the food supply; freed them, that is, from the humorless business of magically propitiating the powers of increase, thereby giving them the leisure and the confidence to play around with dangerous passion. My answer to this objection is that the Mesopotamian discovery of love was in fact a *recovery* and an elaboration of the games we used to play in our innocence, before the fall of alpha-shaman scared us half to death. The fact that we returned to love as soon as we could build some decent walls to keep the lions at bay only indicates how much we were longing to get back to our oldest and best kind of madness. The Sumerians, and to a notable extent the ancient Hindus, in the first flush of urban self-confidence—and unmistakably hot climates—actually elaborated something like a religion of love. In due course, however, cooler counsels prevailed, as Egyptian, Greek, and Jew agreed to sequester such energies in the lady-chapel and/or the gymnasium, much as I imagine our forebears did on the savannah when they got serious about legality.

And so to kinship, about which we can be mercifully brief, having already said something about the incest taboo. What kinship most obviously does is regulate our ancient instincts for promiscuous sexuality; but also, in a world suddenly rendered dangerously prone to collapse by the eating of alpha-shaman, it provides a wealth of ties that bind us one to another in various simple and complex ways. These ties, the most basic of our lawlines, compose a reassuring and invisible structure we shall one day call the body politic, and the thing so constituted is perhaps the most important metaphorical example of the *neuron*'s magical power (noticed in the Appendix) to bring cosmos out of chaos by tying disparate elements together.

It also ministers ingeniously to our basic religious desire for magical increase: simply by being born, and subsequently by getting married, I become much more than I am. Not only can I imagine myself as part of a large and powerful body, but kinship *actually* provides me with privileges and powers, allies to call on when feuding, etc. Another ingenious thing it does is to contain the revolutionary energies of the young men by providing painful ordeals of initiation, rites of passage from youth to manhood whereby the young gain access to the pool of breeding females and full membership in the world of kinship. If I must give up my foreskin and be scared out of my wits in order to become a man, this will tend to make me respect my elders and turn my subversive impulses into fears of my own unworthiness. As Yeats put it, "If violence is not embodied in our institutions, the young will not give them their affection, nor the young and old their loyalty."[39]

I hope this brief excursion into "historical time" has convincingly indicated that there was an inherent conflict between erotic love and kinship from the start, and moreover that this conflict was markedly exacerbated once patriarchal civilization took hold. Although we cannot know when the fraternal bond among hunters and warriors first found homosexual expression, the ethnographic evidence suggests it is not significantly primitive; and such evidence as we have from the historical Near East and Egypt suggests it was a Greek invention.

The general drift of my argument is rather grim: given the close contact of Eros and Thanatos, the overlapping of the energies that lead to love and war (discussed in Section 1), it follows that any malfunction in the one will tend to be reflected in the other. If, as I have suggested, erotic love was marginalized by kinship and then further sequestered by patriarchy, one would expect this to be reflected in a coarsening of the energies deployed in hunting and in war: the rites of lamentation that monitor and refine these energies will fall into neglect. That this was probably the case is suggested not only in the Greek myths we looked at briefly, but also in epic literature generally. Both *Gilgamesh* and Homer's *Odyssey* (which we shall examine in Chapter 8) explicitly see war as the activity (one might almost say "the desperate recourse") of men without women, and the cries of lamentation are strangulated. Homosexuality in this context appears as a decidedly mixed blessing: in its military mode it seems clearly to have whetted the appetite for war, and thus is part of the problem not the solution. But in Plato's hands it is elaborated into a doctrine of romantic love in which the *yin* element is significantly present, and as such it offers to rein in the warrior. That Plato's thought arose from the ashes of Athens' military empire seems perfectly appropriate and not fortuitous.

It remains only to point out that romantic lovers of the beautiful have never been able to outgun the big battalions; but it would be unwise to dwell on this.

6 ı THINKING IN THE THEATER OF THE GODS:
The Magic of Metamorphosis

We reason of these things with later reason,
And we make of what we see, what we see clearly
And have seen, a place dependent on ourselves.
—Wallace Stevens

In the last chapter we focused on three major avenues to ecstasy and the sacred for primitive man: killing, loving, and the contemplation of beauty. This one is again divided into a number of sections, all of which are essentially concerned with the magic of transformation. Since the man nominally in charge of such magic is shaman, we might profitably begin with a brief discussion of his evolution, commencing, as in Chapter 5, with some facts about the Bushmen (or !Kung), some kind of sea anchor to hold against our billowing abstractions.

SHAMAN, HIS MASK AND HIS DRUM

Just as there is no alpha-male among the Bushmen, neither is there an official shaman: all the adult males seek shamanic power, on the dancing ground, but only about half of them succeed in becoming masters.[1] In these dances, which sometimes last throughout the night, the women clap and sing by the fire while the men, with rattles attached to their ankles, dance in a circle around them. As the music and dancing intensify, *pneuma* arises (for which their word is *num,* pleasingly congruent) and some of the masters may fall into trance or "half-death," the state of *kia* in which their souls may journey to the spirit world to acquire luck, healing power for the tribe, and forgiveness for the pain they inflict upon the hunted eland. *Num* is understood as a kind of liquid substance that, when sufficiently heated in the belly, rises up the spine and explodes in the brain (not unlike the Hindu yogi's *kundalini*). It is closely associated with the fire that helps to arouse it, is equally frightening and dangerous, and the ecstatic dancers often have to be restrained from jumping into the flames and picking up the coals. The key to mastery of this experience (which tends to come in one's mid-twenties after many years of practice) lies in having a spirit sufficiently open and receptive to the invasions of *num* and yet strong enough to bear its arrows, which seem to perforate the flesh as the ecstasy builds.

Wherever one turns in primitive culture, one finds a comparable structure of religious perception in the beginning: supernatural power flows somewhere behind the world of appearances, and is to be contacted through more or less ecstatic ritual on the dancing ground. And whether it be called *manitou* (Algonquin), *orenda* (Iroquois), *wakan* (Sioux), or whatever, it is both ineffable and yet comes among us: like the *molimo* to which the Pygmies sing and dance, it seems to be both transcendent and yet all-pervasive. This problem by no means disappears when we become more sophisticated: the nod (*neuma*) that fleetingly animates the Greek statue points to it, as do the Taoists who say "The *Tao* that can be comprehended is not the eternal *Tao*," as do the Buddhists who say "If you meet the Buddha on your path, kill him," as does Meister Eckhart who says "I pray to God that he may relieve me of God." We shall return to this enduring mystery in the third section of this chapter, but at this point might mention an elementary but important distinction shaman devises in the early days to lighten its confusing burden; namely, the division of the world into two realms, the *sacred,* where *pneuma* presides, and the *profane* or secular realm of everyday experience.[2]

At the heart of this distinction is the way in which our rituals on the dancing ground seem not only to transform but actually transport us into another world. Is this another world of *space* or of *time*? Conventional shamanism can answer "Both," since the shaman's trance in every culture is understood as a "half-death" in which the spirit leaves the body and flies to another realm, often either to retrieve some benighted soul or to conduct one of the recently dead to their final resting place. But when we ritualize without trance, and all remain (however decorated and disguised) stubbornly embodied *here* on the dancing ground, it will gradually appear more plausible (not only to the skeptical among us) to suggest that if we go anywhere we go into another *time*, in the beginning indeed, the time in which the world was (and is) created, in which the ancestors emerged from *pneuma* and where they still reside, the "dream-time" (as Australian mythology calls it) to which we all return in death and which we must periodically visit for the renewal of our spirits, for a new start in time. Eliade calls it "that time" (*illud tempus* as opposed to *hic*) and has written several illuminating books on the subject.[3] As the antithesis of profane time, it must be timeless time, a time that is no time and yet gives birth to time, what we shall eventually call eternity.

Among the most important ceremonies in any primitive community are the rites of passage whereby the young are initiated into adulthood. These have been exhaustively studied by ethnographers[4] and need not detain us now beyond the crucial observation that despite local variations they all involve a harrowing return to the dream-time in which the youth symbolically dies and is reborn as an adult. If this, perhaps the most momentous experience of transformation in primitive culture, is thought to involve (like the neolithic New Year's ceremony) a journey all the way to death and back, in order to start a new time, we may expect to find traces of this rhythm in the less violent transformations of the self that shall concern us presently.[5]

When shaman leads us through music and dancing into the dream-time of "that time," he is leading us into the mythic time of "Once upon a time," which the Arabic language genially registers as

"It was and was not so." This expression nicely identifies the principal feature of sacred mythic time, its paradoxical nature: both super-real and unreal, alive and dead, ordered and disordered, serious and playful. It is the time in which the imagination, set free from the compelling profanities of quotidian existence, conceives and emends the lawlines by which a culture is to be governed. It does this (just as our night-time dreams playfully question our personal experience) by means of *symbols*, which represent the relatively unknown, absent or invisible thing, and *metaphors*, which perceive similarity between things apparently dissimilar. In the beginning, mythic time is understood by primitives everywhere as a remembering of what the ancestors and gods laid down. By degrees the *dromenon* (the thing done in mythic time) gives birth to the *drama* (the thing done and spoken in the theater), something remembered but also invented and crafted by a poet not altogether unlike our own. The anthropologist who has recently written most perceptively about the continuities between primitive ritual and the modern arts is Victor Turner (*The Ritual Process*, 1969, *Dramas, Fields, and Metaphors*, 1974). His word for the magical space-time, both real and unreal, which these activities occupy, is "liminal," meaning on the line between here and there, cosmos and chaos. This word, adapted and extended from Van Gennep's classic study (*The Rites of Passage*, 1909), deserves wider circulation.

The first and still the best meditation on the magical nature of poetry and drama is Aristotle's *Poetics*, which begins with the important perception that all the arts (like the sympathetic magic from which they derive) are concerned with *mimesis*, the representation of "action and life, happiness and misery." A great deal of energy has been spent in misunderstanding these four words over the past two millennia, and yet it seems to me that if we approach them "from behind" as it were, in the light of the primitive search for lawlines, they speak with the clarity and simplicity that characterize all of Aristotle's important pronouncements. Toward the end of the *Poetics* he says this:

> But the greatest thing by far is to be a master of metaphor. It is the one thing that cannot be learnt from others; and it is also a sign of

genius, since a good metaphor implies an intuitive perception of the
similarity in dissimilars (1459).

What is striking here (apart from the usual clarity and simplicity) is
that this most phlegmatic of masters has briefly and uncharacteristically raised his voice, almost to excitement. Why? I would suggest
that he has somewhat inadvertently stumbled upon one of the great
unlocking perceptions; that what constitutes genius in *all* the arts
(whether primitive or post-primitive) and *all* the sciences too, is
simply this: "the intuitive perception of similarity in dissimilars,"
otherwise known to mere mortals as the inductive leap.

Being a disciplined practitioner of prose composition, Aristotle
suppresses his half-conscious impulse to shout "Eureka!" and returns
to the unapocalyptic matter in hand—diction in the tragic poets;
and so must we now. My defense for almost raising such weighty
matters at this point is to suggest to the reader that the complex
questions of sympathetic magic and symbolic representation that we
shall presently engage are not simply idle curiosities from our
primitive past but absolutely continuous with the "highest" concerns of the post-primitive mind, be it that of a Beethoven or a
Darwin; and that a good way of keeping one's bearings in such
difficult terrain is to remember where it all began, with shaman
poetical on the dancing ground.

Finally, a word about politics: how much power does shaman have?
This is a difficult matter to generalize about, but with the help of a
few simple distinctions we may draw a rough picture. The shaman
properly so-called is our first and most primitive mediator between
the sacred and the profane, and what singles him out for his calling
is his capacity to fall, both voluntarily and involuntarily, into
ecstatic trances—a disposition that has led some skeptical commen-
tators to see him as a neurotic-epileptoid weakling unsuited for
normal life.[6]

The basics of his art are the drum, which finds the music of ecstatic transport; and the mask, which arms him against the dangerous spirits and ancestral ghosts he must encounter on his travels. I would like to postpone discussion of the drum until the first section of the next chapter and concentrate here upon the mask. It may have originated as an apotropeic device to scare angry spirits, but it is more obviously what transforms the shaman *into* one of the spirits so that they, seeing in him a colleague of some sort, will not take offense at his presence in their domain. The mask's simplest function (which children still fully appreciate) is to eliminate the individual's identity so that other, hidden powers, may take possession; and its rigid features attempt to contain the demonic invasion somewhere this side of "meltdown." To the human eye the rigid features of the mask also declare its bearer unhuman, for we, like the chimps, rely extensively on the subtleties of facial expression in conducting our personal negotiations. Thus a fixed expression is in itself frightening, as it forbids contact and gives no clue to the next moves its body intends. If in addition to fixity one adds a measure of mutilation in the features (which is usual with primitive masks), one has come upon the *monstrous,* a word that originally meant a manifestation of the sacred through a mutilation of the profane. Just as the blasted oak has been disfigured by the divine thunderbolt and hence remains magically potent, so *any* disfigurement of natural form indicates that it has been "touched" by divinity.[7] And yet, as we have seen with the chimp at the waterfall, beauty has been associated with divinity from the beginning; and hence we have no reason to assume that these earliest masks would not *also* have aspired to the beautiful. Indeed one might even suggest that it is precisely here, in the search for monstrous beauty, that the serious arts arise, and that we will have some distance to travel toward unsublime secularism and the tidy mind before we find the theological leisure to pursue the entirely beautiful.[8]

I digress, though not frivolously. With his mask and his drum, shaman travels to the spirit world for various purposes: to seek wisdom, to seek lucky weather and hunting, to placate angry spirits, to conduct the souls of the recently dead on their last voyage, to secure the release of the accursed, and to acquire magical powers that may assist in the presence of disease. In the crudest cultures this last will be his chief function, and as "medicine man" he is sometimes no more than a sorcerer with a rag-bag of tricks and curses, abracadabras with which he oppresses the credulous and extorts their goods: however skeptical and resentful of such sorcery the oppressed layman might be, he will rarely dare oppose it when himself in trouble. This is the aspect of shamanism that has given it a bad name with such as Paul Radin (*Primitive Religion,* 1957), whose lucid angers are reminiscent of Luther denouncing the sale of Papal Indulgences.

The answer to this is that every culture gets the magic it deserves: superstition and extortionate mumbo jumbo always thrive among the decadent, whether they be primitive or not: the !Kung dancers, for example, by no means decadent but decidedly primitive, seem admirable in their piety, and their hope for healing power would appear plausible even to a modern psychologist with no time for *num.* To concentrate on mischievous sorcery in the analysis of shamanism is to ignore what we can still recognize in it, the authentic stirrings of the spiritual life. Many ethnologists of Radin's generation (and before), usually atheistic in temperament but often wishing they weren't (such as Frazer), sought to organize their material (and perhaps initiate their attack upon the invisible powers) by boldly distinguishing between the magic practiced by sorcerer-shamans on the one hand, and the religious spirituality that comes in more evolved cultures on the other; thus magic bad, religion (traces of which may even still afflict my next-door neighbor) possibly OK—at least not manifestly stupid and wicked. But this distinction, as I am seeking to suggest throughout, no longer seems tenable to most thoughtful ethnologists; indeed it never had much to commend it. The chimpanzee is a magician when he grooms, a ritualist when he dances, and virtually a religionist when saying his prayers in the evening chorus; and at the evolved end of the development it is not difficult to discern magical beliefs in even the most spiritual of religions. This means, as I will suggest at length in the following sections of this chapter, that we are stuck with the intellectual untidiness of man the animal of various magics, some good, some bad. The abuses of sorcery can be fairly easily identified as excessive applications of a technology called "sympathetic magic," but even so, drawing the line between good and bad magic is difficult, as we shall see.

I should make it clear that when in these pages I speak simply of "shaman" I am thinking quite generally of "that-which-is-not-alpha," the power spiritual not temporal; and my intention is both to counteract the crude distinction between magic and religion and also to avoid reducing shamanism to mere sorcery. The figure so denoted in my prose may be an entrancing shaman properly so-called, he may be a priest, or he may be more of a poet-cum-dramatist. The question that then arises is, "What can we say about the 'political' power of such a generalized figure?"

In hard-headed "secular" cultures little disposed to pneumatic invasion he will be marginal, perhaps little more than a purveyor of quackery to the credulous. But wherever *pneuma* takes hold of the imagination, as it does in what one might call the "high line" of cultures that lead to the civilizations of Mesopotamia, his authority will be central, and he will be a rival to alpha-warrior for the kingship. Let me hasten to add that by "high line" I do not mean necessarily the best. What I would suggest, not altogether whimsically, is that exposure to *pneuma* tends to be a cultural growth-promoter, a stimulus to love and war and magic and technology; in the background of Greece and Egypt and Mesopotamia, for example, one finds a wealth of complex magical and religious practices. By contrast the Bushmen, like the Pygmies in the forests of the Congo, keep both religious and political power minimal and decentralized in a loose democratic federation. In taking the road less traveled by, they missed the grand opera of *pneuma* and lost the war, but it may nonetheless be true that the road they took was the right one.[9]

LANGUAGE AND THE MAGIC OF REPRESENTATION

In a sense this section is well overdue, since much of Chapter 5 presupposed both the discovery of language and a certain amount of sympathetic magic. I have held it back not only because it involves some of the higher abstractions, of which we had a good deal in Chapter 4, but also from the possibly perverse desire to see if I could address some of the larger issues in primitive life without getting trammeled in the reflexive subtleties that nowadays so often sidetrack serious discussion of matters in which the linguistic factor has a stake.

As to the question of when and under what circumstances language was discovered, I have little to say. My vote goes to *Homo habilis,* though I don't think it much matters, and, as mentioned earlier, I think Darwin was right in surmising that we sang before we spoke. Our playful gatherings on the dancing ground would have invited the voice to punctuate and decorate the rhythmic stomping, and the first love song was probably sung by a mother to her child (though "gibbonites" might propose the marriage bed as the source of serious song). Some scholars have recently proposed the hunt as the original linguistic context, but this seems to me unlikely: too tight, too dangerous to provide the necessary room for experimentation. Furthermore, man has almost everywhere and always addressed the gods with chanting rather than speech when intent on attracting their attention, and this might be a reminder that the powerful mode is the original mode.

But whatever the origin, what is absolutely prodigious about language, and will detain us for some time, is that it enables us magically to make present that which is absent: the word, by "re-presenting" the thing it names, seems to summon it into our presence, so that we can discuss its attributes or decide what to do about it without hiking two miles down the way and gesticulating. At a stroke our cultural and technological business has radically increased its scope and efficiency: not only can we store a great deal more in our memory, but we can teach the young what they need to know in a fraction of the time; which means we can teach them a great deal more. The stories that language stores are not only for business, of course, but also for pleasure: first of our treasure heaps, possibly the best.

Sympathetic magic, which we briefly met in the buffalo dance, is a natural extension of the word's primordial power to summon what is absent by means of symbolic representation. Whether the symbol is a spoken word, a drawing in the sand, or a mimetic dance, the principle is the same: the act of symbolizing, particularly when ritualized, actually "re-presents" its object, which literally means "bringing it before us by calling it back from whatever place it may have reached" (the original sense of the Latin prefix re-, according to the *Oxford English Dictionary*). What gets called back is not the body in question but its soul (*pneuma*), which to the animistic primitive seems a good deal less securely housed in its body than it has since become (hence the prevalence of ghosts and metempsychosis among primitive peoples). Once the soul has been brought before us we may simply enjoy its company, as in representations of the beautiful, or we may seek to act further upon it, for good or for ill, by ritually calling forth other powers, blessings or curses, from *pneuma*'s cauldron. [10]

For the magic of representation to do its work, the ritual setting is important. As we have already observed, the practice of ritual is not an invention of irrational primitives, but is as old as the reptiles, which may mean not only that it is supremely useful but that we are more or less stuck with it. Throughout the animal kingdom, moments of "sacred" encounter, of love and war, tend to be ritualized; that is, they proceed on "automatic pilot" along set lines instinctually programmed. The evolutionary function of these rituals is to make dangerous communications absolutely clear and to minimize bloodshed. It is surely not surprising that primitive man, seeking to put his technology of the sacred on a firm scientific footing, should have agreed with the rest of the animal kingdom that when approaching dangerous powers, ritual is a most important tool.

Even the most "anti-ritualist" of modern scientists is still imbued with this principle: open-heart surgery, for example, proceeds with a set sequence of precise movements, and if this procedure is not followed, anything from dangerous confusion to bloodshed and death may ensue. Of course there are important differences, as everyone knows, but few are happy to recognize the similarities; which is but one reason why, despite the eloquence of Lévi-Strauss (*The Savage Mind*, 1966), few are willing to grant that primitive ritual is an aspect of primitive science, less empirical than primitive botany, certainly, but in no way incompatible with it.

Another reason for resistance is that human ritual clearly has a large element of playfulness in its composition, and since playfulness is not serious, and science is, it therefore follows . . . This is all wrong: Huizinga (*Homo Ludens*, 1955) has masterfully shown that playfulness lies at the heart of most activities we nowadays call serious, and that it is the humorlessness of the age that prevents us from cheerfully acknowledging the playful element in, say, science, for example.

As for the scientific objection to sympathetic magic itself, this turns principally on the laws of motion: Galileo and Newton, the fathers of scientific materialism, taught us that "x" can only exert force on "y" through contiguity (which includes gravity). The primitive, by contrast, says that the power of life and death is with *pneuma,* everywhere and nowhere, and who has seen the wind? Subatomic physics is now exploring the possibility of "nonlocal connections"; of things happening here as a result of other things happening way over there; and thus our classical scientific notion of causality is up for revision. But however such revision may loosen up the scientific mind, we will remain convinced that, for example, beating the tom-tom in order to make the rain fall involves a childish misconception about how the world works; and it is worth emphasizing that the case for primitivism is in no way enhanced by evading this fact.

What we must do is distinguish between the childish and the grown-up aspects of sympathetic magic. Thus, for example, I would propose that grown-ups may plausibly believe in some sorts of word-magic, such as the efficacy of prayer in certain circumstances, and in the magic of representation when it is concerned with evoking the past, the true and the beautiful; but they may not plausibly believe in what one might call "hard-wired" instances of sympathetic magic. No one acquainted with the basics of empirical science can believe, for example, that a band of primitives, however ritually inspired, could successfully curse a foe in the neighboring tribe (unless that foe heard that he had been cursed and was disposed to credit their magical powers); for *pneuma* is far too grand to submit to such mechanical tinkering:

> Nature lets none unveil her: if she refuse
> To make some revelation to your spirit
> You cannot force her with levers and screws.
> —Goethe, *Faust,* Pt. I

Scientists take note. Amen. Selah.

It is possibly unfair to associate scientists with hard-wired magicians, but possibly not: Goethe certainly had such an association in mind when he penned those lines, and one should agree with him wherever one can. In any case I have had my say about science in Chapter 1, at quite sufficient length. What remains to be stressed here is the importance of recognizing how naturally, even "rationally," the belief in ritually clothed sympathetic magic came to the primitive mind; for without such recognition it is impossible to avoid scientismic smugness and do our forebears justice, nor justly inherit what they have truly left us.

One last attempt to bridge the gap. It is a much unrecognized fact that there is common ground between sympathetic magic and what, since Plato and Aristotle, we have called rational discourse: both believe in the magic of representation. For sympathetic magic to "work," the representation must be sufficiently like the thing represented to call its soul before us; i.e., the whole thing turns on the relation of *sameness*. In rational discourse, similarly, for any proposition to be deemed true, the words spoken must be sufficiently like the things they represent for them to grasp or capture the situation—sameness again. How do we know when the exigent demands of sameness have been met? Difficult question: only when we know that we know what we know.

In *Totem and Taboo* Freud welcomed anthropologist E. B. Tyler's definition of magic as "the mistaking of ideal connections for real ones." Less disposed than our Victorian forebears to deprecate the magical, we might modestly amend this to "the taking of ideal connections for real ones," at which point the similarities between magic and rational discourse become more striking than the differences. Let us take an example: when the primitive seeks magical power over his foe, he makes a doll and sticks pins in it. By connecting two representations, pin and doll, he hopes actually to connect pain and his foe. When the philosopher seeks to grasp the nature of the object he's sitting on, he is seeking what we call knowledge, and will begin with the proposition "A chair is a multi-legged bum-raiser." By connecting two representations, "chair" and "multi-legged bum-raiser," he hopes actually to connect the object in question to what Plato called the general idea of chair-ness, the "real" chair, the chair in the sky, the ideal form that every sittable-on object must indeed represent, or at least bear a family resemblance to. (Notice that the word "chair" is thus the representation of a representation: the diagram is not simple.) But where is this ideal chair that every actual chair that has existed, will or could exist, must represent? And who has seen it? Nobody knows; and yet we all feel quite capable of saying whether this is a chair or not. If rational knowledge proceeds through representations grounded in belief in a heaven of eternal ideas that everyone knows but no one has met, can we not say that reason plays almost as magically with representations as magic does? Plato, the father of rationality, certainly thought the situation distinctly odd, and even though he devoted considerable energy to domesticating it, finding the notion of heavenly ideas embarrassingly primitive, neither he nor anyone since has solved the problem, which since his time has been called "the problem of universals." Of course chairs are really neither here nor there, but when one considers that certain mathematical equations not only represent but seem to give us the power to construct a moon rocket . . . well, it's enough to make one think.[11]

The reader will doubtless have appreciated my scrupulous attempt to avoid special pleading for sympathetic magic by taking as my instance the empirically disreputable business of sticking pins into dolls. As I said, I think we should see such tinkerings as understandable excesses of the "properly magical." Where, then, do we draw the line? It is an important and difficult question, which concerns not only improper relations with *pneuma* but what in this century we have learned to call neurosis; that is to say, "hard-wired" instances of sympathetic magic are not only theologically unattractive and scientifically foolish, but also often neurotic in the sense that a child who clings to his teddy bear too long is neurotic. Thus, for example, cursing one's foe with pins and dolls becomes neurotic when it functions not as a ritual release of anger and a warning but as a fearful concealment, from oneself and him, of one's enmity.

Let us agree that man begins his serious quest for control over Nature and himself with representation, with symbols that are thought actually to embody what they stand for, and that select from life's overwhelming abundance certain power points for access and control. In the experience of any child, primitive or not, such control begins with *mimesis*, copying his parents with a view to magically incorporating and hence becoming them. This is the law of life and there is nothing wrong with it. (Indeed, if it is the law of life, *could* there be anything wrong with it?) The trouble begins if and when this project breaks down: if the magical incorporation of parental power goes awry, the child may fix upon certain objects or rituals (the fetishized teddy bear or compulsive hand washing) as a defense against life's fearfulness. At this point the power of representation ceases to work for him and turns against him: such magical practices as compulsive hand washing, which he hopes will enable him to meet reality with purity and courage, in fact do the opposite, distancing him from reality in a condition of cowardice and dependency. Freud was struck by how closely such childish neurosis resembles the primitive's sympathetic magic, and concluded that neurosis in modern man has its roots in aberrant childhood development, and is to be understood as a regression to the magical practices of our primitive forebears.

So far, so good. The bad begins when Freud goes on from there toward a general identification of primitivism with childishness and neurosis, an equation that has had dire effects on twentieth-century thinking. In every one of us, alongside the child we must outgrow is the child we must preserve. The crucial point is to see that neurotic fixities are simply inappropriate uses of the magical powers of representation, the very powers that, when properly invoked, enable the child to grow up and the grown-up to prosper. These powers are diluted but by no means set aside in maturity: any figure of authority, from god to king to priest to guru to hero to lover (and on to the institutions that metaphorically extend them), whom one accepts as to some extent author = augmentor of one's prosperity, enters and authorizes one's acts under the auspices of magical representation—as indeed does any icon (such as a crucifix), poem, or piece of music in which one may foolishly find solace and a temporary stay against darkness and despair.

Are we to label all these childish and neurotic? Clearly not, and yet the idea that we should is implicit in major aspects of Freud's thought concerning the primary and secondary processes, and this has led many post-Freudians to conclude that all authority is bad authority, all poems have designs on us, and apart from the lamentably necessary mimesis of childhood plus the odd bout of transference with one's analyst when things break down, the sane individual keeps his magical doors closed and vigilantly demystifies (or deconstructs) the siren songs that constantly seek to beguile him from every quarter, whether political, religious, or esthetic. [12] This is pernicious nonsense, for man cannot prosper without authors and authorities of some kind; and this means we must live with the ambivalent feelings they inevitably arouse, and accept the risk of binding ourselves to false gods and falling into fetishism. The person who refuses the game ends up hermetically sealed, longing for everything and belonging to nothing—ripe indeed for the fall into abject enslavement, the very condition he is fearfully trying to forestall. It is a vision of paranoia, *the* spiritual complaint of our times, and to call it nihilism is to give it a dignity it does not deserve.[13]

But if we are to avoid its insidious infection we must recognize the truth in Freud's insight, and accept that it obliges us to draw the line between what is life-enhancing and what is neurotic in magical practices. This is by no means easy to do: who is to say, for example, whether a Christian's magical meditation on the crucifix grants him life-enhancing access to the good and evil in himself and others (a reality of which human kind can bear very little) or whether it is a fetishism that constricts his life? I would say that in many cases it is fetishism, but in the right hands the crucifix is life-enhancing: the historical evidence for this is considerable. However, since such an assertion is not provable in any scientific sense, the question of whether we should *believe* in the life-enhancing crucifix, the juju (a West African amulet) or whatever, is a politico-religious one we must answer together on the dancing ground or in the *agora* or in whatever space we set aside for the resolution of such absolutely central matters.

I realize that most readers of this book will be somewhat over-educated, hence atheistic and mildly offended by crucifixes, jujus, and so forth; that is to say, they will have truly passed from the religious to the psychological. To them I would say this: that even if most of us can no longer entertain, in good conscience, the experience of God or the gods, we can at least agree that we are all seriously impoverished by the dearth of symbols through which we meaningfully make contact with our most elusive and profound energies, those that drive us to love and war and the search for beauty. We make do with the reductive and pseudo-scientific barbarisms of ego, id, superego, object-relations, and so forth, but we barely make do. At the heart of this problem is the fact, offensive to the dignity of scientific man, that part of the gift and the curse of mortality is to be *moved* by the invisible and unharnessable currents of *pneuma,* currents that can at best be addressed (not tamed) through tentative symbols that acknowledge their affinity with the playfulness of magic; as Wallace Stevens beautifully puts it in "Sunday Morning,"

> We live in an old chaos of the sun,
> An old dependency of day and night,

and that dependency, which moves us to construct tentative ideas of order, is, as he says, "inescapable." To live with this dependency, we must retrieve the sane irony of the child, who knows that his sand castle is both real and unreal, something absolutely priceless that is nonetheless to be kicked to pieces at sundown. Another word for such irony, particularly apposite since we have lost it, is courage.

Thus what I am advocating is not primitivism but *neo*primitivism, a retrieval of archaic (and childlike) attitudes that takes account of intervening developments. I am not suggesting we simply jettison science and bring out the tom-tom. We must begin at the point where science obviously lets us down, in the representation of the forces that move us to dream of love and war and beauty. We may then go on to discover that pre-scientific man did it better—guided in our travels by our best poets, such as Yeats, Eliot, Pound, and Stevens, who, against extraordinary odds, have never lost the thread. If we then discover that, however sophisticated our science becomes in dealing with objects, we are stuck with tentative magics in our symbolic approaches to the elusive human passions, then even the skeptical among us may cheer up ("If magic is inevitable, relax and enjoy it"). Where we go from there is anyone's guess; e.g., whether we decide the traditionally sanctioned crucifix is compatible with those of our scientific commitments that seem irrevocable, or whether we decide it tarnished by too much association with patriarchal attitudes and fanatical religion, is something we must decide together when the time comes.

But we are not there yet: we live in unprecedented spiritual confusion and would be well advised to think about humility and take short views. As a first step, psychologist, poet, and "proper" scientist might modestly meet in the recognition that significant parts to us *do* live in "an old chaos of the sun" and that it is high time we got back to it. This means getting back to the question of which of our *necessarily* magical practices are neurotic, and which are life-enhancing. As to what should guide us in these deliberations, the above quote from Goethe (himself no mean scientist) points the way: magic, whether primitive or modern, is properly concerned with the playful and reverent evocation of *pneuma*'s ecstasies in the hope not only of a life more abundant, but one less prone to the devastations that occur when the pneumatic catches us unprepared and by surprise. As regards harnessing those invisible yet palpable energies that drive us toward love and war and beauty, the magical singing and dancing we did before science made us skeptical not only have nothing to apologize for, but seem a good deal more effective in every way than the etiolated arts and psychologies that have succeeded them; which is why some of us are saying that the way forward is back.

What crucially gets lost as the belief in magic wanes is the belief that representations have the power actually to summon or partic- ipate in the spirits they evoke. Thus when the Reformation declared the Christian bread and wine no longer consubstantial with the heavenly powers but merely metaphorical, the Passion withdrew. And when music's enchantment could no longer suggest we were in the presence of powers that bind and loose, but merely exposed to what the famous musicologist Eduard Hanslick called "tonally moving forms," there was a falling off. And to catch a glimpse of what symbolic riches we used to enjoy in poetry, consider these festive lines from Shakespeare's *Midsummer Night's Dream*:

> We have laughed to see the sails conceive,
> And grow big-bellied with the wanton wind.

Imagine how much more fun a day's sailing was when we could experience the world this way! But when the poet can no longer reveal to his audience a world literally animated by invisible energies, when he merely traffics in metaphor, he will soon become what he is today, interior decorator to the middle classes.

All this shrinkage in the playful arts, both sacred and profane, is worse than sad; and yet there is in principle no reason whatever why we should not stop the rot and declare the retrieval of innocence as our project for the next millennium. We could if we would.

The discussion thus far has confined itself to the operation of sympathetic magic on objects in *space,* since that is where its vices lie and hence where objections to it are properly addressed. But as I briefly indicated in this chapter's opening section, the more important theater of operations for the magic of representation is upon objects in *time,* the re*presenting* through ritual remembrance of things that were once here but have been absented from us through forgetfulness or the passage of time.

Primitive societies emphasize the importance of remembering because they derive both their moral legitimacy and their cultural practices from a "charter" originally negotiated by their ancestors with the gods; and this charter must be periodically renewed in rituals that recall the ancestral ghosts for a blessing that effectively regenerates the cosmos. In a word, primitive man has no notion of what we call "history," the idea that time present is other than and different from time past (and indeed time future); in fact, such an idea would strike him as not only unattractive but completely insane. [14]

The importance of memory in the primitive's battle against chaos is universally attested, and this helps us appreciate why Mnemosyne, goddess of memory and mother of the Muses, may have been the first goddess of the *nemos,* as suggested in the Appendix. If *pneuma* is what causes things to appear before us and then disappear into the absence of time past, it will occur to us very early on that we can offset this downward drift and help *pneuma* in its renewal of life by participating in its comings and goings: by re-membering the important things that have been, by re-calling them from the past to the present with the magic of re-presentation, we keep what seems to have gone, and actually assist in its reconstruction and repair. Were we not to do this, all of our cosmos, from the sacred patriarchal ordinances to the proper construction of bows and arrows, would slide into chaos. To put it simply, without the magic of memory, time would appear to be irreversible, and everything would drift into death.[15]

This point is very important, and requires a pause for emphasis: the major function of sympathetic magic in primitive cultures is *not* the sticking of pins into dolls, as its detractors would suggest, but saving the cosmos from its "natural" drift into absence or chaos through memory's magical power to recall and repair what is significantly past. Moreover, this magic is still very much alive in modern man: even those of us utterly bereft of ritual access to "other realms" are periodically visited by dead kin, a parent or spouse, for example, who comes either to console, congratulate, corroborate, or chastise our present activities. Scientific materialism will of course decry such visits as mere daydreams spun upon memory traces, but as I have argued at length, we need no longer fear its reductive proscriptions. What is clear is that such visits often feel quite real, the parent or spouse appears in character, expressing what they indeed would express if they were still alive, and the person visited inevitably feels enriched, even if being disturbingly admonished to "Remember me!," as Hamlet was by his father's ghost. To dismiss all such experience as mere fantasy, as many do these days, is contemptible folly; which is not to say that acceptance of such experience involves belief in theories of metempsychosis, ghosts in the night, or whatever. Such theories seem to me on the whole beside the point, infected by the scientific materialism they seek to combat. All one needs, and it is very little, is to recognize what astute primitives everywhere have recognized, that the mind and its powers of representation may have little jurisdiction in space (pins and dolls) but astonishing capacities to neutralize time's tendency to obliterate the past. Having taken this point, a relatively simple one that need carry no supernatural baggage, one might then go on to listen, with a somewhat open mind, to the vast empirical testimony from all cultures and all ages, which suggests that the past can be recalled and renewed in various ways through the use of memory. From there one might go on to discover that in most cultures that have existed, the recall of the past through dream, trance, ritual, and art has been central to the maintenance of cultural and personal sanity. Only in the secular, scientific, "progressive" West has the past been discredited (sometimes quite viciously) and only in the West have certain kinds of cultural and personal insanities consequently flourished.

I rest my case for the moment, and suggest we return to the old days. In Greek mythology Lethe is the river of forgetfulness and her waters are lethal. Mnemosyne and her daughters supervise the magical arts and crafts of remembrance that keep us and our ancestors safe from these waters. And even when we graduate from strictly magical practices to philosophizing, this structure does not alter: the Greek word for truth is *a-letheia*, and it keeps us from Lethe by allowing things to appear (*epiphaino*), which is to say "shine forth" as they truly are and should be, cleared from the polluting waters of ignorance and forgetfulness, and properly hedged by mutability. By thus saving and renewing the cosmos, one also saves and renews oneself. Both Plato and Aristotle believed that philosophy originated in wonder,[16] and to wonder (*thaumassomai*) at the world involves not only astonishment, pleasure, and gratitude, but also the desire to keep what is wonderful safe from those forces of ignorance that would soil and obscure it. One might say that both religious remembrance and the Platonic philosophy seek to renew the world's wonder by re-membering its origins (*anamimneskomai* = to call up through mimesis). This "religious" basis of philosophy was consciously promulgated by the Orphic sects and the Pythagoreans, who drew their inspiration from Thracian shamans in the north and in the south from Egypt, whose priests taught them how the mind can be purified, rectify its mistakes, through the proper representation of *historia,* what has been and is; and though it is widely known that Plato was influenced by Pythagoras and felt traditionally bound to believe that truth (and hence virtue) were to be sought in remembrance (*anamnesis*), rationalists are often reluctant to remember that, like Pythagoras, Plato also thought philosophy was concerned with salvation.*

---

*The bridge between Plato and the modern mind is St. Augustine, for whom

POLLUTION AND CHAOS

We are now ready to attempt a sketch of how divinity might have looked to those shamans charged with the task of devising ritual lawlines for the safe conduct of *pneuma* into our midst. From what we have gathered already, we know that *pneuma* blows both within and without: in the wind, in the thunder and lightning, in the fiery parching sun, in the running of buffalo, and the prowling of predators in the night, we discern a capricious power that may at any time choose to invade, disrupt, or even devastate the precarious order that prevails within the circle of our campsite. But *pneuma* also wells up within the human breast: in anger, in lust, in the evening chorus, on the dancing ground, in the hunt and the war and at the waterfall, we discern a power that expands, unites, and enlivens us, taking us first toward ecstasy, and then beyond that toward delirium, chaos, and devastation—call it pandemonium, which literally mean "demons everywhere."

In the beginning, in the simplicity of our animism, we will see

---

remembering is still the key to integrity and salvation, but whose *memoria* somehow stores in its "vast court" not only the archetypes of truth and beauty but also the personal memories and imaginings through which we find access to them. Gone is the dancing ground, and gone too the leisured spaciousness of Plato's Academy, but we carry *within* us an imaginative power that both refreshes the soul and makes sense of our worldly experience:

> Great is this force of *memoria*, excessive great O my God; a large and boundless chamber! who ever sounded the bottom thereof? yet is this a power of mine, and belongs unto my nature; nor do I myself comprehend all that I am. Therefore is the mind too strait to contain itself. (*Confessions*, Bk. 10, 8).

One might say that Protestantism begins here, and so too does the problem of preserving the transcendent or transpersonal nature of the imaginative powers. When Augustine asks "Does *memoria* perchance not belong to the mind?" he is hoping that it may still be what leads us out of the labyrinth of self and into meaningful contact with *pneuma*. Whether to strengthen one's Jungian faith in the possibility of imaginative access to the archetypes or to counter one's Freudian skepticism about the childishness of the primary processes, Augustine is the man, and Book 10 of the Confessions is the text that both gratefully remembers the innocence of imagination and eloquently defends the sacred seriousness of its mimetic playfulness.[17]

all of these disturbances of normalcy as manifestations of a single, formless, unfathomable divinity that we have agreed for present purposes to call *pneuma*. (Only by degrees will we develop the mental complexity to divide this power into various divinities that we will call gods and goddesses, and then face the considerable difficulty of having to specify how they are related to each other.)[18] If we arrange these instances of pneumatic arousal along a spectrum of innocuousness and desirability, we find at one end the devastations of violent weather and predatorial attack, and at the other the quiet ecstasies of the evening chorus and the waterfall. In the middle we find the ambiguous invasions of love and war, which can be either good or bad. Clearly what determines the position of these experiences along the spectrum is the degree of ritual and artistic control we can exercise: was *pneuma* invoked through representation, or did it come storming in unannounced, unbidden, to blow us away? As we contemplate this spectrum, we recognize the immense potential and importance of the lawlines we entrust to shaman's care.

But can *pneuma* ever *really* be represented? Does it ever actually manifest itself intelligibly to the senses? This, once again, is the profound question of incarnation, about which to generalize briefly is idiotic; but the short answer, as I have suggested at various points, is yes and no. Since representation implies control, and is moreover a *human* undertaking (*pneuma* presents *itself,* man attempts to represent it), one might crudely suggest that the quiet end of the spectrum (ritually controlled representations) tends to foster a belief in an intelligible divinity that incarnates itself in an orderly fashion in Nature and also teaches man to enlist its support in the constructions of his culture. The noisy end of the spectrum (tempests and tigers), on the contrary, tends to foster belief in a dangerous and inscrutable divinity, basically hostile or indifferent to man's culture, and the culture will therefore be chiefly concerned with apotropaic rituals for keeping divinity absent (*do ut abeas* = I give so that you will go away). The latter sort of belief is primitive (*pneuma* blows in the wind), whereas the former might be called progressive or evolved (the gods are quite like us and can be negotiated with). Since the natural history of representation evolves from mimetic dancing to the subtle refinements of word-magic, and the whole question turns upon divinity's submission to (or authorization of) our representative powers, it is not surprising that the theological debate is cast (when it arises) in terms of language: does the *logos* originate with the gods or with man? I think the answer to this has to be "both," and if this were a book on theology, it would be devoted to saying why. Since it is not, I will simply say that in my view the ancient culture that bore down on this question with the greatest intelligence, intensity, and *determination to keep it unanswered* was that of the Jews.

That's quite enough about incarnation, far too complex for the simple primitive tools we are fashioning; and we may legitimately proceed by accepting, for the sake of argument, that whatever *pneuma*'s implicit and eventual intelligibility, we begin our approach to it through the footprints, spoor, or signatures it leaves on the world of space and time. And when we seek magically to represent it, we do so through "symbols," in Jung's sense of "the best possible expression of a relatively *unknown* fact." If we ask ourselves what in our normal experience most resembles *pneuma*, and is therefore best qualified to symbolize it, our first answer is "the wind," and the second is "blood." And if, like our breath and our blood, *pneuma* enlivens when it flows along lines designed to absorb and contain it, but distresses when it spills and overruns those lines into the unbounded, we have drawn a working image of divinity from our oldest object of knowledge, the human body, whose orderly structure is animated by the flow of breath and blood, and distressed when these flows are displaced. Divinity, as I have frequently emphasized, *is* movement or transformation; and the original notion of cosmos, as we saw at the beginning of Chapter 5 with the introduction of lawlines, involves the idea of lawfulness or "everything in its place." When the movement of divinity displaces the cosmos, we have chaos, which, like all epiphanies of *pneuma*, may be a prelude to rebirth, but is essentially experienced as a terrifying portent of death. When *pneuma* spills itself into the foreground, the primitive mind does not say to itself "Ah, glorious Annunciation!" but rather "Ai, pollution!," and takes steps to stem the flow.

The word "pollution," one of the most important in the primitive lexicon, points to something essentially bad, even horrible; and yet, because its root meaning is "a coming into presence of the usually absent divinity," it also carries an ambiguous shadow, the possibility of a spasm that may kill or cure, or kill as it cures; and in the ensuing discussion, which will concentrate on pollution as poison, let us try to bear in mind its paradoxical shadow. Etymology may assist us in this: our word pollution is from the Latin *polluere* = to defile, but close by is *pollere* = to be powerful. Thus I suggest we think of pollution as an injection of strength which disorders. (The etymologist Eric Partridge [*Origins,* 1959] does not think these two words are cognate, and in order not to interrupt our discussion, I shall now pursue him in an important footnote.)[19]

What is absolutely astonishing about pollution is that every primitive culture known to us more or less agrees how it operates. Just as the word for wind or breath (*pneuma*) everywhere means soul or spirit, so the word for pollution in every culture means the bad breath of divinity, an infectious, contagious affliction that calls for the quarantine and cleansing (Greek *katharsis*) of every thing and person who has been exposed to it. The medical metaphors are apposite: primitive pollution operates very much as we understand the modern virus to do, a contagious and effectively invisible life that feeds upon health.[20] And just as today we say that hygiene keeps you healthy whereas dirt spreads disease, so did the primitive: if pollution is a defilement that calls for ritual cleansing or purification, the most obvious material "signature" for such defilement is dirt; and so the primitive adopted it as his major "symbol" of pollution. And just as today we purify the dirt of a wounded body by cleansing with water, so did the primitive magician. Water was the principal agent of *katharsis*, whether a ritual sprinkling of a body recently exposed to noxious influence, or, more importantly, the tears of lamentation through which we sought to purge ourselves of the grief instilled by some calamity. Thus *pneuma* blows in the more or less invisible wind, and the sign of its having overblown and polluted is the more or less visible dirt it deposits—as in a more or less metaphorical sandstorm, for example, or as in the simplest instance imaginable, the appearance of shit where shit should not be, a matter we shall consider at length in Section 4.[21]

The animal origin of the ideas of pollution and cleansing is in grooming behavior. Chimpanzees are not only fastidious about shit, but spend a good deal of time grooming each other; and as one picks out the lice, scales, and bits of shit from another's pelt, so are their social relations purified. The removal of alien matter augments the body's prosperity *and at the same time* repairs lesions in the body politic; e.g., in the aftermath of alpha's periodic charging displays, one tends to find grooming among those whose relationships have been disrupted. As we have seen, these charging displays are the prologues to what we will eventually call the invasive pollutions of *pneuma,* which call upon us to restore order by purifying ourselves of dirt. Thus our first moves into the metaphysical are soberly grounded in the physical.*

Dirt adulterates the thing it dirties, obscuring its identity by contaminating it with foreign matter. More generally, dirt is "matter out of place," as the distinguished anthropologist Mary Douglas put it, and as such it would seem to be an appropriate symbol for that unpicturable but crucial notion, chaos itself. But even though the ideas of pollution and chaos are very close, there is an important distinction: whereas pollution can be imagined as an event in time that arrives to disrupt us, chaos is most readily conceived not as an event but as a state of affairs obtaining in a mysterious some*where,* as the phrase "in chaos" would suggest. If lawfulness is the laying out of things in order, thereby instating a cosmos for the breeze of *pneuma* to animate, and pollution is that foul wind that displaces the cosmos and leaves us "in chaos," there is a sense in which it translates us to another place, a place where things

---

*One might observe that the chief cleansing rituals in our modern suburban houses involve the vacuum cleaner and the bathtub. Both tend to be solitary and done to excess. The obvious suggestion is that we are afflicted by a general sense of pollution that we are not addressing together.

are displaced, a place of displacement, a place that is noplace. Chaos, in short, would seem to be spatial, and yet a place that is noplace is nowhere. This paradox is indeed what we find "in the beginning," the unthinkable precondition of thought, what philosophers sometimes call "the ground of being." The nearest we can get to imagining it is by working back to it from cosmos: a house wrecked by a storm is "in chaos," just over the line from cosmos, here, there, anywhere.

Mythology is easier on the mind than philosophy when dealing with paradox. The Sumerian *abzu* (= deep) is a nowhere place below the ground but just above the underworld (i.e., on the border between life and death, mortal and immortal), where the great shaman Enki presides as snake god of wisdom. In Greek mythology *chaos* (akin to *chaino, chasko* = to open up, gape open) is the yawning womb-tomb abyss from which Mother Earth arose to deliver the cosmos. In German the *abzu* shows up as *Abgrund* (pleasingly congruent), and for *chaos* one can find *Graben,* a deathly hole just waiting to grab the inattentive or unlucky; but in virtually every primitive cosmogony there is in the beginning (and the end) a somewhere of chaotic torpor awaiting animation:

> And the earth was waste and void, and darkness
> was on the face of the deep: and the breath of
> God moved upon the face of the waters.
>
> (Genesis 1–2)

Like the womb from which it must derive, chaos is "originally" static, the quiet before and after the storms of creation and destruction; and yet we also imagine it as a most potent stasis, lying very close to the storms themselves (*Graben* indeed). This can be easily verified by looking into the mind for an image of "chaos": you might see things flying about in the wind, or you might see the debris lying around after the storm. (It is perhaps worth adding that the problem of imagining chaos is by no means for primitives only: the "black hole" in contemporary theories of astrophysics is a nowhere space into which space disappears, and from which it may in due course explosively reappear. The language changes, but the problem seems to endure.)*

This latent potency in the idea of chaos can also be found in the dirt of pollution. Whereas blood flowing from a wound is an example of *pneuma* polluting, the dried blood that stains the clothing of the person wounded is a prime instance of divine dirt, matter out of place indicating that divinity has visited and left us "in chaos." And yet this dirt, itself unmoving and inert, is thought capable of further infecting whomever it touches: thus chaos breeds more chaos. This seems distinctly odd: whereas we found nothing strange in the excitements of a chimpanzee charging display being thought contagious, the suggestion that dirt, the very antithesis of energy, should also have contagious power, seems extremely magical, to say the least.

On reflection, however, one sees that it is a magic we still believe in. What makes a squalid room demoralizing is not the invisible microbes our learned scientists have recently discovered pullulating within the dirt and the grime, but the squalor itself: we instinctively reach for the broom and set about cleaning up, fearing that otherwise our spirits will be infected by the disorder and slovenliness we see around us. And this is not actually strange: the magic that

*The mathematical language of astrophysics enables us to play about with the idea of black holes, which one might think harmlessly naughty since black holes are God's affair, not our responsibility. The case clearly alters however, with nuclear fission, a version of chaos that one should not be able to speak or think without fear and trembling, since its governance comes within our ken. The case alters even more obviously with versions of chaos unmediated by mathematics and instinct with human purpose. Consider the German word *Vernichtungshaus* = the house where nothingness is made. This was the name for the place where Jews were made to vanish in the 1940s. For a language to be able to make such a word is a clear indication of *abzu* genius; but for such a word to be sayable without fear and trembling is a clear indication of schizoid breakage in the soul (not unrelated to our present calibration of nuclear bombs in terms of their "yield"). The primitive would of course maintain that *no* version of chaos should be sayable without some degree of fear and trembling; and the primitive would be right. My defense for writing relaxedly about chaos in these pages is that the modern mind must at some point be induced to address its larger insanities, and that we must begin from where we are; that is, ludicrously unable to *feel* the significance of what we are able to *say*.

enables us to find such disorder "catching" is simply a weakened modern version of the original power of representation actually to call forth the spirits it symbolizes.

Here we see the subtle but important difference between the magic of dirt and the ectasies of pneumatic inflation: the latter, as we have observed at length, are rooted in our primate experience and seem almost "common-sensical," whereas to experience the contagion of dirt requires not only primate energies and ancient memories of grooming but the mediating activities of a large brain that spends a good deal of its time making representations of the world those energies explore. Indeed one might even suggest that in order to discover the polluting chaos of dirt, one must have already spent some time thinking about death.

The distinction I am getting at here has been brilliantly explored by Lévi-Strauss. As he pondered the extraordinary complexity of kinship classifications in primitive societies, it occurred to him that they were a good deal more complex then they needed to be, which suggested to him that we are profoundly moved to construct ideas or representations of order (and disorder), and that this spiritual appetite is sufficiently important to be placed alongside our physical appetites in the analysis of human concern: hence his famous distinction between the "good to eat" and the "good to think"; between, for example, "Unripe figs make you ill" and "Marriage with your first cousin is incestuously polluting." The first of these is bad for the body, the second is bad for the mind. As we move out of primate innocence into the thoughtfulness of culture, the second kind of pollution, which disorders the laws of the mind, becomes increasingly important. Man, in short, is a symbolizing animal, and he lives just as much (if not more) within his symbols as within his body; and although these realms are in principle distinct, the fun begins when one realizes how often and significantly the physical is conditioned and overshadowed by the metaphysical; i.e., how many of our dos and don'ts are dictated not by the exigencies of Nature but by the conventions of culture. (A brief look at the dietary laws of Leviticus, for example, will discover very few unripe figs but a great many items deemed unclean because they are symbolically associated with Jewish representations of pollution.) More generally, this concern with the good-to-think is responsible for the extraordinary formality and decorousness of much primitive behavior. Perhaps because their world is so ill-furnished with material goods, one is constantly struck not only by their elaborate courtesies but also by their profound reverence for the beautiful. It is as if one can see the map in their minds, the compelling Platonic form of how life should be, and it frequently makes one feel spiritually ill-furnished and scruffy.

The gist of all this is to suggest that we are witnessing here another of our falls from Nature into culture: this one might be called the fall into representation. It was fortunate insofar as it gave us some power to harness the mysterious energies of *pneuma* through the lawlines of representation, and more generally, a map of how life should look; but it was unfortunate insofar as it tempted us to obscure the important simplicities of Nature in complex constructions of culture that lose touch with Nature's imperative urgencies and refer only to themselves. To discover that everything that disorders our lives may be systematically understood as divine pollution is potentially liberating: to lose sight of the simplicity of figs in the elaborate diagrams of Leviticus is an alienation from Nature's empiricism that threatens profound confusion. The answer, as so often, is in the middle way, a judicious reliance on representation: some cultures have, and some have not. The point is nicely made in an almost-haiku by Basho, the seventeenth-century Zen poet from Japan:

> How admirable,
> He who thinks not, "Life is fleeting,"
> When he sees the lightning!

SACRED SWARMS

We have frequently noted that the mark of divinity is *movement*: it breaks through the pattern of what is the case, altering what it touches, for good or for ill. The solemn word for this is transformation, the simple one is change.

It is difficult for us these days to respond freshly to the idea of "change," since most of the changes we meet are anticipated, known, and therefore discounted in advance: even changes in the weather have usually been predicted by the weatherman, and eclipses of the sun and moon, which induced apocalyptic panic in our primitive forebears, are barely remarkable, vindications of our knowingness rather than the opposite. Indeed one might even suggest that it is the boring predictability of most of our lives (dialectically conjoined to a deep fear of change) that leads us to disrupt the integrities of modern space and time with the constant incursions of telephones, newscasts, and so forth; as Norman Mailer once memorably observed, the modern age is characterized by *interruption*. But such interruptions are at best pseudo-events, jiggles of distraction to keep the pulse going, and when faced with moments of genuine change, like a sudden death in the family, we tend to look away or fall blankly into a state of shock. Though constantly encouraged to change our lives by advertising jingles and the latest fashions, we are both psychically and ritually ill-prepared when the real thing happens, whether the news be good or bad. Thus, although we tend to think ourselves in some respects more laid back than the primitive, in others we are more rigid, as I think the following meditation will indicate.

This busy rigidity of the modern condition significantly inhibits our imaginative retrieval of the primitive's innocent eye with regard to change, and I mention it here because the matter is so important: not only is experience of change and transformation at the very center of primitive religion—it *is* what pneuma *does*—but in the beginning, when the neocortex was ill-equipped with causal explanations, and life was in any case dangerous, a great many events would have been experienced as mysterious transformations, the ubiquitous incursions of *pneuma*, dreadful perhaps but undeniable, commanding his attention. Only by very slow degrees would such animistic excitements be relegated by the classifying mind to the more or less predictable interventions of various gods and goddesses (which our magical practices may influence), and finally to the causal sequences in which we can discern the prologues to science and technology. Some sense of how slow this process was, can be gathered from the famous assertion of the Greek philosopher Thales that "Everything is full of gods": it would seem that one of the fathers of pre-Socratic science was still imbued with animism.

The general point I am making here is that although this book is principally concerned with those magical transformations whereby *pneuma* invades the soul with ecstatic inflations, what one might call the properly religious experiences (which tend to find us moderns bewildered and uptight), these were perceived by primitive man simply as heightened aspects of the cosmic power that animates all things, a power he must learn to negotiate with, through myth and ritual; and hence in the interests both of "science" (the management of things) and "religion" (the management of souls), the search for what Jung calls "symbols of transformation" was accorded a high priority. If the essence of divinity is the power that changes both the internal and external world, our search for access to and control over this power will begin with the search for symbols of change itself. If shaman can find something that is no-thing but an ever-changing source of what changes other things, he may be approaching the mystery.

And indeed we have already seen him doing precisely this, up a tree in Chapter 4 and studying a herd of buffalo as it thundered by. In this experience of dazzling, generative, contagious, lethal power, he found a symbol of *pneuma* eminently suitable for representation on the dancing ground (which for primitives everywhere is the magician's workshop and playpen). As we have seen, a thundering herd is an epiphany of abundance that gathers the many into one, seeming to weld its disparate elements together by means of the energy surging through it. As such it offers an analogy, symbol, and hence possibly source, of the ecstatic power that amplifies and unites the tribe in abandonment on the dancing ground and in the hunting pack. To dance the buffalo is to represent its *pneuma,* to call its spirit back from where it resides in buffalo-land to animate us here and now.

If a herd of buffalo may represent and induce ecstasy, so, on the principles of sympathetic magic, may other things that are formally the *same,* such as a swarm, a cluster, a colony, a throng, a crowd; and thus we should be less than astonished to discover that in German, that archaic and magical language, the word *Schwarm* means all of these things, and that the word *Schwärmerei* means revelry or ecstasy.[22] To swarm is, above all, to bring forth abundantly: a swarm of bees appears countless in number, and one imagines it capable of endless increase (a swarm of maggots actually *does* increase with magical speed); hence the relation of the swarm to ecstasy, which originates in the orgiastic experience of communal expansion.[23] But swarms are always somewhat frightening, overwhelming (they might swarm all over us), and it is important to remember that our word ecstasy, which now merely means rapturous delight, originally denoted a decidedly mixed blessing: to be in *ekstasis* was to stand outside oneself (or as we would say, to be "beside oneself"), hence to be more or less out of one's mind (or body), which is to say out of control, destination unknown. What if one is indeed overwhelmed and doesn't come back? Ecstasy thus is a marginal state, between increase and loss, pleasure and pain, love and war, sanity and madness, cosmos and chaos, being and nonbeing, sanctity and pollution: indeed I would suggest it is the *original* marginal state, our introduction to the paradoxes of transcendence. The esctasies of transcendence are paradoxical because they are *essentially* ambiguous, for good and for evil and beyond both: even such a seemingly unambiguous word as pollution is no exception to this, as its origins in *pollere* = to be powerful would suggest. No one in his right mind would willingly invoke the pollutions of chaos, and yet everyone knows that from such intimations of death new life does flow, *sometimes*; and it is this essential ambiguity that makes thinking about these things so constantly difficult. And in case there are still some readers aboard who feel this book's preoccupation with ecstasy is rather mushy and beside the point, I should remind them that the word *ekstasis* is appallingly similar to the word existence: Latin *exsisto* = ex(*ek*) + *sisto,* and *sisto* is a causative form of *sto* = to stand. Thus both ecstasy and existence mean "a standing outside." But surely, says common sense, they must be standing outside different theaters? Perhaps: to be in ecstasy is to stand outside *oneself*, whereas to exist is to stand forth from the ecstasy that conceives and scrambles birth and death. And yet the words are also synonymous at some level; which probably means that our forebears, in their wisdom, perceived that the very mystery of Being itself is harbored in the ecstatic conditions of swarming.

Like the other words that symbolize the chaotic realm between life and death, the swarm is something dreadful that may nonetheless be redemptive. Even today, jaded and knowing as we are, who can stare upon a seething cluster of recently swarmed bees—or better, a writhing mass of maggots in an animal carcass—without a sense of dread and "zero at the bone"? First of all, an empirical answer: maggots are in fact the ministers of death that make rotting bodies disappear, and bees are in fact the mysterious creators and treasurers of a food that is registered as in some sense divine in virtually all mythologies. This gives both bees and maggots a good start as symbols of transformation, one creative, the other destructive. Moreover, both were well known to chimp (who raids bee-hives, sometimes successfully) and to hominid man, and hence we have had them in mind for some time. But granting this, we still suspect there is something more to be found in what they symbolize. Why is it that even to the practiced eye today such things are still somewhat awe-ful? The obvious answer is that we fear their contagion, some nightmare of penetration; and yet it cannot be only this, for beekeepers know that a cluster of recently swarmed bees are *actually* in a state of ecstasy, standing literally outside themselves, and will not sting until reality wakes them—but even so they remain awe-ful. I would suggest that what is ultimately disturbing about such orgiastic gatherings is that they represent to the mind the almost unthinkable paradox of "chaotic prosperity": to see so many bodies writhing and smothering, hands and mouths groping for something to touch and tear, is to imagine chaos incarnate, the undoing of all things; and yet this seething mass of either maggots or bees is actually alive and well, prosperous, organized, unified, even ecstatic—these mouths shall be fed. Such a vision, of chaotic cosmos or cosmotic chaos, joins together the two categories that all sane minds keep asunder, thereby constituting an archetypal example of what Lévi-Strauss would call the "bad to think," which betokeneth madness and catastrophe to the primitive mind, and still manages to give us sophisticates a start. To the innocent eye it is literally monstrous, in the original sense of a showing of the sacred through the mutilation of the profane: one's pious instinct is to avert the gaze.

Although the discussion thus far has treated the swarm primarily as a visual experience, at a deeper level it has to do with touch. Not only are the swarming bodies swarming over each other, but our simplest fear is that they might swarm over us, perhaps thereby visiting on us the fate that any hunting pack visits upon the prey it engulfs: thus in a perfectly natural sense we fear death by swarming. More generally, change or transformation, whether of the self or the external world, is announced and transmitted through touch; not only the caress and the body blow, but the more elusive visitations of *pneuma* must enter the body by making contact (we still speak of being "touched" when the heart is moved, or indeed when the mind is unhinged). Since the swarm is a symbol of the transforming power itself, it seems right that it should be instinct with touching.

To revert to terms introduced earlier, a swarm of maggots or bees is a symbol of changeless change, of unmoving movement. To see it as a solid mass or a unit is calming: to then focus on the pullulating movement within this mass is what gives the stomach a turn: again the paradox of flux within substance, anarchy within coherence, chaos within cosmos, no-thing within the thing. Or one might call the swarm a *gathering* that *scatters*: these terms, which we have already encountered at various points, are perhaps the simplest and most important symbols of cosmos and chaos. Long before we gathered crops and scattered seed we knew that cosmos begins when the *neuron* gathers disparate elements together and binds them into unity or substance for the purposes of increase, and that chaos returns when the cord is loosed and the elements are scattered to the wind. It is the oldest rhythm we know, and each term requires the other: when we hear one heartbeat, systaltic, we are not at ease until we hear the answering diastole; and when we admire some cultural artifact, a basket for example, we take pleasure not only in something gathered from coincidence to withstand the elements and increase our substance, but also that it will in time be released from its cultural captivity to rejoin the elements and make way for other baskets. But again, though we are drawn to both poles of the rhythm, we are drawn to them alternately, or in sequence: when they are put together, the world ends.

Something like this is going on in the swarm. Neither quite liquid or solid, the elements embrace and commingle, but neither bind nor loose; or rather, they seem at once to bind *and* loose! It is fascinating, alluring, and dreadful: the swarm seems to be breaking the most basic laws of the mind and the world, of the world-mind. To do this is permitted to the gods, but forbidden to man. And it is here, in the swarm of maggots or bees, that we find the prologue or the inspiration of the religious orgy: bodies that embrace and commingle with endless potency but neither bind nor loose, that bind and loose and yet do neither, are seeking to represent, in ritual time and space, our oldest sense of the sacred power that lies behind and issues in the world of intelligible appearance. It is what the mystic Spinoza would call the sacred realm of *Natura Naturans* (Nature Naturing), which generates and dissolves individual exist-ents in the profane realm of *Natura Naturata* (Nature Natured), and what Nietzsche would identify among the archaic Greeks as the Dionysiac realm that both generates and dissolves the coherent structures of Apollo. And although the Dionysiac orgy seems set a long way back in the imagination, we have all been touched by its comic child, the spirit of carnival: in swarming crowds that gather and scatter, coalesce and dissolve, threaten and rejoice, we find durable witness to our profoundest intimations of divinity.

We shall discuss Dionysus at some length in the next chapter, but here we should at least emphasize his preeminence in antiquity as god of the carnival swarm. Kerenyi discusses in *Dionysos* (Ch. 2) the evidence for his early days as honey god (*Meilichios*) in Crete, but more important for our purposes is his *thiasos*, the band of sacred or carnival revelers forever about to burst into song, dance, drunkenness, or rowdy sexuality. Wherever one meets the *thiasos* or the somewhat less sacred *komos* in primitive Greek rites, and one meets them everywhere, Dionysus is near. We shall return to this.

There is a good deal of swarming in Genesis, though the Hebrew word *sheretz*, which means a creature that swarms, teems, or creeps, is usually translated in the revised version as "creep" for land creatures and "swarm" for the others; thus, as a rule, fish, locusts, and bees swarm, whereas lizards, spiders, and snakes creep.[24] According to Hebrew commentaries, the *sheretz* tends to be continuously moving on or near the ground: thus when the earth teems, look for the *sheretz*. Chapter 11 of Leviticus specifies that almost all creeping things are abominable and polluting, though the swarmers seem to be undefiling. In all this confusion one may discern an incipient tendency in the biblical authors to separate the ecstatic swarmers from the plainly repulsive creepers: such would be consonant with the analysis of creepers I am about to offer. But if there was such a tendency, it seems to have been abandoned at some stage, probably because the whole question appeared too primitive for Pentateuch purposes.

The idea of swarming, as we have seen, has principally to do with abundance, and hence its association with water is a natural one (see Genesis 1:20), as is attested by those primitive cosmogonies that begin with a cosmic serpent being precipitated from the abundant sea-deeps and then generating the rest of creation.[25] Land-based creepers, however, such as mice, rats, lizards, spiders, and snakes, tend to be encountered singly, and their only obvious connection to abundance seems to lie in their prodigious number of legs (the snake being in this context a magical millipede, infinite invisible legs). Could this be so?

Not quite: what is alarmingly abundant about the creepers is not the number of legs (the lizard and the mouse have only four) but the disturbing speed and unpredictability of their movement. Our word "abundance" originally meant overflowing water, and the danger in being exposed to it, as we have seen, is that one may be overwhelmed, which also means drowned; that is to say, the danger is of invasion, penetration, possession by a foreign element; and indeed both folklore and the psychiatric journals attest the enduring power of such creeps as snakes, spiders, mice, and rats to alarm the imagination with fears of penetration and demonic possession.

A room feels creepy when it seems possessed by a malign presence. Creeps can fly, swim, leap, glide, slither, scuttle, and often use camouflage; but they do not stand, much less stand out. Their closeness to the ground contributes both to their obscurity and the unpredictability of their movements. There is a simple sense in which to be is to be perceived, or at least perceivable; and for this one must stand, or at least move in a predictable, intelligible way so that one's contours can be known. The idea of standing underlies not only such words as "ecstasy" and "existence" but also the more sobering "substance." To have "substance" is to have something solid beneath one's stance, which enables one to be under-stood; and to have "standing" is to be known, well known, known to be well, to be as one is known, honest, upright. To creep is not to stand, but to move, stealthily; not in a straight way, but with figure bent for concealment and camouflage, leaning toward the earth and its teeming obscurities, away from the lucid sky. A creep is not straight but bent, affects servility (Uriah Heep-Creep), and insinuates himself (the snake again), the better to bite you when he has reached your heart and you can't see him.

One could go on; but enough has been said to suggest why the first chapter of Genesis adamantly marks out the category of creeping things from both cattle and beasts of the earth (notice the emphases and almost incantatory repetitions in verses 24–6), and then proceeds to abominate them in Leviticus. Creeping things are anomalous, marginal, liminal creatures, neither here nor there, not *belonging* to the clear and distinct categories of creation and/or the mind that seeks to know it; and hence look like sketches of the criminal and the demonic, "more than kin, less than kind."

The king of the creeps is clearly the snake: fastest, most dangerous, seemingly without contour, utterly magical in the means of his locomotion, master of penetration. Equally at home in the trees, on the ground, in the water and underground, all he lacks is wings to fulfill our ancient simian nightmare of ubiquitous threat, which, as we noticed earlier, the Toltecs award him in their winged-serpent god, Quetzalcoatl, and which he carries as the dragon in most mythologies.[26] When the serpent appears as if from nowhere in Chapter 3 of Genesis, he has no wings but seems to be standing upright (a kind of supercobra), clearly a lord of some substance, and ready to perform one of his oldest and best roles, that of the deceiving trickster, for which he shall be made to creep in the dust. We shall return to him in due course.

What mythologically connects the swarm of bees to the creeping trickster are the themes of abundance, possession, transformation, and deceit. The ecstasy symbolized by the swarm offers to dissolve the contours of the self, a promise of death or new life; and since one cannot know which, one may be deceived. Comparably the subtle serpent says "You can be more than you are, immortal perhaps, if you allow me to take possession of you"; and to our fearful timidity he replies "Ye shall not surely die"; and since one cannot know his subtlety, one may be deceived. Despite the mythological continuities, however, the distance between these two is vast: from chthonic thumping on the communal dancing ground in the African savannah to the stark solitary light of Jewish moralism, man standing alone and troubled beneath the law.

In this section I have offered the swarm—whether of bees or maggots—as an epiphany of prime significance for primitive man; not a very empirical offering, admittedly, and some readers may be skeptical. In its defense let me say that, like the buffalo herd, it is adduced in the spirit of myth not history, an important distinction for the purposes of this book, discussed in Chapter 4. The allusion to the creeping things in Genesis is not unempirical, but since Genesis focuses only obliquely, even reluctantly, on the matter, its evidence of a primitive Hebrew swarm-god is less than compelling, though I hope to strengthen this argument when we return to the serpent in Chapter 8. I should certainly mention the famous story in

Judges 14 in which a putative swarm of maggots gives way to a swarm of bees in the carcass of a lion, with magical effects on Samson, for Kerenyi (*Dionysos*, 1976) has found important evidence of a similar motif in connection with the Greek bull of Dionysus (p. 40); and yet the Samson incident (and its magicking riddle) stands out as a primitive remnant in an already primitive tale, and gives us little to work with. Looking across the water to Greece, one finds its myth and ritual rich in Dionysian *thiasoi*, but again distressingly short on swarming *per se* (though one should mention the *erinyes*, that invisible *thiasos* of nemesis and revenge that flies in the wind, like flies indeed, which is what Sartre calls them in his play *Les Mouches*).[27] However, a closer look at archaic Greece does reveal widespread vestiges of the old neolithic bee goddess who survived famously in Minoan Crete; and a very old belief that bees are generated in the carcass of a sacrificial bull (as ministers of renewal) was sufficiently potent to survive into the poetry of Ovid and Vergil.[28] Such scraps tell us nothing about the magic of swarming, of course, but do lend some support to my contention that the swarming divinity is too primitive to have survived into historical times, and hence we must seek it in its evolved metaphors, as Canetti (*Crowds and Power*, 1962) and Bakhtin (*Rabelais and His World*, 1968) have done.

The rituals of carnival are in some respects the most interesting of these, but since they arise from the world of Trickster, Hermes and Dionysus, we shall leave them until the next section. Let us conclude this one with a brief discussion of fire, which is not only a swarming symbol but one that can be, however perilously, grasped. At the center of Lévi-Strauss's elaborate analysis of the mythological mind is the suggestion that what announces and symbolizes our move from the state of Nature into a culture of law and kinship is the domestication of fire. Food that has been cooked promises "magically" to nourish rather than attack us, and in such technology one may see the promethean moment in which man addressed the pneumatic powers with the intention of reducing their sway over his existence. In the orderly, binomial separation and classification of our foodstuffs into the raw and the cooked, the moist and the dry, the sweet and the sour, we can find the beginnings of lawful regulation. Raw nature, symbolized by honey, is the realm of the gods, hedged by taboo, whereas what has been cooked into culture, symbolized by the smoke and ash of tobacco, is man's domain. It is a brilliant insight, and as so often, blindingly simple once one has seen it. On the basis of it, those with empirical tendencies might wish to violate the autotelic purities of Lévi-Strauss's linguistic analysis and blatantly suggest that kinship *actually* (not just symbolically) began with the domestication of fire, and hence the events discussed in Chapter 4 can be dated at around 50,000 B.C., triggering the emergence of *Homo sapiens sapiens* at about 40,000. There seems to me some virtue in this suggestion; for just as, by common consent, the discovery of astronomy, of knowable regulation in the movement of the heavens, gave man the confidence to embark upon the civilizations of Egypt and Mesopotamia, so he would have needed some comparable advance against the ungraspable nature of divinity in order to embark upon kinship. It is difficult to think of anything remotely as significant as the domestication of the cooking fire in this regard; and just imagine how much livelier things would have become on the dancing ground when there was a fire burning in the middle of it!

The characteristics of fire, both actual and symbolic, are remarkably similar to those of the swarm. Its power is limitless: it moves constantly without contour and yet its mass makes it seem thing-like: it feeds on what it touches as if with infinite mouths: it fascinates, attracts, increases, and yet repels with an absolute "Do not touch." Its power to alter and hasten the processes of Nature is essentially destructive, and yet if one even half-follows Lévi-Strauss, once harnessed it symbolizes all that gives warmth to our sense of well-being. In view of all this it is hardly surprising that it should relegate the swarm god and become perhaps the principal manifestation of divinity for primitive man under kinship.

In time, we would learn to think that metals which have endured the rigors of fire have taken on their death and been hardened into immortality. And even today, in our non-mysterious scientific culture, fire remains a principal agent of transformation.*

TRICKSTER AND HERMES: THE GIVE AND TAKE OF THINGS THAT CHANGE

Further traces of the swarming power can be found in a myth that appears with astonishing consistency throughout the world, and that according to Paul Radin (*The Trickster*, 1956), we can confidently place among "the oldest expressions of mankind" (p. ix). Perhaps best known in versions collected from the American Indians, Trickster is an obscene figure who seems to be rising from the depths of unconscious and polymorphous desire toward the light of human clarity and adult separation. Somewhere between monster and child, this inchoate power is instinct with metamorphosis and hence has no determinate shape, but in the admirable version of the mid-Western Winnebago–Sioux, one can at least discern lengths of intestine wrapped around the body, and an equally long penis, similarly wrapped.[29] Thus what we can *see* is a figure defined, encircled, and hence controlled by two bloated appetites, for food and for sex. The third one, which these two together call forth, is the appetite for killing and destruction, and this is symbolized to some extent by the penis as snake and as battering ram, but chiefly by the anus, home of the fart and the turd, located at the end of the intestine. Trickster is more than a little intrigued with this aperture, and tries to engage it in conversation.

Despite such plain speaking, as it were, Trickster seeks to satisfy his desires by more or less elaborate deceits, which he practices by

---

*If we were to consult the Bushman who visited us in Chapter 1, he would of course be pleased to see that fire was still held in some regard, but would be fascinated and appalled by three other things: the pullulating city (Baudelaire's "*fourmillante cité*"), the cancer that swarms through so many of our bodies, and the nuclear reactors where lethal energy breeds from itself in a tightly closed box. All three, he might suggest, are conceived in imaginations insufficiently pious with regard to the swarm god.

means of a protean power to alter his contours and assume any shape he likes. Utterly unprincipled and amoral, he seems to float upon the ever-changing tides of fantasy and desire, and his shape alters to suit the moment. The psychologists would say he is suffering an episode of schizo-manic inflation (the opposite of fetishistic contraction) in which the bounding lines of creaturely finitude are denied in order to accommodate whatever the moment offers—a euphoric trip that will end in madness or depression. Around the campfire, however, we bid good evening to one of our first shamanic sketches, and applaud as he steps forward to announce "Trickster the name, metamorphosis the game."

As creeping thing he is often called spider, and as master of negation ("the spirit that ever denies") he is often seen as a preliminary sketch of the devil. In any case, just as Earthmaker creates and establishes order, so Trickster, either as foolish child or bold deceiver, displays a genius for every kind of disorder. Although he sometimes seems a serious god of chaos, whose home, as we might expect, is somewhere beneath the cosmos of Earthmaker, his anarchy is mostly concerned with laughter that, curiously enough, frequently issues in gifts to mankind. Thus he is best seen as a preliminary sketch for the Dionysiac spirit of carnival that offers us temporary release from the constraints of culture, a gift of considerable dimensions. The importance of this anarchic spirit to the understanding of serious endeavor has been much forgotten in recent times, and we are all indebted to Mikhail Bakhtin for reminding us how it works.[30]

Trickster can also be seen as a preliminary sketch of the shaman and the poet, and as such we would expect him to be at least somewhat at odds with alpha-warrior. In the Winnebago version this is not only so, but we can also find traces of the original division of alpha-shaman discussed in Chapter 4. The Winnebago were among the oldest and most evolved of the Sioux-speaking tribes, and their chief was a kind of supershaman who was strictly forbidden to go on the warpath. Their version of the myth begins with the chief (clearly regressing into the archaic realm of dream and madness) setting off on the warpath after prolonged illicit fornication, various discourtesies, and the ritual destruction of his arrows, canoe, and sacred warbundle (a bag of magical amulets, the warrior's most prized possession). At this point, having blasphemed in all directions, he is abandoned by the last of his followers, and he wanders into the darkness to be transformed into the primordial monstrosity that is Trickster.

The unmaking of culture is a regression that cancels all the separations (such as that between alpha and shaman) that the lawlines enforce. Once beyond culture, one is delivered up to Nature: Trickster discovers he can speak the language of the animals (each of whom he addresses as "little brother"), but with no tools except a knife, he must do the best he can with Nature's tactics of violence and deceit, and the child's fantasy of godlike powers of metamorphosis. Like the child, however (and indeed the early hominids), he is caught between two worlds, having lost the animal's instinctive certainties and not yet found the lawlines of culture. Hence the gargantuan appetites and the lack of control, which leave him so often the dupe and the fool rather than the cunning victor. The power he would fantastically harness is the power of divinity itself, changeless change, metamorphosis, precisely the thing that cannot be grasped.

It is a wonderful story, which has spawned countless progeny throughout the history of literature. In it we see above all the carnival spirit playing with the ideas of blasphemy and inversion, but we also see the primitive mind registering astonishing insights concerning the evolution of imagination and human psychology. Like all good stories of excess, it reminds man of his limitations, even while consoling him over his defeats in the ill-matched struggle with *pneuma*'s elusiveness in the early days. It also offers an admirably lucid perception of the central role of deceit in the satisfaction and frustration of desire.

Although one might think that deceit or craftiness belongs to man's culture rather than the gods' Nature, this is not strictly so. From our earliest days in the hunt we noticed a good deal of camouflage, simulation, and deception in the hunting of one animal by another; and hence what is perhaps the principal skill of the human hunter, that of persuading his adversary that he is not there, is traceable not to human invention but to our emulation of the animals. As Heraclitus said, "Nature loves to hide."

The importance of deceit in human affairs takes a quantum leap with the discovery of language; as the old joke goes, "God gave Adam the power of speech in the garden, and the first thing he did was tell a lie."[31] From that day forward we could bend our skills not only to the disguising of our bodies and our surroundings, versions of metamorphosis, but also to the verbal misrepresentation of our intentions in order to entrap the unwary. Representation itself, after all, is already a simulation, an artifice constructed, in the buffalo dance, for example, to lure the unsuspecting spirit of the buffalo into our midst through skilled *mimesis*; and sympathetic magic, as we have seen, is a technique arising from representation for actually taking hold of some alien spirit through charms, spells, and deceptive simulations.[32] From this it is but a natural step to the kind of dissembling we would today call treacherous; and as our lives came to depend more and more upon linguistic transactions, the opportunities for such dissembling would have multiplied considerably. In sum, it would appear that we came very early to the perception that things are seldom what they seem, and hence that to reach out and grasp what is strange and not already yours is risky, and hence that those gifted with second sight, the ability to predict whether a thing will indeed prove to be as it seems, are to be highly valued. In view of all this, the safest form of appropriation is magical: whereas the hunter deceives his prey into thinking him not there, the magician really *is* absent, and catches his prey by deceiving its spirit through representation.

But there is a further sense, at once simpler and more difficult, in which acts of enticement and appropriation are connected to deceit, and to appreciate this let us return to the hunt, the major context in which for millions of years we learned about give and take. When an animal comes into our ken and we take it, this is both a find, a *trouvaille,* and also something concealed that we capture or steal by stealth and violence. As I suggested in Chapter 5, it is difficult to classify; after all, something that is both a gift of the gods and also stolen, is, to our thinking, a kind of nonsense. And yet the difficulty is more ours than the primitive's, for he did not live within a legal system that sustains the belief that virtually everything is owned by someone or other: indeed his notion of private property, as we understand it, was negligible. In the beginning everything belongs to *pneuma*.

The important point here is that for millions of years our daily acts of appropriation had to do with food, i.e., hunting and gathering; and in both cases success tended to involve stealth (remember the chimps often foraging solo, and hiding with their catch to avoid sharing). The food that we seek is usually *hidden* from view, and we have to find it. Add to this the fact that what looks appetizing may be a trap: he who takes the bait gets caught, and moreover those berries that made us so ill last week were doubtless yet another of the gods' jokes to keep us alert. Thus the idea of taking was associated with concealment, danger, and deception from the outset. Even when we came to think of our taking as a giving of the gods, we would say "The gods decree that the form under which we receive their bounty often involves violence, danger, and deceit." This being so, when we go out to meet them in this dangerous zone of unpredictability, we must keep our wits about us and, like the animals we seek, proceed with caution and stealth. Our prey harbors a spirit that will not easily give itself up to us, and our best tactic is to deceive him into thinking we are not there. But even better than this is *actually* not to be there, to lay a trap for him and stay at home! Less exciting certainly, less than sporting or honorable in the view of aristocratic warriors, but as the neocortex grows it grows clever, and cleverness is difficult to answer. Thus another aspect of "the fall" into braininess.

We shall return to this in Chapter 8. For the moment we seem to have arrived at a definition of appropriation as "a dangerous action best performed by stealth and deceit." To steal is to take without being known, and not to be perceived is in a simple sense not to be there, and hence stealing is a kind of magical invisible taking. We have seen that hunting is involved with both stealing and magical deceptions, and hence it seems reasonable to suggest that the idea of taking or appropriating has been bound up with magic and stealing from the beginning.

The archaic root for theft-words in Greek is *klept* or *klop,* and this root points not to wrongdoing but to the idea of secret or magical action; and the absence of impropriety in Homeric usage suggests that in the beginning it may simply have meant "proper taking," an idea that gains plausibility from the fact that in archaic Roman law codes, acts of legitimate appropriation were still called *furta,* which means thefts (as in "furtive"). In English law we still say that a man is "seized of" his possessions, and this points back not only to the violence of appropriation but also to the simplest sense in which acts of appropriation are magical. To seize or be seized is to be transformed, to have one's identity, even the contours of one's body, changed. The moment I seize an object, take it unto myself and call it mine, my being is altered, instantaneously, and the passive voice used in the legal formulation points to the sense in which one is possessed and altered by one's possessions.

As his wand and flying sandals would suggest, Hermes is the most magical of the Greek gods, which points back to his previous career as a shaman, and beyond that to Trickster himself. The Greek word for tricky is *dolios,* and this, together with the thieving words built on *klept,* were major epithets of Hermes. The third one of importance was *kerdoós,* and though all three in Homeric usage involved the tricky, the skillful, and the magical (all of these meanings survive in our word "crafty"), only the last added the further notion of "gainful." Thus the one who is skilled in magical practices, and the crafting technologies that obviously supersede them, will use these skills for the manipulation and appropriation of objects that will augment our prosperity; and thus Hermes was the god not only of thieves and craftsman, but also of merchants and gift-givers.[33]

This most versatile god is also the messenger, the one who carries things between the gods and man, who is therefore at home in the mysterious marginal zone that separates the two. Thus he is also the god of boundaries, and in the beginning he will supervise and authorize the taking and carrying of food across that first and most dangerous of our bounding lines, the one separating the sacred and the profane, divinity and mankind. As we saw in the previous section, the mind in search of the "good to think" classifies its world into discrete categories, and when the boundary lines between these categories are crossed (e.g., when the not-mine passes into the mine), we are in danger of ending up in chaos. Thus in addition to the physical dangers attending the pursuit of the "good to eat" since time immemorial, we can add, once we start *thinking* about the problem, the metaphysical or mental dangers of violating the laws of the "good to think." To get stuck in the no-man's-land between such categories as the sacred/profane and the me/not me is very bad magic: in physical terms it would mean being caught by the animal one is trying to catch, and hence perhaps *literally* turning into one's prey; and in metaphysical terms it means falling into monstrous absurdity. No wonder we call on such an agile and magical god as Hermes to supervise such transformations.

As we do when we move from the simple appropriations of food to the complex "mutual takings" of trade that, as Brown convincingly argues (*Hermes the Thief,* 1969), were originally understood as "mutual thefts": thus Hermes is also the god of commerce. Marketing in ancient Greece probably began with "silent trade," whereby one object would be left in a lonely spot, a boundary of some kind, and after a suitable interval the leaver would return to collect the object bartered for it. Such "silence" effectively transforms the traded objects from thefts into gifts, and also avoids the risk of violence that arises when taking edges into snatching. The earliest markets (proto-agoras) were also set up in reserved areas or boundaries, to minimize the risks of violence, raiding, and war; and hence Homer could refer to the class of merchants as "professional boundary-crossers."[34] Men also used to cross the bounds for wives, either to seize or to barter for them, again a potentially explosive form of appropriation; and at these marriage-marketing festivals we also find the *agon* (contest or struggle, the root *ag* = gathering), athletic games to contest the women and simply to let off steam; and so Hermes also becomes a patron of athletics, seduction, and marriage. From stone heap to *agora* to *agon* to seduction and marriage, he declares his interest in gatherings. As the new and difficult idea of trade-as-equitable-exchange gradually supplanted the notion of mutual theft, so the danger and the mystery of such appropriation receded, and the market ground moved from the boundary into the polis; and Hermes *agoraios* became a kind of city slicker, patron of merchants and craftsmen.

But he also remained the rustic god of wild and lonely boundary-zones, father of Pan and protector of flocks and wanderers and travelers. Such wild places are dangerous not only because the writ of neither adjoining parish runs there, making them the home of the homeless, the criminal, and the depraved, but also because for the primitive mind, boundaries are always places where chaos lurks— "Here be dragons," as the old maps used to say when they reached the edge of cultural space. Hence the heap of stones gathered together to mark boundaries (like the cairns that still mark our mountaintops) were both markers and magical talismans to ward off bad luck (we still add a stone to the heap for luck). Luck is of course the major gift Hermes has to bestow on man, and he gets his name from *herma* = stone heap or standing stone. At this point we are moving very far back in imaginative space-time, to primordial gestures. What do you do in a wild and lonely spot when you feel the malice of *pneuma* might blow you away? (Suppose you have climbed the mountain in sunshine, and now fog and wind are closing in.) What you do is gather stones together, and build a little heap—a little culture to defy Nature. If you had the time and the technology, you would do better than this, and roll a great big stone onto its feet, a standing stone. This would be a prop and a support, a here-I-am act of defiance; and indeed "prop or support" is the principal meaning of *herma* in the post-magical "civilized" Greece of ancient times. The *herma* was also frequently a milestone, a beacon that gives moral support to the traveler.

The heap of stones takes us right back to the beginning, some "degree zero" of the mind; for it is clearly similar to the primordial bundle (*fascis, phakelos*), which is discussed at some length in the Appendix. Both are primary instances of *gathering* the many into one (the Greek root *ag*, just mentioned), which, as I have emphasized throughout, lies at the heart of the cultural undertaking. This is nicely indicated in Greek, for the verb *neo*, which means to heap up, seems to be clearly present in the magical thing made by the heaping-up of stones, the temple (*neos* or *naos*); and since what we do in the temple is renew our energies by gathering ourselves together in acts that commemorate our origins, both the adjective *neos* and the prefix *neo*- properly designate things newly made or renewed.[35]

Here, I suggest, we can find an opening (*kairos*) into the mystery of the standing stones, the menhirs of prehistoric Europe that were erected from about 5,000 B.C. If one standing stone collects and transcends a gathering of small ones, then *a fortiori* a great gathering of standing stones (such as we find at Carnac in France) will be very powerful magic indeed, a rough draft of the cathedrals we will ultimately construct, places that gather people together for worship, festival, and marketing.

In ancient Greece the *herma* at some point became sexualized: like the Indian *lingam*, it was often cast as a standing stone that represented an erect phallus. Brown in *Hermes the Thief* convincingly argues that such stones, placed at thresholds and crossroads where strangers tend dangerously to meet, were not fertility tokens but good-luck charms, apotropaic symbols to ward off the evil spirits. One thinks of Trickster and the amazing powers (by no means simply progenitive) of his phallus.

It nonetheless seems bizarre that the agile Hermes (who becomes in Latin the *Mercurius* of quicksilver) should have begun life as a stone, despite all that we have learned about how opposites meet in the mythical. Here one should mention the extremely old and very widely distributed myths of *petra genetrix*[36], which work with the idea that stones are the children of Mother Earth, and that humans too are generated from the stoney; and also bear in mind what was

said in the previous section about the importance of "standing."*
Again, one can see the standing stones at Carnac as rows of divine
teeth, those hard and durable bits of the body that proclaim our
seriousness by scattering the flesh that resists them, blueprints for
the flint dagger, our first aggressive declaration of independence
from Nature's tyrannies, which gave its name to the Stone Age. Or
again, one can see them as a stand of "cultured" trees, an advance on
(or precursor of) the woodland *nemos* that was undoubtedly one of our
first temples. Even so, as all of these suggestions indicate, we have
here not only an advance on the cave-painted cathedrals where all
was movement and liveliness (though rendered on stone), but a
move to the opposite spiritual pole. Esthetically, of course, the
move is into crudity, but the new is almost always crude. I think
the explanation of the shift probably lies, as with the move from
the neolithic into the cities of Mesopotamia, in star-gazing. The
evidence seems fairly clear, particularly in places like Stonehenge,
that the stones are disposed along astronomical lines. To see some
pattern in the movement of stars is to see permanence underlying
change, some stand against death; and to erect the dolmens
and menhirs is to align oneself with that permanence, the first
rock of ages. To do this is to see that the gods of chaos may not
only be subdued by stillness, but may be themselves still. In any
case it is a remarkable moment in the coming and going of
human self-confidence, an anticipation of the movement (outlined
in the Appendix) from the wind god of the desert-habituated
Semites to the statuary of the Greeks, through which the gods may
announce their presence to the alerted eye with an epiphanic nod. In

---

*I have heard old countrymen in Suffolk speak of a phallic erection as a "stand"
(in German, *Ständer*). Not unrelated to this, I suspect, is that when appraising the
conformation of a stud animal who must work in the field, such as a ram or a bull,
one looks particularly to his *stance,* the sturdy spread of his hind-quarters.
Conversely, the female must "stand" for his service. Humans on the other hand tend
to "get laid," as eggs do, which might seem either sentimental or tricky but in fact
recalls our oldest word for "getting down to it," what must be done if anything is
to stand. For a discussion of "lay," see the Appendix.

such quickness one is back once again with Hermes–Mercurius, reminded that permanence and change are the two sides of the original coin.

Having followed Hermes back into the shamanic mists, let us now bring him forward and look at the mysterious process whereby the theft is turned into its opposite and its cognate, the gift. We have seen how the taking of food is involved with danger, violence, stealth, and deceit, and surmised that in the beginning there was very little distance between taking and stealing. And yet it is very much in our interest, for obvious reasons, to think that the food we take from the gods is also freely given (a concern that has by no means been outgrown, as the incidence of anorexia among the thoughtful and guilt-afflicted youth of today would indicate). The obvious way to address this problem is with ritual: food that has been obscurely snatched in deception, violence, and anger is clarified and properly named in ceremonies that consecrate it with fire, offer some of it back to the gods, and share the rest decorously among ourselves. As we noticed in the previous chapter, these are perhaps the oldest and most important cultural rites, and we can now see that they also spell out the word gift as a something that only becomes ours as we share it with others. In Lévi-Straussian mode we might say that the food is seized or stolen in Nature, transformed and offered as a gift in culture.

This transformation is crucial, to allay not only our fears but our guilts; for what we have seized may justly be seized from us in turn. Food ingested without ritual legitimation, though safe from seizure, exposes one to the spirits of revenge (*nemesis* to the Greeks, guilt to us). Since the food cannot be returned, the debt incurred cannot be paid, and this leaves one's body "marked" for future punishment, beginning perhaps with a bellyache.[37] Unshared possessions (unknown or at least deplored in most primitive cultures) must be hidden and defended, a more or less shameful business. To privatize is indeed to deprive others, and this needs justifying even in the decidedly post-primitive world of capitalism. To hide what we treasure is instinctive and natural (so much so that we still assume that what is hidden is therefore also valuable);[38] but to display and share with others what we treasure is to overcome the instinctive fear of loss, forestall the guilt of illegitimate appropriation, and transform those around us from potential predators to kin. Thus the gift symbolizes a central triumph for culture over Nature, our faith in its capacity to disarm both the human predator and the guilt-inducing spirits of vengeance.

Something similar occurs with the trading of goods. Those first markets that were held "out of bounds" were potentially wild and orgiastic affairs, prologues to carnival, in which the spirit of deception was at large (one can still sense the spirit of mischief in crowded and noisy marketplaces). Once we moved them to the *agora* inside the walls (in the eighth century in Greece), bartering would have moved toward the ceremonious, a mutual offering of gifts, and "pulling a fast one" would no longer be thought so smart. Again the move from Nature to culture, and the important thing to notice is that deception is to be left outside the walls, in the gods' country. Deceit, one of our first virtues, will now gradually become demonic, characteristic of mischievous gods like Hermes (and Dionysus) and ambiguous heroes like Odysseus: civilized man will endeavor to go straight.

But it is going to be terribly difficult. The pre-philosophical word for intelligence in Greece was *metis,* and it refers to cunning, craftiness, quick-wittedness, and deceit rather than a capacity to think abstractly—altogether Hermes's sort of thing.[39] The goddess Metis was the mother of crafty Athene, and she was so fast with her protean talent for metamorphosis that Zeus couldn't grasp her for sexual purposes, and so had to swallow her, which is why Athena was born from Zeus's head. More important than these, however, is Athena's protégé Odysseus, ambiguous hero of Greek epic, and what makes him so formidable is his peerless talent for cunning and deception. Clearly, skills that were so hallowed by human memory and of such value in a world of violence and warfare could not simply be cast aside. And yet, and yet, culture can't be built on deception.

Homer's *Odyssey* is chiefly concerned with mediating between and finding room for both the innocence of gift-giving and hospitality on the one hand (culture), and the experience of deception and snatching on the other (Nature). We shall examine this question in some detail in Chapter 8 (comparing it with what Genesis makes of the serpent), but at this point we may conclude our discussion of Hermes and also do some groundwork for Chapter 8 by considering briefly what happened to this god when he fell under the sway of post-shamanic, post-magical, Greek "civilization."

The attempt to muzzle him came from two quarters, the military-aristocratic and the moralistic (represented originally by Hesiod the farmer). Alpha-warriors, as we might expect, are skeptical of any magic except the kind they pursue with their swords, and so when Zeus of the thunderbolt arrived from the north with Mycenean kingship, he became king of the gods and Hermes the ex-shaman became his servant. This also served to indicate that aristocratic landowners (the *agathoi*) rule and merchant-craftsmen serve. As for Hermes *dolios,* trickster thief, he retained a certain prestige as long as the aristocrats remained robber barons properly so-called. But when they began to get civilized and form law codes to protect their property, cattle-raiding, which up until then had been their chief pastime (apart from war), had to be proscribed. Even so, raiding was more respectable than thieving: it is worth mentioning that Hermes, who stole the aristocratic Apollo's cattle by night with the aid of *metis*, was seen by both Homer and Hesiod to be in a slightly different class, a lower one, to Heracles and the robber barons who openly and heroically raided by day. Again, the proper arena for the playful exercise of the warrior virtues was the athletic contest (*agon*) in which *metis* was controlled by the rules of the game.[40] The problem of *metis* in war remained a thorny one right down to the fifth century. It was on the whole approved for the navy (slightly lower class) but not for the hoplite army, for which the aristocrats tried (with considerable success) to enforce rules of massed combat by day on fields agreed in advance.[41]

In the works of Hesiod, Hermes *dolios* is gradually reclassified as the devil responsible for the fall of man (not so unlike the serpent in Genesis). There are two major indictments, both contained in the important story of Prometheus.[42] Creator of mankind, cleverest of the giants (*metis* is in his name), the demigod Prometheus learned all the arts and crafts from Athene (*metis* again) and passed them on to man. Zeus became alarmed that mankind was getting above itself, and when one day Prometheus tricked him on an important sacrificial matter, Zeus replied by witholding fire from man. Prometheus countered with another trick and stole it. In revenge, and with the assistance of Hermes, Zeus created woman, "the beautiful evil," Pandora, with whose arrival mortality begins in earnest. Henceforth, in addition to the ambiguous blessing of fire, the previously ungendered man must also learn to live with the ambiguous blessing of the womanly wife, whose fiery beauty will burn him with lust and delusion and trickery; and in case there should arise sage bachelor farmers like Hesiod who might prefer to plough only in the field, Zeus planted the secret of human renewal in the darkness of her belly (*gaster*), so that men who might choose to sleep alone would be condemned to sterility.*

It is worth adding, finally, that in the early seventh century (if that was when he lived), Hesiod was witnessing a profound change in the Greek economy, as it moved from the old village agriculture to the new city crafts and trades. This mercantile economy ripened in Ionia in the seventh and sixth centuries, whence it invaded Athens, where it was legitimized by the Peisistratid tyranny in the late sixth, paving the way for democracy in the fifth. In the significant changes of his era, Hesiod saw the erosion of the old customs and the emergence of the brash new god or devil, money.

With the mention of money we come full circle: not only is it notably Hermetical in that it arises and thrives in the marketplace, but it is also magical, secretive, elusive, fast-moving, and deceitful.

---

*This myth of human origins bears striking analogies to the one in Genesis, but it goes on to associate the fall into sexuality with the institution of animal sacrifice for the tabooing of cannibalism. Apart from its misogyny, it is thus nicely congruent with this book's Chapter 4, and endorses the idea that those "events" are properly associated with the domestication of fire, as suggested at the end of the previous section. For an excellent discussion of Prometheus and Pandora, see Vernant (*Myth and Society in Ancient Greece,* 1980) pp. 169 ff.

Moreover it is notably swarmlike in its tendency to consume what it touches, fascinate and repel with its potent nothingness, and accumulate in amorphous heaps that give the distinct impression of breeding.

Although this section has gone on rather a long time, the mention of money draws us irresistibly to the question of shit, two things that have been suspected of intimate relations since long before Father Freud and the psychoanalysts arrived to pronounce it so. What further qualifies this topic for inclusion here is that it is something we tend to do privately, even stealthily, and about the implications of which we tend to deceive both ourselves and others. Moreover, it is fundamentally involved with giving and taking, and has a long and dishonorable association with the devil of negation.

To begin at the beginning, shit is undoubtedly our oldest instance of "the dirt that pollutes," and our fastidiousness is shared by the chimps, who wipe themselves with leaves when diarrhetic, and are in general quite sensitive about having their bodies contaminated by foreign matter.[43] To carry within us an ever-regenerating source of pollution, which may occasionally slip out unawares (particularly in the fart, which is its comic cognate) and which daily requires correct placement, clearly poses a problem for culture. The fart perfectly parodies "the bad breath of divinity" discussed earlier, and it is surely not surprising to find both farting-guns and apocalyptic shit-baths among the set pieces of Trickster mythology. Clearly, the more hygienic, ethereal, and bodiless a culture becomes, the more such material tends to get repressed, but equally, the more profoundly threatening it becomes. For obvious reasons primitive man was generally more relaxed about defecation than we are, but we should not forget the notorious Chagga tribe, who wear anal plugs to proclaim not only that their shit does not stink but that they don't even do it.

Psychoanalysis has taught us a good deal about the mytho-logic of defecation. The child's first substantial production is the turd, a daily bit of magic in which he both loses a part of himself and yet creates *ex nihilo* something unique, which he may be reluctant to let go. Mother, however, says he must give it away, to her initially, and beyond her to God and the universe. By degrees she suggests to him that though he is extremely clever to create such daily masterpieces, they are also quite worthless, even potentially nasty, not at all comparable to the turd she occasionally retains, gestates, magically transforms and delivers as genuine riches, the renewal of life, for which she is much praised. Somewhat perplexed by this, he gradually discovers that the turd retained not given, converts nicely into the original weapon, a bomb to obliterate the world that either scorns his gift or is unworthy of it. Thus begins the dream of the almighty thunderbolt (as Swift presciently discerned in *Gulliver's Travels*), a dream that originates in womb-envy and can only be contained by persuading the child that generosity and other forms of creativity are better ways of disarming the opposition.* This is quite a load of symbolic freight for any youngster to take cheerfully on board, and it is small wonder that our culture takes such an interest in toilet training.

The first connotation of shit is surplus; and since surplus, superfluousness, and abundance are hallmarks of divinity, shit will be perceived as magical from the start. To be able to generate and shed bits of oneself daily without impoverishment means there is more of oneself than one needs. The obvious suggestion is that it represents a transformation of the food one did not need and could not use: as such it signals both wealth and greed. As wealth it is unquestionably good, indicating not only divine favor but also that God's surplus is to be transformed into something human and given away, a law that Nature celebrates in childbirth and culture celebrates in the ceremonies of potlatch.** As greed, shit is

---

*Following somewhat in Swift's footsteps, the adolescent Jung had a dream of God flattening the local cathedral with a turd. Coming as he did from a pious family full of clerics, he found this deeply disturbing, utterly unfunny. Luckily he made the proper interpretation and decided to become a psychologist rather than a physicist. See *Memories, Dreams, Reflections* (1967) p. 52 ff.

**The potlatch festival has been found to occur in all parts of the world, and is unquestionably bad, indicating that serious pollution arises with the taking of more than one's share, which we will in due course call "original sin." Worse than the wasting of unused surplus is hoarding: the turd retained by the "anal-retentive" character is being held back for future aggression, and it looks very like revenge for the baby it is not turning into. To distinguish the retentive bomber from the virtuous "saver-for-a-rainy-day" is one of the enduring problems of post-neolithic culture.

But there is a terrible joke in the midst of all this seriousness. This manifestly magical stuff, at once good and bad, from which we have drawn the most profound inferences about the human condition, is also just a load of shit, nothing at all. For comic relief from this appalling paradox we think of Trickster, whose frequently shitty exploits often issue unaccountably in gifts to mankind; and in a serious vein we might think of Enki the Sumerian shaman who resides in the *abzu* (= the deep) as snake god of wisdom. Wisdom belongs with nothingness because the profound truths about life and death involve going beyond the phenomenal world in which things appear to be either good or bad to a mysterious realm in which they are both and neither. It is the fascinating, dangerous, and playful realm of dream and poetry, to which certain liminal rituals give us access. Shit is perhaps the simplest and most commonplace thing whose symbolic power points to that realm, and the difficulties it still poses to the enquiring mind give some indication why wisdom has always been in short supply.

To be rich is to have surplus goods, and this is a mark of divine favor: the gods have marked you out from lesser mortals with an abundance of Luck, which is to say power, in the hunting of game

---

a ritual contest in which one clan chieftain seeks to demonstrate superiority over a rival (and enforce his subordination) by showering him with gifts whose value he cannot match in a return bout. It also generally includes some ritual destruction of valuable objects as a kind of libation to the gods, a reminder that whatever enriches our lives is a gift that must ultimately be offered back.

or whatever it might be. A rich man will thus in the beginning be respected by his fellows for his magic; and he calls on this respect in potlatch ceremonies in which the giving of gifts imposes on the recipient the obligation to reply with equal munificence or admit his inferiority, his lesser magic, an admission that often has political implications.[44] But the magical origins of wealth are easily obscured when it comes to be measured in money, even if one remembers that our first "coins" were magical fetishes such as teeth, shells, and feathers, themselves markers or representations of divine favor. In the appearance of a standardized, anonymous coin we see no reference either to its bearer or to the magical thinking that led to its invention; and though this was doubtless very good for trade, it was dangerous for the soul.

We saw earlier that the transformation of "the thing taken" into a gift was one of the important hallmarks of culture. The primitive wisely knows that the wealthy man is not the one who accumulates surplus but the one who gives it away, that to be rich is to divest oneself of riches. This wisdom becomes difficult to sustain in the context of neolithic stock keeping and agricultural surpluses; with the devising of metal coinage in the cities, however, we are in danger of losing it altogether. Can hard currency, being noncorruptible, perhaps be safely hoarded without corrupting its possessor, unlike the shit from which it has symbolically evolved? Can a hardened culture thus outwit its lowly origins and the limitations they propose?

Probably not. The original heap of stones piously proclaims the hope that by gathering together we may build something durably human. When it is superseded by a heap of golden coins secreted in the rich man's treasury, culture is almost certainly in trouble. The heap of golden coins is a frozen swarm, unmoving; and the rich man, though apparently post-magical, will be tempted to fetishize this swarm, secretly to believe that his possession of it has alchemically transformed him from human baseness into imperishable purity that will live forever—in which case he will have by-passed the bowel, acquired the definitive Chagga plug. Thus the worship of filthy lucre is not, as many suppose, the worship of shit but its *denial*; and a denial of such fundamental realities will ultimately poison everything in its attempt to find utterance.* Not only is it clear that hoarded coin sooner or later *does* rot the soul (just as retained feces and fetuses rot the body) but a money-worshipping culture forsakes the chief virtue that flows from gift-exchange: its magical capacity to restrain greed and forestall war.

From time immemorial primitive man has known that the best way to beggar your neighbor and show him who's boss is to paralyze him with presents. The potlatch is the playful solution to the competitive problems that lead to war, and there is ample evidence from anthropology that it works. But when a culture ceases to revere the giving-away of wealth as an incontestable sign of divine blessing, which calls upon the recipient to bow his head, it has lost a priceless treasure, its best game; and soon enough the Big Men in that culture will grasp the alternative, which is to beggar their neighbors by seizing their goods and storing them as heaps of coin in their secret chambers; and since this is less than ontologically satisfying, they will in due course come up with the final solution: heaps of corpses on the battlefield or in the town square. At this point the goddess Paranoia has made her masterpiece: *exeunt omnes*.

---

*Hence the pious capitalist keeps his assets sufficiently "liquid" to remain healthily "circulating": "currency," after all, is what flows. One of the most intelligent explorations of money fetishism is George Eliot's *Silas Marner*.

7 ▪ ACTING IN THE THEATER OF THE GODS:

The Mysteries of Sacrificial Violence

For without a cement of blood (it must be human, it
must be innocent) no secular wall will safely stand.
—W. H. Auden

Like the previous two chapters this one is divided into a number of
sections, and it will conclude our survey of the lawlines through
which primitive man seeks to regulate his exposure to the energies
of *pneuma*. Although this survey has no pretensions to being
exhaustive, it does at least touch on the major themes relating to
love and war, and should enable us to read some important ancient
texts in the concluding chapter with better vision. As the word
"acting" (in contrast to Chapter 6's "thinking") in the title would
suggest, the emphasis is either on ritual (as in the *Bouphonia*) or on
myth that is significantly ritual-related (as with Dionysus and
Isis/Osiris). As the subtitle indicates, our major concern is with
sacrifice, which I shall suggest is best understood as the attempt to
make divinity come into our presence (or leave us) through an act of
mutilation (actual or symbolic). The first section is a somewhat
general meditation on the coming and going of divinity, and hence
makes an appropriate prologue to a discussion of the sacrificial.

HOUSING THE SACRED

The superior man abides in his room.
—Confucius

The reader will recall that one of the cognates of *pneuma* discussed in the Appendix is *neomai* (or *neumai*), which means either to come or to go; and I suggested that the semantic association is very close indeed since divine epiphanies always involve both coming and going. *Pneuma* is originally movement itself, hence its departure is implicit in its arrival (and vice versa), and such coming and going is above all what *pneuma does*. The association with divinity is strengthened by *neomai*'s being a deponent verb, i.e., a passive or middle voice with an active sense, arguably an indication that the process designated was originally attributed to divine agency.[1] Moreover, the presence of *neo* in the verb associates its activity with newness and renewal, the new start in time that, as we saw in the last chapter, is sought in ritual invocations of the sacred. The simple verb *neo* means to heap or heap up, which recalls the heap of stones discussed in the last chapter, and *neos* is the temple that houses the spirit we have in mind when first we gather stones together.

From the paleolithic cave drawings to the artwork of the ancient civilizations (Crete particularly), man's meeting with divinity was conventionally represented by raised arms bent at the elbow with fingers spread (as we do when someone points a gun at us). Such a gesture nicely indicates an appropriate mixture of surprise, greeting, and disarmament, and Darwin (*The Expression of the Emotions in Man and Animals*, 1873) suggests that it is probably our innate expression for astonishment. Its antithesis (as he points out), the expression of normalcy or indifference, is conveyed by hands at the side, with fingers closed and somewhat flexed. If, in the beginning, the thing that comes and goes is *pneuma,* it will still cast its shadow on less mysterious comings and goings when we start to think about them: every discrete *thing* that inexplicably appears (like a baby) and subsequently disappears (like a dead man) will seem to have come from and gone to the sacred realm that lies outside or behind the world of appearances. The usual Greek verb for appearing is *epiphaino* = to shine forth, which carries within it the memory of the animist mentality that experienced every appearance as a more or less divine epiphany (*epiphaneia*). Both Plato and Aristotle attested the common view that philosophy originates not in the will-to-power but in wonder (*thauma*),[2] which is to say that the world we wish to understand calls us in the first instance to arrest our movements, put down our tools, and be properly astonished by its "that-ness" (*tathata* to the Buddhists) before we set to work analyzing its "what-ness." Modern intellectuals and scientists have little time for *tathata*, and their work is consequently much impoverished.

In this section I propose to look briefly at five primitive locations or settings for the coming and going of divinity: the womb, the Jewish Ark of the Covenant, the hearth, the sacred wood at Nemi, and the dancing ground of Dionysus. Though each one is very different, all can be seen as preliminary versions of the temple, except perhaps the last one. Dionysus is both the oldest and the youngest of the divinities canvassed here (to be both primitive *and* sophisticated is almost always a sign of religious genius): he points directly back to alpha-shaman and yet also carries spiritual insights that are still too advanced for the modern mind. Although dancing grounds *are* rough drafts of temple precincts, Dionysus sends his dancers into the wintry wilderness of his holy mountain to call for him; and the ritual sacrifice of his body similarly refuses to be bounded by the altars that are proposed for it (as we shall discover in Section 3). One might say that the ecstasies in his keeping seem almost to mock the worthy seeker of lawlines, and the god himself is surely the most serious joker ever devised by any pack. In his refusal to be housed (except by a mask?) we may find the opening strains of the song that will call us away from the temple and into his theater, which is history. In view of this, it seems only sensible to put him at the end.

The Womb

Temenos in Greek means either an estate, an area of ground sacred to some god, or else the precincts of a temple. Long before we began thinking of temples, however, or even of making rules restricting the use of our dancing ground, we would have realized that Nature herself had provided our first sacred space in the woman's womb: permanently dark, more or less inaccessible, almost always untenanted, it nonetheless centers the storm of human passion, emits a monthly signal of fearful ambiguity, and occasionally opens to announce either new life or bloody catastrophe. It is thus a plausible rough draft for the mysterious place that may be "in chaos," particularly when one remembers that the etymology of *chaos* leads to a verb that *gapes open*.

Not the least of the womb's mystery is that its power comes and goes so absolutely: when the spirits move upon it, it compels those affected with extraordinary force, and yet when the spirits are absent, it is effectively nonexistent, its rumored doorway two unprepossessing folds of skin. Because of this oscillation, and because its potential for social disruption is massive (forcing us to seek shelter within the lawlines of kinship), we shall agree early on that the power involved is a more than natural one. This means that at the very center of a woman's body is a secret space not her own, resting place of the sexual power that comes and goes. With the male, by contrast, only an appendage, the tip or end of the body, is taken over in moments of seizure: though an obviously magical instance of pneumatic inflation, an erect penis is only the vehicle of a passing spirit, drawn to the sacred space to discharge its burden. Both male and female genitals are clearly monstrous, not only because they look (as indeed they are) archaic and unevolved in comparison with the rest of our bodies, but also because they are subject to engorgement and distension. What's more, the female organ appears to be a wound that bleeds, sure sign of divine mutilation: being in this sense more powerful magic, it is more awe-ful, and it seems appropriate that it be hidden. That which is hidden is beyond our reach: it may be treasure or it may be a dangerous predator or it may even be both.

Thus I would suggest that on grounds of theological geography alone, so to speak, we were significantly disposed to locate the sexual headquarters of divinity in the woman's body. Male chauvinists may be dismayed by this suggestion. I would remind them that the phallic *herma* in ancient Greece arose not as fertility symbol but as apotropaic magic, a monstrous mutilation of the profane to scare off evil spirits. This seems to me well judged: however wondrous man's monstrous member may seem to some, the wonder *is* in the coming and going, and to make it stand forever is to move the monstrous toward the farcical, which is why "serious" phallic symbols tend to look more like trees or columns. In other words, the proper icon of fertility is the female torso, and the monstrous supplement is what comes and goes.*

This designation of the womb's centrality has momentous implications. It means that, particularly in neolithic times, we will worship this sacred space as the abode of the goddess, but equally, fear and abhor it as the hidden source of witchcraft and deceit. And if sexual energy ends up between a woman's legs, it probably comes from there as well: "The woman's body is calling to my distended member" says the eternally innocent male, "What can I but obey?" Hence the widespread male skepticism about rape (a skepticism that is still showing remarkable tenacity) and more generally, the tendency of primitive cultures to locate the principal source of sexual pollution in the female body. The fact that this source is thought to be divine, in but not of the woman, mitigates little in the early days when we are chiefly concerned with isolating areas of defilement and

---

*In the beginning, remember, males "ken" the female body as best they can, feeling obscurely implicated in its fruitfulness. In patriarchal times, however, they confidently assert that the womb merely incubates their seed. I am here suggesting that even in those heady days our memories of kenning and our perception of theological geography will undermine such confident assertion; and I would further suggest that such "bad faith" has more than a little to do with man's irrational appetites for war. Needless to say, I cannot prove this, and therefore offer these suggestions in the spirit of serious playfulness.

keeping them clean. By the time the patriarchs take hold in the urban civilizations of the Near East, and the vocabulary begins shifting from the theological to the moral, we are almost ready for Eve the temptress and the sex war as we know it. Feminists have tirelessly pointed out that when men make the rules women suffer the consequences, an important truth whose obviousness seems strangely to have eluded scholarly attention for some centuries. What is less obvious, however, is that quite apart from sexual politics there is a theological disposition stretching back as far as may be, from the womb as sacred space all the way back to the ventral position on the savannah, to locate sexual power in the female: *l'homme propose, la femme dispose.* I say "apart from," which is unprovable of course, but it comes to this: suppose that from day one we had been ruled by alpha-female, would we not still have concluded that sexual power resides (when it does) in the female body? I think so: the womb would still have been sanctified as the opening for divinity, but the regulation of access to it would have been consistently in female hands. What in any case is undeniable is that under patriarchy this divine attribution was turned against woman and she became the scapegoat for all sorts of social and psychic disfunctions. These delusions can be and are being diagnosed, though proper exorcism will take some time. But if what I have said about the basics of our sexual imagination is correct, it means that the new dispensation will be considerably constrained by the old, and that woman may have to remain the major vessel of divine energy where sexual matters are concerned. To do this equitably, to be the sometime goddess but neither the tyrant nor the witch, will not be easy; but it is possible.*

---

*Lest some male readers think I am altogether underrating the male member, let me add that I believe a certain amount of penis-envy to be universal. The piddler who can take aim before he fires is naturally possessed of superior accuracy, and where is the culture that does not esteem accuracy? Squatting, however, only becomes demeaning once chairs are introduced: primitives "hunker" without embarrassment.

The Ark

Kinship and the incest taboo pave the way for the womb's sanctification by regulating access to it: illegitimate entry of the female body is designated a serious pollution. Here, I suggest, we may find the principal origin for the idea of desecration: that the space set aside for the coming and going of divinity must be inviolate, sacrosanct, or else the power it can house will spill into pollution. From here to the idea of a temple is not far: that beautiful clearing in the forest, the stand of trees by the river where we drink and feel strangely well, is an obvious halfway house, as we have seen. Another remarkable one is the Jewish Ark of the Covenant, that astonishingly empty box that was carried by the wandering tribes until it could be set down, surrounded, and oppressed in Jerusalem's temple as the "Holy of Holies." When one realizes that this box is isomorphic with (and was drawn in the beginning from) the female womb, one can better appreciate the fierce dialectic between the holy word the box hopes to entrap and the dove descending with a body for Mary's womb. In other words, the rumored misogyny of the ancient Jews, which Christianity sought to palliate in the gentleness of Jesus, was no mundane matter but based upon a radical perception of the similarity and the conflict between two kinds of spirit that come and go, one Natural, one cultural. To some this perception has seemed mistaken: to others it appears to lie at the heart of Jewish genius.[3]

To say that the Jewish box was "astonishingly empty" will astonish (and even offend) pious readers of Exodus, and so it requires a word. The womb lies in its background, but very far back: much nearer, I would suggest, is another prologue to the room, shaman's drum. What nobody disputes is that the "Holy of Holies" in Jerusalem's temple, that sacred space behind the high altar, was empty; and moreover that this emptiness astonished the infidels who desecrated it from time to time. From this I infer that both the theory and the practice of empty *temenos* was therefore singular to the Jews in the Near East. It was also both primitive *and* sophisticated (to my mind the hallmark of the best Jewish theology, as I shall indicate further in Chapter 8); primitive of course because the divine energies of *pneuma* blow ineffably in the wind, and sophisticated because it takes both supreme intelligence and courage to realize, in a world full of lavishly particularized divinities (as the Near East was by then), that a divinity incapable of visual representation, though it may seem backward and foolish to one's neighbors, is in various ways more compelling than one that lends itself to statuary and ikon.

Whence the emptiness? Here one can only speculate. Imagine the nomadic tribes of Semitic bedouin, wandering the desert sands, time out of mind: shaman carried the drum, in which above all the tribe's capacity to make contact with divinity was concentrated (more than the mask for aural people). Eliade (*Shamanism*, 1964) indicates that shamans everywhere make their drums out of branches taken from the Cosmic Tree (p. 168 ff) and I would propose these hollowed music boxes as man's first essay toward the temple as *constructed* space. I would further suggest that divinity is everywhere most easily contacted through sound, in the beginning, and I say this for three main reasons: the wind is heard not seen (and mystics today still hear the heavenly hum); shaman's drum is everywhere the first sacred construct; and it is universally amplified and extended in the "bull-roarers" of primitive ritual, those frightening wind-generators that even among unmusical peoples both mime and invoke the divine presence. To this one should add that Yahwe is a particularly windy god, and that the Jews are a particularly musical people. Can one not imagine them at some point making a superdrum, not to be touched but always listened to?[4]

Turning to the account of the Ark in Exodus, one is troubled on several counts: first of all the narrative is leaden, often a sign of meddling in the Old Testament. Second, the lavish and fussy design specified by Yahwe seems ill-suited to a band of hungry wanderers, and also theologically dubious (the Golden Calf is only a few chapters away). Third, the function of the Ark is distressingly twofold: both to make "a sanctuary that I may dwell among" (25:8) and "commune with" (25:21) my people, but also as a place to lodge "the testimony [i.e., the stone tablets of the law] that I shall give thee" (25:16) at some later date. This last is curiously offhand; and can one find room among the *gravitas* of graven stone to commune with the Lord?

Such bizarre and pedantic narration makes one suspect the redactive hand, and this is indeed the case. Professor Pfeiffer (*An Introduction to the Old Testament*, 1952) identifies Chapter 25 of Exodus as the work of the "Priestly Code" (p. 189), stitched into the old primitive story in the fifth century when the Pentateuch was being assembled. This was the time of the Rebuilt Temple and the legalists were manifestly in charge, doubtless still remembering Babylon (where all those *texts* seemed to underwrite the city's majesty!). One can imagine them unamused by the altogether undignified and childish rumors of the original ark as a kind of superdrum; and yet the memory of potent emptiness was secured as sacred absence by the Holy of Holies in Jerusalem's temple.

The Hearth

Another prologue to the temple is the hearth, the fire around which we gather to eat together and offer hospitality to the stranger. The hearth is sacred not only because it is a space in which we remember the tribal or household gods, but more simply because it is where weapons may be confidently set aside while the bonds of kinship are ritually renewed in giving and taking. Thus it is a space that must be kept safe from the intrusion of the alien, and hence when hospitality is offered, the stranger's strangeness must be subdued or contained by rites of incorporation. The dangers in hosting an outsider are both real and symbolic: if he is only feigning friendship he may *actually* poison the cup from which we all drink, or else he may do so symbolically, making a mockery of our gifts, our gods, our illusions of civility. Hence the elaborate courtesies and gift-exchange that have attended the hosting of strangers from the earliest days. The ancient Greek goddess of the hearth was Hestia, and her occlusion under patriarchy is eloquent of the shifting of significant space from the hearth to the *agora*, from the *oikos* (home) to the *polis* (city state).

In the simplest terms the stranger at the gate is one who has come from and will return to a land we do not ken and is not kin, perhaps not far from chaos. He is in any event an obvious instance of "matter out of place," dirty in one sense or another, and we fear his pollution. We have no reason to suppose him human, which means he is either subhuman or superhuman; and since the safe bet is sub-, we will probably kill him, return him to the chaos whence he came, perhaps with some ceremony. We might even eat him. In any case it would be fair to say that absolute strangers in primitive worlds (whether chimpanzee or human) generally did not fare well. Given time, security, and religious confidence, however, we will become willing to consider the other possibility: either that he is superhuman or that in him the distance between sub- and super- disappears in monstrous epiphany, and that as an emissary from the gods we should take him in. This is a daunting thought, an important evolution in human morality, and it runs as a *leitmotiv* through Homer's *Odyssey,* finding its theme in the admonition that "all strangers and beggars are from Zeus" (8–557), and its dramatic difficulties at the cave of Polyphemos, as we shall see.

The *Odyssey* clearly illustrates that the offering of hospitality is no less than the bridge that enables man to move from a warring world into one of politics and other peaceful communications. Being such a turning point in human affairs, the word "hospitality" might be expected to have a vexed etymology, and this is indeed the case. Partridge (*Origins,* 1959) suggests that the Latin root *hos* originally meant "food and shelter as a means of preservation." For this root he offers several possible religious sources (including the Indo-European *hsos*) but strangely ignores the Greek *hosios,* an old, important (and itself complicated) word meaning divine ordinance, what Nature (*phusis*) commends as opposed to what man legislates (*nomos*). Since what Nature commends to her creatures is above all "food and shelter as a means of preservation," the semantic fit seems more or less perfect; in which case one might expect to find in the etymons some sense of the difficulties involved in extending this law of Nature into the world of human legislation; and this is so.[5]

Like *xenos* in Greek, the Latin *hospes* means either stranger or host, and this surprising conjunction may point back to the ritual time and space in which host and stranger met in a sacred bond that transformed their secular or profane identities. The host moves toward his own border as the stranger approaches it, and their bond would locate them on the symbolic margins of the host's hearth or heartland; and indeed one notices that both the hospice and the hospital (also shelters with food) tended to be located on the city walls. Akin to *hospes* is *hostis,* also host and stranger, and since strangers are suspected of hostility, *hostis* also means enemy. Akin to the hostile enemy is both the hostage and *hostia* = sacrificial victim offered to the gods. Bearing in mind that *hos* involves food and that in our cannibal days we ate strangers, one can see the sense in eating the Christian *host* (Latin *hostis*) in remembrance of how a particularly monstrous stranger was originally received among us.[6]

The Sacred Wood at Nemi

One of the most haunted and haunting sites in the ancient world was the sacred wood at Nemi, whose savage darkness so fascinated Sir James Frazer that he wrote a long and famous book (*The Golden Bough,* 1922) trying to explain it. This wooded grove, beautifully situated outside Rome on the shores of Lake Nemi, was the principal shrine of ancient Diana (= Artemis) before the Romans consolidated a proper temple for her on the Aventine Hill. The grove at Nemi offered hospitality to no one. The man who guarded her sacred tree was both a murderer and priest. He was called "king of the wood," and his task was to stand with sword drawn on perpetual alert against the arrival of the stranger whose mission it was to desecrate the sacred tree. Even to doze in the small hours was dangerous; for sooner or later the stranger would come, tear a bough from the tree, kill the king, and reign in his stead until he in turn was killed.

The symbolism of this is arresting, to put it mildly. Diana/Artemis, as virgin goddess of hunting and patroness of childbirth, was both killer and protector, as we have seen, and so is her priest. As host, he is mirror image of the *hostis* (stranger, enemy) who calls upon his hospitality, and the sword fight in which their figures merge offers a diabolical parody of the rite in which the welcoming host moves out to meet and merge with the stranger who seeks to visit his world. The sacred space that the priest keeps inviolate is a nowhere place in the sense that its power depends its remaining perpetually absent (i.e., inaccessible) to mankind, and the wombless womb (or super-womb) of this virginal goddess of prosperity is fertilized only by the periodic spilling of priestly blood. The violence that sustains her blessing reminds us that the hunter's prosperity depends on watchfulness and precision in the act of killing, and that when the lawlines are transgressed the goddess of the *nemos* dispenses *nemesis* instead of prosperity. In the violence that drives off violence, one can discern the scapegoat motif: the stranger who tries and fails to kill the protector embodies our own desecrating desires and carries them off with him into death; whereas the one who succeeds and thereby himself becomes "king of the wood" proves that the old king's powers were failing, and thus again the one who dies carries our weaknesses away with him. That both men are symbolically the same man suggests that we are all of us doubled within, carrying both a king-protector and a desecrating stranger; and moreover that both are involved in each other, and the question of which one shall prevail is a matter of luck and timing.

More than this I am unwilling to venture, for though we know that succession to the priesthood at Nemi was still being decided by single combat in the reign of Caligula, much of the story remains obscure. It seems that this extraordinarily primitive hangover was an embarrassment to sophisticated Romans, who visited Diana in her up-to-date premises on the Aventine Hill and chose not to inquire too closely into the background of what was going on a mere sixteen miles into the woods at Nemi. The provenance is clearly Greek in some sense, but this doesn't help much because Artemis, who descends from the Mountain Mother of the Minoans, was already too primitive to sit happily in the Greek imagination: her myths are few (hunting and *childbirth?*) and her shrines offer no clues to the Nemi priesthood. Such mysteries are challenging in their tantalizing untidiness, and this one drove Frazer to write over a thousand pages (in the abridged version!) of fine Edwardian prose in an attempt to unravel it. His learning is prodigious, his rhetoric often persuasive, but I think his bias toward the neolithic (and toward science) makes him uneasy with the difficult paleolithic simplicities in the story. Be that as it may, what little we do know about Nemi is deeply impressive in its starkness and gravity; and I hope to have indicated that it can suggestively illuminate even a brief meditation on the emergence of sacred space and the hosting of its visitors.[7]

Dionysus

To conclude our survey, a brief discussion of *Dionysos Chthonios* (the underground Dionysus) will both introduce us to an "unhousable" divinity and also provide a useful bridge to the next section on sacrifice. I mentioned at the outset that reverence for the womb as sacred space would have been much augmented in neolithic times with the agriculturalists' discovery of Mother Earth as the cosmic womb-tomb that feeds, furnishes, and then reclaims us all. No one disputes the universal distribution at this time of myth and ritual miming the annual cycle of vegetation: life (represented by Dionysus) is born underground, shoots forth in gladness, and is then harvested (dismembered and dispersed) in joy and sorrow as the earth withers into the *morte saison,* from which in due course life emerges once again. There are as many ways of telling this story as there are cultures to tell it, but the basic structure is as constant as the agricultural cycle it represents.

One of the tantalizing aspects of ancient Greek study is the paucity of "hard" evidence about Dionysiac ritual. Of absolutely central importance in the beginning, this god of the pre-Hellenic Greeks and Minoans was resisted by the migrating/invading pastoralists from the north, whose patriarchal "Olympian" theology succeeded by degrees in displacing Dionysus with their altogether more "civilized" and aristocratic Apollo (Zeus masterminding the exchange).[8] Hence, in a very simple sense, we must *dig* for Dionysus. Second, he was above all a god of mystery, and his important rituals were secret. Of the most important of these, his annual death by dismemberment (*sparagmos*) and perhaps cannibalism (*omophagia*), we have no direct documentation; and Gilbert Murray argues persuasively (from Herodotus chiefly) that this is because the ritual of his Passion was for initiates only, its representation tabooed to the uninitiated.[9] The point requires emphasizing: although there are many books that speak as if knowingly of these lurid and fascinating matters, they are in fact speculating; and it is mainly because of these crucial gaps in our knowledge of Dionysus that I do not give him a more central place in this book (over which in many ways his spirit presides). This said, over the centuries (from early in the second millenium B.C.) a good deal of evidence both hard and soft nonetheless did accumulate, and it has been assembled in *Dionysos*, a work of prodigious scholarship (almost 500 pages long) by Karl Kerenyi (1976).[10]

Although the mosaic breaks off in various places, calling for imaginative (and indeed lurid) surmise, a central core does seem to be reliably established, and runs roughly thus: in the winter months the spirit of the earth that Dionysus embodies lies deeply dispersed below, in a sleep so dark and deathly that the female nurses/watchers of the divine man/child must attend his memory with intense devotion in order to hold and gradually gather his fragmented spirit together. This period of anxious tendance and healing was punctuated at Delphi by expeditions to the heights of Mt. Parnassus where the ecstatic leaping of the female Bacchantes (actually called *Thyiades*) would try to help awaken the god and "make him come," as we said in the buffalo dance: the therapeutic thumping of their feet would call through the holy mountain to the dormant divinity, hoping to turn him (and hence themselves) toward life rather than death.

The wildness of this dancing is often thought to have been drunken and sexually debauched, but in fact it usually was not so: Parnassus is over 8,000 feet high and in winter is snowy, frozen, and fierce. The dancing on its slopes was more like a wild and abandoned running (the dancing Thyiades imitating the storm-wind *thyella*) and it seems that the expeditions not only lasted several days, but went on leaping through the night. Needless to say they sometimes got lost, and were on one occasion so badly snow-bound that a rescue party had to be sent up to find them. In short, the Thyiades had to be just as fit as our modern ski-teams (the contrast is instructive), and their ecstasies were of an ascetic rather than sybaritic nature. [11]

The winter period ended with the awakening (*egeiro*) of the god, and this was followed by his arrival (*epiphaneia* or *epidemia*), which the uninitiated might resist, and then as his powers grew (and the word *epidemia* would suggest) by an increasing ferment and delirium that would culminate in an orgy of ritual madness (*mania*), the hunting of the hunter god (*Zagreus*), and the dismembering (*sparagmos*) and perhaps eating of his live body (*omophagia*), usually in the form of a goat (though there is some evidence from Crete of a bull, and rumors everywhere of a human being "in the beginning"). Thus does the nurturing hand of the nursing feminine that fostered this life in its illness and vulnerability reach its predatory conclusion in the hand that tears and feeds upon its flesh. The dismembering priestesses stand in for the Great Goddess, the mothers, and ultimately all of us; and the function of their savage ritual was to recall and bear witness to the cruelties of Nature (both human and divine). [12]

The ritual tearing of the flesh was intended at once to invoke the god's presence, confess the sinfulness of human violence (pollution), and send it off in the scattered fragments of the scape-goat (or bull or human). If these fragments were then eaten, this would indicate the god's blessing upon the proceedings: the frenzied violence transmitted to the torn flesh would be magically transformed and returned as nourishment.

Of all the dying gods inherited from the neolithic era, Dionysus most nearly resembles the story we have told of alpha-shaman. What is new, as we would expect, is the period of tendance and lamentation that precedes his awakening, and also the gearing of the story to the annual cycle of vegetation. On this point it is worth noting that in many parts of Greece (though not Attica) the story was enacted on a two-year cycle, the first devoted to the awakening of the god, the second to his arrival and dismemberment. Such abstraction of the story from the vegetative round helps return it to human keeping, as it were, both recalling the hunting dance of alpha-shaman and illuminating the energies of the relatively new urban life, whose coming and going were still grounded in but no longer completely enveloped by the agricultural cycle.[13]

Also important for our purposes are the various myth/rituals relating to the resistance of the uninitiated to the god's arrival. There are two principal categories of resisters: respectable matrons who might be driven into nymphomania and invited to dismember their own children; and puritanically law-abiding husbands who might be first maddened and then dismembered in emulation of the god whose arrival they refused to accept. Both themes, very old, are woven into the *Bacchae* of Euripides, and will be discussed presently in connection with tragedy. What can be said here is that they clearly illuminate the central teaching of this extended family of myth and ritual: Dionysus in his coming and going recalls us to the origins of the sacred, those animal powers that both manifest our finest energies and threaten to devastate all that we cherish. If you let him into your life, under appropriately ritualized circumstances, you will be deeply disturbed but also deeply enlivened, touched by the sources of good and evil and yet sanely returned to the casual comedy of civil society. If you refuse him entry he will invade, and you will die one of the many deaths he mischievously conceives in his elaborate theater of the mad.[14]

There is another important and confusing point to consider in relation to the abstraction of Dionysus from the agricultural cycle. The agricultural year ends or dies with the harvest (late June in Greece), a natural time to enact the god's dismemberment (the cutting and gathering of the sheaves, the eating of his body); and where the dead season is wintry or prolonged, one would naturally expect a period lamenting his absence. For the sake of simplicity my "agricultural" account has suggested that Dionysus arrives in the spring and dies with the corn harvest in the summer. But with this god simplicity rarely lasts long: when the grape came to Greece from Crete, the corn reverted to the sole keeping of Demeter/Persephone, and Dionysus became above all god of the vine, harvested in the fall. More important than this, however, is the emergence of a myth/ritual in which the two moments, of his death and of his rebirth, naturally separated in the agricultural year, were brought together. This complicates the story a good deal: to say that he is reborn as he dies is to say not only that he comes and he goes but that he comes *as* he goes, even perhaps that he is most vividly present in the moment of his dying. There is no way of knowing when this complicating conjunction was first proposed, but there is some evidence to suggest that the Greeks celebrated it (perhaps movably) in mid-spring, as we do with Jesus, and as the March date of the Athenian festival of the Great Dionysia would suggest. Why then? and what lies behind it?

Much of the answer can almost certainly be found in the very old neolithic ritual, everywhere celebrated among agricultural peoples, of "Carrying out the Old Year" (or Death) and "Bringing in the New."[15] Much of our knowledge of how this rite worked in early Greece comes from the superb detective work of Jane Harrison (*Themis*, 1963) and the story runs briefly thus: each year we appoint a year-spirit (*eniautos daimon*), a man to represent and embody the potency of Nature and the culture we build upon it. At the end of one year and the beginning of the next, the old daimon or King is killed (either actually or symbolically) by the new. (We can see traces of this story in the background at Nemi.)

Such a rite is of supreme importance to neolithic peoples, as it ensures nothing less than the continuity of life ("The king is dead, long live the king"); and it is thematically close enough to the birth and death of the crops for the two stories at some point to have been more or less confusingly conjoined. Thus in the case of Dionysus, for example, he may die either at the hands of the nursing females (standing in for the Great Goddess) or at the hands of a young man (himself nursed by and hence plausibly standing in for the nurses) whose name is New Year, year-spirit (*eniautos daimon*), or Dionysus Reborn; and a natural date for such an event might well be in March (the vernal equinox ultimately), when the New Year was sufficiently awakened (revived) to take on such a manly challenge.

As we think about this fight between Old and New, it will gradually become apparent to us that Dionysus actually takes both parts, being both the challenger and the challenged; which is to say he is the dramaturge who oversees their contest. As dramaturge he is the indestructible spirit of life itself (*zoē*), and he issues a mask to each of the contestants, whereby they represent the two parts (or rather two times) of himself, the waxing and the waning. Thus in the foreground, the lethal play of life against life (*bios* versus *bios*), and in the background indestructible *zoē*, which both gathers and scatters the coming and going of individual existents and promises the reconciliation of *yin* with *yang*. In this way, I suggest, we should understand the origin of the double masks of Dionysus that we find engraved on the old Attic vases, a motif that reaches its conclusion in the two masks that preside over the drama that emerged in the Great Dionysia, one mask for comedy and one for tragedy.[16]

We also find old vases that picture a single Dionysus mask plus a cloak hung on a column, which is how he was usually represented: the mysterious and elusive spirit of this very old god resisted the knowable lineaments of cult statuary. If one sees the cloak as a shaman's costume (which was, according to Eliade, everywhere thought to help protect the shaman from death on his journeys to the spirit world), one can interpret such pictures as representing the spirit of *zoē*, which animates every *bios* but is not exhausted therein; i.e., which is both immanent and transcendent. This motif can be traced back to paleolithic shamanism and the old hunting practice of hanging the quarry's head, horns, and skin on a tree in order to encourage its resurrection.[17] Before he became enmeshed in the annual travail of the vegetation cycle, supershaman Dionysus had enjoyed a long career as Zagreus, the mighty hunter, and so his association with the hanging mask and cloak goes back as far as may be. It provides a pre-agricultural line of descent to the idea of a *yin/yang* divinity that divides itself in two and is then reunited in a sacrifice of itself to itself, hunted to hunter. Such an idea, eminently Dionysiac, was by no means confined to the Greeks, and may be as widely distributed as the practice of shamanism. Consider this astonishing poem from the Icelandic Eddas concerning master-shaman Odin:

> I ween that I hung on the windy tree,
> Hung there for nights full nine;
> With the spear I was wounded, and offered I was
> To Odin, myself to myself,
> On that tree that none may ever know
> What root beneath it runs.[18]

The tree on which he hangs is Yggdrasil, the world-tree itself, and it calls to mind the Tree of Life in Genesis, beside which the First Adam is divided into male/female and then falls into wounding and death; also the second Adam, Jesus Christ, whose death on Calvary's "windy tree" both reminds us of the inevitability of human violence and promises that it can be survived.*

Thus Old Year–New Year, self-sacrificing divinity, the blending of hunter and planter mythologies. There is one more point we must briefly notice in connection with Dionysus: if Old Year is killed by New Year he is killed by someone very like himself—his son, his brother, his double, or the nursing mothers; and though this killing carries with it some of the necessity (*ananke*) of Nature, it also carries the germ of cultural irony, that this killing is in some sense a mistaking, ultimately self-slaughter. We saw the outlines of this perception in the ritual play at Nemi, and we have considered at some length its hunting origins in Chapter 5: for the time being let it sleep.

Housing the sacred? Very difficult when Dionysus comes on stage. Not the least impressive of his primitive credentials (Nature not culture) is the way he would laugh to scorn any attempt to confine him in a temple.[19] In the myth of *Dionysos Chthonios* he tends to be either intolerably present in his bullsiness (ballsiness) or painfully absent in his afflicted dispersion, the deathly god of life indeed; and this is almost enough to make one think that the manic-depressives have got it right. A ludicrous suggestion, of course, and yet its almost-plausibility does point to the dangerous extravagance of this god, his insistence on occupying the most

---

*As with Dionysus, the Advent of Jesus is called for in December ("O come, O come Emmanuel") and it leads to intolerable swelling (*orgao*) and crucifixion in the spring when, like Dionysus, he is torn and eaten.

difficult territory, the border country that separates and confuses cosmos and chaos, sanity and madness, love and hatred. If Apollo is the way of *claritas*, Dionysus is the way of *confusio*. No wonder the Greek patriarchs insisted on marginalizing him; and no wonder this book doesn't offer him more space. The one thing he most certainly does not do is "abide in his room"; and admirers of the Confucian epigraph to this section must ask whether the Chinese sage has wisely outgrown the Dionysiac savagery or whether he has hidden away from the really superior thing. I offer no comment on this; but what *is* clear, I think, is that this god's appalling sense of humor seems to suggest (and to have suggested from very early on) not only that the sacred cannot be housed but that perhaps the human cannot be either, in which case the idea of tragedy is not far off. The only "Western" figures who might answer him are Osiris, whom we shall meet presently, and Jesus, whom we shall not.

SACRIFICE: THE MUTILATING ECSTASY

We are finally in a position to approach the problem that lies at the heart of religious experience. Our first intimations of this mystery arise in the hunting of animals: to apprehend, mutilate, and then consume together the flesh of some creature is where the story begins; as I put it earlier, "To sacrifice means literally to make sacred, and our first way of doing this was to tear living flesh until the blood flowed." Of course we probably did this for millions of years without thinking too deeply about it, even if it was the activity that above all demarcated and distanced us from our pongid cousins; and yet the rhythm of it was doubtless all the while engraving itself upon us, gradually turning one of our first adventures into something between an instinct and a ritual.

However untroubling it may have been during this long period, matters thicken in the aftermath of alpha-shaman. The tearing of flesh can now be perceived not just as an aspect of the hunt but as an avenue to the sacred; for the mutilation of the animal's body can now be perceived as a rendering of the monstrous, giving passage to divinity as it comes among us to augment our weal or our woe. Such mutilation, performed by the hands, is finally what makes divinity come; and as such it is among our first intimations of artistic power, the power to enhance our lives by altering the contours of Nature.

Hence the practice, widespread among primitives, of ritually mutilating the body in the name of adornment. Bones placed painfully in the nose, scarified cheeks, distended lips, and so forth, all make sense when seen in this context. Painful mutilations remind us of divinity's severity, its ultimate association with suffering and death; but when ritually administered, bodily mutilations also indicate a divine blessing, that the gods have favored the mutilated ones with their "touch," a mark of enhanced power. (They may also indicate, subtextually as it were, the eternal enmity of the old for the young—one thinks of circumcision, of which more presently.) It goes without saying that these marks of the monstrous are borne with pride and thought to be beautiful; and if anyone thinks this merely indicates a crude sense of esthetics in the primitive mind he should look again at the animals in the Lascaux caves—not only beautifully modeled, but modeled under unimaginably difficult conditions. Thus we must assume that when the primitive chooses to beautify monstrously, he knows what he is doing: the sacred was ambiguous from the beginning, and ritual scarifications of the flesh bear witness to this fact.[20]

From ritual scarification to the lopping of finger joints (a speciality of the Crow Indians) is not so very far. What are we to make of such sacrificial practices? The modern mind tends to find them abhorrent, and indeed this lies at the heart of our pejorative use of the words "primitive" and "savage." Though the question is a complex one, some cautionary notes about the dangers of ethnocentric tourism can be sounded. First of all, having more or less lost both our religious and esthetic relations with monstrous beauty, we tend to find bodily malformations simply repellent, indications of malignancy rather than blessing, and certainly not both; and whereas a ceremonial bone in the nose may seem to us merely eccentric or weird, an absent finger joint makes us look away. Second, because of this loss and the incomprehension it brings, we tend to concentrate on the subtextual psychological theme—the revenge of the old on the young. This works particularly well on mutilations associated with initiation ceremonies, such as male and female circumcision. Clitoridectomy and infibulation of the female seem indefensibly cruel, the more so when one considers that most female initiation ceremonies are far less violent than the male, for sound sociological reasons. The case against male circumcision, however, is by no means straightforward. First of all, one can see the religious and esthetic sense in enhancing the monstrosity (without damaging the performance) of the already monstrous member. Second, because we barely initiate the young anymore (the cruelty almost altogether subtextual) and are almost neurotically opposed to all forms of patriarchal authority, we find it difficult to appreciate how well most primitive initiation rites (with their attendant cruelties and scarifications) actually worked. On the other hand, one needn't have read Freud to find the practice of male circumcision a little disturbing.

This said, and it is very little, the problem still stands. Do we not think that exposure to a sacrificial divinity, which is quietly commemorated in scarifications of one kind or another, and then less quietly in rituals of a Dionysiac nature, leads to more cruelty than would have been the case without such exposure? My answer to this is yes. Is it not therefore a regrettable chapter in our history? Yes again, but unavoidable: unless the whole argument of this book is mistaken, *pneuma* was waiting for us when we left the garden (indeed we had already kenned it as proto-chimpanzees) and one of its initial impacts upon culture was to augment, theologically as it were, our natural taste for mutilation. It is at this point that the argument becomes truly complex and momentous: do we not also think that man becomes less cruel when he moves beyond scarification[1] and a sacrificial divinity toward an organic or natural esthetic and rational skepticism? My answer to this is "Possibly but by no means necessarily": after all, with unscarified bodies and godlessness we have just endured the most violent century in human history. What pacifies the sacrificial lust is not the *denial* of the sacrificial divinity—for it is undeniable—but the elaboration of the sacrificial urge itself, using its energies to harness its cruel proclivities. Before going on to consider whether this may be so, however, we must look briefly again at warfare (where the sacrificial energies do their worst) and at how the fifth-century Athenians, beyond scarification and almost godless, failed to resist its glamour.[21]

It is important to recognize that all wars are holy wars, not because of theological banners that may or may not be flown, but because the flowing of blood and the ripping of flesh consecrate the ground in the oldest and simplest sense we know. To kill and die on the battlefield, to mutilate and bleed, brings one before the dicing table of the gods, where luck and skill and courage combine to name the players definitively. Some will be chosen to play again tomorrow, some will be wounded and scarred, and some will be mutilated beyond recognition; but all have been gathered in the presence of the most real thing, to know and be known with the utmost clarity in an orgiastic festival of generosity and hatred. Where else can one find the opportunity to employ one's deepest energies, so hedged and constrained as they are by common prose? Where else can one freely offer them up to the gods to whom they so manifestly belong?

Where indeed. Here is the truly savage god, and once one has felt his power, it is easy to see that the fuss we have made through the ages about the cannibal is indeed beside the point—a straw man to be sure, whose tabooing secretly licenses a profounder passion. One might even suggest that the simplest way to address this passion and restrain warfare would be to lift the taboo and insist that every warrior slain must be ceremonially eaten. One might further suggest that this thought may have been a factor in the imposing and brandishing of the taboo in the first place: warfare on any significant scale could not proceed without it. Be that as it may, what is undeniable is that once literature begins to deal with warfare, the mutilating ecstasy is more or less elided, hidden from sight. We come close to it in Homer's *Iliad*, where the language lingers graphically on the mutilation of flesh; but the ecstasy that this induces in the warrior (and in the reader) is not broached, far less rendered self-conscious. It is certainly not identified as the energy that drives us into battle.

By the time we reach the literature of fifth-century Athens, the mutilating ecstasy has receded from view almost altogether (apart from the disreputable Dionysiacs), and the sacrificial aspect of warfare has been moralized into matters of honor, courage, and the giving of the ultimate gift. But the whole question of warfare seems to recede at this time, as these most brilliant people give themselves luminously to the arts of civilization. The lay reader is thus astonished to discover that Athens was more or less constantly at war throughout the fifth century, and by the end of it her glorious empire and the city itself were decimated. Where did such subtle and intelligent men find the time and the energy to be so persistently going off to butcher and die? And since they did, why did they not address the matter more forcefully in their remarkably articulate language? The question is not a simple one, but some part of the answer must lie with what had by then become the almost-unmentionable mutilating ecstasy,

> the blind
> swipe of the pruner and his knife
> busy about the tree of life . . .[22]

(Blinding the pruner is a sublime touch here, since the mutilating ecstasy has everything to do with making the gods visible, as we shall see presently.) Surveying the ruins of Athenian glory from the fourth century, even the wise Aristotle failed to perceive the black hole in the story, something crucially unaccounted for: he was unable to crack the civilized code, unable to separate the rage for war from the rage for order, unable to unravel the dark secret of mutilation. On the contrary, he helped to keep the secret hidden by endorsing the scapegoat alibi—as men have done throughout the ages—that what separates the barbarous from the civilized is not Homeric mutilation but cannibalism, that old bogeyman.*

---

*Notice that what makes cannibalism such an effective scapegoat alibi is its

It is almost enough to make one despair. If the Greeks could not do it, with their unparalleled intelligence and with the relatively plain-speaking Homer in the background (sustained and deepened by the tragedians), how can we? Can we possibly, at this late hour, find a way over the schizoid wall that prevented them from addressing the primitive ground of their own activities? Can our critical powers, no match for theirs but not inconsiderable, succeed where theirs failed? It is not likely, but it is possible. There are three major factors in our favor: first, the mess we have made of the planet in the past century and the urgency of the ecological crisis provide us with both motive power and a measure of humility. Second, unlike the Greeks who clung somewhat rigidly to "culture" in their anxiety to distance themselves from the primitivism they saw all around them, we are disposed to believe (with Dionysus) that primitivism can tell us something about the insanities of civilization. And third, unlike the Greeks again, women today are no longer sequestered, and we are disposed to believe that *yang* is calling out for *yin*, and vice versa.[23]

We may now turn to the question of how the sacrificial may be tamed by the sacrificial. At the crude level, we all do this when energies that would mutilate "the other" are turned against the self, largely through the mediation of what we nowadays call guilt. A less crude and altogether better solution is the discovery that the divinity one meets in violence is better met in the *renunciation* of violence, an offering back to the gods of their mutilating powers— powers that they have inappropriately lodged in the human breast. The mysterious reward for such renunciation (which we might call "meta-sacrifice") is a sweetness undreamed of in the warrior's philosophy, something not unlike kissing the toad and finding the princess, and we caught a glimpse of it in the preceding discussion

proximity to what it conceals. The word clearly focuses on the *eating* of flesh, not the mutilation that necessarily precedes it. It is as if renunciation of the teeth takes care of the other problem; and so it does, releasing it unmonitored into the darkness.

of Dionysus. It is also experienced in sexuality, where the desire to mutilate (and be mutilated by) one's partner is engaged, absorbed, and transformed into gentleness. Although the sexual story is relatively straightforward, the religious versions of meta-sacrifice (or sacrificial sublimation) are not only complex in themselves and constantly in danger of sliding into self-mutilation, but they also differ a good deal from culture to culture. With luck we can keep our discussion intelligible by confining ourselves to the simplest elements, the basic procedure.

We saw in Chapter 5 that the sacrificial ecstasy arises in hunting and in sex, the major difference between the two being that hunting involves the mutilation of *actual* bodies whereas in sexuality the mutilation, death, and rebirth are (usually) metaphorical representations of the energies lethally deployed in the hunt. An equally important difference, to modern eyes at any rate, is that good sex tends to moderate the desire to mutilate actual bodies—make love not war, as the saying goes. Just when and how forcefully this occurred to early man is by no means clear, so we must speculate with caution. In view of this, and because we moderns are so much better informed about sex than killing, I will dwell briefly on the first, and at more length on the second.

Our earliest version of the sacrificial love story comes from third-millennium Sumer, and concerns Inanna and Dumuzi (precursor of Adonis). From the fine translations by Wolkstein and Kramer (*Inanna, Queen of Heaven and Earth*, 1984) of tablets inscribed early in the second millennium, we discover that sexual love begins in visions of abundance and gladness, and then moves into the darkness of the *abzu* where mutilation, death, wisdom, and perhaps rebirth await. As in the hunt, the sex becomes murderous when the lovers mistake each other, or take each other for who they would rather not be. These stories are told with astonishing psychological insight, for which modern equivalents would be difficult to find; and they lie in the background of the widely celebrated festivals of Adonis, whose somewhat unimpressive Greek myth we considered in Chapter 5. We noticed earlier that the Sumerians rather specialized in love, and when we look to Egypt and then Greece, the temperature cools considerably, doubtless as a result of patriarchal seriousness. Still, Osiris is killed for a sexual error, and Isis revives his soul by embracing his corpse and thereby conceiving her son Horus. Dionysus is, as usual, perplexing: although his major rites are absolutely concerned with sexual energies, he neither conspicuously marries nor consorts, except collectively with his *thiasos*, the women who alternately tear him to pieces and then watch over his healing. This is certainly "about" hunting, but is it not also sexual? Whether or not one thinks so, it was clear by the time Euripides wrote the *Bacchae* that Dionysus had become the bearer of profound wisdom concerning sacrificial sexuality, both male and female; and to bolster the Greek holding in this regard, we should remember the Artemis myths discussed in Chapter 5.

I have kept the foregoing paragraph sketchy because the evidence from the early civilizations really is sketchy. What can be inferred? The Sumerian stories (together with the cave paintings discussed in Chapter 3) suggest to me that prehistoric men and women probably understood the analogies and interplay between hunting/killing and sex, and how the latter could attenuate, forgive, and repair the desire for the former. But this understanding is imperfectly and obliquely fostered under patriarchal man as he drifted ever further from the embrace of his woman and into the arms of war itself. This "drift" will be the major concern of our next chapter.

What then of hunting and killing? If what one might call "serious sexuality" was under-exploited by patriarchal man as a way of containing the mutilating ecstasy, what else was available to help him rein in, criticize, and transform his desire to "tear flesh until the blood flowed"? The answer to this, already somewhat discussed in Chapter 5, is "the rites of lamentation"; and they emerge on those days when the hunt or the war miscarries, when the quarry is mistaken, when instead of increasing our prosperity we lose one of our own. On these occasions our killing ecstasy turns instantly to sorrow, and we return to the home-place to bewail our loss.

But the movement toward lamentation (and guilt) can be mischievously blocked by those who would disown their sorrow. To mistake the quarry, either in hunting or in war, is plausibly construed as a sign of divine anger, a loss of Luck. But this divine anger (*phthonos* in Greek) can be interpreted in broadly two ways, either as cause or effect of the bad killing. Opting for "cause" and blocking his sorrow, *Yang* will say "The gods commend killing, but they are angry and made us kill badly today. Let us sacrifice some child or passerby in order to kill better tomorrow and retrieve our luck." To this *Yin* will reply, "We are significantly defiled by bad killing and must seek to purify ourselves through lamentation. Perhaps thereby we may find the source of our mistake." *Yang's* interpretation of divine anger blocks not only his sorrow but any perception of the lust that is ultimately responsible for it. Until he listens to *Yin* he will be unable to approach the mistaking, and will remain bound in a vicious circle where violence can only beget more violence.

We saw something in Chapter 5 of how the rites and energies of lamentation, essentially *yin*-feminine, seek to monitor, attentuate, criticize, dampen, subvert, forgive, and redeem the hunting ecstasy; and we shall return to this matter at some length in the discussion of Isis and Osiris. What needs saying now is that although they have by and large not prevailed on the planet (particularly within the patriarchal epoch), they have from time to time been a match for the hunting mania (as it moves into warfare), and produced commendably pacific peoples (such as the Minoans). Although, as I have just suggested, something almost schizoid overtook the fifth-century Athenian psyche, it nonetheless produced, in the midst of its military adventures, an extremely profound lament for their folly in some of the tragedies. Perhaps the most historically powerful of the religions of lamentation is Christianity, and though it has spent most of its time being hijacked by the hunters, its energies have by no means been exhausted. When William Faulkner was asked what he thought of Christianity he replied, "A good idea: someone should try it sometime."

The general point I am making here is that the energies of lamentation are extremely powerful ones, capable in principle of containing the sacrificial killer. (I would even argue that if the ancient Athenians had had *our* reasons for containing him, they probably would have succeeded.) If this is so, and of course it cannot be proven, it means that the critical moment in the sacrificial process comes not in discovering the sadomasochistic delights of scarification, but when the wounded or guilty or bereaved hunter (or sexual warrior) stops to listen for the sound of lamentation. If he truly hears it, his killing rage will be contained, and he will be moved *by the same sacrificial energies* to repair or redeem what he has inappropriately damaged. If not, he will stop up his ears, sequester his tenderness, and try to repair the damage by doing some more.

This is the all-important moment, for it is precisely here, where sorrow is refused and converted into anger redoubled, that the possibility of healing and forgiveness escapes us. And not only on the primitive battlefield: we modern city-dwellers see some minor version of this refusal every day. The ability to accept life's woundings as grounds for sorrow rather than anger has always been in scant supply: how many people do we know with the courage and the talent to evade sadomasochism and discover genuine sadness?

What makes such sadness possible, opening the door to healing, repair, and forgiveness, is the sound of lamentation. Thus, to return to our initial image, the scarified hunter is disturbing, but not necessarily scarey: he is only human. To know whether his mutilated flesh indicates that he has been vaccinated by divine anger or whether he is about to become the inhuman prey of the sacrificial monster, you must listen to what he hears.

If he cannot hear the *yin*-feminine lament, what must be addressed is not the irrationality of sacrifice but his musical education; for surely it is clear to everyone by now that though we most of us no longer scarify our faces, we have by no means become immune to the dream of holy war and its psychopathologies in everyday life: nor shall we. The urge to sacrifice, like everything *pneuma* evokes in us, is *dangerous*; but since it carries the possibility of salvation right next to the possibility of damnation, the worst thing we can do is switch on the television in the hope that it will simply go away.

The sacrificial rituals of Dionysiac religion starkly present the problem: did they on balance exacerbate human cruelty by encouraging us to believe that the frenzied dismembering of live flesh (however ritually confined) is somehow "natural" and divinely ordained? Or did they, by audaciously identifying and bearing witness to original sin, actually reduce its maddening dispersion by keeping us in touch with it? The answer to this, as I have just suggested, lies in the quality of the lamentations that accompanied such rituals, and from this distance we can hear virtually nothing. Those who are ill-disposed to Dionysus might argue that his ecstatic tendencies were always implicitly excessive, bound to overflow their ritual containers in the end; while those in favor might argue that what led the Greeks into self-destructive bellicosity was not their Dionysus but the Homeric values that elbowed him aside. As clerk of the court, my job is only to point out that we do not here have anything like enough evidence to reach a verdict; but we will have more before the end.

After almost three chapters of lawlines, we are finally in a position to return to Chapter 4 with a crucial emendation. The memory that we both suppress and preserve as we move from the feast of alpha-shaman into totemism and exogamy is not only of sexual excess, parricide, deicide, and cannibalism, but more simply and importantly of the sacrificial energy itself. At the center of what we discover on that mythical day is the abiding sacredness of mutilation; and what makes this knowledge particularly harrowing is that the mutilating energies are preserved—even as they are canceled and raised up—in the sublimations of sacrificial ecstasy commended in the religions of lamentation. Is it any wonder that this should become the deepest and darkest of our tabooed secrets? And is it any wonder that possibly the most powerful of the religions of lamentation should be Christianity, the one through which we can most nearly approach, confess, and abide with this darkness?[24]

THE SCAPEGOAT

The theme of the scapegoat is central to the sacrificial story, and mercifully it is quite straightforward, almost breezy, compared to what we have just worked through. I do not know of any culture in which the scapegoat motif does not figure more or less significantly, and this still seems to me a remarkable indication that there may indeed be narrative archetypes somehow imbedded in the human mind.

The story is briefly this: divine pollution moves within the community. We want to expel it. Since it must have been introduced by some carrier or agent of the divine, our task is to find this carrier and send it or him back to the chaotic realm from which it issued. This divination and expulsion is to be supervised and ritually undertaken by shaman. The simplest instances have to do with human illness, and shaman's task as medicine man is to enter the afflicted body and retrieve the offending object, invariably thought to have been implanted by witchcraft. Such crude narration, wide open to hocus-pocus, is part of what has given shamanism a bad name; and yet despite this inauspicious beginning, even at this stage we can see the outlines of major magic: the offending object (*katharma* in Greek) is a prime instance of divine dirt, the "matter out of place" discussed in Chapter 6, and its ambiguity consists in its being the dirty object that cleanses.

We meet the scapegoat properly so-called when the pollution concerned is abstract and diffuse, more like an invisible plague afflicting all our spirits; and in such circumstances, instead of trying to discover the agent that introduced the pollution, our attention shifts to the finding of a suitable agent to carry it off. An obvious example of such affliction is the general animus of the dead that always hovers over primitive cultures like a cloud (or indeed an invisible swarm of flies), an abstract store of malevolence usually held responsible for whatever goes wrong among us. (This is our first essay on the long road to the notion of individual guilt.) Such malevolence seems to accumulate over time, which is why most primitive new year ceremonies involve a general spiritual house cleaning, an invocation, propitiation, and exorcism of the dead and their anger against the living. Such Dionysian ceremonies often involve the consecrating of a goat (or some other animal, or a human) whom we all touch more or less abusively, thereby transferring to him the divine pollution that moves among us. Then we drive him into the wilderness, or stone him, or in some other way mutilate and dismember him. We may even eat him.

The obvious source for this story is the hunt. First of all, from the very beginning it would have been evident to us that when a pack of predators attacks a herd of animals they cull the weak, and their anger is placated, as it were, by the sacrifice of one member of the herd; and in our hunting we imitate the predatorial pack. Also, however, as we saw in Chapter 5, the hunted animal seems to embody and contagiously infect us with divine power, and the violent excitement is concentrated in its blood, which we drink at the end. Such drinking is a filling that empties, for even as we take in the divine liquid we feel our own violence draining away. Thus one might say the hunt is a sacrificial killing in which our own violence (and intra-tribal hostility) is expelled and transformed in the life-enhancing nectar that unites us.

The overriding problem for primitive culture, as I have emphasized throughout, is the control of inappropriate violence. It is for this reason that primitive man performs all his significant actions according to ritual formulas, and also, incidentally, why he appears to us to carry his body with such grave dignity. Hence it is not surprising that he should perceive the hunt as an almost "natural" ritual with a great deal of magic, magic that invokes, releases, expels, and transforms into triumphal unity much of the violence that hovers as a perpetual threat to concord in the campsite. And hence it is also not surprising that he should take this magic and elaborate it extensively into those myths and rituals that we identify with the word "scapegoat." One might expect to see more of the scapegoat once we become farmers and lose the daily ritual of the hunt; and indeed this seems to be so. The sacrificial rites of *Dionysos Chthonios*, for example, though they remember the hunter (*Zagreus*), are significantly geared to the agricultural cycle.

A classic instance of scapegoat ritual, much discussed by ethnologists, is the Athenian harvest festival of *Bouphonia*, celebrated in late June. This primitive rite had remarkable staying power, not unlike the sacred priesthood at Nemi, as it persisted well into the fourth century B.C., to the certain embarrassment of the progressive element in Athens. Barley cakes, the offering of first fruits, are set out on the altar. Oxen are led in, allowed to wander about, and when one of them decides to munch the cakes he is set upon by two men, the first felling him with an ax, the second slitting his throat. Amid general consternation the murderers fling down their weapons and flee. All then flay the beast and feast on its flesh. After the meal the torn hide is sewn back together, stuffed with straw, and the resurrected ox is harnessed to a plow. A trial is then conducted by the king in an ancient court to determine responsibility for the murder. The maidens who had carried water for wetting the weapons accuse the sharpeners who accuse the butchers who accuse the weapons, which are duly condemned and cast into the sea.

What a play! As principal deity of the neolithic, the ox or bullock (*bous*) appropriately embodies the unpredictable spontaneity of *pneuma*, and may be thought naturally sacred, *hosios* in the ancient sense noted above. The barley cakes, first fruits of the harvest, are reserved (*hieros*) to divinity, whose acceptance of our offering will release and commend the rest of the harvest for general use (making it *hosios* in the more conventional sense). But *bous* has *mistaken* the cakes, thereby disordering the ritual process and releasing pollution. Thus divinity reveals its diabolical face, which must be resisted. But the killing of *bous* is *also* ritually disordered (violence begets violence, pollution is contagious): it is ox-murder (bou*phonia*) not ox-sacrifice (bou*thusia*). Call it deicide.[25]

Flight is our oldest answer to violent contagion. When things calm down we seek purification (*katharsis*). We decide, with great wisdom—which appears as folly—that the *bous*-conducted pollution came from the chaos of divinity, everywhere and nowhere, and we may return it whence it came by discovering and expelling, through shamanic divination, the dirtying object (*katharma*), the matter out of place: hence the weapons go into the sea. The important fact that we are *all* implicated in the violence is ritually attested in both the communal flaying and the communal feasting; as is the even more important fact that our violence has been registered, condoned, condemned, and expelled in what may now be seen as the self-sacrifice of divinity.

I say "now" because part of what is being enacted here is the *instituting* of animal sacrifice, the transformation of bou*phonia* into bou*thusia*, and since the word *bouthutos* means "of or pertaining to sacrifice generally," one can see it is of great moment. Eliade (*Myth and Reality*) persuasively argues that rituals of renewal everywhere involve a return to the beginning, *in illud tempus,* to re-enact the cosmogonic events. This idea works reasonably well in the present instance. The "unscripted" disordering of the altar by the *bous* recalls the disordering leap of alpha-shaman into the center of the circle, and this is followed in both cases by illegitimate murder, confusion, and feasting. Again in both cases order is restored by the institution of lawlines, ritually policed. (To have a ritual re-enactment of the origin of ritual is impressively subtle.) The barley cakes indicate that even under the settled conditions of neolithic piety we are never safe from the energies of desecration; and the plow remembers and commends not only the domestication of animals but also the violation of Mother Earth for agricultural purposes.

Both acts of transgression (the cakes and the murder) are violent mistakings (with the possible implication that all violence mistakes), but they are "corrected" by the instituting of a ritual in which our violence is remembered, shared, harnessed, expelled, and forgiven. Thus sacrilegious murder and theophagy are transformed into the piety of proper food, and the murder can be seen as the god's self-giving, a divine sacrifice that teaches us that the overflowing of *pneuma* can be contained through ritual resistance to it, and that the invasions of divine violence can be met by an answering violence that turns them back upon themselves. There is a time and a place for killing, even deicide, but it must be *cleanly* done, and cleanliness is defined by the ritual process. Thus, what is being called for is a limited war upon heaven, culture drawing a line against Nature.

A significant aspect of the problem addressed in this ritual is that when we become farmers the animals we slaughter are our domesticated friends, not the wildness we ecstatically pursue in the woods: hence the cold-blooded killing looks disturbingly like murder, and the eating reminiscent of cannibalism. The ritual process awakens and channels divinity, converts *bouphonia* to *bouthusia,* and banishes these unpleasant thoughts. The verb *bouthuteo* (= to slay *or* sacrifice) clearly indicates that any animal meal must be licensed by a certain amount of ritual in the killing, however perfunctory.[26]

The blessing of *bous* upon our proceedings is nicely registered in the hay-stuffed resurrection, and his return to the plow confirms his consent to the agri-cultural harnessing of his energies. One might even see here a commending of the move from paleo- to neolithic, animal sacrifice to barley cake: the best way to minimize the spontaneous violence of *bous* is to harness him to the plow, get him stuck into Mother Earth. (The definition of civilized man in the Homeric poems is *sitophagos* = eater of bread.)

The complex structuring of this ritual has the dense texture of serious dreams and profound poetry; and it would be quite impossible without the scapegoat motif that caroms through it like a billiard ball almost out of control. First comes *bous,* chosen at random by the powers of Luck and Unluck to convey the charge of *pneuma,* and die for his pains. Then come the murderers, perhaps also chosen at random, in any case "standing in" for all of us. Then the helpers, handlers and sharpeners of the weapons, and finally the weapons themselves, sufficiently like and unlike us to embody and carry off the violence that has disturbed our orderliness. From this list it can be seen that the scapegoat is not simply a *substitute* for the real culprit, an innocent passer-by framed to take the rap (though in decadent rituals this is frequently the case). To avoid farce he must be drawn from among us in such a way as convincingly to embody violent energies that cannot *in principle* be more specifically identified.[27]

The Greek word for scapegoat is *pharmakos,* and like the dirtying *katharma* that also promises cleansing *katharsis,* it is essentially ambiguous, akin to *pharmakon,* a poison that may be a cure. As with the drugs we obtain from the pharmacy, the dosing of an afflicted culture with a *pharmakos* will not cure but exacerbate the patient's condition if improperly administered. The obvious danger here is the one that attends all dealings with *pneuma*: if the *pharmakos* is improperly killed, instead of sacrifice we have murder (e.g., *bouthusia* reverts to *bouphonia*), and instead of achieving purification (*katharsis*) our pollution is increased. Less obvious but more importantly marked on modern man's psychologized maps, however, is the line that separates the healthy ritual, which *actually* purges, from the unhealthy one that may only mystify and exacerbate the ill-will by offloading (or "projecting") it on to some innocent substitute. Such disavowal is even worse than what we nowadays call "kicking-the-cat syndrome," for the kicker at least confronts his violence and often knows whom he would rather be kicking. And yet drawing this line between the healthy and the unhealthy in the context of primitive scapegoat rituals is not as straightforward as our psychology primers might suggest.

Although the obvious usefulness of scapegoating among primitives is to meet generalized pollutions (there is some evidence that the *Bouphonia* arose to counteract the divine malevolence of drought),[28] it can also be used to arrest a blood feud. The logic of primitive pollution ordains that if you kill one of my kin, I must kill one of yours to achieve purification; which will in turn provoke you to kill another of mine, and so on. This is known as the revenge cycle, and it really did decimate many primitive populations.[29] This problem was not decisively addressed until public systems of justice arrived to monopolize the use of legitimate violence. Before then, however, feuding clans were often reconciled by pooling their pollutions and sending them off on the back of a scapegoat.

It is this practice that has given scapegoating in general a bad name in some quarters, as a childish make-believe prologue to our grown-up courtrooms. There is some truth in this but not much. Let us grant that the blood feud is one of the worst aspects of the belief in pollution, and that it is clearly preferable to understand acts of violence as originating in, and hence the responsibility of, the individual who performs them. (We are, needless to say, still having difficulty with this belief, as the frequency of "diminished responsibility" pleas would indicate.) On the other hand, it is important to emphasize that scapegoating *does* work if both clans agree to let it do so and participate together in a sufficiently solemn ritual. (The *agreement* is the rub, which points to a distinct advantage of the mandatory court.) What's more, we can still discern the scapegoat figure in our courtroom rituals: when we banish the guilty one, either to death or the wilderness, he carries with him some of our violence (provoked by his own) and even some of our guilt ("there but for fortune . . ."). When he goes we feel unaccountably better. This seems to me no bad thing: indeed, all things being equal, a good thing; but it is unquestionably a *scapegoat* thing, and the frequent failure of our jurisprudence to acknowledge this not only diminishes the ritual's efficacy but can also lead us to pervert the evidence in our somewhat unacknowledged eagerness to find a culprit. And finally, the sacred character of the scapegoat, his being "reserved to the gods," is lost in our courtrooms: our culprits are thought wholly noxious, and this is both a crude and a cruel simplification of how violence actually moves in a society.

Even this brief sketch indicates not only that certain scapegoating virtues get lost in the courtroom, but that we can by no means simply say "scapegoating miscarries when the innocent is punished and the culprit goes free." The point, as so often, is that *context* is all-important: while we have all experienced the tendency to disavow and project on to others the violence that moves within us, to then conclude that all primitive scapegoating is simply at the mercy of such psychic disfunctioning is willfully blind. It assumes that primitive man wanders around in such a religious fog that he cannot see the blood on Bloggs's boots when he agrees to blame the goat. In fact however, the contrary is true: primitive eyesight, trained on a more dangerous world than ours, is on the whole a good deal more acute; and when our man agrees to ignore the bloody boot, he is sagely finding discretion the better part of valor in order to arrest the revenge cycle. One might even suggest that cultures with scapegoat rituals are less prone to the disavowal and projection of their violence than those without.

It nonetheless remains the case that all scapegoating practices are dangerously exposed to the corruptions of disavowal, and not the least part of the *Bouphonia*'s genius is that it recognizes this and incorporates within itself a critique of its own procedures. In terms of the cosmogonic declension mentioned earlier, the trial is the latest fixture in the play (later than the plow), and the serious side to its buffoonery is the suggestion that some crimes, pollutions, or misfortunes cannot be usefully tried in the newfangled courtroom but properly remain in the province of the scapegoat; namely, those old and eternal ones that seem to come among us from nowhere, and yet in which we feel ourselves implicated. The Christian term for this is "original sin," and one—not the only—proper response to this condition is a ceremony in which it is collectively owned, and in which a scapegoat is nominated to embody our resolution to bear down upon our affliction and see it off together.

One of the functions of the Christian ritual is to remind us that the man-god Jesus has come among us to wean us from the primitive practice of scaping actual goats: his death has carried off our sinfulness once and for all, and we remember this in commemorating the Last Supper. It is widely thought that this advance into spirituality or metaphor is one of the historical achievements of Christianity; and so it may be, broadly speaking, and yet this advance is anticipated in the *Bouphonia*. By pardoning and recalling the murderers we recognize the materialist crudity of *actually* mutilating the body of the scapegoat, what one might call "the fallacy of misplaced concreteness." In order to register this perception, that we now understand the ritual to be concerned with *symbolic* action, we substitute for our crude human substitutes an even cruder substitute—the weapons; and they recall the *katharma* that shaman used to produce from his patients' bodily effusions in the dim old days. It is a masterstroke of comic invention: by the topsy-turvy logic of the carnivalesque, the way forward is indicated by mockingly moving back.

And so, finally, to the carnival elements in the proceedings. First of all, the atmosphere of make-believe and mummery throughout, the actors acknowledging themselves as such, an irony not usual in primitive ritual. Second, release from the normal laws of consecrated action and the consequent erasing of the boundaries that separate life from its ritual representation. Third, absence of the class and power divisions that normally prevail, in order to indicate that what is being produced, constructed, and represented here is of the people, by the people, for the people. Fourth, a disturbingly grotesque juxtaposition of violence and murder with comedy and laughter, together with the suggestion that the new life that mysteriously arises from death cannot be fully incorporated without such juxtaposition. And fifth, the mock trial presided over by the "king," remarkably similar to the trials conducted by the carnival kings in the medieval Feast of Fools, in which the prevailing order is mocked, inverted, and unmade in the search for an ampler idea of order, one that contains, exemplifies, and suppresses certain kinds of disorder.

I mentioned at the outset that the *Bouphonia* appeared ridiculous to the better classes in ancient Athens, and Aristophanes had little to fear when he mocked it in *The Clouds*. It is sadly ironic that the acknowledged master of the Old Comedy could find nothing in the comic genius of this ritual to nourish his own heroic attempts to counteract Athenian folly. In our time, advocates of the carnivalesque, following Mikhail Bakhtin, are concerned to indicate the damage done to our serious rituals by the suppression of the carnivalesque since the Renaissance. With such thinking I am in full agreement; and if I were asked in general terms where we should begin to look for our lost integrities, I would nominate the *Bouphonia* as one of our most important and strangely neglected early texts.[30]

DIONYSUS AND THE ORIGINS OF TRAGEDY

One of my reasons for dwelling at length on the *Bouphonia* is that I think (and hope the reader has already suspected) that it has much to tell us about the origins of drama. Although certain aspects of this story will remain forever shrouded in darkness, it is generally agreed that tragedy emerged from the annual Passion (*pathos*) of

Dionysus, the ritual play in which the *dromenon*, the thing done, was the sacrificial slaughter of the god, either in human form or as a bull. Before we begin speculating, however, we might add to our supply of facts gathered from the *Bouphonia* some information about the principal Athenian festival of Dionysus, the *Anthesteria*.[31]

This very ancient festival took place in early spring (late February in our notation) and was concerned, as our recent discussion of *Dionysos Chthonios* might suggest it should be, with the awakening of the god. To awaken the god you must open the earth to let him out, and this opening (*kairos*) was achieved with the help of the *thyrsos*, the magic wand briefly discussed in the Appendix. As with new year festivals generally, such an opening of the earth toward the growth to come was also an opening *back* to what had been, and the ancestral spirits would come pouring out. These spirits were somewhat mischievous and thirsty (*dipsios*), and consequently a good deal of wine was poured. And yet despite the wine, the proceedings were somewhat gloomy, or as we would say, spooky: maidens would swing on ropes to bring on the spring, and the men held a drinking contest (in silence!), but the worry about pollution (or as we would say, guilt) seems to have been salient, and carnival violence not far off. The major event was the sacred marriage (*hieros gamos*) performed by the wife of the "mayor" (*archon basileus*) with Dionysus the bull. This took place in the *boukoleion* (the bull's stable), which was situated next door to the mayor's house. Just how she consummated this marriage (while her husband was off judging the drinking contest) was of course a mystery, but one orator referred to her performing "unspeakable sacrifices for the city,"[32] and Kerenyi (*Dionysos*, 1976) thinks it possible that she would mount a stone dildo of the phallic bull, thereby bringing both him and herself back to life (pp. 308 ff). In any case it doesn't seem to have been much fun, as the mythic associations were with Ariadne, whose congress with the Dionysus bull probably killed her, and also with Erigone, the daughter/wife of Ikarios/Dionysos, who hanged herself in despair when her father/husband was torn to pieces for bringing to man the dangerous gift of the vine: all of which suggests that the mayor's wife may have been at some risk, and it also casts some gloom upon the maidens swinging for fertility upon the ropes.

That is enough about the *Anthesteria* (though it also I think suggests that T. S. Eliot wasn't simply being perversely anti-Chaucerian when he wrote "April is the cruelest month"). What it certainly tells us is that old Attica traditionally approached the new year with something less than euphoria, and this in turn suggests to us that as Athenian fortunes improved remarkably through the archaic period, they might well have wanted something a little more jolly. We should also note that in the historical period there was no Athenian festival given over to the death and rebirth of Dionysus—and hence it is not surprising that this was the theme chosen to dominate the new spring festival, held in March, and called The Great Dionysia. This is where the drama emerged, and though its origins have been much debated over the years, I have a simple proposal: since the *Bouphonia* was extremely old-fashioned, and since the gloomy aspects of the *Anthesteria* might reasonably have provoked a desire among the thriving Athenians to open themselves rather more inventively to the spring, in a carnival spirit, a new (very old) festival was established, at the very end of the wintry Dionysiac half of the year, to work upon the archaic but inexhaustible theme of "New Year killing Old Year"; and here we find Thespis, in Aristotle's view the first proper tragedian, composing dithyrambs with one protagonist in the latter sixth century on the theme of Pentheus (which means "the one who suffers"), the king who, in Euripides' version, resists and is dismembered by the "new" god whom he very much resembles. As I suggested in the discussion of *Dionysos Chthonios,* mid-spring (after the awakening) is a suitable period for the killing of the Old by the New, and the theme naturally opens itself to the age-old hunter's quandary of violence turned by necessity upon another, who may be brother, who may therefore in a sense be oneself. By degrees the story would have been freed from the agricultural simplicities of Old Year versus New Year, and Old Year would have enlarged his reference to include "the adversary" or "the enemy," at which point the story could carry a good deal more complexity—notice the implication here that villainy originates in untimeliness. The Athenians in the latter sixth century were gearing up under Peisistratus and his son for an era of remarkable violence (the Persians almost in sight), supreme intelligence, and democratic invention. Is it any wonder that they called upon demotic Dionysus to authorize and entertain their emergent spirit? The warrior virtues of Homer's aristocrats had to be grafted on to the basic root-stock if Athens was to prevail in the Aegean, and the dramatic festivals were to play an important part in the process. Thus was the old disreputable god granted a new license; and once unshackled he first led the Athenians a brilliant dance and then scuttled their ships.

It is well known that the dithyramb was originally a bull-driving song, the song with which you danced and drove the Dionysus bull to slaughter, usually in the spring; and yet the *trag-odia* is a "goat-song," and its singer (*tragodos*) was either dressed in goat-skins or awarded a sacrificial goat as a prize. Jane Harrison's explanation of this anomaly (in *Themis*, p. 204 ff) seems quite convincing: that the bull thrived in the rich pastures of Crete, Thrace, and Asia Minor, but stony Attica is the home of the goat, where bulls come very expensive. Hence Dionysus the goat. To this one may add the old rustic theme of the goat as the natural enemy of the vine: as such he was annually sacrificed by the country people in March, and Vergil believed this was in fact the origin of the tragic song (Dionysus divided against himself).[33]

The rustic elements in the origins of drama should not be underestimated (Dionysus always *demotikos,* god of the people). Most important of these is the *komos,* the swarming throng of revelers who might be men dressed as women, who might be bearing the ritual phallus (in a procession called the *phallophoria*), who might be the young mocking the old, or who might be the poor going in to town to mock the rich with what we used to call "rough music." Akin to *komos* is *komē,* an unwalled village, *kompazo,* originally to boast, and *komodeo* = to mock, whence *komedia* = the comedy. Aristotle reminds us that the dramatic contests originated with the phallic songs of the dancing satyrs, the first goat-songs were indeed rough (mixing the elements of comedy and tragedy), and that it was some time before the genres were separated (Dionysus anachronistically preserves his rough sense of humor in Euripides' *Bacchae*).

Armed with this rudimentary outline, we may return to the *Bouphonia* to see what light it may shed upon the emergence of the variable drama from the fixed ritual *dromenon* (the thing done) of old. The supremely important point for our purposes, which I have been trying to indicate throughout, is that Dionysus is the god of ecstasy and excess, the unhousability of *pneuma*. This is his singularity, what above all distinguishes him from Osiris, whom we shall meet presently (and who was thought by Herodotus [in Book II] to be virtually the same divinity). To put this slightly differently, the distinguishing mark of Dionysus among the dying gods is the mad violence he is disposed to inflict, both on his worshippers (survivable) and on those who resist him (lethal); which is to say that his *rituals* will involve madness, and resistance to them will involve even more. The survivable madness, as we saw in our discussion of *Dionysos Chthonios*, is inflicted on the women who must nurse the divine child through the winter's affliction and then ritually mutilate him (thus being inoculated against madness by madness). The lethal dose is inflicted on those who, like Euripides' Pentheus, piously resist such abominable practices and are in consequence themselves invaded by the dismembering madness. The mythic archetype for this is the pitiable figure of King Lykourgos, who could not bear what the women were doing in the name of Dionysus, and so seized the ax from the sacrificing females at the altar, slew them in a frenzy, and went on to kill his own son and mutilate the corpse under the impression that he was pruning a vine. (The great age and venerability of this myth is indicated by its being cited by Homer—*Iliad* 6:134—who only ever mentions Dionysus under severe compulsion.) As the myth of Lykourgos illustrates, the mark of Dionysus turned savagely mad (*mainomenos*) is the ritual blasphemously mistaken, in which the violent energies overspill the ritual lawlines and mutilate the wrong victim. It has long been recognized that Lykourgos lies behind the Pentheus of Euripides: what is less well known is that there are a number of other important myths and rituals also concerned with violent spillage at the sacrificial altar, some associated with Dionysiac resistance, some not.[34] What I should like to propose is not only that all of them should be seen as authentically Dionysiac but quintessentially so, as bearers of what one might call his leading edge, that mischievous restlessness that would not remain bounded by the lawlines of ritual sacrifice. It is this edge that helped to lead the Greek soul from myth into history, from a world in which the themes of love and war are permanently engraved in the seasonal rituals that repeat and confine them, to one in which those energies have escaped their ritual containers to contest the larger follies of narrative invention "in history." And it is here, I suggest, in ritual overspill, that we find the originating core of the tragic drama. This hypothesis is strengthened not only by the fact that the theme of Pentheus was frequently addressed (by Thespis at the first and by Euripides at the last) but also by the fact that in the *Oresteia* of Aeschylus (the first and perhaps the greatest of the major tragedies to have survived), the catastrophe is also unleashed by mistaken ritual, when Clytemnestra provokes King Agamemnon into walking on the sacred *peplos* (tapestry), thereby symbolically despoiling the *oikos* (household) and anticipating its ruination when the king is butchered in his bath. Thus the *Oresteia* and Euripides' *Bacchae*, the first and the last of the immortal dramas, are both constructed around what I am proposing as the original primitive plot, the restless refusal to abide within the lawlines of the sacred.

Where should we look for the incubating germ of this restlessness? One can only speculate: New Year and Old Year? In view of the singular importance of the contest (*agon*) throughout the annals of Greek ritual (the Olympic games, for an obvious example), it is hard to imagine that Old Year ever ceded to New Year without a fight, as it often did in other cultures.[35] One thinks of the priest-kings at Nemi: something like that; and there is indeed evidence to suggest that the Olympic games were originally staged to decide who should be "king of the year" (or *eniautos daimon*). If Old Year managed to win again he would persist: if not, he was killed (either actually or symbolically) and the new victor crowned.[36] One can imagine, as the Athenian mind freed itself from the agricultural cycle, and lost its faith in the capacity of ritual *agon* magically to contain the energies of *pneuma*, that the idea of unscripted (unritualized) *agon* might come to seem more *real*; and thus it may have underwritten the move from the single protagonist of Thespis in 535 B.C. to the introduction of two protagonists by Aeschylus in 467; and once you have moved from one into two, the house is divided, the story has got loose and will not resolve: for two into one won't go. Such speculation is of course somewhat idle; and moreover to what extent the ritual restlessness of Dionysus was implicit in the pre-Hellenic peoples who fostered him, and to what extent injected by the northern pastoralists who ultimately marginalized him, and to what extent imported from the Near East via Phrygia, also cannot be known (though it is worth noting that Lykourgos was said to be a Thracian, which led many erroneously to suppose that Dionysus was originally a northerner).

The *Bouphonia* is centrally concerned with unritualized violence at the altar, and it is this that constitutes its prime importance for seekers of Dionysus, not the theme of bull-sacrifice at harvest time. The fact that the violence is survived and reincorporated, places it with the tragicomic sensibility from which, as we saw, the original goat-songs emerged. Its basic structure is clearly very old and innocent (altogether bumpkin to the classical Athenian), and yet its comic sophistication suggests to me the elaborating hand of some urban genius. But whatever the truth about its dating and provenance, one cannot fail to find the combination of simplicity and complexity, innocence and experience, crudity and refinement, tragedy and comedy, very impressive. In it Dionysus becomes (for once?) supremely civilized; mischievous enough to rock (and mock) the ritual boat in carnival mood, orderly enough to see us safely home in the end. I mentioned earlier how sadly ironic it was that Aristophanes and Co. could find in it nothing to save their beleaguered souls, and we may now be in a position to see why: it was simply too *late* for such saving grace. The genius of Dionysus had run wild, *mainomenos*, run wild and gone to ground both; was in any case lethally unapproachable, as the mounting corpses of

Spartans and Athenians helplessly indicated. The drama could (and did) to some extent diagnose the disease; but it lacked the ritual power to prescribe a cure.

Or one might say that Dionysus had put to sea (since that is where he absented himself when not under ground) and that the ship of state, having been moved irrevocably into history, was taking water and listing badly. Both Aristophanes and Euripides knew that it would almost certainly strike and sink; and so it did. There was salvage, of course, as there almost always is; but the hope of salvation would not return for some time.

THE LAMENTATIONS OF ISIS/OSIRIS

There is of course a great deal more to be said about Dionysus, but the important point for this book's argument has been made: that whatever powers of lamentation he bestowed upon the nurses who annually butchered him, and they were undoubtedly considerable, they failed ultimately to contain the mutilating frenzy, whose "interests," so to speak, were therefore made over to the Homeric party, as we shall see in the next chapter. Where does this leave our argument? Having suggested that the energies of lamentation are capable *in principle* of containing the mutilating violence, I have also indicated that in classical Greece they did not do so; and hence the reader will justly feel that my argument for lamentation requires something more chronologically apposite than vague gesticulations toward a Christianity that would not appear for another four hundred years and that lies safely beyond this book's primitive assignment. Where would one look in fifth-century Athens for a stronger music of lamentation than the culture was mustering? One would look to the acknowledged source of many of one's major religious ideas—to Egypt; and there one would find Isis and Osiris.

In order for us to do this, however, we must not only sketch the broad outlines of the Egyptian mentality, but first say something more about the neolithic revolution that preceded and made it possible—a task in any case incumbent on a book that aspires to trace the wanderings of *pneuma* from the hunting savannah to its primitive conclusions in ancient Greece. Thus this section will conclude not only the present chapter's argument about sacrifice, but the general survey of lawlines that has engaged us since the fall of alpha-shaman in Chapter 4.

The neolithic revolution began some twelve thousand years ago in the Middle East with the domestication of goats and sheep and the discovery that certain edible grass seeds could be planted and harvested. As a result of this, the world population, which had been stable at one million, soon shot up to a hundred million. The oldest town known to us is Jericho, which was importing obsidian from Anatolia by about 8300 B.C.; but almost as old and far more instructive is Catal Huyuk, a substantial town of about 30 acres situated on a river bank in a rich alluvial plain, some 200 miles inland from the coast of southern Turkey. Here for at least two thousand years the old hunting ways coexisted side by side with the new farming life. As well as the rich soil (which gestated the barley seed first brought down from its native hills around 8000), there was an abundance of deer and auroch and wild pig to keep the hunters happy.[37]

Conditions altered significantly throughout the Middle East around 6000 B.C. when the winds died and the weather became much hotter.[38] Pastures dried up, the game disappeared, agriculture became possible only in the river valleys, and people were thrown together in large numbers. In those places where the labor of the dispossessed was astutely organized by the dominant, cities arose: indeed it would be fair to say that civilization was the human answer to climatic failure. Although Jericho failed to meet this challenge, folding up around 6000 B.C., Catal survived (twelve different towns have been excavated on the site) and it is evident that agriculture overtook hunting there as principal food-supplier around 5800, and the male gods in the town declined thereafter and finally disappeared. Although the bull continued to dominate the animal shrines, the goddesses displaced the gods. Religion was clearly important, as a third of the buildings were shrines. Not only ceramics but obsidian mirrors and daggers and metal trinkets (from about 6000) have been recovered from the site.

Catal offers a unique and uniquely attractive snapshot of the changeover from paleo- to neolithic, in an urban setting moreover, but not much to inform the questions we would ask of the neolithic generally, which are two: what were the religious implications of settling down, and what did the goddess mean? My answers to both these questions are fairly simple and can be briefly hazarded. The giving up of our nomadism was obviously traumatic, for divinity, as I have emphasized throughout, *is* movement, and in losing much of our daily movement we lost those easy and consoling delights of *pneuma* that can still quicken the step as one wanders through the countryside on a Sunday afternoon. This loss, quite apart from the relegation of the hunt, would have afflicted the men more than the women, and the two together would have created a good deal of boredom, which always leads to sex and violence.

Amplifying this alienation from divinity is the growth of technology under urban conditions, nicely symbolized by the town wall (a massive structure both in Jericho and Catal). The wall protects us against predators and invaders, but also subdues the breeze that might animate the midday somnolence. Such *fixity* troubles the mind. If the holy spirit is blowing where it listeth in the winds of *pneuma,* how can we follow it while dug in behind the town wall? The gods build no walls in either woodland or savannah, and it may prove difficult to get their blessing. Where do we find the *nerve* to aspire to such permanence and such power? *The Epic of Gilgamesh* and the stories of the Tower of Babel and Prometheus the fire-thief clearly indicate our unease. The wall also symbolizes the law (as the Heraclitean epigraph to Chapter 5 indicates), the gathering body of regulations, both ritual and technological, that first moderates our exposure to *pneuma* and ultimately threatens to block our access to it (consider St. Paul in Romans 7:9 remembering that "I was alive without the law, once"). Thus the wall we first build to protect and venerate our sacred tree may turn it to stone in the end.

And town life? As the redundant hunters hang about the smithy, knocking up yet another spear to add to their sadly large collection, they mutter darkly about the growing power of the women. In the early days of agriculture, before the heavy plowing with oxen, when it was more like gardening than farming, the implanting and fostering of the seed would have been womanly magic; and since this magic soon became responsible for the bulk of our food, the shrines filled up with goddesses. What's more, the women *liked* the safety of their new houses, easier for raising the children, and they doubtless soon became house-proud—the houses at Catal were kept very clean. More generally, the rhythm of the agricultural year, like the rhythm of child-bearing, has everything to do with patience and passivity, the long waiting for good luck on the day; and the women somehow seemed to be better at this than the men.

Finally, a further word about neolithic sacrifice. The annual mystery for neolithic culture was the life cycle of the corn spirit, born in the green shoots, violently killed in the harvest, and resurrected in the seed sprouting from the dead earth. It is not difficult to imagine considerable anxiety attending this annual cycle, focusing on the new year ceremonies in which humans would participate in the divine drama through ritual representation. As the old year wanes, *pneuma* withdraws (from vegetation and the human breast), the cosmos itself becomes unstable, and the angry spirits of the dead are abroad, threatening mischief and retribution. All in all it is a troubling time, and it is not surprising that in our ritual make-believe we do our utmost in the way of sympathetic magic to represent a decisive termination of the dying year and rebirth of the new.

The mythological evidence (prodigiously marshalled by Frazer in *The Golden Bough*) points conclusively to the widespread practice of annual or periodic human sacrifice, in which the "Old Year" or the "King," as the goddess' seed-bearer and harvest (her consort and her son), would be killed, dismembered, and offered up to her (as his wife and mother) in order to ensure the potency of "New Year." In the case of Dionysus, as we have seen, the dismembering was usually performed by his own *thiasos,* the women who had nursed him as a child. The parts of Old Year's body would often be buried in the earth (as the Osiris myth indicates) and in the feast that followed we would usually eat not his flesh but that of some animal sacrificed along with him as his surrogate or substitute. In so doing we would both confess and seek divinity's blessing upon the violence we necessarily practice in the cultivation and satisfaction of our appetites. It is not difficult to discern the figure of the scapegoat in this story; and behind him, the oldest of our guilty secrets, the feast of alpha-shaman.[39]

In the neolithic New Year's festival we can see the major elements in the story of alpha-shaman recalled, reinterpreted, and disposed in manageable form. The new emphasis on the necessary sacrifice of male potency in the interests of fertility was, of course, full of implications for the sex war; and even when we became sufficiently confident that the new year would come without the *annual* sacrifice of our leading man, he would still be offered up periodically (often on an eight-year cycle). The magical reasoning here was that the "sacred marriage" of the king to the queen as earth mother had to be terminated, "with extreme prejudice," as it were, before his powers had a chance to wane and thus cause the harvest to fail. It must also be admitted that this is a harrowing start for the modern love story.

But it is one thing to say that the sexual play of time versus eternity was represented by male and female respectively (and our discussion of "housing the sacred" in Section 1 would indicate that these roles are the natural ones), quite another to say that the female somehow prevailed. Our best evidence on this important and obscure question comes from Catal: with the arrival of agriculture the goddess prospered, male gods in human form went into severe decline, but even more prosperous than the goddess was the bull (as was the case somewhat later in Minoan Crete, as we shall see). What does this mean? All one can hazard with any confidence, in my view, is that the elemental power of serious violence was being held at the theriomorphic (animal) stage, while the culture's hopes of subduing, surviving, and integrating such violence were being vested in the human form of a goddess. Call for Lévi-Strauss: he would encourage us to say that the bull is mostly Nature, the goddess mostly culture.

The "sacred marriage" of bull and goddess, that universal motif in early days, therefore represents our dangerous gamble with the forces of *pneuma*; that they can enter us, be subdued, sacrificed, and transformed into human prosperity. This gamble is dangerous because if our magic fails, we get what we see, no sacred marriage but monstrous bestiality, the rumor of which swirls about the Athenian *Anthesteria,* as we recently noticed.

The matter of neolithic religious symbolism is not only difficult (we really are in the dark) but highly contentious. Part of what makes it so difficult is that the mythic mind is at this point grappling with huge changes and contradictions (the idea of culture based in crops that are planted and killed and reborn), and is consequently in a highly tentative and fluid state (so many of its timeless paleolithic certainties challenged). What one finds at the beginning of historical culture (ca. 3000 B.C.) are vestiges of androgynous divinities who metamorphose easily from one animal or human form to another, the pantheism of the animist mind moving slowly toward the identification of discrete (and gendered!) gods and goddesses to tell its story. Behind the luminous distinction of the Isis/Osiris myth, for example, to be discussed presently, we catch bewildering glimpses of rioting symbols such as the eye, which is the sun or the moon or the god or the goddess or the cobra or the weapon or the wound . . . ; and the mud, which is the cow, which is the barley, which is the bull, which is the male, which is the female . . . To seek the psycho-logic in such confusion can be great fun as long as one prohibits sharply the tendency of the tidy mind to find fixed meanings where all is in flux. In other words, mythographers should move cautiously among such material, and frequently they do not. [40]

Having spent fifteen years assuming rather uncritically that the prevalence of the goddess around 3000 B.C. (particularly in Crete) meant some discounting of the male, I finally realized that although this may be so, the *evidence we have* suggests that we should begin our argument at an earlier point; namely, the ubiquitous fact of the neolithic goddess abandoning her animal forms for a human shape while the god remains (and even becomes) theriomorphic. This is something we *know* (as opposed to all the things we might conjecture) and it has certainly not been given the attention it deserves.[41]

It can be clearly seen in Minoan Crete, where the art work suggests that the goddess consorts with lion, tree, snake, and bull. We shall discuss the Cretan mystery in some detail at the end of the next chapter, and at this point I want only to make one relatively simple but important proposal: the great goddesses of the ancient cultures are always seen as the direct descendants of the old neolithic (and paleolithic) fertility goddesses, but when they begin to consort (in some kind of marriage) with animals and trees, I suggest that the marriage envisioned is *not* principally of male and female but, as the symbolism indicates, of Nature and culture; and hence what the goddesses *principally* represent (particularly in the presence of an animal consort) is no longer the natural crudities of life and death but rather the cultural complexity that must house and absorb Nature's violence. What makes this difficult to see (and easy to resist) is that they must *also* retain their older designation of womb-tomb-mother-earth (*la femme est naturelle donc abominable,* as Baudelaire sourly put it). To revert to the important discussion in Section 1, the womb as sacred space evolves logically into the "feminine" temple (*temenos*), the place where we both offer up first fruits *and* imagine the culture housed. If it is thus mytho-logical to have the goddess represent both Nature and culture, it is also confusing; and hence to represent the dangerous dialectic between Nature and culture we marry her to the unequivocally natural bull or snake. I suggest that we find this difficult and confusing because they did too (the Cretan bull, for example, rarely appears *with* the goddess, though the more primitive snake does).

Strong support for my proposal comes from the oldest of the great goddesses, Sumerian Inanna and Akkadian Ishtar, who are very interested in love and war (the two flowers of culture) but strangely not in childbirth.[42] Egypt is even more interesting: when the primordial goddess Nut gets beyond being the cosmic cow, she stands over the (masculine) earth and encloses the play of culture with her body by leaning over it and touching the earth with her hands: thus she represents the temple that we hope may contain the movement of divinity as it comes among us. A marked taste for war is un-Egyptian, but love passes to Isis, much the most civilized of the great goddesses. Again, the Cretan goddess, with her jewelry and flounced skirts, appears highly civilized even when playing with snakes. The Greeks are very late, relatively speaking, but four of their five principal goddesses are either warlike virgins (Artemis and Athena) or indifferent mothers (Hera and Aphrodite): only Demeter really *mothers,* and she hardly marries.

What then of the old theriomorphic consorts? Again Crete is the best place to look, since its consorts remained unashamedly and yet thoughtfully theriomorphic for some two thousand years, and we shall address this matter in the next chapter. At this stage, again I have only one point to make: if it is the body of the goddess that houses the sacred play of culture, it is the role of her consort to represent the sacred power that comes and goes. The tree-snake-bull is the power of *pneuma* that comes to shake and fertilize and expire, in the earth mother yes, but more importantly in the house of culture, which we hope will live, as Nature does, forever. There is a marvelous irony in this structure of symbols: the goddess, who takes a human shape, represents a cultural totality we never see but must imagine; whereas her consort, who carries the invisible energies of *pneuma* into our midst, is a tree or a snake or a bull, all of whom can be met (epiphanically or not) on an afternoon's possibly dangerous stroll out of town.

We have all of us labored too long under the masochist yoke of Robert Graves's matriarchal paranoia. Look at Catal, look at Crete: goddess and bull, above all: put them together and what you get is not the maceration of the male (premature anthropomorphism), but good news, the faith that culture may absorb and transform the energies of Nature without killing them off.

Imagine the Nile valley. An immensely long and flat hollow runs from the north to the south of Egypt, almost as barren as a wadi for some of the year. Beyond this valley, on either side, endless desert. On the far horizons to east and west, mountain ranges to seal us off and repel the invader. On either side of the river, cultivated fields rise to a certain level, and where they stop the desert begins. This line is the high-water mark of the Nile's inundation, which annually brings a rich gift of silt out of Africa to make the desert flower. Because the soil thus annually transformed is very rich, it can support a large population, all of whom live closely clustered on the high ground along the river banks—*urbs in rure,* urbanity without walls. There is very little wind (apart from the prevailing northerly breeze) and no rain. Nothing disturbs the stillness of this symmetrical landscape except the sun, which daily crosses it at right angles: the only invader is the Nile, once a year, renewing us all. Is it any wonder that such conditions fostered the most contemplative and enduring of all the ancient cultures?[43]

The Egyptian imagination is a remarkably visual one (the eye not the ear) and its dominant features, again unsurprisingly, are symmetry and monumentality. There are two obvious gods of movement, the sun and the grain-growing river, Re and Osiris, the light and the dark, the dry and the moist, the transcendent and the immanent or emergent. Re (or Ra) was the god of the conquering pastoralists, whereas Osiris belonged to the peasant farmers.[44] A widespread distaste for the first of these has led subsequent visitors to Egypt (such as ourselves) to neglect the genius of the second. Since these gods developed rather different theologies, which marry with difficulty, let us begin briefly with Re and then move on to Osiris. As befits any major deity, the sun is impressively ambiguous, both the joyful source of all illumination and monstrous in his raging heat; moreover, his manifest mastery of the day is challenged nightly when he must cross the underworld waters of Nun's abyss in his boat, and survive the attacks of the dragon-serpent Apopis in order to be reborn the next morning. Thus harshness and kindness, darkness and light, the tenuousness of cosmos, from the beginning. This is emphasized when he subsequently becomes Amon-Re, Amon manifesting the (undoubtedly Osirian) principle of *concealment.* Thus "waving banners in the sun on an overcast day," altogether *yin/yang,* the more impressive when one remembers that Egypt knows almost nothing of overcast weather.

Such wisdom was purchased at a price. As was the case somewhat earlier in Mesopotamia, the first four centuries of Egyptian court culture were characterized by a religious madness that we might as well call sunstroke. Dazzled by the harsh and daily triumph of the sun, with which he identified, totally, Pharaoh would meet his own apparent demise with manic denial: the bulk of his court (mostly women) would be invited to process solemnly into the vast necropolis of his tomb and be buried alive with his corpse, not only to speed and comfort his journey into the sun, but to remind us all that earthlings derive their reality from the King as Sun God. On a good day, some five hundred souls would be rather unpleasantly suffocated in this way, and since they were mostly women, one may suppose that what partly inspired this madness was the desire to obliterate the memory of the bad old days when the king was sacrificed regularly to the neolithic goddess. But sexism aside, what is more generally deplorable here is a kind of materialist fixity of the imagination, a religious stupefaction in which the incorrigibly playful, tentative, and *symbolic* nature of all ritual representations of the dream-time has been quite forgotten.[45]

Although these fixities were much loosened when the sun recovered his shadow side as Theban Amon-Re, there remains something unattractively hieratic and stiff in this "sky-line" theology; and so let us turn to the "water-line" stories that evolved around the figure of Osiris. As the word "water-line" might suggest, Osiris was the god of the people (like his Greek counterpart Dionysus), always associated with moisture, hiddenness, and mystery, and with Apis (or Serapis) the sacred bull: throughout Egyptian history he remained the most revered and significant of the gods. Mythically venerated as the bearer of the grain (and other arts of culture), which delivered the Egyptians from cannibalism, he is the lineal descendent of the old neolithic fertility spirit, sacrificed, dismembered, and buried annually to make the corn grow. But in certain respects he stands head and shoulders above such other inheritors of the corn spirit as Dumuzi, Adonis, and Dionysus, and in my view his story is truly a masterpiece of the mythopoeic.

The widely attested difficulty of Egyptian mythology in general and of Osiris in particular becomes much more manageable in the light of Professor Wilson's observation that "with relation to gods and men the Egyptians were monophysites: many men and many gods, but all ultimately of one nature" (in Frankfort, 1977, p. 66). This is to say that what seems to us a bewildering variety and inconsistency of mythic motifs, and a blithe disregard for proper zoning regulations in the movement of heavenly traffic, are in fact indications not of confusion but of the animist mentality that genially underlay and underwrote the Egyptians' confident explorations in the dream-time of myth and ritual. Not unlike the Greeks and their *phusis,* the Egyptians began with a Nature benign and divinely animated, and this spirit, moist rather than dry, dark rather than light, was concentrated above all in Osiris:

> Whether I live or die I am Osiris,
> I enter in and reappear through you,
> I decay in you, I grow in you,
> I fall down in you, I fall upon my side . . .
> I cover the earth,
> Whether I live or die I am Barley,
> I am not destroyed.[46]

Even here, however, in the relatively early days, his fertilizing power seems to be coming from death, and one can feel the emphasis gathering toward the fall rather than the rise, an emphasis that will gradually increase, particularly in the time of the New Kingdom; and it is, needless to say, an emphasis that we shall now follow, since our interest at this point is in the search for an adequate theology of lamentation. But before we begin it is worth insisting, particularly because we necessarily approach Osiris through many centuries of Christianity, that this dying god was conceived in confidence and strength, not in poverty of spirit. Beginning simply as the barley that comes and goes, he gradually evolved into the power that *comes in its going,* that waxes from its waning; and although he became otherworldly in his decadence, for many centuries he was right here and now, concealed but immanent, present in his absence. It was only because the Egyptians were spiritually so richly settled in a world where the eye was filled with seeing and the ear with hearing that they dared to isolate the dying fall as the most real thing; and one can feel the strength of such richness in the Coffin Text just cited, a text that, despite the notorious difficulty of translating the Egyptian language, is unmistakably impressive.

Although the literature of Osiris is vast, I propose to focus, and only briefly at that, on the two most important motifs, the story of his daily incarnation and the passion play of his death. But can two such stories coexist? How can a god who came and died also be incarnate every day? The question is impossibly large, but something can be said here. Mythic narratives either take the form "Once upon a time something happened, . . ." or "Here is what is *really* going on today and every day." Whereas we moderns tend to find these two forms quite different, even incompatible, the mind at home with the mytho-logical passes quite happily from one to the other, unobstructed by what we would call the temporal contradictions between the two. Thus, for example, Christian theologians have, over the centuries, been much exercised by the question of whether the New Testament is a historical account of a once-for-all incarnation or a story that tells us how we crucify Jesus daily. The same problem arises for us in the case of Osiris, though less pressingly since his Passion is comfortably lodged in the "Once upon a time." Simply to assert my belief that the ancient masters of the mythological were right and the problem is soluble, in the case of Osiris at any rate, may strike some readers as peremptory, even in the light of the foregoing chapters; and to point out that the Egyptians thought the problem soluble even as they were discovering a good deal about the mathematical measurement of chronology might seem evasive. But there, time presses, and we must pass on.

In the story of the incarnate dying god, Osiris becomes visible only in the moist shadows cast by the perpetual struggle between Seth and Horus, two ancient figures from the Ra-royal mythic line. Horus, simplest of the three, is the rising sun, the young King of the new year who initiates and augments prosperity. Seth was originally the noble lord of the desert, brother to Horus, and came to embody the power of darkness, chaos, and negation, ubiquitously emanating from Nun's abysmal waters, which are brackish and salty, hence Seth's dryness. It is important to realize that in the beginning Seth is simply the adversary, Nature's resistance to the triumph of culture, present wherever the energies of Horus are engaged upon increase. Behind Seth as adversary, of course, one can discern the outlines of Old Year versus New Year; but as adversary, the *perpetual* threat to prosperity, he becomes a much more compelling figure, and is locked in eternal combat with Horus, the latter forever losing an eye, Seth forever having his testicles cut off. Whenever one of them seems about to prevail, the other gods step in to restore the balance. In the course of time (which may be to say "When Osiris was brought into the story"), some changes were made: Horus became Osiris's son, and Seth became Osiris's brother, a dangerous move that paved the way for the eventual isolation of Seth as primordial bad guy. Because we moderns are much disposed (to our cost) simply to construe negation as villainy, we must make a particular effort not to do this with Seth, and remember that the pious Egyptian mind venerated his formidable powers.[47]

Although the struggle between Seth and Horus fills the daily foreground, Osiris too is never absent, though it takes a practiced eye to see him (or better, an instructed heart to feel him); for he is the spirit of the life that is always departing, almost absent in its presence, almost present in its absence. He is the setting sun in search of the moon, the wounded or dying King, almost "the notion of some infinitely gentle, infinitely suffering thing."[48] The non-philosophical souls on the banks of the Nile would find him unequivocally twice a year, in the cutting of the corn and the planting of the seed. These are the two dramatic moments of the agricultural cycle, and both were experienced as epiphanies of the dying god, moments in which his presence could be felt as disappearance. The harvested sheaves were the dismembered body of the mutilated god, just as the treading of the seed into the Nile mud was a trampling of the god into rottenness and darkness. In both cases it is we who mutilate the god, and we do it in the hope of life's renewal; and in both cases our violence is accompanied by lamentation.

Taken together, father and son compose a picture of *neomai*, the coming and going of divinity, and their movements are mediated by Seth as Egyptian representative of the *abzu*. For the purpose of clarity I have kept father and son separate thus far, but they must also be conjoined, a two-in-one figure in which the linear waxing and waning of the agricultural year is complicated by the perception that at any point in the year life is *both* waxing and waning: leaves are falling here but soil is composting there, and the one runs to the other. Thus the ever-dying sadness of the father is redeemed by its augmenting the ever-waxing vigor of the son, which in turn furnishes more for the father to undergo. To separate the two is to invite the manic-depressive alternation of brashness and desolation. To keep them conjoined is to find the opening.

One might say that when he was young Osiris too fought Seth, but that would be wrong, because when he was young he was Horus, son of the father. The endless woundings of Horus (and of Seth, come to that) are absorbed and carried off by Osiris, and so the son is forever becoming the father, who dies the son's life, as it were, and so too, one would expect, the father is constantly renewed in the son who lives his death. And yet how can this be? How can the wounding of the son hold and repair, that is, forestall the absolute loss, of the dying father? What is it that prevents the ever-dying Osiris from actually doing so, and tumbling off the map into oblivion?

This is the heart of the mystery, where the agricultural passes into the cultural, and the answer lies with Isis, wife and sister of Osiris, mother of Horus, lunar emanation of Hathor the cow-goddess, herself an emanation of the neolithic fertility goddess, again the amazingly rich mud-banks of the Nile. The clarity of Isis is in the foreground with Seth and Horus, witnessing and occasionally intervening in their struggle, plus of course sponsoring, underwriting, and blessing all the good things that come from the womb of Mother Earth. But she also dwelt in darkness, acquainted with the night, as her lunar designation would suggest (as also would her almost-twin sister Nephthys's marriage to Seth). The moistening eye of the moon is what makes dark things discernible, and this is what Isis does. If, as we have said, the ever-dying Osiris is perpetually on the point of vanishing, difficult to discern even in settled circumstances, we should not be surprised if, at certain times—such as the desiccated season before the annual inundation—he should seem to have disappeared altogether. The one who holds him in her mind is Isis, who knows him as no other does; and when he is lost, as in the dry season, and when the moon disappears, it is she who has to find him. But in the recensions of mythic time, *that* time can become any time and all time; and thus emerges the figure of Isis perpetually losing and finding the man being perpetually lost and found. And thus even when she was smilingly sponsoring church fêtes, and awarding the prize for the largest pumpkin grown this year, she was also in the dark, hastening or sequestered, and sustaining against the forces of manic cheerfulness the idea of her brother-husband lost and perpetually fading, at the edge of oblivion. It was Isis who kept Osiris alive, by remembering him. It couldn't have been young Horus, whose every quiet thought was about how he might outfox Seth in the morning. The central importance of such attention, such bearing in mind, was ritually recognized in the Osirian festivals, usually held in the dry season, in which the searching and lamentation for Osiris seemed to have predominated. (I say "seemed" because most of these rites, particularly in the period of the New Kingdom, were secretive.) And when, in the first centuries after Christ, Isis became the dominant goddess throughout the Mediterranean world, it was not the fruitful womb that stood out but the sorrowing eye of tendance, which promised that the sufferings of violence can be borne and redeemed in the heart that commemorates them.*

*Isis makes one beautiful appearance in the New Testament when Mary Magdalene, discovering the empty tomb, says "They have taken away my Lord, and I know not where they have laid him."

* * *

The monophysitical genius of the Egyptian mind, mentioned above, is apparent in the tale just told: the five characters independently pursue their destinies, and yet they are, like the five fingers of a hand, all members of one family and locked together in perpetual give and take. As an ensemble they constitute the pattern of stillness and movement (stillness *in* movement) with which Osiris aspires, in the Coffin Text cited, to "cover the earth," the reality of *pneuma*'s coming and going insofar as man can follow it. To see the five as one, and yet five, and forever, is not easy; but such is the logic of the mythopoeic whenever it is working at full stretch: as an ancient text (addressing Osiris) says, "If you walk, Horus walks: if you speak, Seth speaks."[49] The *Death of Osiris,* on the other hand, is a much easier story to grasp, because it more or less adheres to the laws of discrete space (here is not there) and linear or irreversible time (this then that).

In the beginning, when he was perhaps still a bull, King Osiris ruled in Egypt. One night, in a passing regal oversight (or perhaps lured by the spirits of desolation), he mistakes his sister Nephthys for his sister-wife Isis, and mounts her darkened body, thereby probably siring Anubis, jackal god of dead substance (in appropriate commemoration of the jackal's carrion talents). Brother Seth, husband to Nephthys, is mightily displeased, and so plots, with seventy-two henchmen, the death of Osiris.[50] The becoffined corpse is thrown into the sea (not the Nile, the anti-Nile) and it drifts to Phoenician Byblos, where it washes ashore and sprouts a sturdy and sweet-smelling erica tree, which the local king duly installs as serious pillar in his palace. The grieving Isis arrives some time later, is taken on as nursemaid to the king's son, and in the evening dusk flies mournfully about the pillar as a swallow. After failing to confer immortality upon the princeling (a story for another time), she makes her escape with the casket and returns by sea to Egypt, probably opening it en route and embracing (in the form of a kite) the corpse of her brother-husband, thereby conceiving Horus of the waxing year (though accounts differ on this crucial moment). Back in the swampy delta[51] she hides the casket, but it is found by Seth on a boar hunt, and he chops the corpse into fourteen pieces and scatters them throughout the realm. With great difficulty Isis searches everywhere, and together with her errant sister Nephthys recovers all but the genital member (always the major wound of the ever-wounded Osiris in the previous tale) and reconstitutes the corpse.* Some say the fish got the member, but I think we should have a word with Nephthys. In any case, Horus grows up to avenge the father, and after the decisive battle Seth is confined to the Sun's cosmic boat, where he nightly defends both Nature and culture against the mischievous attacks of Apopis the dragon-serpent, incorrigible son of chaos. Horus becomes pharaoh, the widow Isis proceeds to a life of more or less good works, and Osiris becomes king of the underworld. All live happily ever after, except that Osiris occasionally complains about the lack of light down there.

My jaunty tone has I hope conveyed my sense of the inferiority of such closed and tidy narrative to the compelling openness of the one that preceded it; and yet it has several strokes of genius, and seems to me unequaled throughout antiquity in its kind. The only point that need slightly detain us concerns Osiris's move into the underworld (*Dat* in Egyptian, not far from *Nun*'s abysmal waters). What he does there is supervise the delivery of the dead, the transmigration of their souls into bird form, and either the recycling of dead substances into the plenitudes of Nature above ground, or else, in some late versions, the passing of judgment upon the orderliness (*maat*) of their earthly existence and the consequent awarding (or not) of eternal life. Insofar as such awarding represents an attempt to extend the pharaonic privilege to everyman, it seems laudable enough, but since that privilege was mistaken in the first place, I find it regrettable. In any case one sees no promising ground for such an egregious narrative move either in the Nile mud or in the flight of birds. What sustains Osiris in his dying is the attentive eye and sorrowful song of Isis: one should ask for no more than this.

---

*As fertility spirit, Osiris was often represented ithyphallically, and hence as dying god one would imagine the reverse. The Fisher King of the Grail legends is an emanation of Osiris, and he, for decency's sake, is wounded in the thigh.

Two final points, one easy, one not easy. The coffin-born tree that sustains for a while the Phoenician palace invites us to think of Osiris as tree-god; and this, given the paucity of trees in Egypt, suggests an impressively long memory of African days in the forest. As pillar it was known as the *Djed* column (*Djed* = stable), doubtless of prehistoric provenance, and such a column was raised at harvest festivals throughout Egypt to represent the indomitable corn spirit (one thinks of the mask of Dionysus hung on a column). Small versions of the *Djed* were popular as amulets, and they undoubtedly originated, like the standing stones of Europe, more or less in the beginning.

Unsurprisingly in such a visual culture, the eye is the most commonplace and important of all Egyptian religious symbols—also the most difficult to construe. Again very old, the eye symbol seems to have originated throughout Europe and Asia as a representation of the Great Goddess, usually in her fierce aspect. But the goddess is the giver as well as the taker of life, and the eye is not only what first warns us of hostility in its bearer, but is also the great receptacle that opens itself to be filled with the world's intelligence and beauty. Furthermore, most self-respecting goddesses have two eyes, just as the cosmos is looked over by the sun and the moon.

And if this is not complicated enough, one must further bear in mind that in the patriarchal takeover many symbols of the masculine and the feminine had to be reversed; and although this was managed better in Egypt than elsewhere, it occasionally led to muddle. Thus, for example, the eye on top of Pharaoh's head was originally the fierceness of the female cobra, but was gradually assimilated to the sun, and hence no longer the gift of his wife and mother.

In view of such confusion, let us again substitute *yang/yin* for masculine/feminine; and let us further agree that in both Egypt and China the solar is mostly *yang* and the lunar *yin*. The Eye of Horus is *yang*-solar in its waxing strength and ferocity, but *yin*-lunar in its wounding and loss. When Seth plucks it out and flings it into the wilderness, the moon goes out, and lunar Thoth (not Isis) sets off to find and repair it. At this point the narrative stream seems to divide: the repaired eye is both returned to Horus and offered to Osiris. And yet what Horus receives, as the moon returns to the sky, is a new solar eye with which to rejoin the battle. (This narrative hiccup is required by the story's endless reiteration, and should not be dwelt on.) What Osiris receives is an eye sacrificed to life's violence, which has been mysteriously repaired and transformed in a process for which our word is forgiveness. Just as the sun dries the land with the heat of its vigor, and the moon moistens it with the dew drops of its tears, so the solar eye becomes lunar through suffering, and the apparently greater is included in the apparently lesser. Osiris, having been "the hidden one" from the beginning, is utterly *yin*, and yet absorbs the sacrificed energies of *yang* Horus.

Here we should pause to recall our earlier discussion of sacrifice, where I argued at length that religious mania originates in the mutilating frenzy. The daily struggle in which genitals and eyes are ripped out provides as clear an image of these energies as one could ask for. Each figure is mutilating the other's powers of mutilation (or better, by fusing the figures, as we have done with other pairings in the myth, we produce a composite image of the mutilating monster mutilated). Why genitals and eyes? The former is fairly obvious, as we have noticed throughout both the swordlike aspects of the male member and the proximity of sexuality to wounding.* But why the eye? The obvious answer lies with the human disposition to imagine power (particularly aggressive power) as emanating from the eye, a disposition we may confidently trace back to simian days. The unobvious answer has to do with the "ocular" nature of sacrificial mutilation, which distinguishes it utterly from murder. To want to make an end of someone is to want to make them no longer visible, no longer separate from oneself. The one I want to murder has something that is mine (or that I absolutely intend to make mine) and the obvious way to achieve this is to incorporate him, enfold him in my arms and hug him "to death" in a closure of the visible. Thus the call-sign of the murderer is, as Othello said, "Put out the

---

*One might also mention that soldiers in the ancient world tended to be armored above and below but not in the middle. Hence emasculation would have been a convenient version of scalping.

light," and its primitive conclusion is cannibalism. Mutilation, on the contrary, is only interested in the mutilated body as a vehicle for divine epiphany, which, as the word suggests, is what appears between the mutilated flesh and the eye that beholds it. Thus mutilation is utterly *yang*, "waving banners in the sun," and to remove the warrior eye is symbolically both to remove the mutilating power and its capacity to enjoy its work. In early days Seth probably ate the eye of Horus.

There is some evidence for this conjecture from what we know of ritual cannibalism, where the body is first mutilated, then incorporated. In Polynesia Captain Cook witnessed a human sacrifice that ended with the victim's left eye being presented to the lips of the king.[52] In the ritual cannibalism of the Brazilian Tupinamba, comparably, the victim's eye was the most potently charged, and reserved to the sacrificer.[53] The Eye of Horus probably originated in such unsavory circumstances, but by the time it is offered to Osiris in the Pyramid Texts, the polarity of its power has been reversed. Instead of conveying to him the mutilating power of Horus with which he may go forth and mutilate others, it is precisely what will heal and protect him from such violence, either in himself or another:

> Take to thyself the Eye of Horus, he brings it to
>   thee: put it in thy mouth.
> Behold, we bring thee the great left eye as healer.
> I have brought thee the Eye of Horus . . . that it
>   may purify thee, that its odor may come to thee . . .[54]

Such an eye, no longer suitable for the work of mutilation, will be used by Osiris to lighten the underworld and comprehend the secrets of the life that leads to death. One might even say that the mutilating eye of the warrior is blinded in the mistaking of its object, whereas the blinded eye of the traditional seer or prophet, such as the Greek Tiresias, is all-seeing in the ungrasping fullness of its vision.

Thus concludes the argument that began early in this chapter's second section with my assertion that the mutilating cruelty that opens our eyes to the monstrous epiphanies of the sacrificial divinity is properly canceled, preserved, and redemptively transformed in the elaboration of a *harness* for our sacrificial instincts, not in some rationalist attempt to close the door on them; and moreover that the harness is to be sought *within* those instincts, and not elsewhere. Some of these pages have been difficult, for which I apologize; but the subject *is* a difficult one. And very important: it seems to me that what above all keeps the modern world from exploring again not only its primitive inheritance but its undeniable religious hunger is the fear that here be dragons indeed. I believe that the ancient Egyptians uniquely met the major dragon, and mastered him/her; and though much of their wisdom was preserved and extended in the Christian genius, much was lost (not least in the suppression of the goddess). The Christian genius has in any case gone rather cold since the early eighteenth century, and calls out for a regenerative return to its sources. Isis and Osiris, mummified and somewhat inaccessible after centuries of dusty neglect, are still there. We could if we would.

One more word before closing. The Eye of Horus, lunarized through the tears of suffering and offered up to Osiris, also belongs to Isis, in whose body as Hathor (which literally means "house of Horus") the drama unfolds. Although she plays her specific parts as sister, spouse, and mother, in another sense she is even more passive or reflexive (middle voice in Greek) than the brother-husband whose sufferings she must bear in mind. In the end it is *her* tearful eye that encompasses and sustains the whole story.

Such intimacy and reconciliation between god and goddess, masculine and feminine, Nature and culture, is unique among the ancient civilizations. The major goddesses of Mesopotamia, Crete, Greece, and India are all formidable and impressive in their various ways, but none of them manages to align either their violence or their tenderness with that of their consorts, as Isis does. The possible exception to this is the ever-mysterious goddess of Minoan Crete, who may have reached some profound accommodation with the bull. We shall briefly consider the evidence for this at the end of the next chapter.[55]

PART THREE

OCCLUSIONS OF THE SACRED:

Moving from Myth into History

8 ı THE ECSTASIES OF LOVE AND WAR

Sad is Eros, builder of cities,
And weeping anarchic Aphrodite.
—W. H. Auden

The essay on Isis and Osiris concludes this book's search for ritual lawlines strong and subtle enough to govern the ecstasies that lead us to love and war. And yet even if, as I have argued, Isis and Osiris *do* provide an answer, and one moreover by which we moderns may still be nourished, it goes without saying that they did not altogether prevail even in relatively peaceful Egypt, far less in the surrounding cultures more exposed to the winds of war and weather.

In this final chapter we shall leave the quiet thoughtfulness of the Nile Valley and engage with the turbulence of Israel, Mesopotamia, and Greece. Throughout the fourth and third millennia, the evolution of neolithic culture around the Mediterranean had been frequently interrupted by the incursions of aggressive pastoralists from the north. Just before 2000 B.C., the planet's climate took a significant heave for the worse: desiccation and famine hit the farmers of the Mediterranean and the Middle East, and fierce, horse-mounted pastoralists from the steppes of Asia launched devastating raids upon the settled agricultural orders all the way from India to Europe.[1] Empires were convulsed, overland trade routes disrupted, and a language that the philologists call Indo-European left its traces everywhere. As a result of these incursions, trade became increasingly sea-borne, and first the Minoan, then the Phoenician Empires arose to dominate traffic in the Mediterranean.

Even monumental Egypt was disturbed by the invasive tendency, being occupied by the Asiatic Hyksos for about a hundred fifty years early in the second millennium. The settled calm in which the vision of Isis and Osiris had been nurtured was gone, and it would not return.

All three of the texts we shall examine in this chapter are later than the story of Isis/Osiris, both chronologically and mythologically; and in all of them the human spirit is seeking and failing to find a place to house its restlessness. Each in its way is concerned with an occlusion of the sacred, and all may be seen as prologues to the birth of tragedy. Before we begin, however, something should be said about the fact that we shall here be dealing with literary *texts* (sacred or secular), with myth rather than ritual, the thing *said* (*legomenon*) rather than the thing *done* (*dromenon*), particularly since this distinction has generated a good deal of scholarly debate recently. (Readers with neither appetite nor need for the higher pedantry are invited to proceed directly to Section 1 on Genesis.)

We saw in Chapter 6 that through the ritual magic of "representation" primitive man seeks to call into his presence (either by words or dramatic gestures or both) such divine energies as he wishes to negotiate with. When such words are no longer embodied in ritual performance but read from a script in solitude, what changes? "Nothing much," say some, "the reader is called on to *imagine* the ritual presence of others to help him call forth the spirits named in the text." "Everything changes," say others; "Since the reader is absent from the ritual gathering of his 'parish,' which is necessary for proper invocation, he can only summon a ghostly simulacrum of the divinities involved, who only *seem* to appear in the theater of his mind, present in their *absence*."

This debate has become extremely complicated in the recent prose of M. Derrida and his cohorts, and luckily we need not enter it fully here. Like so many of our genuine mental problems, this one was first addressed by Plato, who noticed with his abundant common sense (in the *Phaedrus*) that the physical abstraction of script not only renders the written words liable to misinterpretation (thus creating the "Lit Crit" industry, by the way) but also renders memory (the "calling to mind" so essential to religious ritual) more or less superfluous. Thus, at the very least, solitary reading is liable to error and deception, and at the most to a failure of the magic of invocation. As is so often the case, I am not only happy but grateful to agree with Plato in his musings on the (relatively) newfangled technology of script.

I am furthermore prepared to admire (with some reservations) Derrida's *La Pharmacie de Platon* (1968), an extended commentary on Plato's *Phaedrus*. But Derrida's subsequent work, and even more so that of his "deconstructionist" followers, has I think been somewhat swallowed up in its own incipient nihilism, and is doing the intellectual world no good. As briefly as possible, let us return to Derrida's sources, not Heidegger first but the actually more salient Mallarmé:

> Je dis: une fleur! et, hors de l'oubli où ma voix relègue aucun contour, en tant que quelque chose d'autre que les calices sus, musicalement se lève, idée même et suave, l'absente de tous bouquets.
>
> Variations sur un Sujet: crise de vers

> I say "flower"; and forth from the forgetfulness into which my voice relegates all bounding contour, as something *other* than known blossoms, musically arises, the fragrance of Idea itself, that which is absented by all actual bouquets.

My translation is not good, but French at its most French (as this is) does not English well. What Mallarmé is proposing here is that the (properly poetical) saying of "flower" absents all the particular flowers that we might know in order to allow the Platonic Idea or the divine essence of floweriness to be remembered and come before us. Having taken a spectacular front flip, *très moderne*, Mallarmé is effectively agreeing with primitive man about the power of word magic. This is a crucial text for modern poetics (by no means yet assimilated) and I happen to think it not only beautifully said but worthy of our belief.

The deconstructionist error is to fasten upon the absenting of known physical flowers and to ignore the "presencing" of *idée même et suave*. Thus, in their view, words embedded (not embodied) in texts can at best invoke other texts, endless chinese boxes that not only cannot bring life before us, but actively alienate us from it. This is the deconstructors' loss of faith, their nihilism, their jettisoning of the baby and retention of the bathwater. To put it in Heideggerian terms, they have fastened upon the master's *"Destruktion"* and ignored his wonderful meditations on the redemptive possibilities of what he calls "presencing," without which his *"Destruktion"* merely carries us into the void and leaves us there.[2]

Enough said, for present purposes. The matter is an important one, and lies among those things that militate against hope and belief in our time. I am in no sense suggesting that "textuality" is unproblematical. Like other things done in solitude, reading is dangerously open to phantastical imaginings, particularly in the climate of modern alienation; but the *point de départ* I prefer for such exigent lucubrations is Marshall McLuhan's observation that "Schizophrenia may be a necessary consequence of literacy." The deadpan hyperbole here both registers the seriousness of the question and yet also humorously recognizes that the modern intellectual thinks too much, doesn't take enough exercise, and hence tends to get things out of perspective.

In sum, I am suggesting that primitive man was lucky and right to believe in word magic, and that such modern masters as Mallarmé and Heidegger were right to believe that some attenuated version of that magic can be sought in and through our written texts. Properly undertaken, the act of reading is and always has been *actually* magical; as we shall see presently when we find *The Epic of Gilgamesh,* one of the world's oldest texts, not only remarkably accessible to modern man but wonderfully nourishing to his spirit. Less ancient than Gilgamesh but also wonderfully nourishing to the spirit of modern man is the prose of John Milton, which admirably overleaps our present perturbations:

> Books are not absolutely dead things, but do contain a potency of life in them to be as active as that soul was whose progeny they are;

nay they do preserve as in a vial the purest efficacy and extraction of that living intellect that bred them.

Areopagitica (1644)

GENESIS 3: ADAM AND EVE (LOVE)

1 Now the serpent was more subtil than any beast of the field which the LORD GOD had made: and he said unto the woman, Yea, hath God said, Ye shall not eat of any tree of the garden? 2 And the woman said unto the serpent, We may eat of the fruit of the trees of the garden: 3 But of the fruit of the tree which is in the midst of the garden, God hath said, Ye shall not eat of it, neither shall ye touch it, lest ye die. 4 And the serpent said unto the woman, Ye shall not surely die: for God doth know that in the day ye eat thereof, then your eyes shall be opened, and ye shall be as Gods, knowing good and evil. 5 And when the woman saw that the tree was good for food, and that it was a delight to the eyes, and a tree to be desired to make one wise, she took of the fruit thereof, and did eat; and gave also unto her husband with her, and he did eat. 7 And the eyes of them both were opened, and they knew that they were naked; and they sewed fig leaves together, and made themselves aprons. . . . 16 Unto the woman he said, I will greatly multiply thy sorrow and thy conception. In sorrow thou shalt bring forth children; and thy desire shall be to thy husband, and he shall rule over thee. 17 And unto Adam he said, Because thou hast hearkened unto the voice of thy wife, and hast eaten of the tree, of which I commanded thee, saying, Thou shalt not eat of it: cursed is the ground for thy sake; in toil shalt thou eat of it all the days of thy life. 18 Thorns also and thistles shall it bring forth to thee; and thou shalt eat the herb of the field. 19 In the sweat of thy face shalt thou eat bread, till thou return unto the ground; for out of it wast thou taken: for dust thou art, and unto dust shalt thou return.

Both this story and that of Cain and Abel (along with the Tower of Babel and the Book of Job) are usually attributed to the Edomites, those almost-Jewish descendants of Esau who occupied the rough marginal land to the south of the Dead Sea, on the way to Egypt. The Edomites were also metaphorically marginal, as Esau's hairiness (compared to Jacob's smoothness) would suggest, with a reputation among the Jews both for desert uncouthness *and* Egyptian sophistication. Whatever one makes of the Edomite attribution of these stories, their poetic genius is undeniable, and their god is considerably tougher than the one who later makes a covenant with his people; more primitive certainly, but also, arguably, more sophisticated, and this has left problems for Hebrew theology.[3]

We have already discussed some aspects of the Fall in Chapter 4 with regard to alpha-shaman, and in Chapter 6 with regard to swarming; in conclusion now I propose only to gather up some loose ends and say something about the question of unity and separation. If we assume that the tabooed fruit represents food instinctively kenned as poisonous by the untroubled primate, then the questioning of this represents the unlocking of ancient instincts as we move into a world in which we can *choose* what to eat, what to take, what to have and what to have not; and this leads us to the feast of alpha-shaman. When we awaken from this exalted nightmare, we see our newly found freedoms in a context of distressing alienation: we are now free to measure the distance between us and everything we would touch. Milton's famous lines capture the essentials (if one ignores the Puritan "Providence") with an elegant simplicity worthy of the original:

> The world was all before Them, where to choose
> Their place of rest, and Providence their guide;
> They hand in hand with wandering steps and slow
> Through Eden took their solitary way.
> *Paradise Lost*, 12:646–50

The rhythm of the verse here perfectly mimes the human pace, troubled yet resolute. Because the world is newly strange, Adam and Eve wander wonderingly, but also errantly: hence their steps are slow. They are slow also because of timidity and fear and sadness:

their way is solitary now, the natural bond of kin and ken no longer uniting them to the garden's denizens. The prominence of "hand in hand" underlines the importance of this first and uncertain mitigation of human solitude.

What has provoked such saddening solitude is an act of excessive appropriation, ingestive certainly, orgiastic probably ("beguile" is our only clue). Although the atmosphere is undoubtedly lustful, it would be simpleminded to suggest that the sin is merely an act of fornication: we had already been doing *that* forever, as even the Puritan Milton conceded. But since this story is a masterpiece of understatement, drawing much of its strength from what it leaves unsaid, we should respect its shadows; and all we can legitimately infer about the serpent after two chapters of the Bible is that he is lord of the creeping *sheretz,* who serves the swarming power. What this suggests, or so I have argued, is that when the serpent arises among us, we are moved to embrace and commingle, eliminate the space that separates us one from another; and when fully aroused with alpha-shaman, we move upon our own inviolate center, consuming *ourselves* in a moment of irreparable closure. The dream that led us to this is still dreamed by the child who would devour mother's breast, absorb his own source and so become self-begotten and immortal. Original sin is also still original innocence, honestly inherited.

Because we moderns have wandered so far into history's oblivion, I have felt compelled to reconstruct the gross incident in Chapter 4. But imagine the Edomite sages around the campfire, so much nearer the source, so much less insulated by oblivion: "Oh, you don't want to hear that hoary old one about the cannibals again, do you? Disturbingly crude. Here's something more refined, a Lord and a Lady in beautiful parkland, trouble with the tree-god." The crucial word precipitated from these tales, however they are told, is *greed*: the problem, unknown to the primates, of infinite (or at least impossible) appetite. Man is the animal who would *appropriate more than he can bear,* and the penalty we pay for wanting to unite ourselves to too much is that *all* our acts of appropriation and communion become problematic.

It is this that makes the sex go bad. Waking to find ourselves alienated from Nature, we instinctively hold hands with the one who might symbolically restore us to unity. The sexual act is now asked to bear and redeem the loneliness of creatures who not only live increasingly within the symbolic structures they build to replace an instinctual repose, but who have tasted blood with alpha-shaman. Because the meanings of sex are no longer confined to what their surfaces would suggest, the possibility of damaging deceit arises (nicely transposed to the fruit in the story). We discover all this before we meet up with Yahwe in the wind of the evening, and our new garments paradoxically declare both a commitment to the sexual adventure (nudist colonies are unsexy) and also our discovery of a distance between us that we would for most purposes prefer to erase or deny.

The knowledge we will henceforth seek to grasp in compensation for our lost repose will not only be carnal, of course, but techno-logical and scientific. The heart of this matter, as I suggested in Chapter 1, is thunderbolt longing, the desire to absorb the gods by acquiring their power over Nature. The message in both cases (i.e, sex and science) is that we are on our own now: we have within us the capacity to repair some of our separations through certain ecstasies and the weaving of lawlines, but equally it is our responsibility to distinguish between legitimate repair and unions that damage the tissue we would unite ourselves with. Having lost the magical ability to "tell" which good-looking fruits are poisonous to the touch, we must learn to think about it. The history of sexual relations and atomic physics in our time would suggest we still have not thought hard enough; but perhaps at least we are almost ready to supplement Browning's famous remark that "A man's reach should exceed his grasp or what's a heaven for" with "A man's reach always *does* exceed his grasp and that's what hell is for."

Two objections finally, both already mentioned in earlier chap-ters. The first is to the suggestion that there was a law already in place that we knowingly broke on the day; and I have had my say about that in Chapter 4. The second has to do with Eve the culprit: although the unfairness to Eve has much poisoned sexual relations over the centuries (for which revenge is now being taken), it seems to me an egregious structural fault that can be "corrected" without impairing the story's essential genius. One might begin by attaching the serpent to Adam's strangely absented body: this must be gently done, however, or else we will end up with Adam as the culprit, and a tale whose knowledge is confined to the carnal. By "gently," I mean that the serpent should arise equably between the two of them, offering them both a ticket to ride.

The ancient Midrash was a scriptural commentary that sought to illuminate the sacred Jewish stories not by analysis and interrogation but by telling even more stories. As a minor exercise in the midrashic spirit, I now propose briefly to tell the Greek story of the maid-mother Persephone/Demeter—itself a commentary on Isis/ Osiris—to further illuminate Adam and Eve. One day the nubile Persephone was out gathering flowers, and as she plucked the seductive narcissus she fell (or wandered) into a chaotic chasm that gaped open and led her to the deflowering embrace of Hades the underground snake, who persuaded her to swallow the pomegranate seed.[4] Mother Demeter wandered disconsolately in search of her other half (her former and unviolated self), was employed (like Isis—the parallels are remarkable) as nursemaid in the palace at Eleusis, but found no trace of the daughter she had been. In anger she cursed the earth absolutely, and all the green things withered. For a whole year nothing grew, but still she would not relent. Finally, to save mankind from extinction, Zeus intervened and negotiated a settlement whereby the maiden Persephone would be reunited for two-thirds of every year (while the earth flourished) with the mother she was, is, and shall be, but would spend the winter months down below with her husband. For her part Demeter instructed the keepers of her Eleusinian temple in certain mysteries concerning birth and death. Many people were annually initiated into these mysteries, over a period of at least a thousand years, and yet we still have only a vague idea of what was involved. Many ancients believed that they were based upon the mysteries of Isis and Osiris annually celebrated at Abydos.

This may well be so, but what a falling off in mythic terms! Sex is down to rape (however vaguely desired) and married life is in the dark: proper young wives would rather be at home with mother. Although Demeter does lament the loss of innocence, she fails to find it (until Zeus intervenes) and it is the unmitigated rage in her cursing that stands proud. One looks in vain for any sense of the Egyptian faith that lamentation can recover the thing sacrifically mutilated, or the Sumerian faith that the voyage to the *abzu* can be edifying. Although the Greek myth is very old (traces of goddess worship at Eleusis from 2000 B.C.) and hence not easily tampered with, one may suspect the dread hand of patriarchal recension. And yet if this were extensively so, why is the rape not softened somewhat, and why does the Lord Hades not have more than a walk-on part as a thuggish and sometime subterranean jailer? Why has he been substituted for Dionysus, the proper Greek equivalent for Osiris? The probable answer to this, briefly glimpsed in Chapter 7, is that Dionysus gave up the corn when he took on the vine, and Poseidon, the other obvious candidate, was banished to the sea, as we shall discover presently. In any case Hades makes a hopelessly inadequate replacement, and as a result the myth almost founders in a gender imbalance that looks profoundly antimale—and antifemale too, come to that. Whatever the explanation, it is difficult to resist the impression that Greek men and women simply didn't *like* each other very much.

The pan-Hellenic festival of *Thesmophoria* to which this myth was attached was also very old and for women only. On the first day, live piglets were carried down into a snake-haunted pit and offered by young maidens to the chthonic divinity (perhaps in remembrance of former times when the maidens themselves were sacrificed). On their return from the pit they carried the rotted remains of last year's piglets and scattered them in the fields. The second day was given over to fasting (and a certain amount of antimale obscenity); and the third celebrated the "fair birth" of the newly risen corn.[5]

Although the Greek myth is chilly in comparison with the Egyptian one, it is still a good deal more consoling than Genesis. If one sets it beside the story of Adam and Eve, one can see that the first two acts, registering the fall into carnality and the divine curse, are roughly isomorphic (similarly structured) but the third is very different. Demeter finally condones the violation of her body, and suggests that in the return of the agricultural cycle, everything in its season, we may find lawlines to regulate our lives. The piglets are "the things laid down" (*thesmoi*) to represent our violence, and if this is done with piety, they may be transformed, through sacrificial magic, into the laws (*thesmoi*) that recognize and contain the appetites that lead us to mutilate and grind with the teeth and the thighs and the plow. Yahwe, on the other hand, does not rescind his qualified curse upon land or thighs, nor does he offer any lawful guidance to his creatures as he sends them off into history. Such "savagery" becomes more intelligible when one remembers that Edom is not particularly blest with rich soil; and yet, strangely enough, it is this very savagery that commends the Genesis tale to us moderns, for our mythic soil is also not rich. Envious bedouin the Edomite sages may have been, looking east to the Euphrates, west to the Nile, and north to the Jordan; but the desert air is remarkably clear. They could see that the agricultural pieties were no match for man's historical hunger, and that he would sooner or later break out of any paradise-parkland he was lucky enough to find himself in.

GENESIS 4: CAIN AND ABEL (WAR)

1 And Adam knew Eve his wife; and she conceived, and bare Cain, and said, I have gotten a man with the help of the Lord. 2 And again she bare his brother Abel: and Abel was a keeper of sheep, but Cain was a tiller of the ground. 3 And in process of time it came to pass, that Cain brought of the fruit of the ground an offering unto the Lord. 4 And Abel, he also brought of the firstlings of his flock and of the fat thereof: and the Lord had respect unto Abel and to his offering. 5 But unto Cain and to his offering he had not respect: and Cain was very wroth, and his countenance fell. 6 And the Lord said unto Cain, Why art thou wroth? and why is thy countenance fallen?

7 If thou doest well, shalt thou not be accepted? and if thou doest not well, sin lieth at the door: and unto thee shall be his desire, and thou shalt rule over him. 8 And Cain talked with Abel his brother; and it came to pass, when they were in the field, that Cain rose up against Abel his brother, and slew him. 9 And the Lord said unto Cain, Where is Abel thy brother? And he said, I know not: am I my brother's keeper? 10 And he said, What hast thou done? the voice of thy brother's blood crieth unto me from the ground. 11 And now cursed art thou from the earth, which hath opened her mouth to receive thy brother's blood from thy hand. 12 When thou tillest the ground, it shall not henceforth yield unto thee her strength; a fugitive and a wanderer shalt thou be in the earth. 13 And Cain said unto the Lord, My punishment is greater than I can bear. 14 Behold, thou hast driven me out this day from the face of the earth; and from thy face shall I be hid; and I shall be a fugitive and a vagabond in the earth; and it shall come to pass, that whosoever findeth me shall slay me. 15 And the Lord said unto him, Therefore whosoever slayeth Cain, vengeance shall be taken on him sevenfold. And the Lord set a mark upon Cain, lest any finding him should kill him. 16 And Cain went out from the presence of the Lord, and dwelt in the land of Nod, on the east of Eden.

The story of Cain and Abel can be briefly summarized: God accepts Abel's lamb offering, rejects Cain's vegetables, whereupon Cain murders his brother, and is cursed by God but sanctified by a mark to preserve him in his wanderings. Some readers of this story drift into murky waters at the outset by assuming that Cain's offering is inadequate: either he was sinning in his heart or else God is telling his people to keep sheep and not till the ground. The latter idea will not take us very far, even though many Old Testament authors show a preference for Israel's pastoral phase over its agricultural one (so exposed to Canaanite corruption); for in the end Abel the pastoralist dies without issue, whereas Cain, having walked off his curse, builds a city and leaves many famous descendants (no trifling matter early on in Genesis). The former idea, that Cain wrapped his vegetables in dark thoughts, may find *some* support in the riddling verse 7, but not much: if Cain were stupid enough to think he could hoodwink the Lord on such a matter he was quite properly disabused, in which case his anger was not only thoroughly inappropriate but directed at the wrong person: collapse of story in the banalities of Cain.

Which leaves us with only one other hypothesis: that the editors of the "S" document, about 1000 B.C., having just assembled one of the world's finest stories in Chapter 3, may well have known what they were doing when they gathered the various Cain tales together in Chapter 4, may even have composed something structurally similar and almost as good as Chapter 3; and that to see if this may be so we should trust the tale for the time being, and that means assuming, along with Cain, that there is nothing substandard in his offering.

As soon as we do this the story springs to life, and we see that Cain, like Job, is being introduced to the injustice of God. Not that God would use that word: as he explains at length to Job, justice is a human concern, even perhaps something man contrives to *protect* himself from God. But if what has arisen is neither justice nor injustice, does this mean that God is showing Cain his whimsy? Not whimsy either, for the Hebrew wind, at least in Edomite hands, is never whimsical. The word we want is a simple one, but much neglected on the modern tongue—luck; and for an elegant gloss one could turn to Exodus: "I will be gracious to whom I will be gracious" (33.19).

Cain cannot bear it; and surely we are with him. Living as he does in the beginning, he understandably fails to make subtle distinctions between his earthly and his heavenly father, and expects as much justice from the latter as the former. We sympathize because we can remember: is it not true that we all find our most painful childhood memories in the experience of unjust parental rejection, particularly in the favoring of a sibling?

Ah yes, comes the reply, sibling rivalry is indeed a serious matter, but is it grounds for murder? What's more, this is not just a story of murder, but of *the* murder, the first one, the original; and so it invites us to find in it the *essence* of murderousness. Can this most evil flower spring from the apparently ordinary soil of fraternal envy? I think the answer is yes, but it will take some telling. First of all, a hint from ethnology: in almost all primitive cultures, the birth of twin boys is thought to be very bad luck, sometimes calling for infanticide. In exceptional circumstances the contrary interpretation is made, and the boys are marked down for kingship. Thus twinning is clearly monstrous, a sure sign of *pneuma*'s irruption, a promise of either desolation or sacred renewal. But why should twin boys bear the promise of future violence? The old mythic answer would be "Because twin boys sufficiently resemble the Old Year–New Year pairing to threaten us with unritualized violence, an unscripted fight." And indeed such an ancient perspective does enable us to see the structural similarities between this tale and the Dionysiac themes discussed in the last chapter: once again we are confronted with the failure of ritual to contain the envious rivalry of nearly matched figures, and this I have proposed as the hallmark of tragedy.

But this tale, though arguably based in old mythic time, is quite specifically concerned with the *family* as narrative institution; and our discussion might well begin with the question of paternal inheritance, which traditionally goes to the first-born. The practice of primogeniture still survives in aristocratic Britain, where the first-born son not only inherits the estate (thereby keeping the family substance intact) but also the title (thereby keeping the name distinctively defined); and thus he is in a sense more real (royal) than his siblings, the true inheritor. In such a situation one would expect to find resentment in the younger sons (not to mention the daughters); but when the younger son is a look-alike who misses the boat by ten minutes, the whole structure begins to tremble. Number-two son both is and is not number one, and what culture can thrive when its lines of classification are so mocked?

The problem is openly met in Genesis 25–28, where Esau the redskin arrives first (and so is promised the inheritance) but is quickly followed by Jacob with a "hold on Esau's heel." When the fateful day comes, many years later, Jacob successfully impersonates Esau (by wrapping himself in animal skins) and so deceives blind father Isaac's nose, and is awarded the paternal blessing: thus Esau is dispossessed and hatred unleashed. Jacob becomes leader of the Jews, and Esau goes off to become founder of the Edomite kingdom. Shocking behavior from one of the great patriarchs, one might think, and yet we are clearly meant to embrace it. The implication would seem to be that when the arbitrary constructions of culture are questioned by the greater arbitrariness of divine Luck, resourceful rogues will arise to seize the day. In early manhood Esau seemed to be a "cunning hunter" whereas Jacob was "quiet or harmless" (25:27); but mother Rebekah knew that this was not truly so, and helped Jacob to "steal" Esau's cunning (or rather resolve the monstrous ambivalence that twinning represents) and so prove himself the true inheritor. To put it differently, when God throws twins he is throwing dice that break through our orderly surfaces, daring us to throw them back.

The simple function of this story is to tell the Jews why the "aboriginal" Edomites have been pushed on to the poorer land and why enmity between the two peoples shall persist. Cain and Abel, oppressed neither by twinship nor a significant territorial dispute, offer an almost impossibly pure study in fraternal rivalry and the envy it may generate. Such abstraction in the pursuit of mythic universals always rides the edge of emptiness; and although there is in this tale no mention of patrimony, I suggest we must imagine it to be symbolically at stake, implicitly present in its absence, awaiting Cain's envious ferocity, which will call it to mind.

Under patriarchy the father is the vessel that bears and conveys the reality and substance of "the fathers," and if he makes two copies of himself by siring two sons, either they are the same (in which case he is subdivided, diluted, and we move toward the twin problem) or they are different, in which case the simple mind suspects he has poured himself into one and not the other; which means that one is the true copy and the other is some kind of fake or imposter. Parental favoritism will always help this story along; and though the first-born is often given the benefit of the doubt, the younger one is naturally disposed to challenge such arbitrary numerology.

Or one might say that the fight for father's blessing is the fight for the *pneuma* or the *numen* or the numinousness of his name. If both are offered it, then they face each other to fight over the nightmare of twinship. If one is offered it, the other either accepts his derivative status as a kind of appendage or servant of his brother, or else challenges the paternal judgment by donning animal skins (a simulated regression to animal truth) to prove that he is in fact his brother. The smooth and clever Jacob consults the theatrical wardrobe and puts on shaman's costume. Cain, altogether less civilized and clever, can see no metaphorical way of making his point, and so can only become his brother by *actually* incorporating him.

To allow this story to take place in the beginning, we must see the family circle bound absolutely tight (there is nothing outside it) and the challenge within it a radically existential either/or: otherwise we will not credit Cain's sense of total eclipse in Abel's shining. "In Abel's blessing I am cursed" Cain seems to be saying, his identity shattered in his fallen countenance: "Better luck next time" may be the import of God's riddling question in verse 7. "There will and can be no next time, for he has taken my name, and in this darkness I *am* not," says Cain as he moves into the field to consume his brother and plow him under.

I suggested in the discussion of sacrifice that murder can be best understood as the attempt to retrieve some part of oneself intolerably stolen, and that the appropriate gesture for such reincorporation is a bear hug that eliminates the space that separates the parties. The last part of verse 7 throws some light on this, for it uses the same phrase as God employs at 3:16 when he dooms Eve to Adam's rule because of her sexual desire for him. The sin that lieth (or coucheth) at the door is, all things considered, probably the snake, which united (while at the same time forever separating) Adam and Eve in the context of a comparable alienation. If Cain opens the door to such proffered intimacy, he shall become swollen with a power that shall at least appear to do his bidding when he "rises up" against his brother in the next verse. Both the first serious fornication and the first meaningful murder properly begin in wrestling matches exploring the ground of incorporation: from there they move into the dark.

The irony in this tale, clearly discernible in God's voice, is that the absolutely existential either/or is in Cain's mind, not necessarily in God's script, though it *might* be in God's script if Cain assumes it isn't. We shall never know, because we cannot presume to scan the ways of the God who is "gracious to whom [he] will be gracious." The grown-up response to the rejection (as God subsequently explains to Job) would be "Perhaps the Lord is in a carnivorous anti-vegetarian mood: never mind, tomorrow is another day." But there are no grown-ups in the beginning (except perhaps God) and this is both Cain's heroism and his folly: he doesn't have the time to investigate God's tone of voice.

Engorged by the snake, Cain yearns for the ground, to ground his brother in the ground they came from, to cancel God's mistaken rejection by becoming his brother in an embrace that will eliminate forever the space between them. Whether or not one imagines a fumbling toward buggery and cannibalism here, the fumbling is important: this being the first murder, Cain does not know what he is doing, as is indicated in verse 9 when he truthfully says "I know not [where he is]: am I my brother's keeper?" (The irony here is that, having consumed his brother, this is precisely what he has become.)

In the stories of both Chapter 3 and Chapter 4 we are invited to understand the engorging snake as the power that seeks to overcome perceived separations through illegitimate unions or acts of appropriation: love and war, still riding together. But whereas Rebekah, in the later brotherly story, helps Jacob in his attempt to eliminate the blessing of Esau through cunning, Mother Earth is appalled at what Cain has done. She consents to take Abel back (opening her mouth to receive his blood) but she will deny her polluted first-born both her invigorating embrace ("shall not henceforth yield unto thee her strength") and repose at the end of the day ("a fugitive and a vagabond shalt thou be in the earth").

Yahwe knows something of the loneliness and the pain of violent men without women, and senses the seriousness of this heroic fool who was alive enough without the law to do he knew not what but what he had to; and so, because the law is not yet, and because the contagiousness of violence would otherwise find him out as a wound brings flies on a hot day, God scarifies the face, as if to say "This man is a pioneer, has charted unnavigable waters, has mistaken another for himself, and yet has not: self-mutilating scapegoat, he belongs to me."

THE EPIC OF GILGAMESH

What is astonishing about this work of genius is that it was not only the most popular tale throughout the Middle East for some two thousand years but it spent the next two thousand buried in the sands, its cuneiform tablets having been excavated only a century ago. Unsurprisingly enough, it is still having difficulty dislodging Homer's works (relative youngsters at ca. 750 B.C.) from their primogenitive position in the epic pantheon. Although the story evolved considerably in its long life and there is nothing like an official version, I shall now attempt to convey the major shapes, drawing on the two versions that are at present widely available in English.[6]

The quasi-divine "butting bull" called Gilgamesh is King of Uruk, a major city in what is now southern Iraq. The poem opens with praise for the splendidly solid walls he has erected to shelter his people from the winds of *pneuma*. But now he grows bored, missing the wind: none can lock horns with him on the wrestling ground, and he abuses the youth of the city. To prevent him from turning his horns to the walls themselves, the gods send him Enkidu, a wild and wonderful man-god-bull-cow. The fight is terrific, almost a perfect match, a doorpost is smashed and only part of the wall comes down (2:2:50). A breeze can now get through, and peace returns to Uruk.

It is all unashamedly erotic. Gilgamesh foresees the encounter in a dream where he "hugged him like a wife" (1:5:36), and this phrase is repeated many times. But of course there is a price for such consummation: in order to enable the wild Enkidu to fit between the city gates he must be somewhat shrunken to a civil size, and this means seven days and nights on the mat with the temple love-priestess of goddess Ishtar:

> The courtesan untied her wide belt and spread her legs,
>   and he struck her wildness like a storm.
> She was not shy: she took his wind away . . .
>   six days and seven nights Enkidu attacked,
>   fucking the priestess.
>   (1:4:15)

As a result of this

> Enkidu grew weak: he could not gallop as before.
> Yet he had knowledge, wider mind.
>
> (1:4:27)

Not only does his galloping slow down, but the wild animals whom he formerly protected from the hunters now flee from him. As in Genesis, the introduction to serious sexuality is coincident with an alienation from Nature.

The other payment exacted is political, but we can defer its discussion until the bill is presented for collection, later in the story. At this point all seems to be well, and Gilgamesh/Enkidu, their bond of loving-friendship strong as a wall, seek a suitably epic challenge for their heroic energies. They find it in Humbaba, the ferocious monster who guards the Cedar Forest in the north. Undoubtedly one of the masterpieces of the mythopoeic, this creature somehow manages to incorporate most of the elements we have belabored under the headings of *pneuma,* chaos, and the *abzu.* Humbaba, quintessence of metamorphic power, is of course amorphous, and his ferocity is manifested chiefly through fire and wind; but though ferociousness is his major epithet, it is displayed only to those who would invade his forest sanctuary; and although the late Akkadian version (1500–1000 B.C.) tries without success to present him as a force civilized man should hate and abolish, the older Babylonian version (2000–1600 B.C.) sees his "evil" as part of the nature of things (not unlike Seth) and the even older Sumerian sources register his ferocity simply as the furor of battles and storms. An interesting declension.[7]

Even more interesting is that the old sources say nothing about *killing* Humbaba. Thus what began as an epic adventure, perhaps a kind of elemental wrestling match, ends up as a moral crusade in the later versions, a search-and-destroy mission under the aegis of Shamash, bogus god of justice and light. This mutilation of the heroes' mutilating energy almost crazes the poem; for Humbaba's proper title is "Guardian of the Forest of the Living," and within its precincts he is most attentive and sensitive to all the creatures under his protecting care: "When the wild heifer stirs in the forest, though she is sixty leagues distant, he hears her" (p. 71). He is, in short, the *wonder* of the natural world, and hence the attack upon him cannot avoid appearing, as indeed it is, transparently vicious.

There is also a seemingly economic motive for the expedition. Cedar wood was highly prized as a building material in treeless Mesopotamia (as indeed it still is most everywhere). What is magical about cedar wood is that it does not *rot*. Thus, kill the tree god and build his undying body into the pillars of your urban temple, to register *your* immortality. (One thinks of Osiris and the Djed column, an altogether more circumspect approach to the problem.) On inspection, the seemingly economic motive reveals its religious base: wealth is for not dying (as we saw in Chapter 6).

The death of Humbaba, although almost unintelligibly fragmented on Gardner's broken tablets, is handled with remarkable intelligence in the Sandars version. The defeated monster pleads for mercy and offers to become the king's servant. Gilgamesh is disposed to spare him but Enkidu insists on annihilation, to which Humbaba replies with astonishing insight: "You a hireling, dependent for your bread. In envy and for fear of a rival you have spoken evil words" (p. 83). The words "envy" and "rival" at once make us think of the similarity between these two—both of them archaic Mountain Mother-Fathers, guardians of the wild. But if one of them can be enlisted in the service of progress and civilization, why not the other? Because of envy. And why is Enkidu envious? Because he lost the wrestling match, and so became, though friend and brother, the *younger* brother, number-two son, hence servant and appendage of the king. To be a hireling is to be at the disposal of another, that is to say "dispensable," and this awakens the fear of being dispensed with: to be "on expenses" is to be expendable. Thus at one stroke Humbaba identifies not only envy as the source of political hatred, whose logical solution is murder (the retrieving of the intolerably stolen), but also the inability of money adequately to compensate (through representation) the ontological imbalance between boss and employee. The point about envy is made by Cain and Abel, but we have had to await Karl Marx (and Father Freud) to be so clearly reminded of certain things money cannot buy.

Because Enkidu is adamant, no settlement is negotiated. (They could easily have taken a batch of cedars to blazon their triumph in the temple and left Humbaba in charge of a shrunken estate with instructions to send a regularly renewable cedar tribute, much as we are even now trying to arrange in the Amazon forests.) When Humbaba dies, "There followed confusion for this was the guardian of the forest whom they had felled to the ground" (p. 83). His seven splendors are extinguished and the sacred forest shrines are desecrated. Even "the mountains were moved and all the hills" (ibid). Our heroes are clearly in for big trouble.

But since this murder was mostly the work of Enkidu, it is now the turn of his brother to join him in major pollution. When they come back to Uruk, the goddess Ishtar proposes a "sacred marriage" to the king, as custom dictates. Gilgamesh replies by pointing out, quite correctly though highly insultingly, that it would mean certain death, for have not *all* her lovers perished when she tired of them? (Behind this denunciation we hear the bones of all those sacrificial kings rattling in the hero's mind.) Had his refusal been less insulting, Ishtar might have reminded the post-poetical king that although she kills she also renews, and there is no evading her. But since the time for talking is past, she calls down the Bull of Heaven, her theriomorphic consort, and the heroes take him on.

Just as the original Sumerian sources make no mention of killing Humbaba, here too one finds a trace of original playfulness: with the bull's first pass Enkidu leaps aside and vaults on to his back, seizing the horns. One thinks of the Cretan bull-vaulters and also of the bull-vaulting painting at Catal Huyuk: perhaps in the beginning this too was meant to be a kind of wrestling match. But in all the mature versions only death will do, and the killing sword goes into the neck, *bouphonia* not *bouthusia*.

After this, the story declines rapidly. Enkidu's death is decreed by the gods as punishment for the murder of Humbaba, and in mourning his brother, Gilgamesh foresees his own demise. The major aspiration of the epic enterprise, to kill death by glorious mutilations that will be forever remembered, admits defeat. Half-crazed with anger and sorrow, Gilgamesh wanders off in search of some other, older, solution to death's indignity, a reaching back for lost shamanic memories; but it fails to focus.

Both murders look like mistakings of the kind we discussed in Chapter 5 in connection with hunting. By exaggerating Humbaba's legendary ferocity, the heroes convince themselves that he is an alien evil that must be extirpated. But the ecstasy of the chase is cut off before the consummating embrace, and they must stand before their defeated enemy and exchange words. What they see is nothing ferocious but a violated victim, and the focus immediately becomes domestic. Humbaba weeps, takes Gilgamesh by the hand, and shows him his house. Everyone is thinking of families and the evening return to the hearth: "O Enkidu," cries Gilgamesh, "should not the snared bird return to its nest and the captive man to his mother's arms?" (p. 82). But at this point Enkidu sees, both correctly and incorrectly, *himself* in Humbaba, and is moving toward the vision of brothers twinned and at odds: "Because we are so alike, we must compete for the king's favor, and if he wins it I am eclipsed." One might even suggest that Enkidu has not perceived the implications of his lost wrestling match with Gilgamesh until now, when it is being re-presented in Humbaba. And yet his reasoning is also wrong: in killing this other motherless mothering guardian of the wild, he is killing his brother, himself. This is the horror of fratricidal strife and the envy that it exemplifies: that in striking the other who is threatening access to the source of one's being, one is also striking oneself. Thus Enkidu obliterates himself in his brother Humbaba, and the subsequent judgment of the gods merely confirms what Enkidu has already done.

Something similar takes place with the Bull of Heaven. To be truly the *king* of Uruk, not merely its worrisome warrior, involves addressing its goddess, which means not only siring one's replacement (the son who eclipses) but foreshadowing this in her bed. This the bull does, has done, time out of mind; and he stands in the green field as living proof that it can be survived. But "bull-butting" Gilgamesh, cultural man without agricultural faith, can no longer see himself in the bull: cannot see that in striking at the bull he is striking out at his own potency, in search of the steer. Thus Gilgamesh cannot tolerate his resemblance to the bull, and Enkidu cannot tolerate his resemblance to Humbaba (which would involve admitting that he too had lost his kingdom to Gilgamesh). Both men fail to find themselves in their animal brothers because they fear an eclipse of the self; but since the fearful aggression against bull and monster arises in each case from a refusal of their own identities, it ensures the very outcome it is trying to avert—even if Ishtar *is* a whore. In falling prey to envy and fear when addressing their own animal powers, they each reveal the unsound base on which their seemingly equitable friendship was raised; and thus when the gods dissolve the heroic brotherhood, they are merely confirming what each of the men, in their more testing fraternal encounters, has already done.

Since wrestling plays such an important part in the story, one is not surprised to discover that throughout Mesopotamian history the name of Gilgamesh was associated with sacred festivals of wrestling and athletics.[8] Some sense of archaic sacredness can still be discerned in the Sumo wrestlers of Japan, men who live apart somewhat monkishly, their lives devoted to the service of something that is at once art and sport and ritual. When these monstrous men scatter grains of rice and stamp a bare foot, they are invoking the potency that both makes the earth flower and moves the bull forward. The epiphany is brief as the bulls lock horns, and is returned to the ground in the body of the one who is thrown.

It is small wonder that wrestling should commend itself to cultural man not only as the play of the gods but as a civilized way of resolving the crisis that twinship symbolically threatens: these two men on the mat look about the same, and this apparency calls forth a lightning ferocity that resolves the confusion and "grounds" (or "earths") the dangerous energy. Although one of them has prevailed, this is, at least in principle, the luck of the gods, for they might meet again tomorrow with the opposite result. Their violent conjunction is so devised as to establish their separateness; and it is this separateness, the space that comes and goes between them, that paradoxically makes them equal.

The matter is difficult and important. What Cain fears and hates is not the *distance* from Abel but the lack of it. To be without distance is to be the same, and if two are the same, at least in human terms, the danger arises that one will be thought a copy, fake, or impostor of the other. When God favors Abel, Cain feels himself called the not-son, the Abel who is not Abel, swallowed up in his brother's shining, engulfed in conjunction without separateness; and so he strikes out to prove that Abel is the imposter, who *is* not. And yet when he attempts to retrieve the proper distance from Abel, he moves *toward* him in an engulfing embrace, not away; and thus does he enviously mistake his brother. When two men fight in "deadly earnest" to establish their *difference*, there is a simple sense in which they in fact achieve the opposite and become the *same*, all difference abstracted in the hurling of abuse and the simplicity of tooth and claw.[9]

The answer to Cain's quandary, as I have suggested, is to come back and wrestle tomorrow. In order to do this, however, the dancing ground must be consecrated as a wrestling ring, with rules and a judge upon which all can agree. Wrestlers offer their apparent sameness to each other, from which "difference" epiphanically appears. It is because Cain was living in the beginning, without the lawlines of culture, that he did what he did. The lawlines provide a structure (*nomos* = law or melody) in which the various notes may meet, strike, retain their variety, and yet be harmoniously resolved:

> Take but degree away, untune that string,
> And hark, what discord follows! Each thing meets
> In mere oppugnancy . . .

This famous speech from Shakespeare's *Troilus and Cressida* (Act 1) is undervalued today because it praises a hierarchical society; but its deepest wisdoms speak truly of any viable social arrangement, and could enrich our present labors for the democratic ideal by inviting us to consider, for example, the sublime judiciousness of Sumo wrestling.

Still, it must be conceded that wrestling does not stop the rot between Gilgamesh and Enkidu, and this is for two reasons: first, because it may mask but cannot annul the isolating realities of kingly power ("Uneasy lies the head that wears a crown"); and second, because Enkidu's position as the king's favorite is inadequately grounded, and cannot sufficiently repair the ontological damage done by the loss of his animal kingdom (particularly since he refuses to mourn this loss until death is nearly upon him). In sum, all things being equal, the wrestling match can resolve and contain the violence that threatens to disrupt the orderliness of culture; but since we so often carry within us the tragic seeds of envy and self-division, the ritual power of the athletic contest *(agon)* to hold the line often fails to suffice.

Thus it is with Gilgamesh and Enkidu. What their wrestling match *does* provide, however, as its remarkably erotic language would suggest, is a somewhat durable framework of union within which their differences can be explored. Although marked by great affection and embracing, the union is not a sexual one. I say this for two reasons: the first is that the text is quite uninhibited in its sexual explicitness, and had it intended sexual union, would have said so. The second is somewhat abstract, and concerns the inevitable problems of inequity that arise with male (though less with female) homosexuality, particularly between warriors. As we saw in Chapter 5, these problems are essentially anatomical (deriving from the submissive posture of the monkey "presenting" his buttocks) but not wholly so. Since the major theme of the *Gilgamesh* epic is the deeply desired and almost successful attempt to make the long-haired "feminine" Enkidu the equal of Gilgamesh and a replacement for Ishtar, a sexual union would further soften Enkidu, provoke more envious resentment, and hence subvert the tale's tendency. That said, the killing of the Bull of Heaven brings such a conclusion very near: both of them having tasted the emptiness of military conquest and having decisively renounced the goddess' thighs, it is not clear where else they could place their energies. But the gods intervene, with messages of death, and we are spared the adventures of Enkidu the catamite in the court of a limp-wristed and spiteful old queen.[10]

What then of heterosexual wrestling? Everything I have said about the fraternal fight to wrest equality from sameness applies as much if not more to the struggle between man and woman: in the coming and going of sexual intercourse we seek to measure and repair the distance that alone guarantees a union in which one is not swamped by the other; which is to say, both seek an appropriate measure of mastery and submission, somewhere this side of sado-masochism. But when man and woman wrestle there are two chief differences, one a plus, one a minus: although heterosexual copulation must also deal with the problem of buttock presentation, this is offset by the fact (still discernible) that the male member is being admitted to the original temple of birth and death, where he will surely die but may also be literally and/or metaphorically renewed. This is the oldest set of religious symbols we have, and though they are in bad shape at the moment (which is why homosexuality appears attractive to many), they are extraordinarily resilient. Arguments that seek to invoke Mother Nature's immutable intentions are not to the point here, as a number of ancient Greek writers have found to their cost,[11] for the argument *is* a cultural one, about meanings not orifices (or rather, about the meanings of orifices) and these are, to some extent, ours to dispose. Although I see no reason why a mythic symbolism of equity for male homosexuality could not be evolved (and a female one more easily), we do not have one yet, old instincts die hard, and even were we to succeed, it would lack the "natural" advantages of the heterosexual union. On the other hand, given the state of the sex war on an overpopulated planet, a monkish or a monosexual haven is clearly in the interests of the culture at large, as at least a refuge from the hetero wrangle (and this is not to mention the traditional nearness of homosexuality and the arts); but for such a haven to be soundly constructed, the problems of inequitable violence in homosexual contact must be addressed, as Plato does in the *Phaedrus,* and as *Gilgamesh* does on the dynamics of wrestling.

We digress somewhat from the heterosexual embrace: if the womb is its advantage, male muscle power is its drawback. Although men and women simulate a wrestling match when they conjoin, the emphasis is on simulation. This problem goes right back to the savannah and will never disappear. On the other hand, in a sense it *has* disappeared, because we now have laws that forbid the use of the strong right arm against the woman. But even more than this, our present ideology of sexual equality marks the strong right arm as a regrettably monstrous vestige of some previous, ill-considered regime, almost something a man should apologize for still carrying. In fact, our present heterosexual story bears more than a little resemblance to that of Cain and Abel, siblings whose apparent equality is questioned by man-Abel's carrying certain marks of divine favor (the strong arm and its symbols), which are calling forth certain envious resentments and revengeful plotting in Cain the woman. The obvious answer to this one is to live in an urban electronic environment in which arm muscles naturally wither; and so most of us do. But the difference nags, and will continue to do so until we find a story that enables us cheerfully to accept the unchangeable aspects of our evolutionary inheritance.

Both Genesis and *Gilgamesh* suggest that what women lack in physical power they make up in subtlety, *metis* and deceit ("wider mind" as Gardner's *Gilgamesh* beautifully puts it), and I suspect that this is historically as well as mythically true. Is it not plausible to suggest that of the two categories of crime in Greek and Roman law codes, those of force and those of fraud, one is the male speciality and the other the female? The problem is vast, contentious, and this book is about to end. What I have to say about it has already been said, in Chapter 3 with relation to the male baboon and his invisible structures of dominance, man the ritualist and woman the realist (with a disposition to move the goalposts). While I believe there is truth in this argument, and that it is enhanced when one bears in mind the wrestling imbalance, I offer it in a playful spirit. What is distinctly unfunny, however, is the suggestion, evident in both Genesis and *Gilgamesh,* that the problem of deceit and the loss of instinctual rapport with Nature that it symbolizes is somehow woman's *fault.* To say that woman is "by nature" (which is history) the better practitioner of certain arts is one thing: to say that because of this she dooms us all to a world of untrustworthy surfaces is slanderous in the extreme. The slide from one to the other, a bulwark of patriarchal wisdom, is still deeply imbedded in our received ideas; and the difficulty of clearly separating the two in the context of our thinking means that it will continue to afflict relations between the sexes for some time yet.*

HOMER: ODYSSEUS AT THE CAVE OF POLYPHEMOS

A brief discussion of Homer's poetry is an appropriate way to end this book for several reasons. First and most importantly, this poetry represents, much more unequivocally than does *Gilgamesh*, Western man's decisive break with the primitive wisdom we have been trying in some measure to remember in these chapters. The *Iliad* was, is, and ever shall be *the* war story, by which I mean that its influence upon Western culture has been immense, and that it still stands as the soldier's manual and bible. If we are to remove the love of war from our breasts, we must go back to see how this master craftsman so firmly lodged it there; that is to say, go back and listen carefully to the dying cries of the older divinities. Not to the *Iliad*, where the cries are scarcely audible, but to the *Odyssey*, whose embarrassingly

---

*Part of the trouble with "woman the deceiver" is traceable to the difficult ambiguity of the great goddess as both feminine *and* symbol of "the culture." We wrestled with this in the previous chapter and will return to it at the end of this one. Since the move from Nature to culture involves an exponential growth for the possibilities of *metis* and deceit, we naturally assign them to the goddess whose body houses our cultural constructions.

primitive vestiges may help undo our monstrous covenant with the gods of war.

The idea is not a new one. In the 1890s Samuel Butler was so amazed by the "feminine" feel of the *Odyssey* that he decided it was written by a woman. Bernard Shaw was at least half-convinced, but the classicists were unmoved. Butler's arguments were in fact rather silly, but his instincts were timely: Britain was even then certifying her imperial insanity in the Boer War, and thoughtful women were becoming extremely disaffected with the patriarchs. The profoundly buried forces that were leading to the cataclysms of the Great War could almost be heard rustling on the tom-toms. Can the Kaiser be contained in Africa? Can the workers be stayed with nationalism and jam? Can we buy off the women with the vote? A crazing time undoubtedly, altogether too much for the Fabians. Imagine Butler half-dreaming on his couch: "The arguments are straining in every direction. If only we could return to the beginning, and find that the master of war also wore skirts, or rather that the *Odyssey* was written by his wife . . . ."[12]

A hundred years later and the problem remains much as it was, although a number of things have moved in our favor. The returning sanity of the Russian bear has distanced the nuclear threat that kept many of us speechless through the eighties; the ecological crisis is focusing the mind; a much higher percentage of women are now allowed to be thoughtful; and we have learned a good deal about primitivism. But the problem remains formidable: "Make love not war" we said in the sixties, and this was fine as far as it went, which was almost nowhere. It went nowhere because we failed to realize that war is not finally a political or a technological or even a psychological problem, but a *religious* one: we make war because the war gods call us to the field, and to combat this we must first recognize its truth and then remember how we used to dance to a different music.

Although we have traveled considerably in this book, the domestic narrative has remained remarkably constant: in order to get home in the evening the man needs to bring something to please the woman. The first campsites on the savannah were woman's ground, her jail but also her palace, and the man who came and went was both freer to wander into adventure and yet constrained by that freedom (whose reverse side is always unbelonging) to give some account of his wanderings in the evening light. Whatever one thinks of my speculations concerning the early love story, the relatively hard evidence about female lineages (which would ultimately flower in matrilineal kinship) plus male puzzlement over paternity, plus a projecting backward of what we know concerning primitive lamentation, would suggest that even in the beginning the women and their children held a good deal of the important ground.

What the man brings home in the evening is meat for supper and the story of what he discovered in the unknown. When alpha-shaman is split in two, both the story-telling and the symbolical traveling into the unknown tend to devolve upon shaman, and since he stands politically somewhere between alpha and the woman, one might expect him to embody something of her critique of alpha's epic journeys (along with his own) in the stories that accumulate in the tribal memory. Although I am (necessarily) speculating again, something of this sort is required to account for the otherwise puzzling fact that even such vigorously patriarchal heroes as Cain and Gilgamesh (and Odysseus, as we shall see) are effectively savaged by the feminine principle, though somewhat subtextually. Someone is speaking up for madam in these stories, however subconsciously, and since it can't be she, it must be shaman's ghost.

Or one might say it is her voice in his dreams. Although the original hunting motif is discernible in all three stories (dimly in Cain, admittedly), the rift that has opened between the sexes is astonishing. The sometime mockery of the Mighty Hunter that one imagines in the beginning has degenerated into virtual banishment from the hearth. With Cain this is literally so: readers stoutly armed with the knowledge of Jewish misogyny often overlook the fact that the editors of this monotheistic book somehow failed to remove the traces of a mother goddess radically unamused by her son's heroic violence: it is arguably *her* curse that sends him into the wilderness, which the ironizing father ("That's my boy!") mitigates with protective scarification. Although Gilgamesh has an old mother in Uruk he finds the place unbearably claustrophobic, and his epic adventures merely confirm his homelessness by outraging every manifestation of the fostering hand that he meets. The pattern in Homer is similar: because Queen Helen has been abducted or seduced (the distinction is not really important), all of our hearths are polluted, and so we will spend ten years smashing up the other man's hearths and then ten more trying (but also not trying) to return to our own, which by then may well be polluted with adulterous wives like Clytemnestra, cursing our story.

Gilgamesh, as we have seen, spurned the idea of returning to the hearth because he "knew" that Ishtar, his intended, was essentially adulterous; and indeed she *did* curse his Humbaba story, first with the Bull of Heaven and then with a flood that very nearly extinguished mankind. Homer's heroes on the other hand are soberly married men, and *do* try to return; and this is the theme of the *Odyssey*. Will the women curse their story? Of course they will, we say, coming to the question with *Gilgamesh* and the argument of this book in mind. But in fact the answer is yes and no, or rather no and yes; for the "feminine" critique of warrior violence is all but muffled in this poem, and it will require considerable sleuthing on our part to uncover it. Some measure of the challenge can be gathered from the fact that despite Butler's timely instinct and some heartening post-patriarchal activity in classical studies recently, the challenge has not yet been taken on, let alone accomplished: so we shall have to move slowly.

Before we begin, a word on the poem's background to shed some light on the difficult question of how the feminine voice might be both suppressed and not suppressed in a warrior poem. Strange as it may seem, after almost three thousand years of Homeric scholarship we still know remarkably little for certain about the poem's many sources and composition.[13] Both the *Iliad* and the *Odyssey*, though written down in Ionia about 750 B.C., originated as epic songs sometime in the Mycenean age (ca. 1600–1200 B.C.). The Greek-speaking Mycenean lords, of northern provenance, were more warlike than the mercantile Minoans from Crete who first fostered and then submitted to them, and the native farmers whom they subjugated were known as Pelasgians. Although the warlords dominate the songs, all three cultures are at play in them. Troy VIIa seems clearly to have been sacked around 1240 B.C., and this might have been a Mycenean undertaking. If so, it might have been a final burst of folly (like the French to Moscow), for their "empire" soon collapsed, probably much assisted by the Dorian invasions from the northwest (ca. 1200). During the "dark age" (1200–800), many Greeks emigrated to Ionia and kept singing of olden times until illumination returned about 800 B.C. with the archaic period of ancient Greece as we know it. The songs were then edited, collated, and unified by one or two (blind?) poets of genius, and written down in the new alphabetic script.

The crucial difference between myth and "rational" forms of discourse is the former's lack of self-consciousness, its inability to stand back and look at itself critically. Herein lies both its childish inconsistency and its truth-telling genius, a combination that continues to astonish, compel, and outrage modern man in his rationality. The stories are *given* (by the gods), and though each singer has some license to improvise, he cannot tamper; and yet myths clearly do evolve, responding to changes in the circumstances from which they issue. Although the *Iliad* is much the more coherent and less primitive of the two Homeric epics, both often suggest the uncensored and unself-conscious texture of the dream. Particularly in the *Odyssey,* rich symbolic clusters are simply offered without being nudged or interpreted, and juxtapositions are sometimes bizarre. In short, what we seem to have is the dream-time of a people (in fact several peoples); and just as one can sometimes censor one's dreams to a certain extent, so one can occasionally feel the poem being nudged this way or that. It is sometimes suggested that Homer himself intervenes extensively in the poems, but their compelling inconsistencies everywhere belie this: the palimpsest remains rich and open.

First of all a simple and obvious point about the differences between the two poems. Just as cats find it easier to climb a tree than to come back down, so it is much easier on the mind to undertake a war than to come home; hence the coherence of the *Iliad,* in which the enterprise is not finally questioned, and the relative incoherence of the *Odyssey,* in which it is. The latter poem is trying to dream a dream that will at once counter, confirm, and exorcize the dream of war, and the task is beyond it. Cracks open in the structure, and as in any dream worth interpreting, repressed material, old and interesting, comes struggling out. Critics from Longinus to Bowra (*Homer,* 1972) and Kirk (*The Songs of Homer,* 1962) have preferred the *Iliad,* extolling its coherence and undoubted nobility of spirit (though usually keeping a judicious silence on the mutilating ecstasy to which that nobility is tied).[14] Although much of the *Odyssey is* garrulous and dull, its set pieces seem to me more distinguished in purely literary terms (if such exist), and its scope wider, its wisdom lowlier, its value greater; but it is just possible that I may be prejudiced.[15]

What is afflicting such heroes as Gilgamesh and Odysseus is a theology that calls them to the mutilating battlefield in the hope that the dying done there may live forever in the minds of men:

> the gods did this, and spun the destruction
> of peoples, for the sake of the singing of men hereafter.
>
> (*Od.* 8:579)

It is a difficult faith to sustain, particularly when the battle is over and one's thoughts turn toward home, which is one reason why the returning Odysseus spends a good deal of time weeping for his dead comrades. And if the women do not share the faith, it becomes even more difficult to sustain; and if moreover the conventions of our culture and its poem do not allow the women to speak on this matter, nor allow us simply to ask their blessing and forgiveness, we are committed to a good deal of narrative indirection. The poem can admit that the war will not be over until Odysseus sleeps in his bed again; but it cannot admit (what it indirectly confesses) that behind the woman who lies on the bed stands a goddess without whose help the man's violent pollutions cannot be cleansed in proper lamentation.

Circumspect Penelope, though beautifully drawn, is too good to be true. Although she manages (thrice) to speak of the "evil, not-to-be mentioned Ilium," and though she weeps movingly, her tears are not salty enough to find out the heart of the trouble. The only "war-wife" who might be up to it is Clytemnestra; but the poem draws back, as if sensing its inability to contain her voice, and writes her off as simply monstrous. Some three hundred years later Aeschylus saw that she was *the one*, her homicidal adultery at least *partly* to revenge her daughter, sacrificed for a fair wind to begin the military expedition; and he placed her voice at the center of the *Oresteia*. Such frankness from the feminine would be unthinkable in the *Odyssey*, where the women both do and do not matter, and it is this structural ambivalence that makes the poem so fascinating. In the raid on Polyphemos the Cyclops, for example, there isn't a woman in sight, the boys get away with murder, and yet the voice of the feminine not only speaks up but carries the day.

What has made this episode from Book 9 so popular through the ages is not only the "boy's own" element of derring-do (our wily Odysseus on top form) but also, undoubtedly, the mutilating ecstasy—the reaming of the giant's eyeball with a red-hot poker offers all one could ask in the way of quasi-sexual violence. And yet if one reads it carefully, particularly with Humbaba in mind, one discovers not only an anti-Odyssean argument but one of such force as almost to stop the poem in its tracks.

The Cyclopes are a race of one-eyed giants whose natural monstrosity clearly places them on a primitive map somewhere between man and the divinity that surrounds him. Things that dwell in the marginal (liminal) space between two known categories (or places) are inherently ambiguous, as we have seen, and the Cyclopes are consequently mysterious. Are they subhuman or superhuman? Both? The gods on the whole eat ambrosia (raw) whereas man is an eater of bread (*sitophagos*) and meat duly consecrated, both cooked. What do the Cyclopes eat? In the *Iliad* they are said to live on mare's milk and be "the most just of men"

(13:5). But another line of thinking associates them with Hephaestos in the ambiguously demonic work of his smithy; and since they *are* monstrous, might they not also, on occasion, eat the subhuman meal of raw flesh? Let's go and find out.*

Most of the evidence from the Cyclopes' world in Book 9 suggests a kind of pastoral paradise. "Putting all their trust in the immortal gods" (107), with whom they clearly have a special arrangement, their crops are magically self-seeding and self-cultivating. (This fact alone so outrages Odysseus that on the basis of it he calls them "lawless outrageous" (106), a fair indication of what is to come.) Self-sufficient and self-contained on their abundant and well-wooded island, they want neither ships to trade with others nor political institutions for haggling among themselves: each one lives alone and self-governing in a mountain cave with his wives and children and his flock of sheep. They tend their flocks, of course, but this is more like play than proper work (which is what bread-eaters do with plows), and a measure of their self-contained contentment (which Odysseus construes as laziness) is that they don't even bother to visit their beautiful uninhabited adjacent island for picnics, let alone husbandry. In short, a vision of aristocracy without the corrupting presence of servants.

Here is our first glimpse of Polyphemos:

> his mind was lawless,
> and in truth he was a monstrous wonder made to behold, not
> like a man, an eater of bread, but more like a wooded
> peak of the high mountains seen standing away from the others.
> (189–92)[16]

---

*Jack the giant-killer stories are ubiquitous in folklore. One-eyed giants are often associated with fire gods. Dragons are not far off, with their maternal associations. All these themes eddy and swirl about this tale, tempting the nihilist critic to complicate it into meaninglessness; hence it is all the more important to cleave to the text, quite complex enough, which clearly indicates that of all the giant's possible old names, tree-god is the one to watch, as we shall see. For a competent but uninspired discussion of the Cyclopes, see Kirk (*Mythology*, 1971), pp. 162 ff.

Traces of the tree-god, certainly; wonderful, upstanding stone, enviably self-contained. But what about "lawless," appended rather pathetically to the portrait? It seems to me both a dramatically inspired touch *and also* an indication of the poem's inability to contain the monster. Strictly speaking the epithet is accurate: the giant tree-thing living before the fall lives instinctively, and has no need for laws to direct his behavior and curb his appetites, and this is part of his wonder. To say somewhat inconsequentially that his *mind* was lawless nicely gestures toward the almost unthinkable thought that he can somehow exist perfectly well *without* a mind. And yet unstrictly speaking, the epithet points back to "lawless outrageous" and several other similar outbursts with which the poem seems trying to prepare us for the "evil" cannibal who must be attacked. To construe these outbursts as simply pro-Polyphemos ironic put-downs of Odysseus is to overcleverize and tidy up a Homer who is at this point beginning to gasp for breath: as we shall see.

Why have they come? Silence. The answer given by Odysseus is purely formulaic:

> [to] find out about these people . . .
> whether they are savage and violent, and without justice,
> or hospitable to strangers and with minds that are godly.
> (174–76)

This is a white flag he frequently waves, and behind it one can see Homer looking (a little desperately) for a theme to unite these old oral fragments under the aegis of a culture-hero or ambassador for national unity, no mere tourist, certainly no mere rip-off artist. On this occasion, as on several others, the flag is bogus: Odysseus has already (almost a hundred lines before) identified this island as the home of the "lawless outrageous," even though his admiring and envious description of it has made us think rather of the garden of Eden. A NO TRESPASSING sign, however, would not surprise us: if you try to force your way into paradise, either as tourist or hit-man (he had just raided the Kikonians a few days before), your rejection might well appear to your paranoid fantasy as lawless and outrageous.

In any case he decides to have a go, as hit-man in tourist garb; and with a hand-picked squad of commandos (195) he slips into Polyphemos's cave while the good shepherd is out with his flocks:

> We went inside the cave and admired everything inside it.
> Baskets were there, heavy with cheeses, and the pens crowded
> with lambs and kids. They had all been divided into separate
> groups, the firstlings in one place, and then the middle ones,
> the babies again by themselves. And all his vessels, milk pails
> and pans, that he used for milking into, were running over
> with whey.
>
> (218–24)

So much for the lawless outrageous. After due consideration they decide not to burgle the giant straightaway, but to roast a few lambs, gnaw a few cheeses, and await his return "to see if he would give me presents" (not just Odysseus but *poem* almost out of control). The giant returns to a scene out of some Sam Peckinpah movie western, and the rats at the cheese "scuttled away into the cave's corners" (poem back in control). Having closed up the cave, Polyphemos confronts his guests: less than garrulous, as befits a mountain-peak-tree-thing, he comes fairly straight to the point: "Strangers, who are you? . . . Is it on some business, or are you recklessly roving as pirates do . . . bringing evil to alien people?" (252–55). Odysseus replies with a deal of blah-blah-blah (which he even thinks *witty*) and the giant whacks a couple of commandos with a paw and eats them. From here things degenerate quickly: Odysseus dopes the giant with a magical brew (liquor for the Indians) and reams out the eyeball. In the morning the blinded Polyphemos opens the cave door to let his flock out to pasture (life must go on) and is feeling each fleece, both to re-establish contact with his darkened world and also to check for escaping rats (who are in fact hanging to the sheep's bellies). Last to pass him is his prize ram (with Odysseus underneath):

My dear old ram, why are you thus leaving the cave last of
the sheep? Never in the old days were you left behind by
the flock, but long striding, far ahead of the rest would pasture
on the tender bloom of the grass, be first at running rivers,
and be eager always to lead the way first back to the sheepfold
at evening. Now you are last of all. Perhaps you are grieving
for your master's eye . . .

(447–53)

Exit Polyphemos the king, sadder than Humbaba. (Need I add that
the commandos then depart with all of the sheep, leaving the
Mountain-Man more or less utterly bereft?)

Undoubtedly one of the world's great stories, but more than
somewhat disgusting, no? The difficult question, however, is how
disgusted the poem intends us to be. Although my recounting and
the context of this book's argument would say "very," the matter is
by no means so clear. It is in fact quite murky; indeed, if one were
to ask for a snap decision, the court would pronounce that, all things
considered, the poem almost approves the raid. How can this be?

Let us begin with the simplest question, and Odysseus's strongest
card, that of cannibalism, most despicable of crimes in the Homeric
world. I said that the *Iliad* fed the Cyclopes on mare's milk, and
there are traces of this here: at line 249 the milk pails "would serve
for his supper" and at 297 he drinks (to moisten the commandos)
"milk unmixed with water," as if such a heady brew (the ancient
Greeks watered their wine) was getting on for the lawless outrageous, almost outrageously innocent. This in itself suggests that the
cannibalism has been "stitched" into the story once the need for a
villainous monster had become apparent. And yet such stitching
(even were it better done) could not produce a proper villain because
Polyphemos, as epiphany of self-regulating divinity, can cheerfully
cannibalize without corrupting his nature. This wondrous monster
is *phusis* before the fall of alpha-shaman, before the laws of cooking
and sacrificial slaughter were introduced to keep man in line. We

must remember that divinity does it raw, whatever it does, and when aroused, it chomps. In order to become civilized, man must resist the divine ecstasies, the lawless dream of alpha-shaman, by regulating his appetitive intake. On the borderline between man and the gods, Polyphemos seems to enjoy the best of both worlds. Odysseus has come to "humanize" him, and the charge of cannibalism can be upheld only by either denying the monster's divinity or proving that it threatens the human community. [17]

We need not explore such difficult matters at this point; for what the poem makes very clear is that the only justification for despoiling the *home* of Polyphemos would be a charge of cannibalism, and hence it makes the charge, and the charge is gratuitous. Whether as man or tree-thing-shepherd, he is absolutely right (in the absence of a local constabulary) to start snapping his fingers at the commandos. Why does he then go on to eat them, given that his usual supper seems to be milk and cheese by firelight? To say that he is annoyed, and this is one way for a mountain-peak-tree-thing to clear rats from his cave, is already to concede too much, for it overlooks the fact that the narrative does not even attempt to make the cannibalism plausible. To leap from pastoral vegetarianism to its opposite pole requires a little mediation, and the poem offers none. Hence my charge of "stitching" (since this is in most respects poetry of a very high order); and the motive for such stitching is to prevent Odysseus from appearing to us as Polyphemos has seen him to be, simply "a recklessly roving pirate . . . bringing evil," contagious pollution from the Trojan war.

What I am suggesting is that here, in this tale, the "feminine" voice of Humbaba and the fostering hand has beautifully constructed its case against the reckless, roving, wandering warrior-pirate; but the warrior voice that dominates this poem is seeking to mitigate the charge, even unto acquittal, with a bogus countersuit for cannibalism, the heaviest card not only in the Greek but in all primitive decks, as we have seen in previous chapters. It must be conceded that this mitigating voice has succeeded rather well over the past three millennia.

And yet the poem, in its larger structure, sustains the charge against Odysseus. The blinded Polyphemos calls on his father Poseidon to curse the homecoming of Odysseus with danger and suffering, and this Poseidon does. Although this cursing is recounted in Book 9, it is gravely announced by Zeus in Book 1 (68 ff) and chronologically it comes very near the beginning of Odysseus's homeward journey from Troy: the only events to precede it are a perfunctory smash-and-grab raid on the Kikonians and a brief dalliance with the Lotos Eaters. In other words, in the absence of the actual Trojan mutilation, the blinding of Polyphemos is the pollution that provides the fuel that keeps our hero from sleeping in his own bed throughout the poem. Poseidon keeps Odysseus on the run for ten long years, and even once he reaches Penelope, he will not be finally released from taboo until he walks his accursed oar sufficiently far inland that it is mistaken (by locals innocent of reckless seafaring) for a winnowing fan—a sword to a ploughshare. But it is even better than a ploughshare: Tiresias directs that the oar must be *planted, like a tree,* and sacrifices offered there to Poseidon (11–120 ff). The significance of the oar-planting pilgrimage will concern us presently, but it appears to be the forfeit exacted by Poseidon from Zeus, Athena, and the others for a settlement of the feud (see 1–68 ff). Thus, despite the cannibalist whitewash, the poem's larger structure tries to register the crime's gravity.

If it is the blinding of Polyphemos that registers the pollution of Odysseus, it is the meeting with Nausikaa that registers the possibility of cleansing (*katharsis*), the remission of sins. Coming at the beginning and the ending of his wanderings, these episodes gain considerably from being looked at together, for the play with inversions is dazzling. Ironic inversion is already at work in the first episode, where pirate meets cannibal and each accuses the other of being unfit for hospitality: one might almost say each calls forth the criminality of the other, mutually vindicating their suspicions (though as I have indicated, the balance cannot be sustained between man and god-man, and so Polyphemos prevails). The homeless one enters a home saying this is no home, and proves while disproving his assertion: he both wants and does not want to be the other (because he cannot and he must not) and his actions testify to his

ambivalence. By the time Odysseus beaches on the shores of
Nausikaa, however, Poseidon has almost emptied him of his
dangerously muddled confusions, and he emerges from the sea
looking very much like, dare one say it, Polyphemos. In the place
of blindness there is an almost complete physical and spiritual
exhaustion. All his companions are dead, all his gear is gone. But
what we see (after a few hours' sleep to restore the thing he is) is
something like a muted parody of the tree-thing-mountain-peak:

> . . . great Odysseus came from under his thicket,
> and from the dense foliage with his heavy hand he broke off
> a leafy branch to cover his body and hide the male parts,
> and went in the confidence of his strength, like some
> hill-kept lion . . .
>
> (6:127–30)

Thus, he to play Polyphemos, she to play Odysseus (but also vice
versa); and since he then shudders lustfully at the sweet sound of
female voices, and moreover appears "terrifying . . . all crusted
with dry spray" (137), the probably naked* maiden needs an
injection of courage to stand her ground. Her companions all
"scattered one way and another down the jutting beaches" (137),
reminding us of how Odysseus and his companions, similarly
shocked, all "scuttled to the dark corners of the cave" (9–236). But
in his place she stands her ground, thus offering to undo his
Polyphemian disgrace; and although he begins to address her
"blandishingly and full of craft" (6–148) as usual, he is so overcome
by the grace and beauty of her brave acceptance that within a very
few lines he is speaking from the heart, quite transfigured:

*The girls go for a swim (one does not imagine bikinis) and then have a picnic.
Still no need for bikinis, but sunhats are indicated. These are what get thrown off
at line 100 (*krēdemna*, translated as "veil" by both Lattimore and Butcher and Lang,
clearly means headgear). The dancing ballgame was probably a quasi-ritualized
offering to Artemis, as the lovely digression at line 102 might suggest; and we are
surely being invited to think of what happened to Actaeon when he surprised *that*
goddess frolicking naked in the waters. In short, grimy ship-wrecked sea monsters
are not supposed to jump out at naked princesses on the beach. It is a testing time
for all concerned, the more dramatic for being understated.

> Wonder takes me as I look on you.
> Yet in Delos once I saw such a thing . . .
> I saw the stalk of a young palm shooting up . . .
> And as, when I looked upon that tree, my heart admired it
> long, since such a tree had never yet sprung from the earth, so
> now, lady, I admire you and wonder, and am terribly
> afraid to clasp you by the knees.
>
> (6:161–69)

Piety recovered and uncovered by his ordeal in the sea and by this miraculous remission, his voice is cleared and his eye, past lusting, can perceive himself perceived and pardoned in the tree-goddess of old.

Nausikaa had come to the beach to do the washing, but by the time she gathers up her companions and the linen, she has cleansed a good deal more than a week's soiled clothing; and we have been vouchsafed the glimpse of a way through by going all the way back to the almost-forgotten tree-gods. Such a vision of redemption is of course too good to last, and soon after this the poem moves into steep decline, returning us to the Mycenean chop-chop. But wasn't it wonderful?

Some of our larger perplexities may be illuminated by trying to name the two sides (or teams) whose *agon* or struggle composes the epic play. Odysseus is above all the man of crafty words and schemes (*metis*) and his sponsor is crafty Athena (with her father Zeus in the background). As culture hero Odysseus seems to be concerned with promoting a civil unity among the Hellenic peoples by commending the "progressive" arts of agriculture (bread-eating and meat-sacrifice), political assemblies for law-making, ships for trading, and above all the offering of hospitality (rather than death) to strangers, a matter we discussed at some length in Chapter 7. Although this program is sometimes convincingly espoused, the roving pirate (ex-soldier) also lurks within his breast, in no great hurry to get home to the boring old bread-maker.

Ranged against Odysseus and his wandering progress is Poseidon, various baddies, plus the Cyclopes and their almost stranger ex-neighbors, the Phaiakians (who also mediate between the two groups). Who was Poseidon? This very old wilderness god looks to some extent like the Greek version of Egyptian Seth. Bernal (*Black Athena*, 1987) thinks so (p. 20), and moreover has found evidence to suggest that the two major cults introduced to the Greek mainland from the south around 1500 B.C. were those of Athena and Poseidon. This fits rather nicely with the *Odyssey*, over which these two uneasily preside, with Zeus the northerner tagging along behind Athena and offering his services as mediator. Poseidon's domain under brother Zeus's settlement is of course the sea, but his epithet "Earth Shaker" and his rumored congress with grain-bearing Demeter may preserve the memory of a time, in Crete almost certainly, when his wildness was not so confined. In any case he is the sworn enemy of Athena, and is generally presented in Greek myth as irritable and resentful.[18]

I suggested in the last chapter that the "virtues" of chaos, amply registered in the Sumerian *abzu* (from which they successfully emigrated to the east), fared rather badly as they moved north and west. The Edomite sages knew that desert Yahwe could speak wisdom out of the whirlwind, but this notion did not sit well with the orthodox covenanters. Egyptian Seth of the sea and the desert is an ancient and a noble lord, not without his admirers (the Hyksos, for example) but an entirely negative force, certainly not associated with wisdom (as Sumerian Enki was). And when we come to Greek Poseidon, the position is even worse: if one sifts through the rag-bag of post-Homeric mythology, the invention of horse racing is about all we have to be genuinely grateful for with regard to his lordship. This is rather strange for the number-two god in the pantheon and one of the major players in the *Odyssey*. I shall attempt to shed some light on this mystery in a moment.

Poseidon is not only the father of Polyphemos, but the principal god of the Phaiakians. The latter are a good deal less primitive than the Cyclopes, but they acknowledge the relationship (6–4, 7–205); indeed the Phaiakians are the most civilized people we meet in the

Odyssey. They work the fields, as men do, but they enjoy a magically fine climate, harbor the totally magical Nausikaa, and sagely solve the theological problem with "a fine precinct of Poseidon" (6–267) in the middle of town and "a glorious grove of poplars" (6–291) for Athena in the suburbs. It goes without saying that they are magically gifted mariners and are, in short, *ankhitheoi* = relatives of the gods, an epithet Homer uses twice only, both times of them (5–93, 19–279). Since Athena's long suit is crafty *metis* (her mother, after all, was the thing itself), one would expect Poseidon and his team to glory in plain-speaking; and this is indeed the case.

The meeting with Nausikaa is one of the finest things in any literature, but part of what makes it stand out for the *Odyssey* reader is the *relief* we feel at hearing, for a change, speech unconstrained by the prudence and calculating suspiciousness of *metis*. What one needs above all for plain-speaking is no fear of the other's possible hostility; and this, as we have just seen, is what the princess Nausikaa wondrously supplies: which takes us back to Polyphemos the tree-god, who also awakened our hero's "wonder" before it gave way to envious blasphemy and desecration. The giant's speech was also remarkably clear, and by a nice irony, showed itself far more astute than the gabbling verbality of Odysseus (who was thus forced to call upon the magical technology of the *pharmakon*-drug, which poisoned everyone). And going further back to *Gilgamesh,* we remember Enkidu's crafty talk about bird-snaring (doubtless learned from the temple-priestess) as opposed to the crystal-clear insights (and heart-rending cries) of the forest Humbaba, whose ear was so finely tuned to the world of sound that he could hear the heifer stir at sixty leagues.

Metis proceeds by concealment, an obvious necessity to the man who must negotiate his interests with other men. A measure of concealment is also necessary in the ritual representations through which man tries to contact the invisible divinity without being burned by the spillage of *pneuma*. The state of blessedness, on the contrary, would be characterized by uncalculated (unritualized) spontaneous communication between man and the gods, as Alkinoos, King of the Phaiakians, explains:

for always in time past the gods have shown themselves clearly
to us, when we render them glorious grand sacrifices
and they sit beside us and feast with us in the place where we do,
or if one comes alone and encounters us, as a wayfarer,
then they make no concealment, as we are very close to them,
as are the Cyclopes and the savage tribes of the Giants.

(7:201–06)

We have seen throughout this study that the question of concealment is absolutely central to the dialectic of culture, and also
absolutely ambiguous. As "overcast weather" it plays *yin* to *yang*'s
"waving banners in the sun," and as the essentially hidden movements of life's waxing and waning, it is Osiris operating in the
shadows of Re's clarity. As *metis* its ambiguity becomes fully
apparent: with Trickster and Hermes it is associated with *pneuma*'s
powers of metamorphosis, much esteemed by primitive man in his
appropriative undertakings. But as culture moves increasingly into
lawfulness, the ideal of aristocratic openness and plain-speaking
emerges to cast a shadow upon the previously "virtuous" *metis*. And
yet since divinity is in the beginning an absence (or concealment)
that becomes present as unpredictable movement, it would seem to
be incorrigibly akin to *metis,* and hence difficult to invoke as sponsor
for open-handed aristocracy. This problem is of considerable dimensions, central both in Homer and Greek tragedy, and is being
obliquely addressed in the passage just cited, where King Alkinoos
is attempting (not altogether plausibly) to recast divinity as
aristocracy in order to avoid having to declare war on the inscrutable
heavens. I suggest that, having noted the theological difficulty, we
accept the imaginative necessity of his story and pass on.

The point about the solitary wayfarer is less troubling: to travel
alone is to be "not-man" (for man is doomed and sustained by living
socially) and hence it is to be either sub- or superhuman. As we have
seen, the normal assumption is that the stranger (*hostis*) is hostile,
and hence the solitary wayfarer would normally need considerable
concealment (*metis*) of his strangeness to come among us without
violence; but the magical Phaiakians, at least in times past, could

manage clarity and openness even in these dangerous encounters. Such are the privileges of being *ankitheoi,* related to the gods, and they are the privileges of innocence, an undefended openness to experience such as the chimp enjoys at the waterfall. In the dangerous world of humankind, however, such innocence (or spontaneity) is not given but must be acquired, and it becomes one of the major aspirations of aristocratic self-possession. To be self-possessed (like the Princess Nausikaa) is to be fully present, in full possession of what one is, hence fulfilled, not fearing the loss of some part of oneself already occluded (or alienated) in that darkness that men everywhere have called the fear of death. Such self-possession, strangely enough, is instinct with modesty, and another word for it is *grace*; and yet this word, since it tends to revive in us vague memories of religious concerns and aristocratic ideals we affect to have outgrown, is apt to stutter on the modern tongue. The matter is both simple and complex, and the only point I would make here is that grace, whether it illuminates the brachiating monkey or the Princess Nausikaa, is schooled in the shadow of death; by which I mean that its fearlessness arises in the only way it truly can, from a disciplined exposure to the fearful; which is to say that to be fearlessly self-possessed is to be possessed also of one's death, and such possession manifests itself in modesty. Its catechism is wonderfully compressed in Shakespeare's "Rue, the bitter herb of grace," and like so much else of the first importance, it has escaped us; but it has not altogether vanished (I have glimpsed it in ancient Scottish crofters) and we could find it again if we tried.

Odysseus has glimpsed it in the Princess Nausikaa, and sees in her the virtue that has eluded him in his wanderings and could redeem his suffering; and we are now almost ready to say, quite simply, that the occlusion of the sacred that has harried him is clearly registered (present in its absence) in the very "virtue" he has exploited to compensate for its loss—his *metis.* His heroic longing to be more than man, on a par with the gods, able to travel fearlessly alone and to take what he wants, leads him at times to be less than man, *over*crafty; and the punishment for such failed ambition is a certain degree of what we would call self-hatred. This can be seen in the attack on Polyphemos, where his *metis* is both pronounced and uncharacteristically pathetic. What puts him off his stroke from the beginning is an unexplained irritability, a smouldering resentment of Polyphemos, and this makes us think of his name, which derives from *odussomai* = I hate. [19]

That envy is the matter comes across with much subtlety in the almost charmingly childlike way he describes the improvements he would make on the Cyclopes' spare island if only someone would let him show his stuff. Envy is perhaps the worst of all the human devils, best understood through the twin-brother motif: I want to grow up to be like big brother, in fact I want to *be* big brother, in fact I *am* big brother and he is not. But envy always backfires: by desecrating the home of big brother Polyphemos, the unhoused Odysseus merely exacerbates his own homelessness. Big brother Polyphemos is indeed big, a self-possessed and plain-speaking antecedent of the aristocratic Alkinoos, in whom the stately virtues of the massive tree-god are elaborated and refined in human gracefulness. When measured against such stateliness, Odysseus is forced to see his devious craftiness in the light of the creepy-crawly *sheretz,* who stands for nothing, definitely low-down. This point was first made when the rats at the cheese fearfully "scuttled away into the cave's corners" (236), again when he calls himself a "Nobody," and finally in the parting exchange of insults, when Polyphemos explains that he had been warned in a prophecy that he would one day be blinded by Odysseus:

> But always I was on the lookout for a man handsome
> and tall, with great endowment of strength on him, to come here;
> but now the end of it is that a little man, niddering, feeble,
> has taken away the sight of my eye, first making me helpless
> with wine.
>
> (513–17)

I suggested earlier that the problem of *metis* was one of the *Odyssey's* major themes, and so it is too in the *Iliad,* where the aristocratic Achilles (its central character) says pointedly to Odysseus: "He is hateful to me as the gates of Death, that man who conceals one thing in his heart, and says another" (9–312). Like a great tree that opens itself utterly and fearlessly to the wind and sky, Achilles has nothing but contempt for the little man's ploys of cunning, the deals that get done in the marketplace; and yet the danger for the aristocrat who talks only to the gods is that he might lose the common touch, and when the world of other men insists upon negotiating its interests with him, he may find himself maddened by his incapacity to meet it. This is indeed what happens to Achilles, and a related objection is made in the *Odyssey* to all those islanders who live in seemingly solitary splendor. The verbal trickery of *metis,* as I have said, is the mark of man fallen into the necessity of politicking with his fellow man, and its dialectic with the open-handed ideals of godlike aristocracy is taken into the heart of Greek tragedy, sublimely so in the *Philoctetes* of Sophocles.[20]

FINALE: POSEIDON AND THE CRETAN SEA-BULL

What emerges clearly from the foregoing is that Poseidon's team gets the best parts in the *Odyssey.* They speak openly and speak the best poetry, they are older, more primitive (and more civilized), more magical, more peaceable, more feminine, and seem oddly to produce trees at key moments. Why should this be so? My answer is as simple as it is unprovable: they come from Crete, and many of the poem's best energies, which we have up until now discussed as the gentleman(woman)ly critique of piratical violence (and the cunning that suits it), are better understood as a dialectic between the vanishing wisdom of the Minoans and the ascendant pugnacity of the Myceneans. This suggestion becomes more plausible when one remembers that as the balance of power shifted from Crete to Mycenae (in the sixteenth century), many of the best craftsmen were drafted to the mainland to civilize the new brutality. As a result, the two styles blended a good deal, and yet most of the fine Mycenean pieces can be confidently identified by the scholars as Minoan work.[21] Something similar must have taken place with regard to myth and religion, but since we know so little about Minoan religion, we would be well advised to hasten slowly in our speculations. What we do know is that the Cretan goddess, even more than her counterparts in Egypt and the Near East, was given to worshipping and marrying with a tree-god, whose periodic death she would mourn. We also know that the Myceneans, ill-at-ease on the sea, nonetheless took Poseidon very seriously (he dominates the excavations at Pylos, for example). Much of the rest, concerning the Cretan imagination of violence and its influence on the Mycenean mind, we can only guess; and hence this meditation must proceed very largely in the dark, which is perhaps an appropriate way to end a book that has spent much of its time there.

Let us begin with Minoan religion, a tantalizing subject because it may represent, perhaps even more wonderfully than do Isis and Osiris, an actual historical answer to the problems of sex and violence that have concerned us throughout this book. Civilization arose in Crete only a little later than it did in Egypt and Mesopotamia (about 2500 B.C.), fostered, as was its previous neolithic settlement, from the shores of Asia Minor. Hence the major reference initially is not to Egypt but to Catal, its fine craftsmanship, its remarkably naturalistic artistic styles, its goddesses, its horns of consecration and its vision of bull-vaulting. All of these prevail in Minoan culture, and mark its provenance as more Asian than Egyptian. For a summary of what we can infer about its religious practices, what better authority to harness my enthusiastic tendencies than the grumpy but incorruptible Professor Nilsson:

> In spite of limitations imposed by the nature of the evidence, certain characteristic traits of Minoan religion do emerge in contrast to the Greek. One is the preponderance of goddesses and of female cult officiants. Masculine deities are, in contrast to feminine, very scarce . . . and it is likely that this preponderance of the female sex accounts for the emotional character of the religion, which appears particularly in tree cult scenes. . . . All phallic symbols, such as

abound and are so aggressive in numerous religions—including the historic religion of Greece—are in Minoan art completely missing.[22]

We know little about Minoan culture generally because we have decoded neither their original hieroglyphic script nor the succeeding Linear A; but it may be, since Linear B (broken in the 1950s) has revealed so little of interest, that the Minoans were in any case not very scriptural. (I say this because of all the major cultures they seemed to have feared death the least, and writing is above all an answer to such fear.) Despite this ignorance, however, what we do know is that about 2000 B.C. some rather brilliant *daimon* entered their souls and moved them to outshine their Cycladic cousins and establish a maritime empire that traded all the way from the Levant to Britain, where Professor Atkinson has detected their influence in the constructions at Stonehenge.[23] We also know that their opulent palaces were neither surrounded by battlements (as the Mycenean palaces were) nor much decorated with scenes of violence or war. But though they managed to prevail without much warfare, their sailors were undoubtedly tough as well as remarkably adventurous; Thucydides, for example, alludes to the formidable achievement of the Minoan navy in clearing the Aegean of pirates.

Unfortunately for our purposes, the Minoan palace walls are rather reticent on the subject of theology. Cretan works of art are marked by gaiety and exuberance, not by mythic preoccupations with the mysteries of death; and one can imagine the visiting Egyptian ambassador smiling ruefully, "Ah these divine children, blest with a light step, but lightweight in the end." He might be right, but he might not. Our inquiry must begin, in the absence of a story line, with the flowing line of their art, a natural ease first glimpsed in the paleolithic caves, and then again at Catal, in marked contrast to the monumental stiffness (or "stillness," to its admirers) of the Egyptians (and to a lesser extent, the Myceneans).[24] Here esthetician Wilhelm Worringer's well-known distinction between abstraction and empathy can help: artistic styles move between the abstract, which seeks control over the flux of organic life by distancing itself from it, and the empathetic, which, seemingly negligent of death, abandons itself to the organic line: roughly speaking, Father's law versus Mother's eternal reassurance. When Professor Nilsson alludes (more than a touch distantly) to "the emotional character of the religion" in the passage just cited, he is directing our thoughts to the empathetic pole of the human imagination and its mystical conclusions.

Also, as he says, to the "tree cult scenes," the two most celebrated of which are reproduced and discussed at length in Campbell (*Occidental Mythology,* 1964).[25] Each of these seems to be suggesting that a life focused with sufficient piety on the goddess and her tree-god need not fear the roar of her mountain lion, nor even perhaps that of her bull, nor even the slither of her snake: which calls to mind the Tree of Life in the Garden of Eden, withdrawn forever from the reach of greedy mankind, sent forth to labor unhappily under the sun-lion's pitiless gaze. But the even more interesting and difficult comparison is with Egypt, where the harshness of the sun-lion-falcon-cobra is sufficiently alienated from the feminine touch in the virtual absence of trees to call forth the despairing mania of pyramids, mummification, and an abstracted style, and yet sufficiently unalienated to call forth the genius of Isis/Osiris. I can imagine the newly arrived Egyptian ambassador attending some tree-cult ceremony and saying "Affecting certainly, but childish and naive, no? We too used to worship trees in the beginning, our first home after all, millions of years in the African forest. But life is more complicated now, and one really must address the violent energies set forth in the feast of alpha-shaman. The snake-handling episode was charmingly primitive, but what does your goddess make of the buffalo-bull?" And here, at this crucial moment, the sound track dies, for the Minoan excavations tell us very little about this; and the difficult question we must now pursue is whether the Minoans were simply brilliant children who chose to ignore the dark side of the moon, or whether they may have addressed its terrors even more wisely than the Egyptians, but took their secrets with them.

It seems to have been conventionally agreed in Crete that matters of sex and violence were on the whole not suitable subjects for the decorative arts. The nearest we get to the goddess and her bull (and it is both very near and far) are the pictures of boys and girls leaping playfully over the bull's horns. The idea of leaping is prominent in the etymology of "playing" in most languages,[26] our simplest expression of exuberance, the flashing forth of *pneuma*. Together with its contrary, the stamping foot (an earth-shaking gesture that is either calling up chthonic energy or scattering it), it constitutes the basic grammar of the dance whose ritual purpose is the augmenting of prosperity, as this lovely hymn, found inscribed on stone in eastern Crete, would suggest:

> Io, Kouros most great . . .
> Lord of all that is wet and gleaming . . .
>
> To us . . . leap for full jars,
> And leap for fleecy flocks,
> And leap for fields of fruit,
> And for hives to bring increase.
>
> . . .
>
> Leap for our Cities,
> And leap for our sea-borne ships,
> And leap for our young citizens
> And for goodly Themis.

The leaping dancers are calling on the bull-god to come and leap for them; and though the dating of this hymn is uncertain, the material is as old as may be, as Harrison in *Themis* (1963) convincingly argues.[27] I cite it here because there is nothing in it that would be out of place in our imagining of the ritual invocations that doubtless preceded the bull-vaulting contests. Notice Themis at the end, particularly apposite to my arguments in Chapter 7 about the goddess as symbol of culture, for this is precisely what Themis was—symbol of the abstract totality of our customs and practices, the piety (*eusebia*) that gives us good order. She rightly comes at the end, collecting all the elements of prosperity for which we leap for the leaping bull.

What the hymn does not mention, but the bull-vaulting makes abundantly clear, is that our leaping must survive the risk of serious mutilation if it is comprehensively to represent the play of culture and Nature. It does this with extraordinary gymnastic skill, courage refined by precision into grace under pressure. Much more dangerous and properly theological than the wrestling matches we have discussed, the bull-vaulting game sublimely proposes the human wager with divinity. If one of our dancers is gored, and this is quite likely in the circumstances, it indicates that the culture has not measured up to its highest aspirations today; and if the bull is sacrificed at the end (as in the Spanish bullfight), it indicates that he has consented to offer up his perpetually lethal energies to the dance of our designing.

This, I think, is as far as we may legitimately speculate about the bull's violence on the basis of Minoan evidence. For the rest of the story we must turn to Greek mythology, the *textual* record of what the Myceneans made of their unspeaking Minoan inheritance. Here the fun really begins, for the gaps, occlusions, perversions, and significant silences are everywhere apparent, and we really must do some leaping if the story is to be pulled together. Before we start, a little thread to help the reader keep track: I suspect that the Cretan bull was quite possibly a match for his cousin Osiris, and that his major mysteries were imported, distorted, dispersed, and shared out among Zeus, Poseidon, and Dionysus, the three Mycenean bull gods.

First of all, in view of the scarcity of male figures in Minoan art, let us call on the unimpeachable Burkert (*Greek Religion*, 1985) to dispense with the fantasy of Cretan matriarchy: "The real political and economic power lay, as in the parallel Bronze Age civilizations, in the hands of a king: his throne room and throne form the dynamic centre of the palace" (p. 38); and indeed the throne at Knossos, excavated by Sir Arthur Evans, was flanked by two griffins (snake-bird-lion monsters), not very feminine. Second, given that the scholarly "problem" of Minoan culture is its seeming singularity, its *difference* from that of both Egypt and the Near East, let us give ample prominence to two of its *known* singular features: the Minoans were the world's first great sailors, and their buildings were regularly destroyed (about three times per century) by earthquakes and tidal waves (the last and largest of which, when nearby Thera exploded—about 1450—with ten times the force of Krakatoa, seems to have finally broken their spirit). These two astonishing facts seem to me obviously related. To the primitive mind throughout the Mediterranean, the sea is the wilderness, and only spirits inured to the experience of chaos would conceive the altogether outrageous project of trying to be at home there. Thus I would propose the Cretans as first masters of the abyss, and would suggest that such mastery has everything to do with their men's ability to forego the macho reassurance of phallic jujus and be suitably impressed (not threatened) by the strikingly attractive women who dominate their art works in those distinctively flounced skirts. I would also suggest that since the Cretan men managed to be at home on the sea (without losing sight of the flounced skirts), they were content to subdue its pirates, grow rich from trading upon it, and yet on the whole resist the temptation to pillage and enslave the people who lived on its shores.

The sea is the wilderness of Seth, terrifying to the interloper; but within its divinity, creatures are nourished with a motherly care, just as Humbaba guards the "Forest of the Living." The task of a seafaring people is to enlist its tolerance, even its blessing, so that it will show them, say, its dolphin and not its raging sea-bull. But this is already too advanced: Humbaba, remember, is mostly wind and fire to the interloper; not simply protean but shapeless, unimaginable, and cedar forests are a good deal less chaotic than the original wilderness of the sea. Thus I imagine the Cretan sea-god to have begun as simply wind and darkness, wind in the darkness, death in the windy darkness; and from unimaginable *pneuma* he would have progressed to something almost intelligibly protean, like the Greek "Old Man of the Sea," dolphin on a good day, sea-bull-griffin in a gale. And of course he would have been originally indistinguishable from the earth-shaking volcanic power that periodically knocks us down. Imagine Thera and those other mountainous islands that rise from the deep: where else might the volcanic power reside but way down *there,* beneath the bottom?

I flail in the darkness here because neither violent sea-gods nor earthquakes are ever represented in Minoan art;[28] and this seems to me to involve more than the visual difficulty, more than the decorums of good taste, something indeed more like taboo: "These dreadful things we know intimately, and do not speak of them in public." To have lived serenely, as it seems they did, so near the abysmal edge, required a singular combination of courage and skill. The sailor who survives the storm is the one who ties the knot *correctly* as he's almost being washed overboard; and he tends not to talk about it afterward. One may discern some trace of this in the elegant bodies arching nonchalantly over the bull's horns; and I am reminded of Nietzsche's wonderful remark in another context, "How these people must have suffered to have become so beautiful!"

And now, as briefly as possible, to the three Greek bulls, Dionysus, Zeus, and Poseidon, from whom we may learn something of their Minoan forebear. Dionysus is in many respects the most interesting, also the most obscure, and he virtually defies the summarizing mind. He was usually associated with Osiris by the Greeks themselves, and the obvious line of transmission is through Crete.[29] Sacrificial master of the mysteries of life and death, androgynous and supple in his protean ability to enter and disturb all forms of life, violent and subtle, he is above all the original pan-theist, and patron of our most harrowing and sublime irrational moments. Mystic god of enthusiasts and wine drinkers, born with horns and a headful of snakes, he was particularly worshipped by women, and was the only Greek bull with a pronounced tendency to turn into trees. He also had a pronounced tendency to materialize magically from the sea, and like Osiris was at home in the marginal marshes. All of these characteristics are plausibly Minoan, and none of them would have commended him much to the post-theriomorphic and anti-mystical disposition of the Greek Olympians, who only admitted him to the pantheon in the fifth century, when his genuine religious powers had declined sufficiently for him to be safely recognized as respectable. Despite his obvious relevance to the concerns of this book, and despite my having admired him for some twenty-five years, constraints of space and balance have forced me to choose between him and Osiris for sustained discussion, and I have preferred the latter for two main reasons: unlike the Greek god, Osiris is lamentably ill-known in the West and calls out for publication; and second, we do have direct access to the primitive origins of Osiris's story, which moreover dominated Egyptian culture for almost three thousand years. Dionysus, by contrast, was labeled subversive and was resisted by "official" Greek culture from the beginning, with the result that we have very little *accurate* knowledge of his primitive origins; for example, much the best source of information about him comes from Euripides' heroic attempt to revive his memory at the end of the fifth century in the *Bacchae*.[30] That said, it is important here to recognize that any serious attempt to reconstruct the Cretan bull from Greek sources would have to spend a good deal of time with Dionysus. In addition to the points I have outlined, there are three well-known myths that recount his adventures as a tree-bearing sea-bull-lion-dolphin, and there is the further important matter of his association with religious "mysteries" that also seem to have originated with the Cretan bull.[31]

Greek literature frequently refers to the Cretan mysteries, doubt-less related somehow to the Egyptian ones, and most often associated with Dionysus the bull. Although one would dearly love access to these mysteries, nothing I have read on the subject (and I have read most of it) suggests that anyone has much idea of what was going on. Mysteries, after all, are supposed to be *secret*, and the Greek Eleusinian rites, which persisted for over a thousand years, perhaps qualify as the world's best-kept secret. So what can be said? No one disputes Evans's claim to have found evidence of ritual regicide in ancient Crete. This would tie in with the many rumors associating Dionysus the bull with the Cretan *omophagia*, the feast of raw flesh, to give us a glimpse of alpha-shaman. The seasoning for such proceedings may well have been provided by the goddess, whose undisputed predilection for the poppy seed suggests that Cretan mysticism was sustained and enhanced by the ritual ingestion of opium. More than this need not be ventured for our purposes, which are only to sketch the outline of an answer that (had we but world enough and time) could be made to the Egyptian ambassador's sense of the all-too-bearable lightness of being Cretan.[32]

And so to Zeus and Poseidon, a less interesting story, but the one we want. If Dionysus was awarded the indigestible aspects of the Cretan bull, the digestible ones on the whole went to Poseidon, though since there was some jostling for position between Zeus and Poseidon, the story has its complications. Here again I must summarize rather brutally. Imagine the Mycenean power waxing as the Minoan power wanes. Not unlike the Romans and the Greeks, the younger power must take religious and esthetic instruction from elder brother, but also make such changes as are necessary to establish its dominance. If the Cretan bull was amphibious, as I am suggesting, one might expect to find a Mycenean myth of an old land-bull who was subsequently and resentfully confined to the sea (which the Myceneans didn't much care for); and this is exactly the story of Greek Poseidon, the major god mentioned in the Linear B texts recovered at Mycenean Pylos.[33] As bull of the land he was married to Demeter, the earth goddess (even perhaps siring Persephone), and as sea-bull he is constantly scrapping with Athena (Zeus's daughter) in an attempt to regain lost territory. Zeus is etymologically Indo-European, descending from the north with horses and chariots and the Mycenean lords. His bland personality marks him as a newcomer (all the interesting parts already spoken for), but if he is to be number one, Poseidon, the earth-shaking sea-bull, has to stand down and become number two. Zeus holds on to his warlike thunderbolt, consents occasionally to dress up as a bull, but since he spends most of his time in court settling disputes, perhaps gives Poseidon his horse, which in any case ill-suits a sky god (and doesn't suit a sea-bull very well either, but a gift horse is a gift horse). Like forcibly retired divinities everywhere, Poseidon then gradually acquires a bad reputation, absorbing the disavowed and projected thuggery of the Mycenean upstarts.

There is one story of the Cretan bull that Zeus clearly had to wrest from Poseidon because it was too important to be left in his keeping; and it concerns the origin of human life on Crete. If Crete was to become a Mycenean colony it was obviously important that its life be seen to originate with the Mycenean god; and thus even though this story centers on the sea-bull, which I am proposing as the Cretan trademark, his name is Zeus. In this tale, unquestionably of Cretan provenance, the Phoenician princess Europa was picking flowers by the seashore one day. The bull emerged from the sea, raped her, and swam back with her to Crete, there to sire Minos, the legendary King and culture-hero; who married divine Pasiphae, who subsequently conceived an adulterous passion for a beautiful bull sent by Zeus or Poseidon to Crete. Concealing herself inside a magical metal cow (crafted by Dedalus) she had her way with the bull and produced the monstrous minotaur, human body with the head of a bull, who was sequestered in the labyrinth and kept quiet by a periodic meal of Athenian youths sent as tribute to their Cretan masters. Pasiphae's unmonstrous child was Ariadne, who inverts her mother's crime by betraying the bull for human congress.[34] The minotaur was certainly no Greek invention, for he appears on Minoan seals and coins, though whether he in fact required the sacrifice of Athenian youths (on the bull-vaulting ground or in the labyrinth) is something we shall probably never know.[35]

What is left to Poseidon are various old theriomorphic tales in which he moves among the dolphins and sires various sea-monsters. Perhaps his most widely known appearance is as the sea-bull who stampedes the horses of Hippolytus; but most significant for our argument is the old myth of his being nurtured as a youth by the "evil" Telchines, secretive smiths and magicians who dwelt underground (underwater?) at Rhodes.[36] What is the wilderness god doing with mysterious craftsmen in the deeps? One has to go back to Enki in the *abzu* to get any purchase on this one, but if we remove the envious charge of "evil," the myth will sit well with Cretan sailors who know that a fully provisioned sea-god must authorize the "secret" nautical skills and magical lore with which they seek to survive his wildness. Although the *Odyssey* tries lamely to associate Poseidon with the technical skills of the Phaiakians, it has clearly forgotten how the thing is done; and the Greek myth of the Telchines similarly expires in disapproving vagueness. The richness of the *abzu* may well (as I believe) have reached Minoan Crete, but it failed to negotiate Greek waters, which is the main reason why the Greeks were never at ease on the sea.

With this glimpse of a lost cultural aspect of Poseidon, we come very near the heart of my argument, which is not only that the extraordinary Cretan bull was severely lamed when parceled into three by the Greeks, but that in separating his wisdom from his violence much was lost; for much of wisdom can only be learned in the context of violence. In the Greek myths and in much of the *Odyssey* Poseidon is simply "Earth-shaker," the sea-deep volcanic power that heroic eaters of bread might be tempted to provoke but wise men avoid. Almost like Seth one might think, the mutilating wildness that civilized men shun; but Seth is one of the family, and his daily struggles with Horus engage our constant attention. Similarly, in my proposal, the Cretan bull, either as earth-shaking volcano or maritime gale, never escapes the Minoan mind, as the bull-vaulting pictures would suggest. The lovely women in flounced skirts must dance with their sailor-boys in the opulent palace tonight in the knowledge that tomorrow the palace may be flattened and the sailors drowned. Such abysmal discipline soothes the savage breast and keeps us all from the needless pettiness of human violence. When it is lost, as it is lost in the Homeric poems, the savage breast turns the mind to mindless mutilation on the high seas and the battlefield: where else are the serious gods to be found?

What makes the best parts of the *Odyssey* so poignant is the sense of this old discipline almost still within reach, but not quite—a Poseidon whose violent strangeness may still almost be touched by a woman and returned to the innocent strength and sturdy suppleness and beautiful leafiness of a tree. Vestiges of this faith can be discerned with Nausikaa, and though it *is* in the *Odyssey*, it is not Greek: which means it must be Minoan. Perhaps the best evidence for this is a recurrent motif in Minoan art, bull's horns with a tree sprouting up between them. What can this mean if not that violence can be transformed into leafiness through the mediation of the goddess who consorts with both? And there it is, concluding the *Odyssey*, as the seafaring oar whose improper violence is renounced and returned as foliage. Like the widespread myth of bees emerging from the carcass of a bull, the tree-bearing horns seem to speak of a faith in the redemption of violence which the *Odyssey* has almost lost and which the Greeks will not significantly retrieve until they undertake the foolishness of Jesus.

Thus, I propose, the oppressive weight of the Cretan bull was dismantled in the Mycenean mind. Some of his best secrets went to Dionysus (who was then often deemed primitive, foreign, lower-class, and irresponsible), and most of the rest of him went to Poseidon, formidably powerful as befits number two, but thoroughly bad-tempered and thuggish. Part of what makes the *Odyssey* feel so old is that in places it preserves memories of a time when Poseidon was more than a thug. With all this in mind, let us now again approach the theological strangeness of the *Odyssey*. Athena with her shield, her snakes, and her sacred trees looks very like a suitably bellicose transciption of the Cretan goddess, expounding the new order of Zeus; and Poseidon looks like a suitably demystified reduction of the Cretan bull, whose magic has escaped us and which we therefore largely wish to deny and forget. It is important to remember that Cretan sea-magic was not inherited by the Myceneans: the maritime empire of the Minoans passed to the Phoenicians, and along with it, one imagines, the secrets of how to be at home on the sea (which may in any case have come to Crete from Phoenicia in the first place, as the myth of Europa would suggest).*

---

*Matthew Arnold got this mythic pattern right. Look at the conclusion to his beautiful poem, *The Scholar-Gipsy*. The Phoenician skipper, seeing "the merry Grecian coaster" sailing onto his erstwhile patch, "Freighted with amber grapes,"

Hence we have the *Odyssey* as a poem about land-lubbing Greeks who undertook the maritime challenge, provoked its deity, and paid dearly for doing so, as would their Athenian descendants some centuries later. What haunts their dreams are memories of a people (the Phaiakians) who somehow managed to sail the sea and trade upon it without provoking and being provoked by its abysmal emptiness to acts of mutilating desecration. The secret of the Cretan poise has escaped the singers of this song, but they remember that it crucially involves a kind of manly competence that allows the feminine to prosper; and in the redemptive moments of the *Odyssey*, with Nausikaa and in the planting of the oar, this almost un-Greek memory surfaces again, centering the play.

The Phaiakians are usually associated with Corfu by the scholars, astonishingly enough,[37] and yet even so late a figure as Plato (in the *Critias*) remembered that the Utopian myth of Atlantis was built upon memories of Crete. Quite apart from their seafaring alliance with Poseidon, the artistic accomplishments of the Phaiakians look altogether at home in Crete, where they testify to an enduring Greek memory of Minoan superiority (a memory that Evans's discoveries at Knossos would suggest is accurate as well as mythopoeic). The crafting energies of the plain-speaking Phaiakians find expression not through *metis* in the mouth but through skilled precision in the hand, either in the workshop or at sea (or further back, one might add, on the bull's horns); and such precisions, magical but not

---

realizes that he has lost this relatively local market (the Aegean Isles) to these "light-hearted" upstarts, and so calls out the serious nautical skills that prove the sea his "ancient home"; and lays a course "To where the Atlantic raves," far away, taking his dark skin and even more mysterious goods to inform and greet the primitive European soul

There, where down cloudy cliffs, through sheets of foam,
Shy traffickers, the dark Iberians come;
And on the beach undid his corded bales.

To have come up with this in the heyday of the British Empire was a quite remarkable gesture of deviant patriotism, for which Arnold was never sufficiently thanked.

deceitful, are clearly related to their graceful bearing and equable temperaments. Odysseus is deeply impressed by their ability to be so at home on both land and sea. Like the British whose maritime empire subdued the world while dreaming of the sweet safe softness of the villages at home, Odysseus wants to go a-roving and yet remain *sitophagos,* an eater-of-bread, centered upon the woman who waits. The thing was never easily done, for the caverns of the sea call upon man's emptiness. The ones who did it first and best were the Minoans, and their secrets still remain part-published in the Phaiakian shining.

And where did those secrets come from? The reader will have guessed my answer. The tree-bearing sea-bull who ended up as a sea-horse knew something of Seth's negations but even more of how they could be survived by Osiris in the barley; and before that, he knew of Humbaba's rich forest silence and Enki's wisdom in the *abzu.* The virtues of the void came north and west to cosmopolitan Crete, largely *via* Phoenicia, teaching her children, both boys *and* girls, to vault the bull instead of simply killing him; to use their *hands* to manifest gracefulness instead of fighting the darkness with darkness. In Crete these virtues went to ground, and took most of their secrets with them, lingering through Poseidon's creatures in the *Odyssey* as half-remembered traces of some tree-borne graceful thing, and occasionally surfacing centuries later as an even dimmer sense of something powerfully good, source of the life-enhancing precisions. Yeats heard it beautifully in one of Sophocles's finest poems, so let us give him the last word:[38]

> Because this country has a pious mind,
> And so remembers that when all mankind
> But trod the road, or splashed about the shore,
> Poseidon gave it bit and oar,
> Every Colonus lad or lass discourses
> Of that oar and of that bit;
> Summer and winter, day and night,
> Of horses and horses of the sea, white horses.

APPENDIX:
Etymologies of the Sacred in the Ancient World

I placed a jar in Tennessee,
And round it was, upon a hill.
It made the slovenly wilderness
Surround that hill.

The wilderness rose up to it,
And sprawled around, no longer wild.
The jar was round upon the ground
And tall and of a port in air.

It took dominion everywhere.
The jar was gray and bare.
It did not give of bird or bush,
Like nothing else in Tennessee.
                        —Wallace Stevens

In the beginning supernatural power is experienced by primitive man as energy that interrupts or intensifies the normal flow of events—an obvious example is the thunderstorm. By degrees, through the use of ritual and sympathetic magic, he seeks to harness this power so that it may animate and sustain the fabric of human orderliness that we call culture. And even when, through history's attenuations, modern man no longer turns naturally to gods and goddesses, as in the poem cited above, one still finds traces of the original design; but for Stevens the power that magically awakens, absorbs, and subdues the wildness in Tennessee is thought to be esthetic.

What are we to call this power? If we are to follow its major tracks through the early days of mankind, we need a word that will be as appropriate to a group of hominids thrilling to a herd of buffalo on the African savannah as to some rather sophisticated Athenians dancing a sacrificial dance at the Festival of Dionysus; and it must also be not altogether out of place when approaching the jar in Tennessee.

The word favored by anthropologists since Durkheim's *The Elementary Forms of the Religious Life* (1915) is "the sacred," denoting a range of experience set apart from and opposed to the everyday "profane" or "secular." The further back one goes, the more disturbing, even violent, sacredness becomes: that which sanctifies is always potentially polluting, the divine infusion may become lethal if the dose is not properly regulated by the rules of art and ritual. "It is a fearful thing to fall into the hands of the living God," said the preacher (Hebrews 10:31): "The only thing worse is not to," was D. H. Lawrence's wonderful reply. In sum, the sacred is awe-ful, dread-ful, *dangerous* (as the Hebrew *qadosh*, Greek *hagios*, and Latin *sacer* attest).

The dangerousness of divinity was obvious to our forebears, whether one thinks of those hominids hiding in the African trees as the buffalo thundered by, or a group of Cretans in 2500 B.C. taking great care over the ritual sacrifice of a bull, that it be performed just so; or indeed, to refine the point, a group of Jewish bedouin invoking their god by carefully not naming him. Divinity only seems innocuous to those from whom it has withdrawn.

Modern poets do not easily remember much of divinity's danger (Stevens's jar, though wonderfully neo-primitive in certain respects, would seem to underestimate the Tennessee rattlesnake); and hence we should be the more grateful to ethnologists—Robertson Smith (1889) the pioneer—for having gradually opened up, in the past hundred years, a broad highway back to our primitive ancestors and their sense of the sacred. When one is lost or confused, it is often best to return to the beginning; and with the question of divinity I feel sure that this is so.

At the outset of her important book *Purity and Danger* (1966), Mary Douglas observes (p. 7) that "primitives make little difference between sacredness and uncleanness [i.e., pollution]." To realize this is not to realize that the primitive is a confused child (as numerous ethnologists have supposed), but that he is exposed, unlike us, to the *mysterium tremendum* in all its distressing ambiguity. Needless to say, cultures as they evolve take the necessary steps to separate the sacred from the unclean so that they may not become confused. And yet, as this book argues at length, such separation must at the same time preserve the original ambiguity it is at pains to abolish. If it fails in this dialectical undertaking, if, that is, it succeeds too well in separating the sacred from the unclean, both terms lose their potency, and religious experience withers away. Christianity offers a good instance: when in the eighteenth century its heaven and its hell had ceased to animate each other with the proper ambiguity, so that, for example, one could no longer readily see the possible saintliness of a sinner, the culture had fallen into what Blake called "single vision and Newton's sleep"; and the time had come once again to call for "the marriage of heaven and hell," a marriage we are still trying to consummate.

Whatever the contributions of science and secularism to eighteenth-century blandness, the Romantic rediscovery of the primitive was accompanied in esthetics by the rediscovery of the somewhat terrifying "sublime" as opposed to the merely "beautiful." Figures as diverse as Kant and Burke were suggesting that we ballast our pleasant perceptions of baroque harmony with the ragings of the sea, awe-fulness to help us recover some sense of the sacred. Two centuries on these suggestions still seem timely, and still difficult to pursue: the word "sacred," for example, stares at us somewhat blankly, having lost much of its "dreadfulness" through its long association with a Christianity of moral uplift. The problem is nicely exhibited in a line of Mircea Eliade's that Douglas quotes: "The sacred is at once sacred and defiled" (p. 8). Apart from the intrinsic difficulty of thinking a paradox, one sees trouble here: the first sacred translates the Latin *sacer*, which, until it too became decadent, carried the twofold meaning; the second sacred is the whited sepulcher of our day, emptied by single vision, which Eliade is even here trying to revive. Ethnology's answer to this tangle in the late nineteenth century was to import the Polynesian word *mana* to denote divine energy, the stuff itself, which may then be either sanctifying or polluting, depending on the circumstances. There is much to be said for *mana*: it is short, travels light, sounds good. The problem, as the look of it suggests—one thinks of manna—is in its cheerfulness: at its most relaxed it is the animistic energy that moves through all creation, which then builds up at certain points and in certain individuals to a "supernatural" concentration of Luck. One has to read closely in Durkheim (1915), for example, its chief proponent, to find that *mana* calls for fear and respect as well as thanks; and more recently, Mary Douglas (1966), who has helped us all to understand pollution better, is still somewhat lulled by its friendliness.

Instead of *mana* the word I use in this book is *pneuma,* an ancient Greek word that carries like *mana* the notion of divine energy, but along with it some degree of "awefulness"; and in what follows I shall discuss the etymology of the three principal words built upon *neu*: *pneuma,* wind or breath, *neuma,* nod, and *neuron,* sinew. From these three rather elementary and apparently unpromising notions much of our fundamental experience of the divine can be seen to evolve. What they share is *movement,* the radical aspect of divinity, that it breaks through the pattern of what stands; and changes it, for good or for ill.[1] Wind is movement itself, a natural opening for the divine: when the god nods he unleashes power that brings order or disorder; and when the sinew ties or unties, things are made either to stand anew or to fall. The wind is perhaps man's oldest divinity, and behind the nod I shall identify the bull, and behind the sinew, the snake. Thus wind, bull, and snake, aboriginal magic. Although the discussion of these three will necessarily be abstract and somewhat discontinuous, I hope it will both provide a general introduction to the subject and convince the reader that *pneuma* is well qualified to stand as the word evoking our engagement with the supernatural.

2

Let us try to begin at the beginning. For perhaps two million years, man wandered the African savannah without much more than his big brain to distinguish him from his chimpanzee cousins. Why he didn't use this brain to build much more than baskets and hand-axes is a question that still troubles ethnology; but even though he didn't build anything that we would call "culture" until very recently, relatively speaking, he was quite certainly learning to think.

The most important, the most interesting, and the most difficult thought we have ever pursued is the one about divinity. Ethnologists agree that man everywhere first meets the divine as that which *animates* the world, provides its zest, sparkle, energy, power, oomph—that invisible something that distinguishes the quick from the dead, the vivid from the dull, the waxing from the waning. What animates the world is *anima,* Latin for soul or breath (corresponding to the Greek *psyche*); and if man's soul is his breath, then the world's soul is God's breath (*ruach elohim* in Hebrew), the wind in fact, the breath of life, *pneuma biou.* [2] According to Professor Cornford (*From Religion to Philosophy*, 1951, p. 189), the absolutely important Greek word *phusis* = Nature (akin to *phusao* = to blow and *phuo* = to grow or generate) was originally understood as the almost liquid energy that animates all things—much like Polynesian *mana.*

Imagine yourself back on the savannah. A light wind rustles through the trees in the heat of the day, lifting the oppressive stillness: a bird flickers, dull spirits revive; life is returning. In the foreground perhaps, an expiring animal: the chest rises and falls, and then is still; life is departing. Invisible, ubiquitous, unpredictable, formless, the breath of life may well convey our first intimations of divinity.

In historical times the idea that man's soul is his breath is very old indeed, as old as the creation stories in which man is fashioned of clay and breathed into life by the gods. The idea that the world itself may issue from the mouth of a breathing god arises not, as one might think, with the god of Genesis, but some two thousand years earlier in Egypt when Ptah renounced spitting and masturbation as creative techniques and replaced them with words issued by the tongue.[3]

If the breath of god may carry the ineffable world-creating words, and indeed the music with which man mimes it, it more obviously knows a harsh register in the winds of mockery and destruction. Fair winds scatter the seeds on their way to rebirth and speed our bonny boats to the place we desire; and yet they can turn foul in a moment, leaving life simply devastated. Ever-present yet invisible, instantly changeable and unpredictable, ranging from the sweetest caress to the most tempestuous blast, the wind has always been one of divinity's favorite names.

The Jews have always known this, and Yahwe was basically a wind god, as befits a desert people tuned to the ear. Zeus too began as a weather god, but the Greeks got beyond such primitive (one might even say "existential") theology as soon as they decently could. They preferred to house their gods in temples, where they could keep an eye on them. And yet, when the Jewish Jesus came to blow down what was left of their temples (with what St. Paul called "foolishness to the Greeks"), the ancient *pneuma* was waiting in the wings, ready for another distinguished career as *hagion pneuma*, the Holy Spirit of the New Testament. The bias of this book toward the primitive should be evident throughout. Thus proper gods are weather gods, and when they become too sophisticated and urbanly grand to bother with the weather, something crucial gets lost (and they tend to stop dancing). Country people (and sailors) still know that they meet divinity daily in the changing weather: town-dwellers tend to forget this, and when they do they get muddled. Thus to Nietzsche's sage advice that we should "Never trust a god who doesn't dance" (the epigraph to Chapter 4), one might add "Nor one who ignores the weather." Christian theology has over the centuries been uncomfortable with the unpredictable windiness of the Holy Spirit, and Jesus does not dance. This I personally find regrettable since Jesus has so profound a hold on my own imagination; and I would venture to suggest that this primitive "absence" dismays a good many other people as well. However, Christianity comes chronologically too late to be seriously addressed in this book: the nearest we get to Jesus is Dionysus and Osiris (in Chapter 7), but that is nearer than one might think.

3

"Pn" is a somewhat breathy sound, perhaps not congenial to the Greek tongue. All but one of the few other words beginning in this way concern the throat and its passage of breath.* Perhaps the "pn" blew in from Africa, long ago, kindness of Egyptian Ptah. In any case, by removing the "p" one removes the breathiness, and one is left with *neuma,* the nod whereby a god makes his will known to the eye. By erasing the "p" we move from the wind god who is heard to the temple god who is seen. But though *pneuma* is stronger magic than *neuma,* it is much simpler; and so, perversely perhaps, we move from a brief discussion of the wind to a lengthy and rather complex treatment of the nod.

Nod? One tends to smile, thinking immediately of noddy, noddle, and nodding off, the foolish carnivalesque parodies of something most serious. And yet one can still find something serious in the idea of being "given the nod": one thinks of a courtroom—or a gang of Mafia thugs—and the time for talking is past: in some very simple and important sense one is about to be either affirmed or struck down.

The ambiguity is crucial. In olden days when the emperor nodded he inclined his head, deferring ever so slightly to something (not us): in giving us the nod he gave us either our life or our death, which meant they were his to bestow. His giving may well be a

---

*The possible exception is the *Pnyx,* the sovereign assembly (*ecclesia*) of all the Athenian citizens: perhaps so called because here the *voice* of the people was heard.

taking, or at least a commanding, that we now go and do what the court has prescribed. But to command is also to commend, both deriving from the Latin *mandare*, literally to give to the hand, to entrust: *mandamus* is an ancient legal form that orders us and thereby gives us order, giving into our hands something for safekeeping and execution—and at the same time, threatening us if we fail. The same thing happens (in reverse, as it were) when we *mandate* a politician to do our "bidding" (another word that means both to order and to offer).

The ambiguity of the nod is nicely mirrored in the hand that does its bidding. The open hand that gives is yielding and nourishing, whereas the closing hand that takes is aggressive and debilitating. Perfectly ambiguous is the hand that holds, which may either be keeping something safe from loss or arresting its freedom of movement (as a prelude to something worse). Thus two hands originally, the mothering hand that feeds and protects, and the predatory hand that grasps and mutilates; and it may be of more than passing interest which of these two is reflected in a culture's language. One can see both in the Germanic languages, where the old Germanic *mund* (which means both hand and protection) gives way to *hand* (which derives from catching and grasping). The Greek hand, *cheir*, is remarkably predatory and disturbing in its etymology (as a quick glance at its cognates will indicate), whereas the Latin hand *manus* would seem to be the opposite (Latin *mamma* = breast).

It is tempting to notice in this connection the ancient Germanic alternation from wooded mysticism to remarkable ferocity, the Greek tendency to associate handicrafts with slaves and foreigners, and the early Roman reverence for husbandry, Cincinnatus with his *hands* on the plow; but such thoughts are both playful and unscholarly. In any case we were discussing the head and its nod, and the important point for us moderns to grasp is that although the head was "above" the hand for the ancients, more venerable and more significant, this was not because it harbored what we revere as brain power. Early Latin and Greek both located what we would call "consciousness" and "will" in the chest area of heart and lungs; but what the head *was* thought to contain and produce—perhaps commemorating our early taste for raw brains—was the seed of life, both the actual generative marrow, which is "blown" down the spinal cord and into the genitals, and also the abstract powers, *pneuma* indeed, the force that gathers and scatters.[4] Thus sneezing, for example, was seen as a divine disturbance that called for "Bless you!," and the nod was seen as a mysteriously controlled or voluntary sneeze, an activation of the immortal parts essential to godly oath-swearing. From sneeze to nod is a long way, from being the passive creature of the higher powers to being actively on terms with them. When man is sufficiently confident ceremonially to swear an oath and seal it not just with a hand but with a nod (the verb *neuo* means both to nod and to promise), he aspires to be in touch with the higher powers that control time future; and culture is truly looking up.

The process whereby the early Greeks and Romans acquired such confidence may be traced in the gradual elevation of man's executive center from the moist and breathy chest cavity (where the ancient *pneuma* blew upon his *thumos*) to include the head where some of the imperishable stuff was actually generated and contained in the divinity of his *psyche*. This complex story has been well told by Professor R. B. Onians in his much underrated *Origins of European Thought* (1951). What can be said here is that throughout the early ancient world the hand was the mortal servant of the "mortal soul" in the chest cavity, and that heads were the sacred vessels not of the "brain-power" we moderns revere but of what one might almost call "wind power," the unfathomable divinities of life and death in the realm of *psyche*. Such high-powered heads were of course not ours but the gods', and our attempt to take possession of them began in the temples where we propitiated the nodding heads of the divine statues.

4

It was suggested earlier, somewhat unseriously, that the nod is what you get when you remove the breathy "p" from *pneuma,* a linguistic mimesis of the process whereby the ubiquitous wind god is housed in a temple, given local habitation and a name, and thereby rendered visible and negotiable. The serious matter behind this is the shift from the wind god of the aural and iconoclastic Jews to the temple gods of the visual Greeks, unfortunately beyond the scope of this work. What we can ask, however, is why a god who is thought to be at home in a temple should be so concerned with nodding.

Greek temples address themselves to the eye, and so too does the statue of the god within. These statues were originally aniconic (faceless), but in the end all the features were portrayed. Given that the gods are, to the primitive mind, essentially invisible and discarnate, "pneumatic" one might even say, the boldness of such visual representation is very striking—and troubling. Is the god in the statue? The answer has to be yes and no, he comes and he goes. Can the wood or the stone be alive? Sometimes. When it is, its liveliness will be registered in the most minimal of gestures, the miraculous nod that fleetingly animates the inanimate, and will be perceived only by those who have piously called it forth. This is not easy for us moderns to imagine, but since the statues were originally made of wood, recalling the trees that had preceded them as objects of worship, one might see behind the nodding statue the stately tree sometimes animated by its rustling leaves, the divinity of *pneuma* in the wind. The Romans were even more taken with the nod (*numen* in Latin) than were the Greeks, and *numen* is cognate with Numa, the legendary king who was said to have been the original lawgiver of Rome, and to have visited the great goddess in her sacred wood (*nemus*) for counsel and inspiration. The goddess was called *Nemorensis*, and *nemesis* was what she unleashed on those who violated her order. The temple in question was at Nemi, which the reader may recall as the centerpiece of Frazer's *The Golden Bough,* and which is discussed in Chapter 7 of this book. A *nemus* (Greek *nemos*) was a woodland grove, and Nemi with its sacred tree recalls the very old practice of tree-worship, prevalent throughout Europe. The evolution from tree-sanctuary to temple proper represents an important shift from Nature to culture, nicely commemorated in the treelike stone pillars of the temples: Arthur Evans found ample evidence of a "tree and pillar" cult in Minoan Crete, and Burkert (*Greek Religion*, 1985) suggests that nearly all Greek temples were originally tree-sanctuaries, usually sited near running water.[5]

A stand of trees (*nemos*), which especially in hot climates often appears by the waterside, seems a natural place to begin. Offering shade and refreshment to the shepherd and his flock, it invites us to pause in our labors and give ourselves briefly to simple enchantment. The trees stand rooted with enviable strength in the earth, and yet their upper branches are soughing gracefully in the wind, harboring birds and perhaps memories of when we used to live there, before things became complicated. To stand among them is to stand sheltered and protected, hidden from without, partaking of some secret within. It will occur to us that only a privileged being, unlike us, could dwell at ease in such a favored spot, and that we should be properly grateful visitors, which we might indicate by pouring a libation to the presiding spirit. To this simple notion of gratitude will soon be added the countervailing idea of punishable trespass if we fail; and as the notion of propriety expands into property, we shall seek to guard this lucky spot from those who are not our kin.[6]

But what essentially guards our Luck is piety, the gratitude we remember to express whenever we visit the sacred precincts. Heidegger believes that giving was originally not a giving-away (of surplus) but a giving-to or accession, a rendering up of what belongs.[7] This seems right: in the libation we give back to divinity some part of itself, commemorating chiefly our gratitude for the food it furnishes, through which both our luck and our life itself (also its gifts) are sustained. One might call this "original piety," and it is easily seen that it consists principally in *remembering* something we might be disposed to forget. Hence *Mnemosyne,* the mother goddess of Memory, may properly come to dominate our woodland grove, as the *nemos* in her name suggests. There is aptness here, for trees not only live a long time but keep a remembrance in their rings of the passing weather. Mnemosyne, daughter of Heaven (Ouranos) and Earth (Gaia), associated with water, mother of the nine dancing Muses, is perhaps the most important of the goddesses who suffered neglect under the Olympian dispensation.

Our word "memory" is from the Latin *memoria* and *memor* = mindful, the act of calling to and bearing in mind. That such calling and bearing is essentially involved with gratitude is something we have largely forgotten, even though it survives in such cognates as memorial and commemoration. That the Greeks remembered Mnemosyne as mother of the Muses would suggest that the arts originate in grateful remembrance of what we have been given, and that indeed they call upon us, as the Psalm sings, to "make a joyful noise unto the Lord, all ye lands."[8]

Remembrance remains central when we come to establish the law, which is concerned with *keeping* what has been laid down. Keeping, like the "laying down" of the law which we shall discuss presently, is an extremely important word, and it takes the *Oxford English Dictionary* five pages to do it justice. Its etymology runs from seeing to desiring to grasping to nourishing to protecting to cherishing . . . and on and on: in short, it seems to carry within it a veritable essay on man's estate. I mention it here because its relations with both appetite and regulation (mediated by the hands) provide a good setting in which to consider briefly the origin of the principal Greek word for law. The word is *nomos*, very close to the woodland *nemos*: like her Latin counterpart at Nemi, the tree goddess of the *nemos* will commend to her people a just dispensing (*nomē*) and apportioning (*nemein*) of goods, rights, and ranks. One of the first and most important things to be apportioned among a pastoral people is indeed pasture, which is the original meaning of *nomos*, that portion of food-bearing land (we still call it "keep") through which my sheep may safely graze.[9] With a supremely judicious sense of metaphor, the Greeks also used "*nomos*" to designate song or melody, that portion of structured time through which my emotions (and perhaps my dancing body) may safely range in search of nourishment without fear of being ecstatically carried away.

The word that comes after *nomos* in the lexicon is *noos* or *nous*, the mind, and though the etymological links are obscure,[10] others are less so. If *nomos* is the divinely appointed place where first my sheep and then my socially constituted being may abide and range for their enrichment, *nous* for Plato was the place where my reflective or spiritual being may abide and range over the idea of Justice, what was left of divinity in classical Athens. To abide is not only to dwell but to remain true to, and such constancy in our relations with both *nomos* and *nous* is instinct with remembrance.[11] Unsurprisingly enough, pre-eminent among the things remembered by *nous*, according to Plato, is *nomos*:

> There is, in truth, no study whatsoever so potent as this of law . . . to make a better man of its student—else t'would be for nothing that the law *which so stirs our worship and wonder* [italics mine] bears a name so cognate with that of understanding. (*Laws* XII, 957)

To be stirred to "worship and wonder" one must be studying something more than the local pasturing by-laws: indeed one may be studying a Platonic dialogue in which all local considerations soon yield to the search for the divine laws of truth and beauty. Such arcane worship is a long way from the temple (where bodies perform ritual actions) and in the view of many "right-thinking" citizens is not worship at all (one remembers Socrates, executed for impiety). This passage from *The Laws* was written in old age, and its hyperbole suggests a man somewhat anxious about the distance his earlier "thoughtfulness" may have taken him from traditional piety—indeed *The Laws* often have a penitential air. The movement from religion to philosophy as mediated in Plato's dialogues lies outside the scope of this work, but one can easily see that the move from *nomos* to *noos* is a radical one, involving much more than the removal of an "m"; and hence one can understand Plato's anxiety that his earlier "thoughtfulness" may have wandered too far from the ritual certainties of the body politic, may even have offended the divinities he had hoped to serve. (Modern secularists scandalized by the very idea of associating thoughtfulness with piety should be reminded that the Old English for thought is *thanc*; and modern soi-disant philosophers scandalized by the very idea of associating

Plato with religiousness should be reminded that Plato was much influenced by Pythagoras, who was not only a brilliant mathematician but also a shaman.)[12]

Something more can be said here of *noos'* religious background, its links with *neuma*. Onians suggests *neomai* as the etymological bridge that may help us to understand how thinking (*noeo*) was a kind of praying for Plato. *Neomai* (which contracts to *neumai*) means either to come or to go. One word for such contraries? Ah, but nodding (*neuma*) is similarly a sign of either greeting or departure, of bidding or dismissal. Taken together, they give us the essence of the temple (*neos* or *naos*) as the dwelling place of the gods who come and go, whose going is implicit in their coming, mysteriously present in their absence, and absent in their presence. What calls the gods forth into our presence, animating the inanimate statue, is the invocation: we call upon (bid) them to call upon us, a complex mutuality in which each commends what the other commands. Something similar happens at the dismissal: "O Lord, now lettest thou thy servant depart in peace," even as we release thee from our calling. And whenever the Christian encounters his god in the church, either visually in the altar cross or verbally in naming him, he bows his head.

One should not be lulled by the dulcet tones of the now venerable *Nunc Dimittis* into forgetting the enormity of what is at stake here. To invoke divine power is always dangerous because it may overflow the container provided by the ritual invocation, cursing instead of commending the human presumption that called it forth. If the ritual be improperly conducted, blasphemy is near, and overspill virtually certain. A somewhat grotesque reminder of this concludes Mozart's *Don Giovanni*, where the nodding statue of the Commendatore, called by the Don to supper, almost scares Leporello to death before it seizes the soul of the blasphemer. However improbable one finds this religious irruption onto the secular stage, it calls forth some of Mozart's finest and most harrowing music.

The earliest gods were invoked by a ritual act (*dromenon* = the thing done) such as a sacrificial dance, commemorating the fact that our life begins and ends when they call upon us. Subsequently the thing was said (*legomenon*) as well as done, and the *dromenon* was on its way to becoming the *drama*. Once speech within the temple precincts has been endowed with the power of word-magic, we have "the invocation" properly so called. But the calling forth of the gods is also a calling to mind, a remembering; and in such calling, as Heidegger persuasively argues, we may find the origins of poetry, the making of significant speech, *Dichtung*.[13] By the time we get to Plato, what is invoked by significant speech are the eternal forms of truth and beauty, called by memory before the mind, recalled. From *dromenon* to *legomenon* and from *nomos* to *noos,* what remains constant is the coming and going (*neomai*) of divinity, always dangerous; for just as ritual blood improperly drawn pollutes all present, so the logos improperly thought casts the thinker away from truth (*aletheia*) into the polluting waters of the river Lethe, the oblivion of ignorance, death to the spirit.

Whether directed at the gods, the forms of truth, or one's fellow man, calling originates. To call is both to summon and to identify: they meet in the notion of calling as vocation, in which one is summoned to take up a working identity or profession. To be called is to be named, to be granted being, to become substantial. When a thing is given a name it is drawn within the clearing of intelligibility as something that is ordered and disposed to act in certain ways. Conversely to lose one's good name is to fall from grace, to become disordered, to be banished from the clearing of what is known and commended. Ultimately, calling or naming is what separates what is from what is not: as the rite of baptism still suggests, it comes at the beginning. To be given a name (*onoma* or *nomen*) is to be granted pasture and abode (*nomos*), an ordering of one's affairs that gives access to and grounds for fearing the law (*nomos*). It is what the nod essentially does: *numen nominat*, the nod names.

If calling is the aural equivalent of the nod that names, one would expect it to have a reasonably impressive etymology; and indeed this is so. The Greek verb for calling is *kaleo*, and in its middle-voiced perfect tense (= to have been called) it simply means "to be." The *kal*-root in *kaleo* makes one think of *kalos* = beautiful or good, which might suggest to the inquiring mind that what the gods call forth in the beginning is the goodness of the beautiful. Could this be so? I think it very likely. The first thing the gods call forth is the *kosmos*, a word that includes the idea of beauty in its etymology, according to Professor Guthrie (1957, p. 107); and then within the cosmos things are called upon to "appear" (*epiphainein*), whose literal meaning is "to shine forth."

If to appear is to shine forth, this presupposes a surrounding darkness (or chaos) from which the shining thing emerges; and such appearances, like the stars, have always been thought exemplary in their beauty, and hedged by divinity, as our word epiphany still indicates. When one adds to this the fact that beautiful things that appear in the *kosmos* are mortal and do not stay long (*mors longa, vita brevis*), one comes near the notion that things that are named into being are called from their usual hiddenness to shine forth in their beauty. Thus, in the beginning the real *is* the beautiful, and it was only sometime later, as Hesiod relates it, that Zeus released among men, in punishment for Promethean excess, the unreal but thoroughly disagreeable apparitions of ugliness and villainy. Plato stands firmly within the archaic inheritance of his language when he asserts that Beauty, Truth, and Virtue are the divinities that alone call upon man's best energies, and that the ugliness of villainy should never be accounted "real."

Lexical support for the antiquity of such thinking comes from the fact that only two radical verbs are built upon *kal*: *kaleo* = to call, and *kalupto* = to cover or conceal. Are these not primordial contraries? The *-upto* in *kal-upto* is akin to *uptioo* = to turn over, and *uptios* = with the underside uppermost: thus to cover or conceal something is to conceal that which enables it to shine forth, its *kal-*, its beauty; and you do this by turning its underside uppermost, inside out, or back to front. At this point we are not far from the idea (discussed in Chapter 5) of beauty as something normally hidden that may be induced to reveal itself to the lucky pilgrim or the diligent man of culture.[14]

5

With these glimpses of Plato and some sense of how speech gradually usurps the role of action and silence in our relations with divinity, we have got ahead of our story. Let us then reverse direction and push back toward those conjectural beginnings that compose our central concern. The gap that separates *numen* from *nominat* may at first seem small but it is radical: from silence to speech, from gesture to language. Before we fell into verbality, before we began talking in the temple, indeed before we even began thinking of constructing a temple, there was a god in whose almost imperceptible and certainly beautiful nod we found ourselves utterly challenged, to find at once a name for him and for ourselves. Who was it?

It was the bull, the major god of neolithic culture, standing still and staring at us. If he decides we are worthy of his closer attention he drops his horns a fraction, bidding us then to reveal with what grace we can bear his intimacies. So long as we run we are as nothing in his sight; but the day that we stand our ground is an extraordinary day, when we dare to make ourselves *manifest,* to show what our hands can make of his head. What finer show could be imagined, what better reply, than to place our hands on his head or his horns and spring over him? This seems to be exactly what the Minoans did in ancient Crete.[15]

The lowering head is a gesture whose meaning is deeply imprinted throughout the animal kingdom—even today's overdomesticated dog understands it. Its human equivalent is the lowering brows, the frown, the contracting of the corrugator muscles. Our word lower, or lour, derives from the Middle German *luren* = to lie in wait—the element of fatal attraction emerges in the English lure and lurid. The bull's lour is the finest in creation: which is surely one of the reasons why he dominated the field in Europe and the Near East from early neolithic times until the theriomorphic (animal) gods consented at last to appear in human form. And even when they did so consent, many of them long continued to be crowned with horns. Thus the dangerousness of the nod reaches back for thousands of years, as far as may be.

Almost as disturbing as the bull, at least to the primitive Greeks, and even more primitive, is the snake. Although the bull's horns look like rearing snakes, ready to lower and strike, the bull and his horns *stand* in a way the snake never does: indeed the snake's magic derives essentially from his almost-liquid shapelessness, his refusal to stand. Almost utterly formless (or as we would say, utterly flexible) with no legs to stand on, he nonetheless moves with incredible speed and lethal accuracy. Mostly unseen, and when seen, unintelligible, known only when he bites you, he is the most flagrant meditation on power itself, the immediate movement from nothing to one. [16]

As the bull is to the nod, so the snake is to our third and final meditation, the sinewing *neuron*. The most snake-like aspect of the human body is the spinal cord, the major sinew, though the analogy may be less apparent to us than to the Indian yogis who, from earliest times, located "the serpent power" in the backbone and focused their meditations upon it. The Greeks believed that the spinal cord transmitted the generative marrow from the brain to the genitals and after death turned into a snake. [17] We believe that it centers and animates with amazing speed the movements of the body; and that along with the lesser nerves and tendons, it structures, orders, and enlivens the various members. Both parties would agree that, though themselves virtually shapeless, the sinews shape and bind the parts of the body into a functional unity.

Outside the body, animal sinew is like a piece of string, a cord, a shapeless bit of nothing much that may have been our first tool, particularly if, as scholars increasingly think, we began with baskets for collecting berries rather than axes for chopping at what resists us. Sinew then, or cord, though nothing itself, is the original tie that binds, that gathers the many into one, whether it be rushes into basket, wood-burning sticks into faggot, ax-head to handle, or three staves into tripod. Thus even without the serpentine analogy, or indeed any knowledge of anatomy (which would have come fairly early), the sinew is strong medicine. As the material equivalent of the nod, it calls the world of artifacts into being, provides the structure that orders the parts of a thing into an intelligible shape, making it nameable and portable. (The first versions of Wallace Stevens's jar would have been baskets bound together by sinew.) Conversely, when the sinew is loosed, it returns the thing to chaos; and although it does not move with the speed of a snake, it does possess the uncanny power to change instantaneously the thing it ties or unties from a nothing to a something, or vice versa. In view of all this, it is not surprising to find the sacred knot as an important symbol in all the ancient religions.

The Greek word for sinew is *neuron*: together with *neuo* (to nod or promise), it exhausts the list of radical words built upon *neu* in the lexicon. As with the small number of *kal-* words, one is tempted to imagine that in the ancient days they threw off such an aura, such strong magic, that the Greek tongue was forbidden to use their sound to form any other words. This aura is discernible in the fact that the sinew particularly denoted by *neuron* is the one we have long called "the Achilles tendon," the one that disables. Readers of Robert Graves's *White Goddess* will remember that the hobbling of Hephaestos (the Greek smith) looked back to the very ancient practice of hobbling the smith-king (like blinding the seer) in order to ensure humility, to prevent the fire-magician from forging himself wings, Icarus-like, to challenge the gods.

The next meaning of *neuron* is metaphorical—"strength, vigor, nerve"; which recalls the yogis and their serpent power.[18] After that comes the bowstring (and the string that ties the arrowhead to its shaft). The bow and arrow are very old, perhaps fifteen thousand years, and again, very magical: not only do they "name" their targets with inordinate fluency, but imagine how suddenly the bowstring abstracted and distanced man from the object of his violence, how certainly it gave him intimations of godliness, immortality. He-who-strikes-from-afar, an Homeric epithet of Apollo, is surely one of the first names for the sky god: on a good day the bowstring must have made even the snake look pedestrian.[19]

The final meaning of *neuron* is the musical string. Which came first, the bow or the lyre? We might well wonder, but will never know. In any case the Greeks associated them, from earliest days, as emblems and instruments of transformational magic. The bow (*biós*) is taken from the tree of life (*bíos*), deals death, which in turn feeds life: hence the Heraclitean aphorism "*biós*, *bíos*." The musical string, analogously, requires a dismemberment to procure the *neuron* and the tortoise shell on which it may be strung[20]; and yet it produces the sweetest thing man knows, which may nonetheless lead him astray. Moreover, the extraordinary airborn immateriality of music, together with its capacity to charm and entrance, properly associates it with fairyland and the spirit world, as the Orpheus story suggests. Thus both bow and lyre, precision instruments that invisibly master the air, surprise and disarm the objects of their attention, "take them out of themselves" as it were, and embark them on a voyage that may lead, in one sense or another, through a death to new life.[21]

Kairos, a wonderful Greek word, referred originally to the opening or cleft that an arrow must find with sufficient precision and power to reach its destination. From there it became "fitness" or "appropriateness," either in space (the proper spot) or in time (the right moment, in season). Metaphorically it came to mean an opening or opportunity, a passage to new life. As such it rides the string of music as happily as the bow, and the sexual note appears crude by comparison.[22] Aristocratic Apollo, perhaps the most formidable of the Olympians, was known as *neurocharays*, delighting in bowstring or lyre, and in his hands the two instruments became almost interchangeable. Very soon after his birth he gravely announced to the attendant goddesses: "Dear to me shall be lyre and bow, and in my oracles I shall reveal to men the inexorable will of Zeus."[23] To be master of both bowstring and lyre is to be some kind of warrior-poet, uniting those virtues whose separation is discussed in Chapter 4 with regard to alpha-shaman; and the aristocratic Apollo is an obvious inspiration for the Renaissance courtier, the gentleman who makes both love and war.

Both lyre and bow meditate magically on the straightened sinew that also moves, and behind both of them is the simple stave or stick, our first weapon and venerable symbol of culture's power to subdue chaotic movement (still evident in the king's scepter). Just as the backbone houses and disposes the serpent power that runs in the spinal cord, so the stave symbolizes our aspiration to arrest the dangerous movements of the foreign and the unintelligible (and it actually protects us from snakes as we walk along the path). Hermes's magic wand was the snake-entwined caduceus, and the musical worshippers of Dionysus carried the almost-serpentine *thyrsos*, a lethal wand entwined with ivy and vine leaves. Just as the snake is revered for his ability to enter dark, secret, and inaccessible places through small or invisible openings, so the magical wand is much concerned with opening doors (as the etymology of *thyrsos* would suggest) that are usually closed or forbidden, most obviously the door into the ground between life and death, but also the one between present and future. Thus wands, bows, and lyres are all concerned with *kairos*, opening the door to what is not here.

6

Before we leave the *neuron* there is one more matter to consider. If, as I have suggested, sinew as "the tie that binds" lies at the very beginning of human culture, the world we *make*, one might expect to find it figuring prominently in the etymology of law-making, which becomes perhaps the most important of our abstract artifacts. That is to say, just as one finds the letters *neu* shared by the primitive *neuron* and the commanding *neuma*, so when one comes to the relatively late idea of law, one might expect to find some trace of the sinew preserved in it. This is indeed the case in Latin, but in Greek the sinew is difficult to discern.

In classical Greece the main word for law was *nomos*, which, as we have seen, derives from the allotted pasture within which my flock may freely range. In this we can see the fundamental idea of orderly apportionment, but nothing either complex or harrowing; and that is because *nomos* can be traced to the nomadic pastoral Hellenic invaders, violent and cheerful. Buried beneath it, as it were, is the older Pelasgian *thesmos*, the law of the pre-Hellenic farmers, a much more cautious, even fearful, undertaking bound by curses and taboos. Crudely put, crops are more fragile than flocks, settlers more anxious than nomads. Draco's laws, "written in blood" as they said, were *thesmoi*: Solon's, far less anxious, were *nomoi*. In sum, though the *nomos* carried the day (as the invaders always do), it had to miscegenate with the darker defeated *thesmos*—and also with the bonds of fate, *peirata,* as we shall see presently.

Thesmos means literally "a thing laid down," a live piglet planted as fertility token along with the seed at the most ancient of annual Greek festivals, *Thesmophoria,* which literally means "the carrying of the thing laid down." Why emphasize the carrying? Because seed must be carried to the place of its planting, just as the harvest must be carried, stored, and again brought forth before it can enrich our bodies.[24] In fact, the idea of carrying or bearing is contained in the idea of fruitfulness in Greek, Latin, and English: the tree *bears* the fruit that we then *bear* home in our basket. The pun is absolutely intentional, perhaps because the carrying to and fro is the contribution of our hands to the mysterious process whereby the earth enriches us.

But there is also a pre-agricultural strand. From our earliest nomadic days, wealth was the surplus you could carry, and plunder was what you could carry off and hang up on some tree as fruitfulness and display, or on an oak post, as early Greek warriors did.[25] The inverse of booty is the gift you bear, a thing carried, manifested, and laid down before the recipient. More generally, in both ritual and epistemological terms, for a thing truly to *be* and be valued, it must be shown, figured forth, brought forward into the light or the sacred circle and set down.[26] And even further back, in the beginning, to be is to be animated, which means movement: my liveliness is most certainly manifest as I carry my body over the ground. One could doubtless go on with this, but enough has been said to indicate that wealth, that which increases our life and substance, is something that must be both carried and laid down. And so is the law, that which orders us and gives us authority, conceived as the origin of everything that sustains and increases our substance and thereby keeps us safe from deprivation. What the law *authorizes* will *augment* our state, since both words derive from *augere* = to enlarge or increase.

Greek, Latin, and English agree that the law is that which is laid down, and the reason for my seemingly digressive remarks on carrying is that both laying and legislating preserve, as we shall see, the idea of handling and bearing. The Latin for law is *lex, legis,* from *legere* = to lay or assemble, and English law, which we are disposed to "lay down" when aroused, does indeed come from "lay." The Greek equivalent and parent of *legere* is *legein,* which issues in the *logos* and all things logical. *Legein* means to lay, gather, assemble, set forth in order, hence also to speak. Clearly the idea of laying lies as near the heart of culture as may be, and even a necessarily brief look at it now will give us some sense of its relation to binding.

The OED devotes no less than ten pages to its meanings. The most important for our purposes, a sense it shares with both *legein* and *legere,* is "to dispose or arrange in the proper position": laying a table is a daily ritual whose miscarriage threatens no more than bad manners in the management of greed, but impropriety in the laying of a keel or a foundation threatens something like original chaos to the religious mind—as indeed it does in the laying out of a corpse. Things improperly laid out or down are liable to be "laid into," one of the many violent senses the word carries. And before we have law we have ritual, that activity in which ghosts are laid (or raised) as things are set forth in order.

In all three languages laying involves gathering, which points to the storing, the laying down, of a harvest or buried treasure (and subsequently the depositing, the laying aside, of money): all of these bring to mind the idea of keeping, which we met in connection with *nomos*. And just as a keel or a foundation is laid for the construction of shelter whereby life may be kept safe, so a "lay" is a lair or lodging or bed—even marriage-bed (Greek *lexos*)—where the seed may be safely planted and nurtured, where the mother may "lie in" with the child she carries, and where life, whether animal or vegetable, may be renewed through rest. Not least of the rich ambiguities in this notion is that it points not only to the darkness where treasure may be laid down for safekeeping but also to the light of legality (and the dinner table) where propriety may be set forth and made visible to all; and whereas the light side of this word is instinct with actions that originate and take hold, the dark side has to do with passivity and letting go. The dark side is clearly dependent on the light—one would not lay treasure, wine, or oneself down without protective steps having been taken—but is the light also dependent on the dark? Must one let go in order to take hold? Ancient piety would tend to say yes, whereas modern secularism would tend to say no. Heidegger, of the former tendency, is particularly concerned with the laying exemplified in speaking (*legein*), and argues persuasively that we should understand it as a "letting-lie-together-before." I think he overemphasizes the passive (or receptive) moment in the Greek making of linguistic order, but I also think that in view of the unbending modern mind he is rhetorically right to do so.[27]

The Romans took the law (and the hand that bears it) more seriously than the Greeks, and hence it is not surprising to find them binding it explicitly with sinew. Consider the following verbs:

lego   *legere*—to gather, assemble, lay
lego   *legare*—to legislate
ligo   *ligare*—to bind

Ligo provides the ligament that binds what has been gathered by *legere* into the legislating of *legare*. More dramatic is the very primitive symbol of the Roman body politic, the *fasces,* that bundle (*fascis*) of sticks bound together by a sinew or ligament and carried by the *lictors* (*ligo* again) before the chief magistrates. When Roman laws were made they were carried (*latum*), as the lictorial procession would suggest, and hence the English lawmaker is a legis-*lator,* a carrier of the law, which in turn gives us our bearings, those lines that direct us to our proper place. Thus the law regulates orderly movement, movement that ensures rather than disrupts stability as its magic ligament gathers and binds the many into one body. And just as law issues originally from the temple, so religion (*re-ligio*) arises as that body of words and gestures whereby we ritually renew, by remembering, the bonds that tie us to each other and our ground. What gets put together in this way is the public thing, *res publica*.

Behind the metaphors of an elaborated culture, a primitive bundle (*fascis*) tied into thinghood by a ligament. Among the earliest representations of it are the sacred reed bundle, symbol of Sumerian Inanna (ca. 3000 B.C.) and the strikingly similar sacred knot of the Minoan goddess.[28] Partridge links the root *fasc* to Middle Irish *basc*, a neck-band or collar, hence perhaps basket, which, as we noticed earlier, may be the original thing made, the ultimate carrier. What he doesn't mention is *fas*, a much stronger Latin word than *numen* for divine command. To command is to collar, to tie up, to unify: what unifies the *fascis* is what literally puts a collar around it, so that the bundle may be carried or stored. It seems sensible to propose that this collaring is the commanding *fas* in *fascis*. This becomes more likely in view of the fact that the only other *fasc* words in Latin concern fascination, the casting of a spell over someone, which involves metaphorically "tying them up" and ordering them about. It becomes even more likely when one considers that the Greek equivalent and predecessor of *fascis* = bundle is *phakelos*, from which the important Latin verb *facio* = to make, would seem obviously to derive.[29] Thus *fascis* and the fascinating are the only things made in Latin that insert the "s" into the basic stem fac-, and this suggests to me the intervention of divine *fas*.

Lying nearby is *fingo* (past participle *fictus*), originally "to fashion in clay." The potter's wheel comes much later than the utterly primitive ligament, and its capacity to throw in quick and magical succession pot after similar pot brings to mind the idea of copying and simulation. From simulation to dissimulation is no distance at all, which is why *fingo* picks up all the makings of make-believe that end in deception, leading to the idea of *fiction* as the invented unreal. But *fingo* and *facio* coexisted happily enough in Latin to meet in compound verbs of virtuous making that usually end in -*ficere*. The problems of deceit and fakery that arise with the making of copies from some original are of central importance in the construction of culture, and the question of twin sons detains us at some length in

Chapter 8. (Stevens's jar in the epigraph poem, though gray and bare, is an original, "like nothing else in Tennessee," which suggests that the wilderness it dominates will not be troubled by the problems of copying and forgery until some time later.)

But let us return to *fas*. Whether or not one thinks it belongs in *fascis,* it is manifestly a word of great strangeness and antiquity: monosyllabic, indeclinable, deriving from an old irregular deponent verb *fari* (to speak), it simply means "the gods permit" (commend and command), which, as we have seen, is the burden of the original nod. Its opposite *nefas* points not only to the forbidden but further back to the abominable. Man's life is portioned out between the *fas* and the *nefas*, and this we call his *fate* (also from *fari*), which in the very ancient Greek myth is represented by a line or thread of a certain length, which the three Fates, the *Moirai,* spin, measure, and cut. To represent human life as a length of sinew certainly recalls the *neuron* as serpent power, but it also points to the tying and untying of one's mortal substance: in effect, the length of your allotted sinew determines how big a bundle you can tie and carry, the size of your thing, what your hands can make of the nominating nod.

This myth incontestably originates in pre-patriarchal neolithic Greece, if not even further back, and its hold on the imagination was such that the Indo-European Zeus never managed to usurp the powers of these three goddesses; i.e., he could not alter the length of a man's allotted span, the day of his death. Homer is understandably unhappy about these three women but recognizes their power, particularly that of Atropos, the oldest, smallest, and nastiest, the killer woman. While the other two weighed and spun the thread, she it was who wove and knotted it into a net that she then threw over the individual as an encircling bond and bound, his luck and his unluck. The thread is of a gossamer fineness, visible only to the seer, but the knotted bonds, the *peirata,* are unspeakably strong. We register them still when we say of some enterprise "It is *bound* to fail." In the fate of Laocoön and his sons, the *peirata* are turned into python-like snakes, a brilliantly effective way of imagining the terrifying onrush of violent death, the closing of the net. Not unlike the serpentine *neuron, peirar* is originally rope or knot, the binding sinew of unalterable law that one looks for in vain in the background of the shepherding *nomos*. Like the *thesmos* at which we glanced earlier, the *peirata* issued from the old, Pelasgian farming culture, which the breezy Olympians came to overrule. The obvious metaphorical meaning for the *peirata* to take on is of boundary or limit, most significantly the line that demarcates the end or edge of the cosmos, separating it off from the boundless beyond, the *apeiron* that figures so importantly in the thought of Anaximander.[30]

Before leaving this myth we should notice that it lies behind not only the binding of unalterable law, man's mortality, but also the less drastic bindings or magical spells that are cast with such abundance throughout Greek mythology. Since the gods are immortal they cannot kill each other, and hence in their quarrels they settle for the next best thing, the physical incapacitation of the enemy with more or less elaborately magical sinews. In such stories we may trace the "negative" aspect of the *neuron*'s magical history, its harmful note: for just as when it "positively" binds three staves into a tripod it confers substance on chaos, liberates it into intelligibility for human use and carriage, so when it is applied negatively as a fetter upon living tissue it imprisons a life, reducing it (temporarily) to thinghood, paralyzing it for abuse. The ultimate refinement of such magic is the curse (*katodo* = I bind you down) wherein the crude material technologies of the *neuron* are superseded by what we call "word-magic," the voice rising above the hand to master the elements.[31]

7

The life-enhancing homologue of the curse is the promise, and by the time we get to Homer, the nod had evolved from its creative "nominating" origins to take up its central position within culture as "promising." When a god promises (*neuo*), he undertakes now how things shall stand in time future: it is effectively to bind time with a sinew, to prophesy, verbally to cast things now into the shape they will assume later. To do such a thing is clearly very powerful magic, and hence in Book I of the *Iliad* when Zeus seals his great oath with a nod, "the mightiest witness I can give," all of Olympus is shaken. This incident is alleged by several ancient authors to have been the inspiration for Pheidias's huge ivory and gold Zeus at Olympia, possibly the most impressive religious statue in the ancient world.[32]

Less cosmic in its implications is the promise one man makes to another. When he does so he binds himself now to a certain state of affairs later, and in such an undertaking one can discern the origins not only of lying and deception but also of human law. To be bound by the law is to promise over a certain period of time either to do or not to do certain things. In this sense the promise goes hand in hand with the curse, which is the promise of retribution.[33] I use the word "hand" advisedly, because this side of Olympus both promising and cursing take hold of time future, arrest its movement, with the hand as well as the head. Just as the long arm of the law arrests the accursed with a hand, so the promiser may give his hand as his gage, and this is the hand that carries the *thesmoi* (laws) that it lays down and keeps. This ambiguity of the sinewing hand is one of our simplest hominid memories, recalling the parental hand that cradles and protects as well as the predatory hand or claw that grabs. Such ambiguity is what the law enshrines as it moves the promise from the godly nod to the human world of earthly hands.

This discussion of the law's origins in carrying, keeping, binding, cursing, and promising is nicely collected in the Hebrew *akedah,* the knot that binds man to God and forms the covenant from whose carried Ark the law and the prophets will exfoliate. The first of these knots comes after the flood, but the most important in Jewish thinking is the sacrifice of Isaac, a binding in which the curse becomes a promise. In Christian thought Isaac is a figure for Christ, whose sacrifice combines and confounds the promise and the curse even more disturbingly.

In conclusion, let us remember *pneuma* and its proximity to nodding *neuma.* The "p" that distinguishes the wind god who gathers and scatters from the nodding statue in the temple points ultimately to a profound shift in religious experience: from Nature gods to culture gods, from ubiquity to localization, from the invisible to the visible, from the ear to the eye. But the disappearing "p" in fact alters the word very little, and this may remind us of the remarkable similarities between the gods denoted. Both nod and breath confer life (or death) in minimal gestures that lie just this side of speech, gestures that supply (or withdraw) the sources of animation. The nod silently calls as the breath invisibly sounds: like the *neuron* that lies before them, their business is with the tying of bundles into functioning integrities—and when the time is right, their untying. Perhaps it is because this tying and untying is at once so simple, so mysterious, and so significant, the bridging of being with nonbeing, that the Latins spoke of the *numen ineffabile*.

8

Last of our etymons, an appropriate coda for an extremely wordy essay, is the English neum (Latin *neuma*), a word that intends the undoing of words. As an element in medieval plainsong, the neum derives from *pneuma*, perhaps because it is sung in one breath, and it is defined in the French *Dictionary of Music* as follows:

> NEUM. s.f. A term in church music. The neum is a kind of short recapitulation of the air in a mode, which is made at the end of an antiphon, by a simple variety of sounds, and without joining to them any words. The Catholics authorize this singular custom on a passage of St. Augustine, who says that, no words being possible to be worthy of pleasing God, it is laudable to address him in a confused music of jubilation. "For to whom is such a jubilation suitable, unless to an ineffable Being? and how can we celebrate this ineffable Being, since we cannot be silent, or find anything in our transports that can express them, unless unarticulated sounds?"[34]

Itself a kind of coda, the neum both reiterates and abolishes (disarticulates, to be precise) the musical structure that precedes it, just as the words of the plainsong are disarticulated by the sounding of plain sound, the breathing of the breath of life, *pneuma biou*.

The neum is not only manifestly wonderful in itself, but singularly useful here as a reminder that what we have been discussing must in important ways elude us—the breath of life, after all, carries no words to fragment and imperil its precious cargo, just as the nod is both far too grand and far too busy to stop and explain itself. There are various ways of putting this: Augustine says God is ineffable, philosophers say existence is no predicate, and Derrida (following Mallarmé) says that words absent the things they name. What I would say, since this essay is now ending, is that it's perfectly all right to discuss the etymons of the sacred at considerable length so long as one ends with a neum reminding one that the thing itself has once again, luckily, escaped.

Kyrie eleison.

NOTES

SMALL CAPS

INTRODUCTION

1. Lyall Watson in *Heaven's Breath* (1985) says this is so in *every* language (p. 253).

2. As Lévi-Strauss (1964) says, "All ritual tends towards magic" (*Totemism*, p. 57).

3. For a lucid account of Frye's position, see Chapter 1 of his *The Great Code* (1982).

4. The Gulag, though somewhat Slavonic in derivation, was sufficiently like the Nazi death camp for both to be found substantially foreshadowed in Kafka, for example; but sufficiently unlike for me to confine my remarks here to the German instance.

5. For Plato and Aristotle on music see below (Chapter 5, note 21), but Milton said it perfectly: "Such sweet compulsion doth in music lie."

6. The immensely learned Rosen (*The Classical Style*, 1971) admits the "difficulty" both physical and structural of the post-Hammerklavier works, but this seems only to increase his admiration for them. What can one say? He should read Nietzsche, to be reminded that music is not primarily notation but something heard, and deeply heard. Or he should read Anthony Burgess, who knows about notation and yet also hears the horror in late Beethoven.

7. "For a multitude of causes unknown to former times are now acting with a combined force to blunt the discriminating powers of the mind, and unfitting it for all voluntary exertion, to reduce it to a state of almost

savage torpor. The most effective of these causes are the great national events which are daily taking place, and the encreasing accumulation of men in cities, where the uniformity of their occupations produces a craving for extraordinary incident which the rapid communication of intelligence hourly gratifies. To this tendency of life and manners the literature and theatrical exhibitions of the country have conformed themselves. The invaluable works of our elder writers, I had almost said the works of Shakespear and Milton, are driven into neglect by frantic novels, sickly and stupid German Tragedies, and deluges of idle and extravagant stories in verse" (Wordsworth, Preface to the *Lyrical Ballads,* 1802).

8. For a harsh but intelligent critique of Riefenstahl, see Susan Sontag's essay "Fascinating Fascism" (*Under the Sign of Saturn,* 1980), which also issues a general warning against the dangers of Romantic primitivism.

9. George Steiner addresses this question compellingly and at length in *Real Presences* (1989).

10. W. B. Yeats (*Explorations,* 1962), p. 212. The truly muscular critic of the decadent body in nineteenth-century language was Yeats's friend Ezra Pound, who called for a return to the musicality (*motz et son*) of the medieval troubadour's *canzone* as early as 1910 in *The Spirit of Romance.*

11. This speech has recently been adulterated by a Hollywood script-writer. The authentic version, which I have followed, can be found in L. T. Jones, *Aboriginal American Oratory,* Los Angeles, 1965.

CHAPTER ONE

1. Including also contemporary physicists, it seems. Stephen Hawking (*A Brief History of Time,* 1988), having some years ago tried to prove that the universe began in a "singular" fashion at some point, now takes the view that in a profounder sense it is eternal. The philosopher Derrida (*Of Grammatology,* 1982) argues that every supposed origin carries a "supplement" (what I have called "antecedent traces") without which it is unintelligible, and hence we can never begin in the beginning. Although one cannot but respect his formidable intelligence, one cannot but deplore the nihilist timidities he has fostered among many of his admirers.

2. Mircea Eliade is the expert on primitive beginnings. My favorite example comes from Indian construction rites: to make the foundation of a building secure, a stake is ritually driven into the ground in such a way as to peg down securely the head of the primordial snake, which is chaos. See Eliade, *The Myth of the Eternal Return* (1954), p. 19.

3. Much the best treatment of this subject is by Huizinga (*The Waning of the Middle Ages*, 1924).

4. Contradictions abound, of course. Newton was both a Christian and an alchemist, and spent his last years trying to construct a chronology of the universe, as if to atone for his perpetual motion machine.

5. For a discussion of Bacon's imagery see Merchant (*The Death of Nature*, 1982).

6. The story of ballistics and modern physics is told intelligently and at length by Jack Lindsay (*Blast Power and Ballistics*, 1974).

7. On Swift's standing in London and the reception of *Gulliver's Travels*, see Nokes, *Jonathan Swift* (1985) Pt. 4, especially pp. 300–17.

8. See Sheldrake (*The Presence of the Past*, 1988), pp. 4–13.

9. And hence a criminal body radically polluted by the devil would be spectacularly dismembered (hanged, drawn, and quartered, for example) in order to scatter the diabolical, drive it out with pain.

10. The Hegelian mind might see in these rites an important transformation of the spectacular dismemberments performed on the scaffold, a "sublation" (*Aufhebung*), which cancels, preserves, and heightens (or intellectualizes) the previous practice.

11. To see how radically subversive of the new orthodoxy this painting was, one might compare it with the earlier one in which, since it was the young painter's first major commission, he was at pains not to give offense. Could that mass of bunched figures looming over the corpse be hungry predators closing on their prey? Surely not: this is food for thought—the feast will come later—as one can infer from the thoughtful and civilized faces, only one of which is looking at the dissected forearm; and there by the corpse's feet is the open book of anatomical science, authorizing the proceedings. Such vestigial uneasiness as one might still feel is offered distraction in the elegant fingers of the dissecting Professor Tulp, and in the rich softness of his beautiful black hat. Although nowhere near the later painting either technically or imaginatively, it is nonetheless a somewhat spooky performance, not least because of the painter's evident perplexity. For an extensive analysis see Heckscher (1958). F. Barker's *Tremulous Private Body* (1984) should be approached only by those already inoculated against Derridean dislocations.

12. For a discussion of Swift vs. Bacon, see Young, *Out of Ireland* (1975), Ch. 3.

13. *Poetics* 1451 b.

14. In contemporary particle physics, the line between fact and fiction

has become virtually impossible to draw, as the smallest particles of matter cannot be perceived without being distorted by the perceiver: i.e., the matter of facts melts into fiction. See Capra (1982), Ch. 3. The word "fiction" is not from *facio* but *fingo* = to fashion in clay, a later kind of making than the first of *facio*'s artifacts. The two meet up in compound verbs for making, which usually end in *-ficere*. For a discussion, see the Appendix.

15. For an extensive discussion of the discovery of nuclear fission, see Easlea, *Fathering the Unthinkable* (1983).

16. The quotes from Blake are from "The Marriage of Heaven and Hell" (1793).

17. This story is recounted in Van der Post (*The Heart of the Hunter*, 1965), p. 133.

18. I am thinking particularly of Niels Bohr dreaming the structure of the atom. On scientific hypotheses see Barfield (*Saving the Appearances*, n.d.) Ch. 7 and Kuhn (*The Structure of Scientific Revolutions*, 1962), particularly pp. 89–90.

19. Heisenberg cited in Sheldrake, *The Presence of the Past* (1988), p. 31. Also relevant here is the extraordinary story being told in contemporary physics about the "big bang" with which the universe began. Could it be that physics, having become bored with the planet it has taught us to destroy, is moving into theology? Equations that describe the emergence of the universe (from a black hole?) in a fraction of a second would strike the layman as even more fictitious than the rather sober account one finds in Genesis. The layman might be right. See Hawking (*A Brief History of Time*, 1988).

20. Still, the poetical news here is mixed. The butterfly hurricane *is* wonderful, *does* expand our notion of causality, but is nonetheless strongly flavored with science's traditional search for determinate sequences: given the flickering wing, we can now *track* the hurricane. For the truly life-enhancing perception of *contingency* one must look elsewhere, to Gould (1989) for example.

21. An elementary point, one might think, and yet the illustrious Hawking (*A Brief History of Time*, 1988) is looking for a theory to end all theories; i.e., he thinks physics may be about to discover the absolute truth about the universe! Dare one suggest that this physicist of genius should read some philosophy of science, Kuhn (*The Structure of Scientific Revolutions*, 1962) for example? That Hawking could make such a mistake indicates that scientism is indeed still alive and well.

22. See Darwin (*The Voyage of the Beagle,* 1906), pp. 369 ff.

23. Stevens's poem of poems is "Notes Towards a Supreme Fiction." For Plato, see the *Timaeus* above all, but also the *Gorgias* and the *Protagoras*. For Aristotle, see the *Metaphysics* and the *Nicomochean Ethics* and the *Politics*. The whole question is impressively surveyed by the late and insufficiently lamented Professor Guthrie (*In the Beginning,* 1957, passim). For a superb eighteenth-century rendition of the *nomos-phusis* controversy, expounded by Messrs. Thwackum and Square, see that wisest of novels, Henry Fielding's *Tom Jones* (Book III).

24. A recent example is Richard Dawkins's widely praised but sadly reductive *Blind Watchmaker* (1986). His enthusiasm for Nature is manifest, his prose lively, and yet he fails to see that his computer games are part of the problem, not part of the solution. What seems to be constraining his incipient piety is not only his unphilosophical background but a fear of the moral majority descending on his lab at Oxford, mischievously armed with stout Bibles. His reductive approach is nicely criticized by Gould in *The Panda's Thumb* (1980), pp. 72 ff.

25. I say "her days off," but sexual selection is big business, as Darwin recognized when he made it the focus of *The Descent of Man* (1870). This emphasis has been understandably played down in the literature of evolutionary science, where attitudes are perhaps more than usually patriarchal.

26. See Darwin (*Autobiography,* 1958), p. 138.

27. One might further speculate that had the clergy been *per impossibile* open-minded enough to accept his work and see God in Nature (as they can now), his "random" would have appeared less vicious and hence his remorse would have been reduced.

28. On the relation between evolution and ecology, see Gregory Bateson (*Steps to an Ecology of Mind,* 1972; *Mind and Nature,* 1980).

29. Capra (*The Turning Point,* 1982) tells the story of President Johnson calling in the physicists for advice on the Vietnam war.

CHAPTER TWO

1. The notion of ontogenetic recapitulation originated with the nineteenth-century anatomist Ernst Haeckel. On its standing in contemporary science, see Sagan (*The Dragons of Eden,* 1978) and Gould (*Ontogeny and Phylogeny,* 1977). Conrad's formulation in *Heart of Darkness* is memorable: "The mind of man is capable of anything—because everything is in it, all the past as well as all the future."

2. See Sheldrake (*The Presence of the Past*, 1988), Ch. 9. Also, Neo-Darwinians speak of patterns of thought having been selected for evolution, much as patterns of muscles were. See Edelman (*Neural Darwinism*, 1986), summarized in Rosenfield (*Neural Darwinism*, 1986).

3. One obvious exception to this rule is the squirrel, an arboreal rodent.

4. Recent ratings of mammal intelligence give the rat .8 and the squirrel 1.5. Dawkins (*The Blind Watchmaker*, 1988) suggests that the complexities of arboreal navigation may be responsible (p. 189).

5. On the braininess of brachiation, see Carl Sagan's *The Dragons of Eden* (1978), pp. 83-4.

6. Washburn reports that infant baboons are instinctively afraid of snakes, falling, and the dark. See Sagan (*The Dragons of Eden*, 1978), p. 137.

7. The bird and the snake are also principal deities of early Neolithic Europe and they are fused in a bisexual bird-snake that evolves into the great goddess. See Gimbutas (*The Goddesses and Gods of Old Europe*, 1982), Ch. 7.

8. "Chimpanzees and gorillas brachiate quite rarely in the wild, unless in intimidation displays, or when they are still young and playful" (Kortlandt, *New Perspectives on Ape and Human Evolution*, 1972, p. 15).

9. See Gribbin and Cherfas (*The Monkey Puzzle*, 1982), pp. 144-48.

10. Cited in Leakey (*The Making of Mankind*, 1981) p. 48.

11. Cited in Leakey (*The Making of Mankind*, 1981) p. 52.

12. Goodall's figures cover a twenty-two-year period, and suggest that about half the expeditions are unsuccessful: thus a total of about four expeditions per month. See Goodall (*The Chimpanzees of Gombe*, 1986), pp. 169, 273.

13. See Fox (*The Red Lamp of Incest*, 1980), p. 85.

14. See Goodall (*Gombe*, 1986), pp. 290 ff.

15. On chimp contagion see Goodall (*Gombe*, 1986), pp. 319, 330.

16. Cited in Koestler (*The Ghost in the Machine*, 1967), p. 281.

17. Chance's theory of "equilibration" confirms this. Dominant monkeys are less programmed, more able to *decide* a course of action, than their inferiors. The key to such grace is the emotion-suppressing amygdala in the brain. See Fox (*The Red Lamp of Incest*, 1980), pp. 111-17.

18. See Eibl-Eibesfeldt (*The Biology of Peace and War*, 1979), p. 38.

19. Lorenz (*On Aggression*, 1966), p. 19.

20. And yet he too can be formidably bellicose. Observing hamadryus and geladas baboons in Abyssinia, Sanderson (*Living Mammals of the World*, 1955) witnessed "terrific battles, amounting almost to organized warfare—with sur-

prise raids, the taking of prisoners, wide manoeuvers, and other grossly human tactics."

21. At Gombe, the "southerners" who lost the war had before its outbreak seceded from the union into a bananaless territory. Hence desire for improved access to bananas could have played no part in the "northerners" strategic objectives. Jane Goodall told me (in conversation, 1990) that her conscience remains clear on this point.

22. See Fox (*The Red Lamp of Incest,* 1980), pp. 129 ff. On the importance of "arms races" between predator and prey for the evolution of braininess, see Dawkins (*The Blind Watchmaker,* 1986), pp. 178 ff.

23. Goodall (*Gombe,* 1986), p. 529. Civets and servals have also been killed and abandoned.

24. See Goodall (*Gombe,* 1986), pp. 298–99 and Kortlandt (*New Perspectives on Ape and Human Evolution,* 1972) p. 88. One thinks in this context of the Hungarian Jansco's films.

25. The Greek myth of Prometheus almost got it right, and the Chinese Taoists, for example, had no doubt about the evil potential of metallurgy (see Needham, *Science and Civilization in China,* 1956, vol. 2, p. 108). In modern times Rousseau has addressed the matter eloquently in his *Discourse on Inequality* (1755) and for a general discussion of primitive man's failure to contain the destructive power latent in the smithy, see Eliade (*The Forge and the Crucible,* 1962).

26. Goodall (*Gombe,* 1986), p. 448.

27. We shall return to this in Chapter 5. On the incest taboo in man and animal, see Fox (*The Red Lamp of Incest,* 1980) passim: in the chimp, see Goodall (*Gombe,* 1986, p. 451). The incest taboo has also been observed in the macaque, the rhesus, and the olive baboon (ibid; p. 466).

Chapter Three

1. Primatologists in recent years have discovered that chimp and baboon are more similar than they had previously supposed.

2. In both cases, however, and among primates generally, it seems dominance is conveyed and sustained through the binding structures of attention that keep alpha in touch with omega. See Chance and Larsen (*The Social Structure of Attention,* 1977).

3. Goodall (*The Chimpanzees of Gombe,* 1986), p. 170.

4. All of this paragraph is based on Goodall (*Gombe,* 1986) most of it on pp. 134–232. Kortlandt (*New Perspectives on Ape and Human Evolution,*

1972) observes that Bantu tribes also drum in the darkness (p. 75). On the baboon and macaque I am following Chance and Jolly (*Social Groups of Monkeys, Apes and Man*, 1970) and Fox (*The Red Lamp of Incest*, 1980).

5. As Konrad Lorenz puts it: "The characteristic which is so vital for the human peculiarity of the true man—that of always remaining in a state of development—is quite certainly a gift which we owe to the neotonous nature of mankind." Cited in Gould (*The Panda's Thumb* 1983), p. 91.

6. Lee (*The !Kung San*, 1979), pp. 450–51. The average figure for contemporary hunter-gatherers may be about 50 percent meat. See Fox (*The Red Lamp of Incest*, 1980), p. 247.

7. Thoughtful evolutionists would agree, and point to random mutation as the cause. I have suggested in the previous chapter that we can as scientists accept random mutation but as philosophers must realize that Mother Nature *does* desire reproductive success and teaches her children to want it too.

8. Some primitives *do* deny the father's role, but then so do we in the story of Jesus, as Edmund Leach wittily pointed out. Such denial has to do with ensuring the ideological purity of matrilineal descent, and not with stupidity. See Fox (*The Red Lamp of Incest*, 1980), pp. 69–76.

9. This survey, of 849 human societies, was conducted by G. Murdock, and is discussed in Daly and Wilson (*Sex, Evolution and Behavior*, 1978), Ch. 9.

10. On the gorilla, see Schaller (*The Mountain Gorilla*, 1963) and Fossey (*Gorillas in the Mist*, 1983) and Chance and Jolly (*Social Groups of Monkeys, Apes and Men*, 1970). The gorilla's love life may owe something to the orangutan, also ecologically doomed, who has also been observed spending fifteen minutes in the ventral position, hanging from a tree branch. See Hrdy (*The Woman That Never Evolved*, 1981), p. 137.

11. The evidence for neolithic matriarchy presented by Gimbutas (*The Goddesses and Gods of Old Europe*, 1982) might be serious but she presents it unseriously, i.e., tendentiously (see below, p. 351–52, notes 40 and 41). I have no doubt that a better case could be made on the basis of the artifacts she examines. My own view of the matter is that we probably came quite close to matriarchy at this time, may indeed have slipped over the line here and there for a while, but that had we been *significantly* matriarchal, some agricultural communities would have remained so into the historical period and been visited by some version of Herodotus. Working against the notion of neolithic matriarchy is the evidence (summarized in Leakey,

1981) that when certain elements of the African !Kung were forced to move from *paleo-* to *neo-*, the position of women actually declined.

12. See the Wilhelm/Baynes translation of *The I Ching*, (1967), p. lvi of Wilhelm's introduction.

13. The bonobo chimp, a serious lover, specializes in the love-gaze. See Hrdy (*The Woman That Never Evolved*, 1981), p. 137. One might propose the love-gaze as an instance of what Niko Tinbergen (1951) calls "innate releasing mechanisms," perceptions that instinctively trigger certain responses.

14. One who does is Rousseau, in his "Discourse on the Origin of Inequality," and he can be a formidable ally.

15. See Sagan (*The Dragons of Eden*, 1978), p. 142.

16. The contemporary expert on the neurophysiology of dreaming is Jonathan Winsom (*Brain and Psyche*, 1985), who focuses on the dream as the theater where new memories with significant survival value for the individual are selected and engraved in the long-term memory by a complex process in the hippocampus which Winsom calls "neuronal gating." There is good crude evidence (from hippocampal lesions) to suggest this process takes three years; and since we dream in images not words, if Winsom is right in proposing the dream as the royal road to long-term memory, this would indeed suggest that our forebears were correct in insisting on the original and enduring importance of poetry, where images are made intelligible. Without poetry verbal man forgets how to construe his own most important memories, and hence ends up on Sigmund Freud's couch.

17. Youthful footprints have been discovered in several caves. See Leroi-Gourhan (*Treasures of Prehistoric Art*, 1967), p. 181.

18. One notices that among the abstract symbols for male and female, hers are the more substantial. She begins with a pubic triangle or oval and progresses to quadrangular forms that were originally interpreted as huts; whereas he is at best a line (spear or phallus) and often shrinks to a dot. Cf., our discussion of the abstract males and solid females in Ch. 2, and supra, pp. 76–9.

19. The one animated human figure in cave art is the sorcerer of Trois Frères, but he only seems to be an exception: with his antlers, owl eyes, bear paws, and bushy tail, he's not very human.

20. On birds and shamanism see Campbell (*Primitive Mythology*, 1959), Part 3. Most of the shamans depicted in cave art have animal heads (usually antlers).

21. Among those who do are Thompson (*The Time Falling Bodies Take to Light*, 1981) and Campbell (*Primitive Mythology*, 1959), the latter of whom briskly identifies the bird-man as "certainly a shaman" (p. 301), but then goes rather uncharacteristically astray since he was laboring without the French code-breakers to tell him the bison was feminine.

CHAPTER FOUR

1. From *The Mentality of Apes*, cited in Campbell (*Primitive Mythology*, 1959) pp. 358–59.

2. See Fossey (*Gorillas in the Mist*, 1983).

3. Fox's book is the more impressive for challenging the dreadful decorums of academic specialization, which ordain that more and more gets said about less and less. Freud's speculations have been resented on this score, Fox was little thanked for his book, and I have no doubt that the present work will not much enhance my academic reputation.

4. Fox, to be precise, votes for the parricide but remains strangely noncommittal on the cannibal meal, perhaps sensing, as I do, the implausibilities in Freud's account.

5. On these patterns see Rosenfield ("*Neural Darwinism*," 1986).

6. Lévi-Strauss (*Totemism*, 1964) attempts to discredit the very idea of totemism (which has rightly fascinated ethnologists for the past century) by focusing on such anomalies as the mosquito. A reader of his book would have no idea that the overwhelming majority of totems are animals or plants, nor that there is general scholarly agreement on animal totemism as the original form. See Radin (*Primitive Religion*, 1957) pp. 203 ff.

7. Those who want to hear the whole case of Lévi-Strauss contra Freud will find it not unsympathetically reviewed in Fox (*The Red Lamp of Incest*, 1980).

8. Going in the other direction, one finds an important origin of all this in the "attention" paid constantly by subdominant to dominant in monkey troups, discussed in Ch. 3.

9. Partridge (*Origins*, 1959) disagrees (pp. 553, 562) and yet recognizes that English real is from medieval French *real*, which means both real and royal (hence realm). The obvious and agreed source is Latin *res* = thing, and the real question is whether Latin *res* = thing and *rex* = king originally conspire. From Indo-European *re* = property and Sanskrit *revan* = rich, come a host of words signifying the valuable. In the beginning those things are valued that hold us together and we hold together: hence

res publica, the thing that is all of us (as in Icelandic, where "the thing" is the legislative assembly). A sacred king is the most real thing because all of our reality is vested in him. The suggestion is that reality is composed of things not given but made. The thing is what we make together; and where there is no-thing, there is God. Thus the declension from *rex* to *res* is both politically and metaphysically plausible.

10. The Greek version of the Fall, which centers on Prometheus and Pandora, includes the theft of fire and the institution of animal sacrifice to forestall cannibalism. It is briefly discussed in the final section of Chapter 6. For a Fall-myth which centers on the cannibalizing dance, consider Hainuwele of the South Pacific, ably discussed by Campbell (1959) p. 170 ff.

CHAPTER FIVE

1. Professor Guthrie (*In the Beginning,* 1957) also finds the idea of beauty in the Greek etymology of "*kosmos*" (p. 107).

2. I am following Lee and Devore (*Kalahari Hunter-Gatherers,* 1976), Lee (*The !Kung San,* 1979), Leakey (*The Making of Mankind,* 1981), Konner (*The Tangled Wing,* 1982), and Van der Post (*The Lost World of the Kalahari,* 1962, *The Heart of the Hunter,* 1965), though only Konner and Van der Post manage to bring them to life.

3. See Van der Post (1962), pp. 247–48 and (1965), pp. 206–7.

4. A reasonably intelligent version of the anti-Tarzanist, pro-scavenging line can be found in Gribbin and Cherfas (*The Monkey Puzzle,* 1982).

5. Traces of this taboo seem still to be with us. I am very reluctant to eat any of my farm animals who die of natural causes, and all the farmers of my acquaintance share this reluctance. The meat we buy from the supermarket, though violently killed somewhere else, and hence not carrion, is nonetheless sufficiently estranged from our own occluded bloodlusts to make some people think about vegetarianism.

6. Consider this passage from Eugen Herrigel's *Zen in the Art of Archery:* "The archer aiming at himself—yet not at himself, in hitting himself—and yet not himself, and thus becoming, simultaneously, the aimer and the aim, the hitter and the hit." Cited in Campbell (*The Way of the Animal Masters,* 1983), p. 76. One might add that certain murderers have been known to dream of turning into their victims.

7. Catlin, *North American Indians* (1844), vol. 1, letter 18.

8. And moving back in time, one thinks of the chimpanzee drinking the blood of his prey, described in Chapter 3.

9. Such demoralizing secularization is a fairly recent development. In the early seventeenth century, while discovering the circulation of the blood in the name of empirical science, William Harvey was still sufficiently pious to take the view that "the blood is the genital part, whence the soul primarily results."

10. The ethnological evidence would agree. See Campbell (*Primitive Mythology,* 1959), passim.

11. Canetti's work (*Crowds and Power,* 1962) is frequently suggestive, and he is good on lamentation, pp. 170 ff.

12. Egyptian Osiris is the odd man out here, since his major mythic responsibilities are to the agricultural cycle; but behind the neolithic calendar one can discern the hunting story from which it grew, a man killed by his own hunters for mistaking a woman. His troubles begin when he mistakes his brother's wife for his own in the night and get worse when he subsequently agrees to climb into a coffin in the mistaken belief that it was intended for someone else's body.

13. Cf. Edwin Muir's excellent poem "The Combat." He dispenses with the mournful eyes since his combat is inter-animal, but he nicely registers the hunter's "despair" as he contemplates the undignified mess that is his victim.

14. As one would expect, Eros and Thanatos remain commingled and confused in the warrior culture of ancient Greece. See Vernant's excellent essay ("Feminine Figures of Death in Greece," 1986).

15. For an equable discussion of these lines in their context, see Dekker (*Sailing After Knowledge,* 1963) pp. 62 ff, whose strictures against Pound's "foulnesse" seem to me fair-minded, if perhaps somewhat lenient.

16. See Harrison (*Themis,* 1963), p. 139.

17. It has often been observed that the sexual appetite is best understood in ingestive terms. Where has it been more beautifully rendered than in the Old Testament's *Song of Songs*?

18. See Hulme (*Colonial Encouters,* 1988), passim.

19. The loony book is by Arens (*The Man-eating Myth,* 1979) and it has unfortunately had some influence among the ill-informed. Had the author been content to point out that rumors of cannibalism in the next valley have always been exaggerated, he could have stayed on firm ground. But his attempts to discredit *all* reports (both eye-witness and inferential) take him beyond crankiness and personal abuse into the foothills of paranoia.

Thus, for example, he begins with the "hardest" evidence of ritual anthropophagy that we have, that of Hans Staden among the Tupinamba in the sixteenth century. Not only does he fail to engage Staden's book (quoting only a few unilluminating phrases for the purposes of mockery) but the classic works on this subject, by Alfred Métraux, *La Réligion des Tupinamba* (1928) and *Réligions et magies indiennes d'Amerique du sud* (1967), are not even cited in the bibliography.

20. This story does not appear in Goodall, strangely enough, but can be found in Konner (*The Tangled Wing*, 1982) pp. 431–32. Miss Goodall has told me (in conversation, October 1990) that chimps have been frequently observed doing the waterdance, but they are almost always male: females have been observed only twice.

21. Aristotle believed that music surpasses all the other arts in its powers of *mimesis*, a term that has perplexed subsequent thinking about esthetics because its primitive, magical overtones are usually underestimated. See his *Politics* (1340a). Plato agreed with Aristotle about music's power (see *Phaedrus*, 259).

22. W. B. Yeats (*Collected Poems*, 1950), p. 213.

23. Rilke, "First Duino Elegy," my translation, definitely free; metrically hopeless, but then so is the original. My major liberty is in putting "sublimity" for *das Schöne* rather than "beauty," which in English doesn't usually behave with the violence Rilke has in mind (see Appendix); and more generally I have tried to cool down the overheated *fin de siècle* element to allow the wonderful *zerstören* to stir us properly.

24. On the troubadours, see Waddell (*The Wandering Scholars*, 1927) and for a good general account, de Rougemount (*Passion and Society*, 1960).

25. As the saying goes, "Man pursues woman until she catches him."

26. The singular exception is *The Hippolytus* of Euripides (very late in mythic terms) where she mercilessly punishes those who have mistaken their sexual choices.

27. See, for example, Herodotus denouncing the Babylonian practice of temple prostitution, Book 1, 199.

28. This point is discussed by Friedrich (*The Meaning of Aphrodite*, 1978), p. 70.

29. The most readable discussion of these practices and the myths they generated is still in Frazer (*The Golden Bough*, 1960). Less reliable but often inspired is Graves (*The White Goddess*, 1961). I shall examine them briefly in Chapter 8. For an altogether amazing poetic transcription, see Pound's *Canto* XLVII.

30. Burkert (*Greek Religion*, 1985) emphasizes the contrast between the somewhat antimale gloominess of the Greek *Thesmophoria* and the Oriental sexiness of the Adonis festivals, pp. 242 ff.

31. For an amusing mockery of this festival, see Aristophanes's *Thesmophoriazusae*.

32. In Alexandria Adonis dies on his wedding night in the Spring and rises (to heaven?) the next day; not far from Jesus. On Adonis, see Frazer (*The Golden Bough*, 1960), pp. 381 ff, interesting but confused, Vernant (*Myth and Society in Ancient Greece*, 1980), and Detienne (*The Gardens of Adonis*, 1977, *Dionysus Slain*, 1979), passim. For an intelligent and extensive discussion of Aphrodite, see Friedrich (*The Meaning of Aphrodite*, 1978).

33. Homer's account of Zeus and Ganymede, thought by many to license homosexuality, says that Ganymede was beautiful but says nothing about Eros. See *Iliad* 20: 231–35.

34. This latter, from Crete in the fourth century, probably an aspect of initiation rites, seems to be exceptional in its crudity: no other instances are on the record. See Dover (*Greek Homosexuality*, 1978) p. 189, and on the "Sacred Band" of the Thebans, p. 192.

35. Buggery as degradation ceremony for the hunter who fails in his attempt to invade another's territory is plausibly examined by James Dickey in his novel *Deliverance*.

36. Unlike our contemporary homosexual culture, where the degrading aspect of sodomy (what we call the problem of sadomasochism) is often ignored, even denied, which leads to considerable confusion. For some clarity and plain speaking on this matter, see the works of Jean Genet, *The Thief's Journal*, for example.

37. For example, although the Greek vases mostly depict intercrural intercourse, it was assumed by Aristophanes and the other writers of comedy, as well as by the Hellenistic poets, that homoerotic desire is for anal penetration and the intercrural was a compromise. See Dover (*Greek Homosexuality*, 1978) pp. 99, 145. As for the "courtly fiction" of the unaroused *eromenos*, this is questioned by the vases that regularly depict the *erastes*'s hand reaching toward the genitals of his beloved.

38. Exigencies of space and theme can be the only excuse for so truncating one of the world's great poems. The outstanding translation of the *Phaedrus* is by Hackforth (*Plato's Phaedrus*, 1952). For a somewhat secularized but often impressive discussion of Platonic love, see Nussbaum (*The Fragility of Goodness*, 1986), Chs. 6 and 7. I hope to have indicated

that gender plays no essential part in Plato's argument. His lovers are male because the females were unavailable: a century earlier, on less sequestered Lesbos, Sappho seems to have anticipated much of his thinking in an exclusively female "Academy" for dancing and poetry. But what *is* essential to the argument is that however the lovers touch or do not touch each other's bodies, they make no babies.

39. W. B. Yeats (*Explorations,* 1962), p. 441.

CHAPTER SIX

1. In the following discussion, I am following Lee and DeVore (*Kalahari Hunter-Gatherers,* 1976) and, with caution, Campbell (*The Way of the Animal Masters,* 1983).

2. For deepening our understanding of this Durkheimian distinction, we are much indebted to Mircea Eliade, who has addressed it in many books. For a general survey, see *Myth and Reality* (1964a).

3. See Eliade, *The Myth of the Eternal Return* (1954), *Birth and Rebirth* (1958), *Shamanism (1964), Myth and Reality* (1964a).

4. See, for example, Eliade (*Birth and Rebirth,* 1958), Van Gennep (*The Rites of Passage,* 1909), and Turner (*The Forest of Symbols,* 1967).

5. Initiation is everywhere a more serious and elaborate ritual for the male than the female. One thinks of the baboon troups discussed earlier, where the young females slide into the breeding pool at menarche whereas the young males have to fight their way in (and many don't make it). But more important, and apart from sexual politics, there is a biologically based point here concerning *time*: a woman's adult life is naturally divided into three periods by her womb (leading to Robert Graves's Triple Goddess of nymph, mother, and layer-out), not to mention her monthly periodicity— thus she is by nature a walking clock. Man, by contrast, is at sea with time, and hence needs ritual demarcations of various kinds in a way that she does not. Imagine the male ritualist, continually drumming for ceremonies to tell the time, and nervously regarding the skeptical female who simply embodies it: father of today's clock-watching male, he is watching the original clock. No wonder he called her goddess, with some reluctance....

6. Even the pro-shamanic Eliade (*Shamanism: Archaic Techniques of Ecstasy,* 1964) seems somewhat worried by this possibility, though he suspects that much of his copious evidence about shamanism comes from decadent cultures. The reply to the scoffers in any case is that the *serious* shaman has a sanity that can be acquired only in the overcoming of

madness, and a strength that can be acquired only in the overcoming of weakness.

7. Traces of such religious thinking survive in our speech today when we sometimes describe a fool as being "touched." The *locus classicus* of such touching in the Old Testament is Jacob's thigh, disfigured in his wrestling match with God, a properly ambiguous mark of divine blessing. See Genesis 32:24 ff.

8. One can hear a faint echo of those monstrous origins in Francis Bacon's famous observation that "There is no excellent beauty that hath not some strangeness in the proportion" (*Of Beauty*). But where, one might ask, is the strange proportion in the excellent beauty of the cave paintings at Lascaux? The answer, I think, is "In the caves themselves," access to which involved considerable distension of the body and scarification of the spirit. The female figurines almost contemporary with these paintings, and not located in the caves, are monstrous indeed.

9. The Pygmies, perhaps even more ancient than the Bushmen, are comparably democratic and even less disturbed by *pneuma*. Their mildly hallucinogenic singing and dancing to the forest *molimo* seem to combine piety and humor in a most attractive way. See Turnbull (*Forest People*, 1961) and Sagan (*The Dragons of Eden*, 1978).

10. The most obvious example of the primitive belief in word-magic is the widespread reluctance to use each other's first names, for fear of "taking them in vain." The symbol's power to summon is enhanced by the flowing or contagious nature of *pneuma* in the primitive mind. A man's fingernail is suffused with his *stuff*, and so, less obviously, is his name. This is called *pars pro toto* in the schools: literary critics call it "synecdoche."

11. I have rather rushed over the problem of universals, but those who are intrigued could consult the lively prologue to I. A. Richards (*Beyond*, 1974) or even myself (*Out of Ireland*, 1975), pp. 11–16. Those who are deeply disturbed by it may be tempted by the still somewhat fashionable complexities of Jacques Derrida (*Of Grammatology*, 1982). He is so outraged by the unlocatability of the original chair that he wants to impound all the objects we sit on. Without a license from the original maker (God the father *absconditus*), there is no way of distinguishing the genuine copy from the fake, and hence the only prudent course is not to sit down at all. One wonders how Derrida manages to cross the street in the rush hour. Such philosophical fastidiousness is humorless, slightly paranoid, and needlessly

nihilistic. It is also rather sad, for at his best he is impressively provocative (*La Pharmacie de Platon,* 1968).

12. Notice how an exception must be made for therapeutic "transference," a decidedly magical practice of which Freud was the chief priest: "Thou shalt have no other gods but me," said the patriarch. While in mildly anti-Freudian mode, let me mention a most astonishing fact: in the general index to the Standard Edition of Freud's collected works, there is no entry under the word "forgiveness." For the virtuous aspects of post-Freudian thought, see the works of English psychoanalyst Charles Rycroft (*Psychoanalysis and Beyond,* 1985, et al.). Despite his having cogently indicated, over the past forty years, that Freud mischievously underrated the imagination, the point still seems to need emphasizing. This can only be because the fear and the envy that led Freud to attack the poetical in the name of scientific seriousness are still alive and well in Western culture.

13. For a brief discussion of its contemporary background, see Young ("Living with Armageddon," 1985). For a sustained analysis of the relations between magic and neurosis, see Becker (*The Denial of Death,* 1973). The original diagnosis of twentieth-century paranoia (still unsurpassed) is Kafka's *The Trial.*

14. On the nature of time in the primitive cosmos, Eliade is still the expert (1954, 1958, 1964a, supra).

15. The basic structure of this thinking is mirrored in Kleinian psychology's emphasis on the importance of repairing through grateful remembrance gifts one may have enviously attacked in one's youth.

16. See Aristotle's *Metaphysics* (982b12) and Plato's *Theaetetus* (155d).

17. With Augustine (as with the Bible) it is important to avoid recent translations. I have quoted from Pusey's version (1838) of the *Confessions,* itself a revision of Watts (1631). For the complex fate of *memoria* in Renaissance Neo-Platonism see Frances Yates's *The Art of Memory* (1966). On the religious aspect of Orphism and Pythagoreanism and its influence on Plato, see Harrison (*Prolegomena to the Study of Greek Religion,* 1962) passim but especially pp. 506–34 and, more soberly, Dodds (*The Greeks and the Irrational,* 1957), Chs. 5 and 7. The antireligious animus in contemporary philosophy is most apparent in the "deconstructive" ambitions of Derrida and his followers, who say that since our true origins can never be found, those who seek them can only be seeking a traditionally sanctioned ideology for oppressing their fellow man; and hence the only purifying remembrance they will allow is that there is no such thing. Such

a paranoid and nihilist attack on the past would deliver us resourceless into the hands of today's advertisements, which we must then deconstruct, etc., etc., forever. Luckily, the banality of the deconstructive wickedness is being increasingly recognized, and so I can confine most of my objections to footnotes.

18. An impressive empirical study of "pre-theological" primitive divinity is Godfrey Lienhardt's book on the African Dinka (*Divinity and Experience*, 1961).

19. Once again the master has followed the conventional line on an important religious term, and once again I am bound to suggest that had our philological forebears read some anthropology they would have written better dictionaries. On this occasion they have not even considered the semantically obvious cognate, doubtless because it did not seem obvious to them: pollution, after all, to the mind unschooled in its paradoxes, seems more like a weakening than a strengthening, like a *di*lution indeed, an injection of foreign matter that simply disorders and contaminates. Whether for this reason or some other, Partridge is at sea with "pollution," and his argument, very similar to that of Lewis and Short (1879), manifests its tendentiousness and admits its weakness: it proposes *pol + luere*, where *pol* is "apparently" a mild corruption of *por*, itself a "presumed" variation on *per* = throughout (or *pro* = toward); and *luere* is taken to mean "to make dirty," a remarkably truncated rendering of an important word whose chief meaning is "to unharness or let loose." My proposal, by contrast, is simplicity itself: *poll + luere* = the letting loose of strength. Of absolute interest is the proximity of *poll* = strength to words like *pollen* = a fine cereal powder, a strengthening dust (like the flower pollen that botanists praise). The notion of dust or dirt comes through the Greek and Latin roots *pol* and *pul*. Strengthening dirt? A paradox indeed, pointing not only to cereals but our origins ("for dust thou art") and also to the fact that dirt is *the* primitive image for pollution (as we shall see presently). Thus the collocation of *poll* = strength and *pol* = dust, to make strong dust, is a semantically perfect background for pollution. *Luere* is also quite at home in this cluster of meanings: like the Greek *luein*, its basic meaning is "to unharness or set loose" (*very* theological, like a thunderstorm), and to primitive man this would usually mean chaos and death (*luein* in Homeric usage = to kill and Latin *lues* = plague). By degrees, however, ritual learns how to ride such stormy weather (fighting chaos with chaos) and *lu*-words move toward the *lava* family to form words that designate the loosing of the waters and hence *washing* (thus ablute, dilute etc.—see

Partridge, p. 340) and on to the metaphorical cleansing of expiation. To set loose the waters can drown as well as cleanse, of course, but *lu*-words in both Latin and Greek are predominantly cleansing and redemptive. To find that *polluere* carries incipiently within it the antidotal notion of cleansing is astonishing, but no more so than that the Greek word for the polluting object (*katharma*) carries within it the notion of *katharsis* = purification, as we shall see. To the richness of *luere* we add the richness of *poll*, which brings in the notions of both strength and dirt; and all three vibrate ambiguously in a word that won't lie down.

20. Modern scientific pollution, of which the ecologist speaks, is much the same: when he says that Lake Erie is polluted by eutrophication, he is saying that excessive exposure to a kind of animation is responsible for the contagious affliction of the life that moves within it.

21. The best general accounts of primitive pollution to my mind are by Van Gennep, *The Rites of Passage* (1960), and Douglas, *Purity and Danger* (1966), *Natural Symbols* (1970).

22. For a sustained meditation on swarming, see Canetti (*Crowds and Power*, 1962), a brilliant work to which I am much indebted, but that unfortunately slides toward the paranoid condition it is trying to diagnose and exorcise. One might say it undervalues the carnivalesque: in simpler terms, it undervalues kissing.

23. Some traces of bee-divinity persist even in our technical talk. Unrelated to swarming, simply to communicate well-being, bees in the hive will embrace their neighbors and perform what is called "the joy dance." To "make increase," arguably *the* mythological event for which all life longs, is how beekeepers describe the splitting of a bee colony into two or more minicolonies.

24. I say "as a rule," but there is little consistency: the Jewish authors were plainly puzzled (see Psalm 104:25). Another word, infrequently used, is *remish* = reptile.

25. The Mayan hieroglyph for water is the wavy serpent, which makes the point nicely. See Bayley (*The Lost Language of Symbolism*, 1951), pp. 199 ff.

26. For a genial introduction to the dragon, see Huxley (*The Dragon*, 1979).

27. Speaking of Sartre, his meditation on viscosity in *Being and Nothingness* is quite similar to my analysis of swarming.

28. The Latin passages are cited and the neolithic bee goddess discussed

in Gimbutas (*The Goddesses and Gods of Old Europe,* 1982), pp. 181–90. See also Kerenyi (*Dionysos,* 1976), Ch. 2.

29. The details in the following discussion are mostly taken from the Winnebago version, which is fully recounted in Radin's book (1956).

30. For those who do not know his books, perhaps the best one to begin with is *Rabelais and his World* (1968), particularly Ch. 3.

31. Chimpanzees are so clever that they can tell lies even without the power of speech. See Gribbin and Cherfas (1982) p. 222.

32. Thoughts such as these lead to radically iconoclastic theologies, such as the Jewish one, with a tendency to taboo all divine representation.

33. The work that best unlocks the secrets of Hermes is Norman Brown's much underrated *Hermes the Thief* (1969).

34. Cited in Brown (Supra, 1969) p. 45.

35. Cf. Genesis 31:45 ff where Jacob "took a stone and set it up for a pillar" and his brethren "took stones and made an heap," a magical heap to mark the boundary between the land of Jacob and that of Laban, and to "witness" their nonaggression pact.

36. See Eliade (*The Forge and the Crucible,* 1962).

37. Rumors of this problem can be heard in the German word *das Gift,* which means poison.

38. A friend tells me that the Russian word for treasure, *sokrovishche,* clearly means "something hidden."

39. The book that has drawn our attention to the importance of *metis* is *Cunning Intelligence in Greek Culture and Society* by Detienne and Vernant (1978).

40. Still, drawing the line between craftiness and cheating was not easy. Homer addresses the problem in Book 23 of *The Iliad.*

41. See Vidal-Naquet (*The Black Hunter,* 1986) Ch. 5.

42. See Hesiod's *Theogony* (ll. 535–616) and *Works and Days* (ll. 45–105).

43. They have even been observed wiping off the traces of unwelcome contact with another's flesh. See Goodall, *The Chimpanzees of Gombe* (1986) p. 517.

44. For an intelligent discussion of the potlatch ceremony, see Huizinga (*Homo Ludens,* 1955) pp. 58–75.

CHAPTER SEVEN

1. Thus, in this instance, *neomai* is a kind of coming that happens to us even though we are more or less implicated as agents. The question of

deponency (middle voice in Greek) is interesting and obscure. Verbs were originally so designated by Latin grammarians who thought they had "laid aside" their passive sense while retaining their passive form. The major subsequent view is that what was laid aside was not passivity but reflexiveness. In many cases this is a fine distinction: to make myself glad or sad is still to be gladdened or saddened, and one may still believe (without being thought mad) that the gods or fate chiefly govern these processes. But the major argument in the case of Greek is a structural one: if in the beginning there were three voices, the one in "the middle" between agency and passivity, partaking of both, *must* have been important. And yet in the classical age its major function was merely to indicate that the action designated was done *for* the agent or with reference to him or his belongings. Thus *luo* = I set loose becomes in the middle voice *luomai* = I set loose for myself, neither interesting nor distinctively voiced nor even remotely passive. Such muddle in such a great language? Very unlikely; and it disappears as soon as one remembers divinity: thus *luomai* = I set loose the elements in and through myself, or rather they are set loose in and through me, and hence one is unsurprised to discover that this verb also meant "to kill" in Homeric usage. In sum, the middle voice in archaic and classical times is the archeological remnant of that crucial middle ground on which primitive man had negotiated with the gods for control over his actions. Having by then become virtually redundant, this ground was rented out for various purposes of a post- or subreflexive nature, and by the time the first grammarians started reflecting on the question, they seem to have forgotten its theological origins altogether. An exemplary tale, to be sure.

2. Plato, *Theaetetus* 155d and Aristotle, *Metaphysics* 982b12.

3. I shall in Section 4 indicate that this conflict between the spirits of Nature and culture, consciously addressed by the Jews, is just emerging in the older great goddesses, who confusingly represent *both* Nature *and* culture.

4. The aural bias of the Jews was probably shared by the Sumerians, whose word for "ear" also means "wisdom." For a discussion of bull-roarers, see Harrison (1963), pp. 63 ff. On Jewish mysticism see Gershom Scholem (1961).

5. The word "hosios" is itself complicated because it can refer either to the sacred or the profane. Plato agreed this was confusing. I have a simple suggestion: that *hosios* (like the Latin *fas*) goes way back to animist times before theology when divinity is simply Nature (*phusis*) and what Nature

commends and commands is *hosios*. When the discovery of evil requires the protecting elaboration of gods and rituals, they occupy a separate and tabooed realm that is called *hieros* = sacred (originally "strong" according to Burkert, p. 269), and the rest becomes profane (*hosios*). But this complex separation never fully supplants the old pantheism, the sacredness of *phusis* never dies, and so *hosios* remains profoundly ambiguous. One can also discern the old sense of *hosios* in the Orphic use of the word to describe the fully purified mystic, beyond the need for protection from the hieratic, hence released from taboo, *identified* with *pneuma* and thus free to flow in its winds without fear. Such a one has recovered original innocence and been assimilated to divine *phusis* before the fall. Thus *hosios* points back to the unity that precedes the fall into good and evil, and as such provides a suitable background for hospitality as the search for unity between host and hostile stranger. On *hosios* see Harrison (*Prolegomena to the Study of Greek Religion*, 1962), pp. 500 ff and Burkert (*Greek Religion*, 1985), pp. 269 ff.

6. Partridge (*Origins*, 1959), on robust form, strengthens the religious connection by suggesting links between *hospes*, *sospes*, and Greek *soter* = savior, and also by pointing to the Germanic shift from guest to *Geist* to ghost (p. 297). To make a ghost of your guest, to eat him instead of feeding him with your substance, is one of our oldest jokes; and like most important jokes it covers a wealth of pressing anxieties. On the ritual incorporation of strangers, see Van Gennep (*The Rites of Passage*, 1960) Ch. 3.

7. My objections to Frazer center on his evasion of Diana/Artemis as virgin goddess of the *nemos*, the hunt, and of childbirth. With startling tendentiousness he moves her toward Juno, who might be eligible for a sacred marriage to the priest-king if he usurped her *nemos* and revealed himself as thunder-god of the oak tree. This is Nordic, sexist, and irresponsible. What *little* we do know about Nemi is that it was *her* grove, she was not for marrying, and she was a formidable huntress who also protected the newly born, however implausible that conjunction might seem to post-neolithic thought. Moreover, her priests (runaway slaves apparently) killed and died for her but never touched her secret sacred places. To so distort the few poor facts is to wander into the night. What I do accept, however, is that the idea of the priest as "king" does indicate a neolithic accretion, referring to the tradition of sacrificial kingship, which clearly makes no sense in paleolithic terms. In the wake of Frazer's massive work, few have been willing to address the strangeness of Nemi. See Grant (*The History of Rome*, 1979) Ch. 2, and Cornford (*From Religion*

to Philosophy, 1957), pp. 31–35. As to Artemis herself, how can a goddess of fertility be a virgin? I have already offered some suggestions in Ch. 5, but one can also see in her sexual abstention the evolution in religious thinking from the womb *per se* to the empty space (so rigorously abstracted in the Jewish Ark) as source of prosperity—a move from Nature to culture. Such a move, involving negation and paradox (hence my phrase "wombless womb") brings us within range of renunciation and sacrifice, to be discussed presently. In any case the empty-full womb of Artemis associates her with *abzu* thinking, uncongenial to the Greeks.

8. The provenance of Dionysus is still disputed. Burkert (*Greek Religion,* 1985) lends his weighty authority to the Minoan-Mycenean view (p. 162).

9. In Harrison (*Themis,* 1963), p. 342.

10. I disagree with several of his interpretations, particularly with regard to the feminine, to which he often seems insensitive, but the bulk of his *evidence* seems to have been scrupulously gathered, even if he frequently fails to mention whether the evidence he is discussing is of the hard or soft variety. Hence I suggest the reader of his book should "proceed with caution." Two other significant works on Dionysus in English are by Jane Harrison, (*Prolegomena to the study of Greek Religion,* 1962) and (*Themis,* 1963), sometimes misleading but often first rate.

11. See Kerenyi (*Dionysos,* 1976), pp. 217 ff.

12. Here is Blake's version of the Dionysiac:

> And if the babe is born a boy
> He's given to a woman old,
> Who nails him down upon a rock,
> Catches his shrieks in cups of gold.
> "The Mental Traveller"

Here Blake's surrealist imagination, moving *very* fast, first combines Dionysus with Prometheus, and then trumps it with Revelations. Giddy eclecticism or good poetry?

13. For an extensive discussion of the two-year cycle, see Kerenyi (*Dionysos,* 1976) pp. 189–272.

14. Dionysus's concern with initiation clearly points back to the rites of passage for the young warrior, which I shall ignore as they would overload a discussion already sufficiently complicated. They are extensively discussed by Harrison (*Themis,* 1963), Chs. 1 and 2.

15. The early European versions of these movable feasts are readably discussed in Frazer (*The Golden Bough*, 1960), Ch. 14, pp. 61 ff, and their Dionysiac background in Greece by Cornford in Harrison (*Themis*, 1963), Ch. 7.

16. These vases are reproduced and the dialectic between *zoē* and *bios* extensively discussed in Kerenyi (*Dionysos*, 1976). The twin masks are also carried by Janus, who presides over our month of January.

17. Burkert (*Greek Religion*, 1985) mentions in this connection that early Greek warriors used to hang their booty on an oak post (p. 267). The rituals attending the mask and cloak hung on a column are discussed by Pickard-Cambridge (*The Dramatic Festivals of Athens*, 1968), pp. 30 ff.

18. Cited in Campbell (*Primitive Mythology*, 1959) p. 121.

19. He *did* have a temple in Athens, the *Limnaios* = in the marshes, but it was opened only briefly on one day a year, during the *Anthesteria*. See Kerenyi (*Dionysos*, 1976), p. 292.

20. An etymological conjecture: Latin *sacer*, an extremely important word, is extremely ambiguous, meaning both sacred or consecrated and horrible or accursed. Partridge (*Origins*, 1959) cannot find its source; but quite close to *sacrificare* = to make sacred is *scarificare* = to scarify, cut the skin of. Partridge finds "influence" at work in their similar endings (p. 597), and I would suggest we might also look for it in their beginnings. For millions of years we habitually encountered the sacred by cutting the skin of the animals we hunted, and this is remembered in the ritual scarification of the primitive body.

21. Warfare is not so very different from the ritual killing involved in human sacrifice, but since this latter involves the idea of the scapegoat, discussion of it will be deferred until the next section.

22. Robert Lowell, "Waking Early Sunday Morning," *Near the Ocean*, London, 1967.

23. My account of fifth-century Athens appears oversimplified because I am speaking of the mainstream, the quasi-philosophical perceptions that prevailed in the *agora*. There were, of course, exceptions. Euripides in the *Bacchae* urged his amnesiac compatriots to remember the holiness of Nature, the beauty and the wildness of our Dionysiac beginnings, and how the one might give us the courage to master the other; but this play was the last testament of an old man who had gone north to die, disillusioned after years of Athenian neglect. When he wrote it, Athens' fate was already sealed. By the time it was performed he was dead, and it won first prize. Among the influences on this extraordinary work were the Orphic sects, of

shamanic and Egyptian provenance, whose secret initiation ceremonies apparently involved a Dionysiac "feast of raw flesh" (*omophagia*) followed by a vow of vegetarianism. The idea here is that impure violence can be expunged through confession and rites of exorcism that return it to its proper place, and the Orphic *omophagia* points directly forward to the Christian communion meal. In fifth-century Athens, however, Orphism was matter for mockery, as one may gather from Aristophanes's *Clouds*.

24. Three major writers on the sacrificial have recently ended up in trouble. Unlike D. H. Lawrence, who survived a bad period of thinking he was Jesus to write remarkably well about sacrifice in the end (*St. Mawr, The Man Who Died*), Norman Mailer began well and slowly sank from sight (*The Executioner's Song, Ancient Evenings*). The other two are academics: Norman Brown (*Life Against Death*) and René Girard (*Violence and the Sacred*) also both began writing well (or at least promisingly) and went on to write madly (*Love's Body* and *Des choses cachées depuis la fondation du monde* respectively). Contemplating this list while I was writing the above section reminded me that the sacrificial is *actually* dangerous, and made me realize why I was having more than the occasional sleepless night.

25. There were several other Greek rituals that addressed the contagious "spilling" of sacrificial violence. See Detienne ("Apollo's Slaughterhouse," 1986), pp. 46 ff.

26. The scapegoat theme is incorporated in the standard Greek ritual of animal sacrifice (*bouthusia*) by the communal and somewhat aggressive throwing of barley groats (or even stones) at the animal just before he is slaughtered. The killing that then takes place is greeted with a scream from the women. The thigh bones (and other untasty parts) are then burned and offered up in restitution, for the resurrection of the dead animal. Then the feast. For an authoritative discussion, see Burkert (*Greek Religion,* 1985), pp. 56 ff.

27. Unspecifiable violence is the most contagious, hence the most dangerous. At Athens the *Pyrtaneos* was the court that dealt with crimes that could not be limited to the responsibility of one agent. It was probably this court that tried the *Bouphonia*. See Detienne ("Apollo's Slaughterhouse," 1986), p. 51.

28. Hence perhaps its strange emphasis on water. See Harrison (*Themis,* 1963), p. 173.

29. A vivid ethnological account can be found in Henry (*Jungle People,* 1964).

30. I say strangely neglected because I can find no account that does it justice, which is why I have dealt with it at some length. The ancient source is Porphyry, readably discussed by Frazer (*The Golden Bough*, 1960), pp. 540 ff. Harrison, not on good form, discusses it twice (*Prolegomena*, 1962, pp. 111 ff; *Themis*, 1963, pp. 142 ff). Burkert (*Greek Religion*, 1985) is perfunctory, Hubert and Mauss (*Sacrifice*, 1964) unilluminating (pp. 67 ff). On scapegoating generally, Frazer's (1960) long and detailed work remains the most readable. Girard (*Violence and the Sacred*, 1977), though frequently suggestive, begins not with hunting but with the "sacrificial crisis" induced by intra-tribal violence, and this significantly unbalances his discussion.

31. My discussion of this festival chiefly follows Burkert (*Greek Religion*, 1985), pp. 237–42. The most informative works in English on the birth of tragedy are by Jane Harrison (*Themis*, 1963) and Karl Kerenyi (*Dionysos*, 1976), which should be read against the often brilliant rhapsodies of Nietzsche (*The Birth of Tragedy*, 1956).

32. Cited in Burkert (*Greek Religion*, 1985), p. 239.

33. See Kerenyi (*Dionysos*, 1976), pp. 319 ff.

34. Some of these are discussed by Detienne ("Apollo's Slaughterhouse," 1986), pp. 46 ff.

35. A striking instance from Southern India: when the old king's time was up he would ceremonially dismember himself with a knife, casting aside as many pieces of his body as he could endure, until, about to faint, he would slit his throat. Cited in Campbell (*Primitive Mythology*, 1959), p. 165.

36. This argument is cogently presented by Cornford in Harrison (*Themis*, 1963), Ch. 7.

37. The classic work on Catal is by Mellaart (*Catal Huyuk*, 1967).

38. A crucial fact not mentioned in Mellaart. See Watson (*Heaven's Breath*, 1985), pp. 85 ff.

39. The basic dynamics of neolithic sacrifice are extensively discussed by Campbell (*Primitive Mythology*, 1959). See his Part II, particularly Ch. 5, a good example of the high spirits and high intelligence that distinguish much of his writing on the mythological mind. He and I do, however, have our differences: I find him not at ease with either the Greeks or the Jews, and also disposed to underestimate the paleolithic origins of both sacrifice and lamentation. In a word, his hunters are often too childish.

40. Gimbutas (*The Goddesses and Gods of Old Europe*, 1982), for example, overrates the capacity of the neolithic goddess, even when she becomes

unequivocally female, simply to absorb into her ample body anything that might look resistantly "other," not to say masculine; and one is left wondering how the neolithic male ever managed to look his wife in the eye, let alone complain about her cooking. A simple instance: on p. 169 Gimbutas proposes the neolithic dog as "epiphany" or "double" of the Moon Goddess. It soon becomes apparent, however, that the dog is not *itself* the goddess, nor even contained by her, but at least "belongs" to her, and is in fact both aggressive and unequivocally male. One is disturbed not only by the quick slide from epiphany to ownership, in which the (emergent?) masculinity disappears (the goddess as Jewish mother?), but also by the fact that none of the twelve dogs illustrated is even in the *vicinity* of a female (and yet the author nowhere admits that her assertions about the dog-goddess relationship are highly speculative). This is both muddled and sexist. The possibility that some of these fourth-millennium creatures might have been disposed to nip the goddess in the butt if she happened by, is not of course entertained.

41. Thus, for example, Gimbutas (*The Goddesses and Gods of Old Europe,* 1982) gives several illustrations from the patriarchal era of a human goddess flanked by or consorting with lions and snakes and bulls; but she strangely fails to wonder why the dreaded patriarchs would have been content to humanize and elevate the female principle while keeping the male rough, primitive, and unevolved. If these symbols were seriously commenting on the sex war (as she frequently implies), the patriarchs would surely have held the goddess as a farrowing pig and dressed the god in finest linen.

42. For an intelligent and extensive discussion of the great goddesses, see Friedrich (*The Meaning of Aphrodite,* 1978), passim.

43. My description is following Wilson in Frankfort et al. (*The Intellectual Adventure of Ancient Man,* 1977), Ch. 1. He also notes that the pattern of population distribution persists to this day, and a calculation made in 1946 concluded that since 96.5 percent of the country is uninhabitable desert, the habitable strip is the most densely populated place in the world (at 1,300 per sq. mile). For a sense of the soil's richness, think of the labor it released for the construction of Cheops's pyramid, 6.25 million tons of stone, the heaviest structure in the world.

44. See Otto (*Egyptian Art and the Cults of Osiris and Amon,* 1968), p. 26.

45. Joseph Campbell (*Oriental Mythology,* 1962) aptly calls it "mythic inflation" and offers a readably stringent critique in his second chapter.

46. Coffin Text 330, cited in Rundle-Clark (*Myth and Symbol in Ancient Egypt*, 1959), p. 142.

47. On the original designations of Seth and Horus, see Otto (*Egyptian Art and the Cults of Osiris and Amon*, 1968), p. 28 ff.

48. T. S. Eliot, "Preludes," *Collected Poems 1909–35*, London, 1936.

49. Cited in Otto (*Egyptian Art and the Cults of Osiris and Amon*, 1968), p. 31.

50. Here again, as Otto (*Egyptian Art*, 1968) points out, the moralizing tale needs a villain, and it can only be Seth (p. 29).

51. Dionysus too was associated with the marginal swampland. The cult actions of the *Anthesteria* took place in the temple of *Dionysos Limnaios* = Dionysus of the Swamp.

52. See Cook's Journals, Sept 1 and 2, 1777, cited in Campbell (*The Mythic Image*, 1974), p. 439 ff.

53. See Huxley (*Affable Savages*, 1956), p. 257.

54. Pyramid Text 39, cited in Campbell (*The Mythic Image*, 1974), p. 450.

55. The ancient Greek source on Isis and Osiris is Plutarch's long essay in *Moralia* (vol. 5 in the Loeb Classical Library), not brilliant but worth reading. Some sense of the Romanized view of Isis-worship can be gathered from Apuleius's somewhat silly *Golden Ass*. On Egyptian culture Frankfort et al. (*The Intellectual Adventure of Ancient Man*, 1977) are helpful, but apart from a few pages in Campbell (*Oriental Mythology*, 1962; *The Mythic Image*, 1974) and a chapter in Otto (*Egyptian Art*, 1968), the only recent book I have found significantly rewarding on Isis and Osiris is by Rundle-Clark (*Myth and Symbol in Ancient Egypt*, 1959), who says in his Preface that "The study of Egyptian religion is still in its infancy" and that "courage is really needed" by those who would interpret its genius (pp. 12–13). Some explanation of why this should be so has been recently provided in a stimulating and intelligent book by Bernal (*Black Athena*, 1987), who demonstrates that although such ancients as Herodotus, Pythagoras, and Plato acknowledged the Greek indebtedness to Egypt, and studied there, European scholars have sought to discourage the Egyptian connection since the mid-eighteenth century, in the interests of our Greek patrimony, Aryanism, and white skins. Let us hope that this noxious trend may now be reversing.

CHAPTER EIGHT

1. On the climatic change, see Watson (*Heaven's Breath*, 1985), p. 8, and Bernal (*Black Athena*, 1987), p. 17.

2. The best introduction to Heidegger on "presencing" is his *Early Greek Thinking* (1975).

3. On the Edomite question, see Pfeiffer (*An Introduction to the Old Testament*, 1952), p. 35 f, 166 f, 682 f.

4. The ancient source for this myth is the Homeric Hymn to Demeter, indifferently translated by Boer (1970), ably recounted by Kerenyi (*The Gods of the Greeks*, 1951) and Graves (1955).

5. The liveliest and most extensive discussion of *Thesmophoria* is in Harrison (*Prolegomena*, 1962), Ch. 4. Although she has virtues that seem to have disappeared from the scholarly world, she also does get carried away. The sober authority is Burkert (*Greek Religion*, 1985), pp. 243 ff. Campbell (*Primitive Mythology*, 1959), not always reliable, is on top form, and instructively compares the Greek myth with that of Hainuwele from the South Pacific (see Chapter 5).

6. These are by Sandars (*The Epic of Gilgamesh*, 1964) and Gardner (*Gilgamesh*, 1985). My quotes from the first are identified by page references, the second by three sets of numbers referring to column, tablet, and line. Gardner's rendition is better edited and translated, but the late version he follows is incomplete, and almost entirely omits the crucial fight with Humbaba. Much the best scholarly book on *Gilgamesh* is by Tigay (*The Evolution of the Gilgamesh Epic*, 1982).

7. See Gardner (*Gilgamesh*, 1985), p. 113.

8. See Gardner (*Gilgamesh*, 1985), p. 100.

9. The fraternal problem in myth becomes the problem of universals in philosophy. How to avoid fakes in the derivation of copies from the original object is addressed by Plato, refused by Derrida, and briefly discussed above in the second section of Chapter 6. On the fratricidal see Girard (1977) Ch. 2.

10. Be it noted that I am not saying that a male marriage cannot in principle achieve equity, but that *these two* could not have.

11. Winkler (*The Constraints of Desire*, 1990) writes amusingly about this in his first chapter.

12. The idea that the two poems had different authors has been believed by many, including me.

13. The present position is ably summarized by Professor Kirk (*The Songs of Homer*, 1962), Pt. 3 and Pt. 5.

14. Bowra's preference crystallizes on p. 138 and Kirk's is elaborated throughout his Ch. 17.

15. For a stalwart advocacy of *The Iliad*, see Griffin (*Homer on Life and Death*, 1980).

16. I am using Lattimore's (1965) translation throughout.

17. A problem common to many monster stories, the search for pious adventure. The proper solution to this narrative quandary is offered by the man-eating tigers that prey on Indian villages: some villagers still piously pay their respects to the corpse after it has been shot.

18. On Poseidon, see Graves (1955), pp. 59 ff and Kerenyi (*The Gods of the Greeks*, 1951), pp. 181 ff.

19. See Partridge (*Origins*, 1959), p. 448. The significant role played by envy in human affairs has been underrated in modern times (perhaps because its presence has become so pervasive). Two illuminating correctives are Melanie Klein's *Envy and Gratitude* and René Girard's *Deceit, Desire and the Novel*. Girard cogently argues that when modern man loses the fiction of an exemplary demi-god as an impossible object of emulation—Jesus, for example—his hero becomes his rival, and envy consumes the story. This fits nicely here: as demi-god Polyphemos can be admired and somewhat emulated by mortal man, but when Odysseus forgets the distance between them and seeks its elimination, the envious devil gets loose, and mischief is made.

20. For a fine essay on the *Philoctetes*, see Knox (*The Heroic Temper*, 1964), Ch. 5.

21. See Higgins (*Minoan and Mycenean Art*, 1967), passim.

22. From Nilsson's two volume *Geschicte der griechischen Religion* (Munich 1955 and 1961) vol. 1, p. 303, cited in Campbell (*Occidental Mythology*, 1964), p. 61.

23. Atkinson (*Stonehenge*, 1960) quoted and discussed at length by Campbell (*Occidental Mythology*, 1964), pp. 65ff.

24. For a brief but scholarly introduction to this line, and its Mycenean stiffening, see the well-illustrated Higgins (*Minoan and Mycenean Art*, 1967).

25. See pp. 51 ff and 71 ff. For a general introduction to tree worship, see Cook (*The Tree of Life*, 1974).

26. See Huizinga (*Homo Ludens*, 1955), p. 35 ff.

27. She translates it in full and discusses it in detail pp. 1–29; but actually the whole of her book (over 500 pages) is a sustained attempt to do it justice.

28. Evans (*The Palace of Minos*, 1921) produces a dog-headed monster who may be pursuing some swimmers, but he is so unfrightening as to be the exception that proves the rule (vol. 1, p. 697).

29. No one *knows* where he originated, and learned arguments have been proposed for Thrace, for Phrygia, for Crete, etc. I don't think it much matters: since his ancestry is clearly very posh, a direct line to *the* Lord Shaman, versions of him naturally crop up everywhere. However, his association with the vine would naturally identify his *historical* persona (i.e., post-3000 B.C.) with the Cretans, the original wine-merchants.

30. And much the best commentary on the *Bacchae* is Dodds's edition of the Greek text (*Euripides' Bacchae*, 1960).

31. These three myths are recounted in Kerenyi (*The Gods of the Greeks*, 1951), pp. 263–72, the most scholarly and readable authority on Greek mythology. One of them is the focus of Pound's famous *Canto II*.

32. Those who would pursue this path further might want to consult Wunderlich (*The Secret of Crete*, 1975), who argues with totally plausible implausibility that the palace at Knossos was in fact a giant necropolis.

33. The actual references to Poseidon are cited in Campbell (*Occidental Mythology*, 1964), p. 47.

34. For this story, see Kerenyi (*The Gods of the Greeks*, 1951), pp. 108 ff.

35. Evans argues persuasively from the visual evidence that the bull-vaulters were not foreign but native and even "of gentle birth." See *The Palace of Minos,* vol. 3 (1930), pp. 227, 232.

36. See Kerenyi (*The Gods of the Greeks*, 1951), pp. 182 ff. Smiths were very serious once upon a time. The precursor of the Greek word for king, *basileus,* is translated as "chief smith" in Linear B. See Burkert (*Greek Religion*, 1985), p. 241.

37. And yet not so astonishingly. As noticed earlier, Bernal (*Black Athena*, 1987) reminds us that Aryan scholarship has long resisted the idea of southerly dark-skinned influence on (not to say superiority to) our noble Greek forerunners. Also, to be fair, Evans only started publishing his six-volume work on Crete in 1921, so the scholars have only had seventy years to think about it.

38. W. B. Yeats (1950), p. 246, transliterating a choral poem from Sophocles's *Oedipus at Colonus* (668–720).

<small>APPENDIX</small>

1. This was widely believed by the ancients: e.g., when Aristotle wrote that the primary function of *psyche* was movement, he was summarizing the consensus of previous philosophers. See *De Anima* 403b, discussed in Onians (*The Origins of European Thought*, 1951), p. 196.

2. Sanskrit *prana*. For a genial history of the wind, see Lyall Watson's *Heaven's Breath* (1984). According to him, the words for "wind," "soul," and "breath" commingle in every language (p. 253). For the strange and difficult etymologies of *anima* and *psyche*, see Onians (1951), p. 93–174.

3. See Campbell (*Oriental Mythology*, 1962), pp. 83 ff.

4. Onians (1951), p. 119.

5. See pp. 39 ff and 83 ff. The divine statues in Greek temples were originally all wood, and even the chryselephantine cult statues of the fifth century were built around a wooden core (ibid., p. 91). Cornford (*From Religion to Philosophy*, 1957), pointing out that the words for "temple" and "ship" derive from the same root, says that "both seem to have been hollow trees" (p. 31).

6. There is evidence of tree worship throughout the ancient Mediterranean and Near East, but nowhere more impressively than Crete, perhaps because it was so well wooded in the third millennium B.C.

7. See Heidegger (*Early Greek Thinking*, 1975), p. 43.

8. "Gratitude is the first law of magic," as Ken Kesey has observed, manfully trying to make us *remember*. Some twenty years ago I ended up at a rustic wedding feast in the depths of Southwestern France: "Lou-ez, Lou-ez, Lou-ez," they sang and cried, through a long and bibulous afternoon. *That* was a joyful noise. ("Louez" means "Let us praise, admire, commend.")

9. See Cornford (1957), Ch. 1, especially pp. 26 ff.

10. Onians (1951) favors *neomai* and *pneuma* (p. 82).

11. As regards *nous*, this is something of an understatement: Plato's entire theory of knowledge is built upon recollection. The German word for remembering is *Erinnerung-an innering* (which usually warms) permeated by the still somewhat sacrilizing prefix *er-* (much concerned with beginnings and endings). Thus to remember in German is to renew one's inner sanctum with what has been and is, thereby opening one's self to the abiding and often mysterious *er*-realm where things begin and end (not dissimilar to the godly realm designated by the Greek middle voice, see note 1 to Chapter 7).

12. On Pythagoras the shaman and his influence on Plato, see Professor Dodds (*The Greeks and the Irrational*, 1957), Chs. 5 and 7.

13. Readers of Heidegger will be aware of my indebtedness to his profound thoughts on "calling." See his essay on "Language" (*Poetry, Language, Thought*, 1971) and also *What Is Called Thinking?* (1968), pp. 116–20.

14. It is also worth noting that four of the five radical nouns built on the root *kal-* are among the first things called into the human world: a basket (*kalamos*), an urn (*kalpis*), a rope (*kalos*), and a stalk of corn (*kalamē*). Like the root *neu-*, *kal-* is sparingly used; and its magic is clearly dispersing when the "a" is elided and we move into the often noisy and violent (not to say "clamorous") world of words built upon *kl-*.

15. The idea is very old indeed. If you look closely at the painted bull's horns in Fig. 48 of Mellaart's *Catal Huyuk* (1967), you will see a man upside down between them. What the Anatolians dreamed in 6000 B.C., the Cretans performed in 2000.

16. It is no idle fancy to see the horns as standing snakes. Horns were widely associated with potency because they grow at the period of sexual maturation from the head, where the generative "marrow" is produced (and from where it moves down the spine to the genitals). Horn, then, is concentrated potency, and the snake is potency itself, the very stuff. Hence the ubiquity of horn shrines, Arthur Evans's "horns of consecration." See Onians (op. cit., 1951), pp. 236–39 and for a picture of a horned neolithic snake, Gimbutas (*The Goddesses and Gods of Old Europe*, 1982), pl. 57. In Euripides' *Bacchae*, Dionysus is crowned with both horns and snakes (line 100).

17. Burkert (*Greek Religion*, 1985), p. 195.

18. *Neuron* ends its magical career, in Plato and the comedies, as a penis.

19. On the translation of this important epithet of Apollo, see Burkert (op. cit., 1985) p. 146.

20. Cf., the bark of the alder that must be "flayed" from the young shoot before being reborn as a pan pipe: Robert Graves (*The Greek Myths*, 1955) vol. 1, p. 81.

21. Cf., Socrates: "When the Muses were born and song came into the world, some of the men of that age were so ravished by its sweetness that in their devotion to singing they took no thought to eat and drink, and actually died before they knew what was happening to them" (*Phaedrus*, 259).

22. On *kairos*, see Onians (op. cit., 1951), pp. 343–49.

23. Homeric hymn cited in Kerenyi (*The Gods of the Greeks*, 1951), p. 134. In the hands of Odysseus, the great bow becomes a lyre for a moment before it is strung to kill the suitors (*Odyssey*, 21:405).

24. Thus the ritual involves both the carrying down of this year's token into the womb-pit of Mother Earth, and the carrying back from the store of last year's crop, well rotted piglet to fertilize the fields. The symbolism is impeccable. See Harrison (*Prolegomena to the Study of Greek Religion*, 1962), Ch. 4.

25. See Burkert (op. cit., 1985), p. 267.

26. Eliade (*Shamanism: Archaic Techniques of Ecstasy*, 1964) speaks of "a 'law' well known to the history of religions: *one becomes what one displays*" (p. 179), which derives from the simpler "To be is to be displayed."

27. On the "letting lie" of *legein*, see Heidegger (op. cit., 1975), the essay on Heraclitus.

28. On this resemblance, see Levy (*The Gate of Horn*, 1948), pp. 231–32. And for an old Chinese poem on the primitive bundle, see Pound (*The Confucian Odes*, 1959), p. 56.

29. Lewis and Short (*A Latin Dictionary*, 1879) unaccountably prefer *phaino* = to appear, the humble *phakelos* perhaps appearing too humdrum.

30. That Anaximander's insensible *apeiron* is essentially spatial is persuasively argued by Burnet (*Early Greek Philosophy*, 1930), p. 58 n. For an extensive discussion of the *peirata*, see Onians (op. cit., 1951), Pt. 3.

31. On Greek spellbinding, see Detienne and Vernant (*Cunning Intelligence in Greek Culture and Society*, 1978), Ch. 10.

32. Burkert (op. cit., 1985), p. 125.

33. On cursing as the origin of law, see Harrison (op. cit., 1962), pp. 138 ff.

34. Cited in J. Derrida (*Of Grammatology*, 1982), p. 249. I cite the French definition not because they invented the neum but because the godless *Oxford Companion* has forgotten about Augustine and speaks only of notation.

BIBLIOGRAPHY

Adams, H., *The Education of Henry Adams*, New York, 1918

Arens, W., *The Man-eating Myth*, New York, 1979

Atkinson, R., *Stonehenge*, Harmondsworth, 1960

Augustine, Saint, *Confessions*, (trans. Pusey), New York, 1966

Bacon, F., *The Advancement of Learning*, London, 1604

Bakhtin, M., *Rabelais and His World*, Cambridge, MA, 1968

Barfield, O., *Saving the Appearances*, London, nd, (Faber).

Bateson, G., *Mind and Nature*, London, 1980

———————, *Steps to an Ecology of Mind*, London, 1972

Bayley, H., *The Lost Language of Symbolism*, London, 1951

Becker, E., *The Denial of Death*, London, 1973

Bernal, M., *Black Athena*, London, 1987

Boer, C., *The Homeric Hymns*, Dallas, 1970

Bowra, M., *Homer*, London, 1972

Braithwaite, R., *Scientific Explanation*, Cambridge, 1963

Brown, N., *Hermes the Thief*, New York, 1969

Burkert, W., *Greek Religion*, (1977) Oxford, 1985

Burnet, J., *Early Greek Philosophy*, London, 1930

Campbell, J., *Oriental Mythology*, New York, 1962

———————, *The Mythic Image*, Princeton, 1974

———————, *Primitive Mythology*, New York, 1959

———————, *The Hero with a Thousand Faces*, Princeton, 1968

———————, *Occidental Mythology*, New York, 1964

——————, *The Way of the Animal Masters,* San Francisco, 1983

Canetti, E., *Crowds and Power,* London, 1962

Capra, F., *The Turning Point,* London, 1982

Catlin, G., *North American Indians,* 2 vols., London, 1844

Chance, M., and Jolly, C., *Social Groups of Monkeys, Apes and Men,* London, 1970

Chance, M., and Larsen, R., *The Social Structure of Attention,* London, 1977

Cook, R., *The Tree of Life,* London, 1974

Cornford, F., *From Religion to Philosophy,* (1912) New York, 1957

Daly, M., and Wilson M., *Sex, Evolution and Behaviour,* North Scituate, MA, 1978

Darwin, C., *The Origin of Species,* London, 1859

——————, *The Descent of Man,* London, 1870

——————, (Barlow, N., ed.), *Autobiography,* London, 1958

——————, *The Expression of the Emotions in Man and Animals,* London, 1873

——————, *The Voyage of the Beagle, London,* 1906

Dawkins, R., *The Blind Watchmaker,* London, 1986

Dekker, G., *Sailing After Knowledge,* London, 1963

de Rougement, D., *Passion and Society,* London, 1960

Derrida, J., *La Pharmacie de Platon* (tr. in *Dissemination,* Chicago, 1981), Paris, 1968

——————, *Of Grammatology,* London, 1982

Detienne, M., *The Gardens of Adonis,* London, 1977

——————, *Dionysus Slain,* Baltimore, 1979

——————, "Apollo's Slaughterhouse," *Diacritics,* Summer, 1986

——————, and Vernant, J. P., *Cunning Intelligence in Greek Culture and Society,* Brighton, 1978

Dodds, E., *Euripides' Bacchae,* Oxford, 1960

——————, *The Greeks and the Irrational,* Boston, 1957

Douglas, M., *Purity and Danger,* London, 1966

——————, *Natural Symbols,* London, 1970

Dover, K., *Greek Homosexuality,* London, 1978

Durkheim, E., *The Elementary Forms of the Religious Life,* London, 1915

Easlea, B., *Fathering the Unthinkable,* London, 1983

Edelman, G., *Neural Darwinism,* New York, 1986

Eibl-Eibesfeldt, I., *The Biology of Peace and War,* New York, 1979

Eliade, M., *Myth and Reality,* London, 1964a

——————, *Shamanism: Archaic Techniques of Ecstasy,* Princeton, 1964

—————, *Birth and Rebirth*, New York, 1958

—————, *The Myth of the Eternal Return*, New York, 1954

—————, *The Forge and the Crucible*, London, 1962

Evans, A., *The Palace of Minos*, London, vol. 1, 1921; vol. 3, 1930

Fossey, D., *Gorillas in the Mist*, London, 1983

Foucault, M., *Discipline and Punish*, London, 1977

Fox, R., *The Red Lamp of Incest*, London, 1980

Frankfort, H. et al., *The Intellectual Adventure of Ancient Man*, (1946) Chicago, 1977

Frazer, J., *The Golden Bough*, (1922) New York, 1960

Freud, S., *Totem and Taboo*, (1913) London, 1950

—————, *Civilization and Its Discontents*, London, 1963

Friedrich, P., *The Meaning of Aphrodite*, Chicago, 1978

Frye, N., *The Great Code*, Toronto, 1982

Gardner, J., *Gilgamesh*, New York, 1985

Ghiglieri, M., *East of the Mountains of the Moon*, New York, 1988

Gimbutas, M., *The Goddesses and Gods of Old Europe*, London, 1982

Girard, R., *Violence and the Sacred*, London, 1977

—————, *Deceit, Desire and the Novel*, London, 1966

Goodall, J., *In the Shadow of Man*, London, 1971

—————, *The Chimpanzees of Gombe*, Cambridge, MA, 1986

Gould, S., *The Panda's Thumb*, London, 1983

—————, *The Flamingo's Smile*, New York, 1985

—————, *Ontogeny and Phylogeny*, Cambridge, MA, 1977

—————, *Wonderful Life*, London, 1989

Grant, M., *The History of Rome*, London, 1979

Graves, R., *The Greek Myths*, London, 1955

—————, *The White Goddess*, (1946) London, 1961

Gribbin, J., and Cherfas J., *The Monkey Puzzle*, London, 1982

Griffin, J., *Homer on Life and Death*, Oxford, 1980

Guthrie, W., *In the Beginning*, London, 1957

Hackforth, R., (trans.), *Plato's Phaedrus*, Cambridge, 1952

Harrison, J., *Prolegomena to the Study of Greek Religion*, (1903) London, 1962

—————, *Themis*, (1911) London, 1963

Hawking, S., *A Brief History of Time*, London, 1988

Heckscher, W., *Rembrandt's Anatomy of Dr. Nicolaäs Tulp*, New York, 1958

Heidegger, M., *What is Called Thinking?*, New York, 1968

—————, *Poetry, Language, Thought*, New York, 1971

—————, *Early Greek Thinking*, New York, 1975

Henry, J., *Jungle People,* New York, 1964

Higgins, R., *Minoan and Mycenean Art,* London, 1967

Homer, *The Odyssey,* tr. R. Lattimore, New York, 1965

Hrdy, B., *The Woman That Never Evolved,* Cambridge, MA, 1981

Hubert, H. and Mauss, M., *Sacrifice: Its Nature and Function,* London, 1964

Huizinga, J., *The Waning of the Middle Ages,* London, 1924

——————, *Homo Ludens,* New York, 1955

Hulme, P., *Colonial Encounters,* London, 1988

Huxley, F., *The Dragon,* London, 1979

——————, *Affable Savages,* New York, 1956

Jung, C., *Memories, Dreams, Reflections,* London, 1967

Kaufmann, W., *The Portable Nietzsche,* New York, 1954

Kerenyi, K., *The Gods of the Greeks,* London, 1951

——————, *Dionysos,* Princeton, 1976

Kirk, G., *The Songs of Homer,* Cambridge, 1962

——————, *Mythology,* Cambridge, 1971

Klein, M., *Envy and Gratitude,* London, 1957

Knox, B., *The Heroic Temper,* London, 1964

Koestler, A., *The Ghost in the Machine,* London, 1967

Konner, M., *The Tangled Wing,* London, 1982

Kortlandt, A., *New Perspectives on Ape and Human Evolution,* Amsterdam, 1972

Kuhn, T., *The Structure of Scientific Revolutions,* Chicago, 1962

Laming-Emperaire, A., *Lascaux,* Harmondsworth, 1959

Lattimore, R., (trans.), *The Odyssey of Homer,* New York, 1965

Leakey, R., *The Making of Mankind,* London, 1981

Lee, R., and DeVore, I., eds., *Kalahari Hunter-Gatherers,* Cambridge, MA, 1976

Lee, R., *The !Kung San,* Cambridge, 1979

Leroi-Gourhan, A., *Treasures of Prehistoric Art,* New York, 1967

Lévi-Strauss, C., *Elementary Structures of Kinship,* Boston, 1969

——————, *Totemism,* London, 1964

——————, *The Savage Mind,* London, 1966

Levy, G., *The Gate of Horn,* London, 1948

Lewis, C., and Short, C., *A Latin Dictionary,* Oxford, 1879

Lienhardt, G., *Divinity and Experience,* Oxford, 1961

Lindsay, J., *Blast Power and Ballistics,* London, 1974

Lorenz, K., *On Aggression,* London, 1966

MacLean, P., *A Triune Concept of the Brain and Behavior,* Toronto, 1973

Mailer, N., *Cannibals and Christians*, London, 1967

Mellaart, J., *Catal Huyuk*, London, 1967

Merchant, C., *The Death of Nature*, London, 1982

Métraux, A., *La Réligion des Tupinamba*, Paris, 1928

——————, *Réligions et magies indiennes d'Amerique du Sud*, Paris, 1967

Montagu, A., *Coming into Being Among the Australian Aborigines*, London, 1974

Mumford, L., *Technics and Civilization*, London, 1934

Needham, J., and Ling, W., *Science and Civilization in China*, vol. 2, Cambridge, 1956

Nietzsche, F., *The Will to Power*, New York, 1968

——————, *The Birth of Tragedy*, (1870), New York, 1956

Nokes, D., *Jonathan Swift*, Oxford, 1985

Nussbaum, M., *The Fragility of Goodness*, Cambridge, 1986

Onians, R., *The Origins of European Thought*, Cambridge, 1951

Otto, E., *Egyptian Art and the Cults of Osiris and Amon*, London, 1968

Partridge, E., *Origins*, New York, 1959

Pfeiffer, R., *An Introduction to the Old Testament*, London, 1952

Pickard-Cambridge, A., *The Dramatic Festivals of Athens*, 2d ed., Oxford, 1968

Plutarch, *Moralia*, Loeb vol. 5, London, 1936

Pound, E., *The Confucian Odes*, New York, 1959

——————, *The Spirit of Romance*, New York, 1968

——————, *The Cantos*, London, 1964

Radin, P., *The Trickster*, London, 1956

——————, *Primitive Religion*, London, 1957

Richards, I. A., *Beyond*, New York, 1974

Rosen, C., *The Classical Style*, London, 1971

Rosenfield, I., "Neural Darwinism: A New Approach to Memory and Perception," *New York Review of Books*, Oct. 9, 1986

Rousseau, J. J., *Discours sur l'origine de l'inégalité*, Geneva, 1755

Rundle-Clark, R., *Myth and Symbol in Ancient Egypt*, London, 1959

Rycroft, C., *Psychoanalysis and Beyond*, London, 1985

Sagan, C., *The Dragons of Eden*, London, 1978

Sahlins, M., *Stone Age Economics*, London, 1974

Sandars, N., ed., *The Epic of Gilgamesh*, London, 1964

Sanderson, I., *Living Mammals of the World*, London, 1955

Schaller, G., *The Mountain Gorilla*, Chicago, 1963

Scholem, G., *Major Trends in Jewish Mysticism*, New York, 1961

Sheldrake, R., *The Presence of the Past*, London, 1988

Sontag, S., *Under the Sign of Saturn*, London, 1980

Smith, W. Robertson, *Lectures on the Religion of the Semites*, London, 1889

Spencer, B. and Gillen, J., *The Northern Tribes of Central Australia*, London, 1904

Steiner, G., *Real Presences*, London, 1989

Stevens, W., *Collected Poems*, London, 1965

Swift, J., *Gulliver's Travels*, (1713) London, 1921

Thompson, W., *The Time Falling Bodies Take to Light*, New York, 1981

Tigay, J., *The Evolution of the Gilgamesh Epic*, Philadelphia, 1982

Tiger, L., *Men in Groups*, New York, 1969

Tiger, L., and Fox, R., *The Imperial Animal*, St. Albans, 1974

Tinbergen, N., *A Study of Instinct*, Oxford, 1951

Turnbull, C., *Forest People*, London, 1961

Turner, V., *The Forest of Symbols*, London, 1967

——————, *The Ritual Process*, London, 1969

——————, *Dramas, Fields, and Metaphors*, London, 1974

Van der Post, L., *The Lost World of the Kalahari*, London, 1962

——————, *The Heart of the Hunter*, London, 1965

Van Gennep, A., *The Rites of Passage*, Paris, (1909) trans. London, 1960

Vernant, J. P., *Myth and Society in Ancient Greece*, Brighton, 1980

——————, "Feminine Figures of Death in Greece," *Diacritics*, Summer, 1986

Vidal-Naquet, P., *The Black Hunter*, London, 1986

Waddell, H., *The Wandering Scholars*, London, 1927

Watson, L., *Heaven's Breath*, London, 1985

Wilhelm, R., and Baynes, C., (trans.), *The I Ching*, Princeton, 1967

Winkler, J., *The Constraints of Desire*, London, 1990

Winsom, J., *Brain and Psyche*, New York, 1985

Wolkstein, D., and Kramer, S., *Inanna, Queen of Heaven and Earth*, London, 1984

Wunderlich, H., *The Secret of Crete*, London, 1975

Yates, F., *The Art of Memory*, London, 1966

Yeats, W. B., *Collected Poems*, London, 1950

——————, *Explorations*, London, 1962

Young, D., *Out of Ireland*, Cheadle, 1975

——————, "Living with Armageddon," *London Review of Books*, vol. VII: 17, 1985

INDEX

Abel. *See* Cain and Abel

Abstraction: and cave paintings, 114; and empathy, 97, 386–87; and erotic love, 97; and imagination, xxxviii; and language, xxxii; male, 97; and poetics, 7; and science, 12, 13, 16, 24–25, 32, 36

Abundance, 239, 244–45, 246, 293

Abzu, 234, 235n, 265, 293, 326; and the Cretan sea god, 394, 395, 398; Humbaba as, 355; and the *Odyssey*, 379

Achilles, 383–84, 417

Actaeon, 176, 377n

Adam, 252, 286

Adam and Eve, 157–59, 341–47, 352

Adams, Henry, 29

Adonis, 174–75, 176, 197–98, 199, 205, 293, 322

Adornment, mutilation and, 288

Advancement of Learning (Bacon), 10

Aeschylus, 176, 311, 312, 370

African walkabout hypothesis, 100n

Ag, 255–56, 257

Agamemnon, 176, 311

Aggression: in chimpanzees, 63, 65, 66, 67, 68–69, 70–71, 85, 122, 169; and the dancing ground, 130; Freud's views of, 73; and gender, 66; and hedonism, 84; and hunting, 169; and the R-complex, 68; ritualized, 122, 130; and sex, 78; and territoriality, 72; and *yang/yin*, 101–2. *See also* Violence; Warfare

Agon, 255–56, 261, 311, 312, 361, 378

Agonistic mode, 84

Agora, 256, 260, 276

Agriculture, 266, 317, 406, 420; cycle of, 280, 282, 283, 299, 316, 347

Akedah, 426

A-letheia/aletheia, 228, 413

Alienation, xviii, xxx, xxxi, 14, 237, 315, 340, 352, 355

Alkinoos, King of the Phaiakians, 380–81, 383

Alpha-shaman: and the buffalo dance, 142, 146, 148–49, 155, 157, 171; and cannibalism, 138, 142–43, 144, 146, 147, 153–55, 158, 184, 185, 206, 317, 341; and the dancing ground, 127, 129, 130–32, 140, 144–45, 146, 153–54, 157, 282–83; Dionysus compared with, 270, 282; divinity of, 140; and dominants, 142–43; fall of, 157–59; as hero, 155–56; and history/poetry, 145; and hunting, 154; love after debacle of, 195–96; murder of the, 142, 143; and mutilation, 144–45; and *pneuma*, 130, 154, 157; and power, 143, 149, 153, 154–55;